PRETTY

FILM AND CULTURE

Rosalind Galt

PRETTY

FILM AND THE DECORATIVE IMAGE

COLUMBIA UNIVERSITY PRESS   NEW YORK

COLUMBIA UNIVERSITY PRESS

Publishers Since 1893

NEW YORK   CHICHESTER, WEST SUSSEX

Library of Congress Cataloging-in-Publication Data

Galt, Rosalind.

Pretty : film and the decorative image / Rosalind Galt.

p. cm. — (Film and culture)

Includes bibliographical references and index.

Includes filmography.

ISBN 978-0-231-15346-1 (cloth : alk. paper)

ISBN 978-0-231-15347-8 (pbk. : alk. paper)

ISBN 978-0-231-52695-1 (ebook)

1. Motion pictures—Aesthetics.   I. Title.   II. Series.

PN1995.G245 2011

791.4301—dc22

2010045025

∞

Columbia University Press books are printed on permanent and durable acid-free paper.
This book is printed on paper with recycled content.

Printed in the United States of America

c 10 9 8 7 6 5 4 3 2 1
p 10 9 8 7 6 5 4 3 2 1

CONTENTS

ILLUSTRATIONS

ACKNOWLEDGMENTS

THIS BOOK HAS BEEN MANY YEARS IN THE MAKING, AND THE development of my ideas has been helped by more people than I can easily list. Karl Schoonover has been both an incisive, generous reader and a source of truly invaluable support. Corey Creekmur, Nicole Rizzuto, Michael Lawrence, Louis-Georges Schwartz, and John David Rhodes read drafts of various parts of the book. Their astute suggestions have improved the book immeasurably. Other important interlocutors were Lynne Joyrich and the readers at *Camera Obscura*, which published an early iteration of the project. Together they challenged me to push on the intellectual histories of the pretty and to refine my claims. The readers for Columbia University Press also offered rich and perceptive responses to the manuscript and provided me with helpful advice for revisions. Thanks also go to my editor at Columbia, Jennifer Crewe, and to John Belton for their support of the project, as well as to copy editor Annie Barva and to editor Irene Pavitt for shepherding the book through production.

Throughout the research and writing of the book, my colleagues at the University of Iowa and the University of Sussex have been incredibly supportive. Department heads Steve Ungar and Sue Thornham nourished my research, and my colleagues Rick Altman, Lauren Rabinovitz, Rosemarie

Scullion, David Wittenberg, Sasha Waters Freyer, Kembrew McLeod, Kathleen Newman, Andy Medhurst, Thomas Austin, Catherine Grant, Dolores Tierney, Sara Jane Bailes, Daniel Kane, and Gordon Finlayson offered insight, expertise, and sometimes food. Also indispensable have been the brilliant graduate student communities with whom I have discussed many theoretical sticking points in various seminars. Anastasia Saverino helped locate and organize material during the early stages of research. Dennis Hanlon very kindly shared his research on Jorge Sanjinés. Isabel Machado dos Santos Wildberger introduced me to some fascinating Brazilian films. Swarnavel Eswaran Pillai was an erudite source of guidance on Tamil film and culture.

Many people listened to parts of this project, offered suggestions, posed questions, and provided encouragement, including Louis Bayman, Mark Betz, Ed Branigan, Chris Cagle, Francesco Casetti, Sarah Cooper, Tim Corrigan, Susan Courtney, Jane Elliot, Sally Faulkner, Susan Felleman, Anne Friedberg, Bishnupriya Ghosh, Elena Gorfinkel, Andrew Higson, Akira Lippit, Adam Lowenstein, Colin MacCabe, Laura McMahon, Nadija Mustapic, Brigitte Peucker, Michele Pierson, Duncan Petrie, Brian Price, Sergio Rigoletto, Bhaskar Sarkar, Steven Shaviro, Christine Sprengler, Sarah Street, Meghan Sutherland, Belén Vidal, Amy Villarejo, Janet Walker, Liz Watkins, Charles Wolfe, and Michael Zryd. The folks at the University of Pittsburgh were massively generous with their hospitality and critical energies, as were audiences at the University of California at Santa Barbara, Kings College London, the University of Toronto, York University (in Canada), the University of York (in the United Kingdom), Temple University, the University of South Carolina, the University of the West of England, the University of Exeter, and Molekula arts center in Rijeka, Croatia. Jennifer Wild invited me to participate in the fascinating CinemArts workshop at Society for Cinema and Media Studies (SCMS) 2010 and gave me the opportunity to talk aesthetics with Tom Gunning and George Baker. And audiences at the SCMS, World Picture, Popular Italian Cinema, and Colour and the Moving Image conferences challenged and inspired me as I developed the project.

Thanks also go to the staff at the Billy Rose Theater Collection in the Dorothy and Lewis B. Cullman Center at the New York Public Library for the Performing Arts, the New York Public Library at Bryant Park, New York University's Bobst Library, the British Library, the British Film Institute, the V&A Museum, the Solomon R. Guggenheim Museum, the

Rhona Hoffman Gallery, the Albertina Museum, as well as the University of Iowa library's Special Collections Department. The chapter on Derek Jarman was kindly supported by the University of Iowa's Arts and Humanities Initiative grant, which allowed me to work with James Mackay on viewing rare films and archive material. James's advice and generosity came at a crucial point early in the project. The book was finished with the help of an Arts and Humanities Research Council research leave.

Some of my ideas on the pretty were first worked through in "Pretty: Film Theory, Aesthetics, and the History of the Troublesome Image," *Camera Obscura* 71, no. 24/2 (2009): 1–42. A version of chapter 2 is to be published as "'Brash . . . Indecent . . . Libertine': Derek Jarman's Queer Colours," in *Color and the Moving Image*, ed. Sarah Street and Liz Watkins, AFI Film Reader (London: Routledge, forthcoming). Part of chapter 3 was published as "Between the Ornament and the Corpse: Adolf Loos and Classical Film Theory," in *European Film Theory*, ed. Temenuga Trifonova, AFI Film Reader (London: Routledge, 2008), 195–210.

Conceived in New York and written in Iowa City and Brighton, this book has been supported by the enthusiasms and good cheer of an international gang of friends, family, filmmakers, and cinephiles. Thanks are due to Loren Noveck, Cyrilla Layland, Shannon McLachlan, John Mhiripiri, and Tracey Sinclair for their hospitality during my research trips. Jill Bradbury, Natasha Zaretsky, Pedram Navab, Pearl Ng, and other friends far and near were much appreciated online cheerleaders when I was stuck at the computer for too many hours. Katy Hoffer kept my spirits up with cinematic visions of Amazonian hoghunters, and I probably would not be thinking about the pretty at all without Evelyn So. Most of all, I thank Adrian Goycoolea for his Madame X–like call to "gold—love—adventure," without which this book and much else would not be possible.

PRETTY

The Pretty as Troublesome Image

INTERSPERSED THROUGHOUT THE NARRATIVE OF CATALAN DIRECTOR Joachín Jordá's avant-garde film *Dante no es únicamente severo / Dante Is Not Only Severe* (1967) are several explicit shots of a surgery performed on a beautiful woman's eye. Jordá has described the film as a provocation of the audience and the surgery shots as an attempt to counter what he terms "aesthetic drowsiness."[1] The shots are certainly arresting, but more striking is Jordá's contention that a visually unpleasant or ugly image is necessary to fend off the seduction of the aesthetic. For him, the visually attractive image can only work against true radicality, and this danger—overtaking even his own film—must be countered with violent measures against the image itself. This filmic example crystallizes a mode of thought that is all too common in film theory. Jordá's claim, in one form or another, runs through the history of writing on film, intertwining an often implicit aesthetic judgment with a usually explicit political critique. This judgment is present even in writing that aims to avoid the aesthetic as a measure of significance, and it leads to the political critique. Moreover, as this example makes plain, the unspoken aesthetic judgment hardly lacks for political implications. In subjecting its fashion model protagonist to on-screen dissection, *Dante* reminds us of the old gender trouble of the avant-garde—once again, slicing up eyeballs is necessary to guard against the aesthetic danger of women.

In this book, I effect a little dissection of my own to open up the body of film's theoretical and critical history and to look, like Stan Brakhage, at the colors and patterns of its insides. If all of this talk of bodies and blood seems far from pretty, that is indeed the point. The rhetoric of cinema has consistently denigrated surface decoration, finding the attractive skin of the screen to be false, shallow, feminine, or apolitical and locating truth and value instead in variants of Jordá's uglified film body. We might think, for example, of the resilience of "empty spectacle" as a figure of critique in film writing from journalism to high theory.[2] I suggest that this critique itself must be interrogated. That is, in positing the pretty as an aesthetic field in cinema, I am not so much selecting a body of texts or techniques to be placed alongside a transhistorical Kantian schema of beauty as proposing a method of reading that troubles this rhetorical history. The pretty is already present in film theory, naming the often unspoken bad object of successive critical models. In naming it, we can trace a thread, a structuring assumption, about the relation between form and content that institutes aesthetics as a problem in and for cinema. By staking a claim on the pretty as a category, we might reimagine the contested terrain of aesthetics and politics as well as open up film histories that have been hitherto unassimilable by the critical canon. And if rendering this discourse visible might involve cutting, reading the pretty demands that we move away from the rhetoric of blood and guts.

In citing the seduction and shallowness of the aesthetic image, we locate film theory within a philosophical history that dates from Plato's separation of idea from image. For many readers of Plato, the word or idea is primary, with the image at best a copy incapable of articulating philosophical reason and at worst a deceptive and dangerous cosmetic.[3] The very language of Western aesthetics is not only logocentric, but also, as a corollary, iconophobic, and it finds the image to be secondary, irrational, and bound to the inadequate plane of the surface.[4] As Jean-Luc Nancy explains, "The image is degraded as secondary, as imitative and therefore as inessential, as derivative and lifeless, as deceitful and weak: nothing could be more familiar to us than this motif. In fact, for the duration of the West's history, this motif will have resulted in the alliance (and it is doubtless this that has so decisively marked the West as such) forged between the principle of monotheism and the Greek problematic of the copy or the simulation, of artifice and the absence of the original." In a nod toward cinema, he adds that this alliance continues in our present day as a "deep suspicion regarding 'appearances' or 'the spectacle.'"[5] Dudley Andrew has directly connected this philosophical tradition to film theory, pointing to "the more passionate diatribes of Marxists and feminists, who have to be counted among the chief iconoclasts of our era."[6] So how do we reconcile a medium based on images with this intellectual inheritance of iconoclasm, the tearing down of images?

For art historian Jacqueline Lichtenstein, the image, banished by Plato from the realm of metaphysics, "was never effectively suppressed, for it has haunted philosophy ever since, as the dead man's figure haunts a criminal: just a shadow."[7] With this dramatic figure, she instigates a hauntology of the image, tracing the secondariness that follows the image from the realm of philosophy into art history. Because art history is obliged not to reject the image altogether, it reframes the debate to one of *disegno* and *colore*, prizing the line's signifying properties and relegating color to the lesser realm of emotion. To this trajectory, I add film studies. If classical aesthetics created a binary of word versus image and art history replicated this hierarchy *within* the image, then I hope to show how the cultures of cinema inherited both Plato's suspicion of the image itself and a modern visuality enmired in iconophobic aesthetics. Writing on film thus very often polices line and color or narrative and mise-en-scène as avatars of, on the one side, purity and reason and, on the other, primitivism and deception.

That this history speaks also to film might be suggested by nineteenth-century French critic Charles Blanc's assessment of the dangers of color for painters of historical battles: "In passionately pursuing the triumph of color, the painter runs the risk of sacrificing the action to the spectacle."[8] This concern for (active) meaning over (passive) spectacle surely resonates with cinematic discourse. For example, in a nearly perfect repetition of Blanc's critique, Anton Kaes argues in *From Hitler to Heimat* that the battle scenes in German war films attempt to present an antiwar narrative, but that "moral messages evaporate when up against visual pleasure and spectacle."[9] Across the major strands of film theory, this same impulse works to exclude certain categories of film as cosmetic or overly visual, whereas others may be redeemed by their linguistic elements or by linguistic critique. We might consider Christian Metz's focus on cinematic language as an instance of the latter and Michel

Chion's attack on what he terms the "neogaudy" style of postclassical cinema as one of many examples of the former.[10] For Chion, the neogaudy film uses a surface play of colors and glossy cinematography—for example, in the French *cinéma du look*—to replace an older engagement with the world itself. In other words, surface replaces depth, images replace meaning, aesthetics replaces philosophy. In his demand for a less pretty image, Chion's text takes as read the identity of "less pretty" and "more significant."

Of course, in proposing this inheritance, I do not mean to suggest a wholesale identification of film theory with Platonic aesthetics. The diversity of scholarship on cinema precludes any universalizing claims. But the problematic association of the image with the overly aesthetic and therefore with the inferior is complexly and persistently intertwined with the history of cinema. Denigration slides from the image as such to specific kinds of images (too colorful, too seductive, too cosmetic), in each case modeling the image that is too imagistic for its own good. These slippages make the pretty difficult to discern: it emerges in the gaps between values or as an unspoken counterpoint to critical assertions. Some of its resonances have explicitly countered aspects of the anti-image heuristic model; for example, feminist arguments for the critical value of the surface or the detail and queer theories of drag and the performative are all significant antidepth epistemologies to which I return as models for transforming dominant regimes of value. But my focus here is on why the denigration of the aesthetic image nonetheless remains such a standard critical practice, how it comes to be received wisdom for theorists who do not agree on much else, and, indeed, how the radical revisions of feminist and queer theories have reenacted this inheritance as often as they have countered it.

For Lichtenstein, "An entire tradition, of which we are the heirs, takes cosmetics to mark an original defect, to veil an ugliness always sensed beneath the virtuosity of masks, to signal an imperfection that art seeks to dissimulate. Moral puritanism and aesthetic austerity, along with resentment and an old, stubborn, and underhanded desire to equate drabness with beauty, thus make their righteous alliance and take delight in a constantly reiterated certainty: only what is insipid, odorless, and colorless may be said to be true, beautiful and good."[11] Film studies, as much as art history, is heir to this aesthetic tradition. This is the terrain that film theory has conceded before it begins, producing the pretty as the necessary exclusion of successive claims on a meaningful image. This book traces the history of film theory's inheritance from aesthetic thought, examining the anti-pretty structures and rhetorical tropes that have proved central to film culture. If the philosophical rejection of the image has been constitutive of Western thought, as Nancy and others argue, then it should come as no surprise that we can find anti-image discourse even at the heart of the moving image. But the pretty is not merely an extension of philosophical or art historical discourse into a new medium.

Cinema produces a unique concatenation of forces around art and international commerce, forcing those invested in visual aesthetics to consider the possibilities of a popular art and the significance of globally transited images. The problems of Plato's cosmetic and Kant's universal beauty are reinvigorated by the perceived dangers of the popular taste for spectacle and the mobilization of a global audience. Aesthetic theories depend on constructions of gender, sexuality, and race to regulate what kinds of bodies and images can be beautiful and who has access to value itself. Cinema condenses the sexism and racism of traditional aesthetics, but it also poses new questions about the pleasures of the image and the geopolitics of a global image culture. It embraces the gaudy and colorful, the pretty face of this year's starlet, at the same time as it elaborates a battery of anti-pretty critiques to keep the medium's essential qualities distanced from such secondary charms. Thus the pretty emerges as a problem in cinema in a way that it does not in art history or literature. Cognate qualities may certainly be found in other media—and I find common ground in the analyses of scholars such as Lichtenstein and Naomi Schor who have uncovered related histories in literature and art—but what compels in the pretty is how closely it is woven into the institutions of cinema and indeed into the constitution of the cinematic itself.

This book seeks to uncover the anti-pretty rhetoric of cinema, analyzing how ideas of the cosmetic as feminine, the Asiatic as effeminate, and the colorful as secondary have saturated film culture from the beginning. It argues that theories of cinematic specificity, realism, and ideology as well as the discourses of film criticism and international film culture depend on the exclusion of the pretty even where they espouse political and ethical values that seem entirely opposed to the prejudices of earlier aesthetic models. At the same time, it examines the pretty as a cinematic practice and a perspective for analysis: What does it look like when films take the disprized features of what I characterize as the decorative image as an aesthetic principle? Can the pretty be put to critical, even political, use? Further, if the pretty is usually rejected as too feminine, too effeminate, and too foreign, it can surely provide aesthetico-political friction for queer or feminist film or for cinemas engaged with but geopolitically distanced from Western aesthetic traditions. Might prettiness in cinema be uniquely able to develop a politics that engages gender, sexuality, and geographical alterity at a formal level rather than simply as a problem for representation?

To read the pretty image is to answer a call, to respond to a question traced across the body of film history. Such a call is many faceted: it must engage the broad history of aesthetics that grounds modern visual theories, and at the same time it must situate film form and style within local economies of place, time, and culture. This book argues for a *longue durée* of anti-pretty discourse in modernity, complexly imbricated in the period's encounters with its racial and sexual others. Close reading of difficult to categorize, noncanonical, and aesthetically problematic film texts determines the stakes of this process and its potential for resistance at the local level. To focus on this history is a political act, rereading bodies of film as well as the politics of the film body.

Why "Pretty"?

Why write on the pretty? The word implies taxonomies of beauty: on the first page of Umberto Eco's *On Beauty*, he includes *pretty* alongside *graceful*, *sublime*, *marvelous*, and *superb* as terms that indicate something we like and something good.[12] *Pretty* is not the same as *beautiful*—the other words are not exact synonyms, either—but it is part of a related cloud of terms. But *pretty* is different from those other words in the disapprobation it attracts. Pretty things do not have the status of beautiful ones. My choice of terminology is a polemical move because *pretty* so immediately brings to mind a negative, even repugnant, version of aesthetic value for many listeners. Feminists hear in the term its diminutive implications; a pretty girl is one who accedes to patriarchal standards of behavior and self-presentation. Marxists think of prettiness as a quality of the commodity fetish, a central function of ideology's ability to veil real relations. Many critics hear in the term a silent "merely" in which the merely pretty is understood as a pleasing surface for an unsophisticated audience, lacking in depth, seriousness, or complexity of meaning. To defend the beautiful or the ugly might be a heroic or radical task, but the pretty is precisely defined by its apparently obvious worthlessness. So to advocate the pretty is an uphill task of lexical redemption. In the course of researching this book, I lost count of the number of interested but confused interlocutors who assumed that the only thing I could be writing about the pretty is how reprehensible it is. I do not mention this critique to garner sympathy: the apparent obviousness of the pretty's inferiority is exactly what makes *pretty* the perfect term to describe the structural devaluation of the decorative image in cinema.

As we shall see throughout this book, prettiness is consistently evoked as a lesser quality, a gesture toward what goes wrong with aesthetics rather than toward its positive qualities. It is therefore fascinating to pay close attention to this rhetoric and to note exactly what (and who) is being excluded from aesthetic value. The history of the word itself traces the terms of such a political inscription. Derived from the Old English *prætt*, meaning "a trick, a wile or a craft," the word *pretty* and its earliest meanings involve cunning and art. One should not make the mistake of supposing this craft to be neutral, however, for its metaphysics is close to witchcraft. This sense is maintained by Siegfried Kracauer, who conjures a hypothetical poorly made but realistic film. "Nevertheless," he argues, "such a film is more specifically a film than the one which utilizes brilliantly all the cinematic *devices and tricks* to produce a statement disregarding camera-reality."[13] Such cunning tricks are very different from the meanings of *beauty*, a term whose French origins connoted nobility and truth. Beauty is a proper form of image to admire, whereas prettiness is at once a lesser, feminine form and, like the Greek icon itself, inherently deceptive. Here we begin to discern the unique value of the pretty for thinking about cinema. As an aesthetic category, the pretty contains within itself the ambivalence about the truth status of the image that underwrites film theory. Moreover, with its implication of witchery, the word *pretty* bonds suspicion of the aesthetic image to the gendered political terms of its embodiment.

It is important to understand that this book is not an etymological study: although individual instances of the word *pretty* and its synonyms are often telling, my creation of *pretty* as a critical term aims to name and thus to render visible a cluster of ideas that are by no means tethered to a single word. The pretty is not an aesthetic category with a long history of critical engagement like the beautiful or the sublime, and it is therefore not possible (or desirable) simply to review the ways that previous cultural critics have deployed the term. Nor is my aim to create a new category, along the lines of the sublime, that would delimit and reify a particular set of aesthetic practices. Rather, I want to tease out a persistent and labile work of exclusion on which the creation of aesthetic categories entirely depends. Categories of value work by defining beauty against certain kinds of image (or certain kinds of body) that are not beautiful. And writing on cinema, I argue, enacts a persistent gesture of rejection of the overly pretty image. Thus to bring this work of exclusion into view, we must look for the various terms and rhetorical moves with which it has been constituted. The exclusion of the pretty in cinema encompasses such a range of theoretical vocabularies and historical contexts that a single term is needed not to flatten out difference, but to highlight the shape of a discourse that was hitherto (as ideology always is) taken for granted. Thus what I am calling "the pretty" is described in a variety of ways across film cultures, with terminology varying not only by language, but also by theoretical context and critical register.

The investigation of the pretty thus encompasses a twofold linguistic imperative. The first move is to gather together under one heading a hitherto dispersed array of critical terms and dismissive gestures that, I argue, operate to produce a consistent space of exclusion. We need a word to render this process visible, and to name these excluded images as "pretty" is to make clear that they have been excluded systematically, not haphazardly, and for reasons that political analysis can bring to light. Because the word *pretty* did not name an aesthetic concept before my harnessing of it, there is no reason to suppose that critics will consistently use it to flag the ideas I am interested in exposing. But by translating these various rhetorics into the language of prettiness, I am able to visualize and describe the stakes of this devalued aesthetic field. The second move counters this synthetic impetus with an attention to the rich historicity of aesthetic terms. The pretty intersects with various concepts—the decorative, the ornamental, the colorful, the picturesque, and the like—whose own cultural histories and linguistic specificity shed light on the problem of the pretty. These linked and often contested areas of visual studies help to describe the historical terrain of the pretty, and each of them plays a major part in this analysis. Each chapter highlights particular terms and examines what role those terms play in the constitution of the pretty. Critical concepts such as the ornamental and the arabesque do not collapse into a generalized pretty, but work to locate in the connected and overlapping shapes of this terrain a category with a unique potential for reimagining film aesthetics.

Because the cinematic pretty is a definitionally international question, we must also consider how the term translates beyond the Anglophone context. There clearly can be no one-to-one correlation of words that translate aesthetic and critical concepts directly across languages, and this impossibility accentuates the need for an analysis that is not tied to a specific lexicon. But the difficulties of translation should not prevent us from thinking about the global transits of film cultures. Just as classical narrative, neorealism, and art cinema have traveled the world—to say nothing of the institutions and counterinstitutions of the studio system, the film festival, and Third Cinema—so the exclusion of the pretty recurs in complex ways across international film culture. Equivalent terms to the English *pretty* appear in many languages to perform similar critical labor. In French, *joli/e* is often used in a very similar way to the English *pretty* to indicate a feminized and secondary variant of *beau/belle*. In Italian, *carino* does the same work, with *cinema carino* naming a sweet and feminine style of filmmaking in the 1990s that is almost always dismissed by critics as inferior to the political cinema of an earlier era. The Japanese *kirei* is closer to *pretty* than to *beautiful* and in *manga* culture marks a more sexualized femininity than the more familiar *kawaii* (cute).[14] Thus although we cannot expect the same word to exist in all of its manifestations across languages, we can use *pretty* to evoke a constellation of qualities having to do with beauty, value, and femininity that resonate across many sites of modern aesthetic thought.

Once having established the choice of term, we might still ask why it should be desirable to read from the perspective of the pretty. Given the suspicion that many film scholars have for *any* form of aesthetic inquiry, it might seem perverse to focus on such an apparently trivial and unintellectual category. Sianne Ngai has responded to similar questions in her work on the cute, in which she argues for the historical reevaluation of "minor taste concepts." Ngai contends that "while prestigious aesthetic concepts like the beautiful, sublime, and ugly have generated multiple theories and philosophies of *art*, comparatively novel ones such as *cute, glamorous, whimsical, luscious, cozy,* or *wacky* seem far from doing anything of the sort, though ironically, in the close link between their emergence and the rise of consumer aesthetics, they seem all the more suited for the analysis of art's increasingly complex relation to market society in the twentieth century."[15] Like Ngai's minor terms, the pretty is undoubtedly imbricated in the consumer aesthetics of popular and art cinema, not to mention industrial design, art, tourism, and so on. As she goes on to make clear, it is not enough simply to condemn these categories as co-opted or secondary. By mapping the rhetorical opposition of the sharp and pointy avant-garde to the soft and infantile cute, she draws out a political analysis of Gertrude Stein's babbling language in terms of gender, sexuality, and modernity. Like the cute, the pretty is rarely seen as worthy of close examination, and yet it is a recurrent concept in both commercial and avant-gardist cinema.

Naomi Schor's work offers another important insight into the significance of minor categories. In *Reading in Detail*, she undertakes a feminist archaeology of the detail, attributing the suspicion with which the detail has been viewed for much of Western history to its association with femininity. Whereas neoclassicism favored the Ideal, freed from any particularity, the rise of nineteenth-century realism brought the detail to the center of modern aesthetics. She argues that the detail was still not valued, however, and that its place between the ornamental (linked to effeminacy and decadence) and the everyday (linked to domesticity) explains its lack of status.[16] This argument shares a methodological spirit with my own, and it also speaks implicitly to the continuing exclusion of the pretty. The everyday and the domestic have been thoroughly rehabilitated by critical theory and cultural studies, but the ornamental half of Schor's equation remains largely disprized. Whereas the detail is now valued, and even the cute enjoys a subcultural hipster caché, the pretty may be the last target of traditional aesthetic disgust. What is important in both examples is the claim that a minor category might be particularly suited not only to rereading specific texts, but also to generating theories of an art form as such. Like the role that Ngai assigns to the cute in lyric poetry and Schor to the literary detail, I find that the pretty emerges as uniquely relevant for thinking cinema's aesthetic terrain.

Insofar as commercial cinema is constantly dismissed as too pretty—as empty spectacle, surface without depth—we might view the pretty as the aesthetic concept that best describes cinema's articulation of visual culture and twentieth-century capitalism. And yet the pretty also names those excluded images that both film theories and, on occasion, the economic institutions of cinema have found impossible to admit. Kracauer's cunning film lacks the realist qualities of the truly cinematic, and we can hear an echo of this rejection of the decorative image in the difficult histories of Max Ophüls's *Lola Montès* (1955) and Zhang Yimou's *Ying xiong / Hero* (2002). Cinema depends on a certain nexus of consumerism and aesthetic seduction, but it also finds a highly decorative image to be unassimilable. In this apparent contradiction lies the pretty's reflexive ability to draw attention to the nature of the cinematic image: a recurrent taste category *in* cinema, it also speaks directly to the question *of* cinema. The pretty bespeaks a theoretical anxiety about the modern image, but it also names practices of image making that trouble aesthetic dogma.

How can we separate the places where prettiness guarantees capitalist inclusion from those that articulate aesthetic or political exclusion? This double-edged sword precisely figures the pretty's unique relation to cinema: no other aesthetic category assumes such dominance at the same time that it delineates such a diverse history of rejection. To understand this paradox, which is precisely what interests me in the category, we might begin by describing certain formal strategies in cinema as pretty. Without reifying an aesthetic category, we will find it is nonetheless useful to list the kinds of images that we are talking about: colorful, carefully composed, balanced, richly textured, or ornamental. As discussed in later chapters, pretty qualities include deep colors, arabesque camera movement, detailed mise-en-scène, and an emphasis on cinematographic surface. The pretty is self-evidently designed, refusing notions of cinematic chance, but it is also measured, stopping short of transgressive excess. By the standards of realism, the pretty image is "too much," but it is also not enough to be redeemed as radical excess. Not quite beautiful or sublime, it is also not camp or countercultural. The pretty image precisely troubles these categories of cinematic value, demonstrating their commonality by providing a common enemy for sometimes unexpected bedfellows.

The troublesome qualities of prettiness are vividly illustrated in Santosh Sivan's film *Theeviravaathi / The Terrorist* (1998), which constructs the psychic space of a young Tamil woman training to become a suicide bomber by means of a highly aestheticized attention to her immediate environment. Sivan was a successful cinematographer before turning to directing, and critical reception of the film often focused on the exceptional light effects created out of lead actor Ayesha Dharkar's face in close-up and the jungle through which her character, Malli, travels.

J. Hoberman, for instance, compares the effects to those of Carl Theodor Dreyer's *The Passion of Joan of Arc* (1928), and M. G. Radhakrishnan finds the images to be "stunning, lyrical and almost picture perfect. In short, beautiful."[17] The film is frequently described in aesthetic terms, with words such as *beautiful, dazzling,* and *sumptuous* bandied by many reviewers. But it is often found to be too beautiful or beautiful in the wrong way: its aesthetic qualities mark it as cinematic, but they also mark it as ill at ease in the world, somehow difficult to value properly. Thus Hoberman describes the bodily movement of a prisoner being tortured as "a disconcertingly fabulous arabesque" and Sivan's "too gorgeous" cinematography as "mannered" (for the geo- and body politics of the arabesque, see chapter 4). A. O. Scott in the *New York Times* finds that "Sivan's taste for extremely tight close-ups—and his tendency to decorate Malli's face with raindrops and tears—feels annoyingly arty," a critique that makes clear the role played by the decorative in turning artistic images into "arty" ones.[18] And Rai Paramjit suggests that "while the movie is humanistic and sensitive, the striking visuals at times feel empty,"[19] illustrating how even in the context of a positive evaluation of content, pretty images lead inevitably to the specter of empty spectacle.

The pretty describes exactly this quality of discomfort with a style of heightened aesthetics that is too decorative, too sensorially pleasurable to be high art, and yet too composed and "arty" to be efficient entertainment. To some degree, this awkwardness is the condition of the art film, and as we will see in chapter 5, there is a strong affiliation between prettiness and art cinema. Where a more robust and masculinist art house style can engage discourses on uncensored realism or ambiguous psychology, the pretty aspects of art cinema speak to the tinge of suspicion that we find in many critical and spectatorial responses to the field. Such awkwardness is accentuated in *The Terrorist* because postindependence Indian cinema has developed little institutional space for the concept of the art house. Even though Satyajit Ray is a foundational figure in the growth of international art cinema, the dominance of the Hindi popular film industry has stifled indigenous art cinemas and, to some degree, has prevented Indian films from accessing the film festival circuit. Moreover, the art cinema movement of the 1960s and 1970s emphasized screenwriting over visual style so that Sivan's films, which attempt to overturn this association of Indian art cinema with visual impoverishment, are often viewed as too glossy. Thus *The Terrorist* is an institutionally troublesome film: an art film in a country whose industry has little space for art cinema, a Tamil film in a country dominated by Hindi-language cinema, and a highly aestheticized Indian film that eschews the popular decorative aesthetics of the musical. This is exactly the territory of the pretty.

The film raises several foundational questions of prettiness and cinema. It is decorative in its style: carefully composed, deeply colored, an orchestrated system of sound, music, and image design that creates the arabesques of Hoberman's review. It is also centered around the body of a young woman. Close-ups of the female face and body have a privileged place in film history, and we might thus move to place *The Terrorist* into a category of reactionary prettiness in which large-scale images of conventionally attractive female stars embody consumable visual pleasure. Moreover, the film's close-ups of Dharkar might be accused of enabling a fetishistic relationship to the "exotic" brown-skinned woman whose mission as a suicide bomber places her both at odds with acceptable codes of femininity and entirely within discourses of the dangerous and unknowable non-Western subject. As Gayatri Chakravorty Spivak points out in regard to the female suicide bomber trope in contemporary politics and fiction, this character is a subaltern who does not speak but acts in silence and loses all possibility of active citizenship.[20]

The ambivalent staging of gender and political violence in *The Terrorist* helps us perceive the difficulty of the pretty: its frequent association with an aestheticizing (and hence potentially exploitative) deployment of the feminine, the nonwhite or non-Western, along with an aesthetic strategy that is hard to categorize generically. But it also brings forward the exclusionary gesture with which prettiness as a critical rhetoric operates: even where reviewers found the film to be politically astute or nuanced, the prettiness of the form rendered the film less meaningful. There is a hint here of a metaleptic figuration of the pretty itself in the film's disconcerting focus on Malli's too-pretty face (figure 1). How can one see the ugliness of political violence in a pretty image? And yet what reactionary heuristic believes that such a feminized image is incapable of serious meaning? To limit a properly political account of intercommunal violence to a realist, gritty, or sparse visual style would not only be prescriptive but also insist on a masculinist aesthetic, steeped in colonial ideas about simplicity of form and the primitive qualities of ornament. *The Terrorist* deploys an international art house style to figure a Tamil

FIGURE 1 *Theeviravaathi / The Terrorist* (Sivan, 1998)
Light effects and close-ups locate a traumatic politics on the surface of the screen.

and international politics otherwise, forcing the spectator to take up a different perspective.

Its prettiness makes *The Terrorist* difficult to read or too easy to dismiss, but it is also essential to the film's project. The picturesque Sri Lankan landscape through which Malli travels bespeaks for Tamil audiences a traumatic history of political violence, just as the woman's body evokes both the culturally resonant figure of the female poet and the specter of the systematic use of rape as a political weapon against Tamil women. *The Terrorist* foregrounds both landscape and the woman's body as a strategy to represent this disjunctive and traumatic Tamil experience of violenced belonging. The film cannot articulate these traumas directly but evokes them in the formal tension between the beauty of the landscape and of the woman and the ugliness of the historical events that both irresistibly figure.[21] The film's composed close-ups articulate the interiority of the would-be killer, refracting her intense focus as well as her distance from the worldly across a visual field composed precisely of the world she plans to leave. The "arty" material details of raindrops, leaves, and rice are Malli's only encounter with life and the spectator's only index of her subjectivity. Far from evading politics, these details saturate the screen with it. We do not hear debates about Tamil independence shoehorned into expository dialogue or narrated through instrumentalized relationships. Instead, the debate plays out across the surface of the screen on the affective territory of a contested landscape and on the body of a Tamil woman who is about to die.

The film neatly appropriates the lack of access to rational discourse that philosophy has ascribed to the colorful and imagistic in order to visualize the emotional landscape of political exclusion as a meaningful and destabilizing force. Sri Lankan Tamil also tellingly contains a lexical distinction between the pretty and the beautiful: whereas a natural landscape might be judged *azhagu* (beautiful), a film would more likely be complimented as *vadivu*. The latter is close to the English *pretty* but literally translates to "shapely" or "well formed." There is a feminizing connotation to the shapely and well formed that echoes European vocabulary as well as a sense of the *vadivu* as a diminutive aesthetic form. But it is the well-formed film that can articulate the traumas contained in the beautiful landscape, and *The Terrorist* never lets the spectator forget the exclusionary violence that is written into the aesthetic.[22] The term *pretty* forces us to think about aesthetic value. It bespeaks a supposed value that has devaluation encoded within itself. As with *The Terrorist*'s focus on the "pretty" body, the concept of a secondary and diminutive variant of beauty, limited to the pleasing surface and lacking access to nobility or complexity, demands that we look for the traces of political exclusions inscribed into the history of aesthetic thought.

THE POLITICS OF PRETTY

François Truffaut famously wrote that "if at any moment one becomes aware of the beauty of an image, the film is spoiled."[23] This anti-aesthetic impulse continues to dominate thinking about cinema, whether it supports the classical invisibility of commercial cinema, the radical aspirations of countercinema, or the neo-neorealist art films of directors such as Jia Zhangke and Abbas Kiarostami. Films that emphasize narrative identification may seem to have little in common with those that refute dominant ideologies or those that value openness and contingency, but partisans of each of these traditions construct their positive values in opposition to films that make the spectator aware of their pleasing visual style. (This is not to say that these examples cannot be experienced as aesthetically pleasing, even beautiful, for they clearly can be. But their beauty is of a kind that is valued as discreet, natural, or internal rather than self-promoting and superficial.) Truffaut claims in "A Certain Tendency of the French Cinema" that ten or twelve films "constitute what has prettily been named the 'Tradition of Quality,'" and his sneer at the nomenclature is just as surely aimed at the films' own style.[24] Thus *prettiness* becomes a term of abuse aimed in Europe at the French New Wave's despised predecessor and at the British heritage film and in Asia at the Hong Kong New Wave of Wong Kar-wai and Stanley Kwan and the Chinese Fifth-Generation directors Zhang Yimou and Chen Kaige.

These examples point us to the way in which pretty films are deemed to be less politically valuable: repeatedly and in different critical contexts, we see films that are understood to be pretty also accused of being reactionary, ineffective, or just plain apolitical. Thus although Merchant Ivory films are highly successful and canonized as British classics, they are also widely viewed as nostalgia for colonial power and rigid class segregation. Similarly, Zhang Yimou's *Ju Dou* (1990) has been accused of exoticizing Chinese history for Western audiences, and *Hero* was widely viewed as using its highly stylized color scheme in the service of a reactionary Chinese nationalism.[25] In countering this critique, I do not want to suggest that prettiness automatically makes films politically complex or positive. Manifestly, form does not lead directly to content in this way. One can undoubtedly find many examples of vapid and meaningless prettiness, just as one can find examples of vapid classicism, vapid modernist posturing, and so on. My point is to unravel why prettiness is so commonly presented as a bad object, what is at stake in making it so, and what gets changed when we remove this assumption.

An anti-aesthetic refusal of the image's plasticity is not the only model available for engaged thinkers and artists. Theodor W. Adorno finds in the aesthetic a space of critique, potentially free from capitalist rationality, and in his debates with Walter Benjamin we find an incredibly rich account of the relationship of aesthetics to politics.[26] Or, to take an example from contemporary art practice, South African artist Zwelethu Mthethwa uses bright, saturated colors in his photographs and paintings of shantytowns outside Cape Town. Speaking of his transition to color after beginning in black-and-white photography, Mthethwa says:

When I looked at the work that I shot before [my study of color], I was shocked. I was shocked that my work seemed to perpetuate the myth that poor people are miserable and down-and-out. The history of black-and-white as a medium, as well as the angst it lends to an image, gave nothing to the images. The photographs missed the colour context. . . . I decided I would employ colour to represent the colour of the places my subjects inhabited. Colour is just so beautiful. When you see beauty you think less of poverty. You think of design and composition. Colour really forces you to look at things that way.[27]

Mthethwa's deeply colored images do not ignore or forget poverty—his work focuses in great detail on representing conditions in the Paari settlement. But the prettiness of his colors demands that we realize there is something else to see besides "poverty." In refusing the ethnographic gaze of the black-and-white documentary photograph, he demands that the spectator also see agency in the lives of his subjects. Moreover, in asking the spectator to engage Paari as both an aesthetic and a communal space, he exchanges a colonial charitable gaze for a postcolonial intersubjective exchange. Thus prettiness can offer its own politics—one with as much potential as an anti-aesthetic to change how we view the social world.

This kind of aesthetico-political engagement is never entirely welcomed in cinema, though, where representations of social malaise are always susceptible to criticism if they exhibit a pretty style. A popular example is the Brazilian film *Cidade de Deus / City of God* (Meirelles and Lund, 2002), which is set in one of Rio de Janeiro's favelas. The film narrates the history of the favela through a visually rich and complexly edited account of a group of kids who grow up surrounded by gang violence. Color design moves us from warm oranges and ochers in the early days of the favela to colder blues and grays as guns and drugs take hold, and the film's disjointed and asynchronous editing emphasizes its young protagonists' sensory experience of being surrounded by violence. For many critics, these compositional techniques mark *City of God* as aesthetic rather than political. João Marcelo Melo finds that the film's Achilles' heel is "the exploitation of poverty—in other words, the aestheticisation of the harsh realities of Brazil's slums." In a key anti-pretty claim we will see repeated throughout this book, a self-consciously aesthetic treatment is seen to be less appropriate for representing social realities than a no less mediated but aesthetically muted vision. Melo accuses the film of "doll[ing] up the slum"—in other words, of using feminine and deceitful cosmetics to mislead the viewer. For him, pleasurable images are "a form of seduction" and necessarily imply "the impoverishment of content."[28] We find here an either / or logic in which images must be ugly to be meaningful, and any appeal to the aesthetic is a deceptive cosmetic incapable of showing truths.

Karen Backstein's *Cineaste* review exemplifies a move that many critics made in its evocation of Glauber Rocha as a contrast to Fernando Meirelles's film. Backstein suggests that *City of God* is "far more 'aesthetic of postmodernism' than what Cinema Novo director Glauber Rocha called the 'aesthetic of hunger,'" and she goes on to ask rhetorically what Rocha would have thought of a film whose engaging imagery and fast pacing threaten to overwhelm its sociopolitical concerns.[29] In a similar vein, Luiz Carlos Merten cites the argument made by critics including Ivana Bentes that films such as *City of God* and *Madame Satã* (Aïnouz, 2002) replace the aesthetics of hunger with a *cosmetics* of hunger, essentially prettifying the inheritance of Cinema Novo.[30] These references indicate how anti-pretty analysis often cites 1960s and 1970s Marxist countercinemas as the preeminent model of aesthetics and politics. By this standard, contemporary filmmaking will almost always fall short because the color palette, camera movement, and editing strategies of more recent world cinema rarely continue untouched the strategies of Latin American Third Cinema or the European avant-gardes. However, although the contrast of flashy postmodernism with the serious political films of a previous generation is a commonplace one, the comparison lacks nuance. Even Cinema Novo had no single coherent style, and as Merten argues, Rocha never intended the aesthetic of poverty to be a prescriptive blueprint for all future filmmaking in Brazil.

To approach *City of God* from the perspective of the pretty, then, we might consider the use of the fabulous—the fairy-tale structure and dreamlike images—in Rocha's own films and the way that nonnaturalistic mise-en-scène has formed an important way to mesh anti-imperial politics with Afro-Brazilian and indigenous histories. An aesthetics of poverty is still an aesthetics, and Rocha's films draw fully on the expressive qualities of cinematic space. Lúcia Nagib discusses the importance of "trance" as a concept in, for example, *Terra em transe / Land in Trance* (Rocha, 1967), finding the film's hypnotic and fantastical qualities to evoke simultaneously aesthetic beauty and political crisis.[31] The allegorical opening of Meirelles's film, in which a chicken escapes from immi-

FIGURE 2 *Cidade de Deus / City of God* (Meirelles and Lund, 2002)
A chicken escapes death in a phantasmagoric, rapidly edited opening sequence.

nent death (figure 2), uses pulsing colors and a fantasmatic sense of threat to suggest an iteration of trance discourse reimagined in the favela's drug-fueled dystopia. Another context for the film's aesthetic is the vibrant and saturated comic book style of contemporary agitprop. A film such as *Cronicamente inviável / Chronically Unfeasible* (Bianchi, 2000) is much more politically direct than *City of God*, but its bold colors and scenic structures, joined with larger-than-life class types, are echoed in *City*'s panorama of favela types, as are the miniature histories interspersed throughout its narrative. In both films, heightened representational strategies make an economic process visible through an aesthetic one. Each of these features has been dismissed as MTV aesthetics or the aestheticizing of poverty, but if we remove the lens of anti-pretty bias, we can find in *City of God*'s style a textured engagement with histories of Brazilian political cinema.

These contexts may not persuade us that *City of God* is a radical film, but they should prompt us to ask different questions—to read a pretty aesthetic with as much subtlety and historical care as we would read any other formal strategy. Nagib, who mounts a compelling defense of the film, begins from the proposition that its form is central to its social engagement, arguing that unlike the contemporary American cinema of attractions, social content is not pushed into the background.[32] But even in taking seriously its form, Nagib is forced into the defensive. She explains the extensive work done by the filmmakers with hundreds of young people from Rio's favelas that led to the casting of nonprofessional actors in the film and that also set up community theater spaces that continued beyond the film's production. This community engagement is a fascinating part of the film's production history, but it is telling that Nagib has to explain it. Meirelles and codirector Katia Lund went far beyond any industrial norms of research, preparation, and investment in local communities, and yet they are still critiqued as exploitative and exoticizing because the film's aesthetic is pretty. Grittier-looking productions that take little time to interact with their subjects are rarely subject to such rigorous investigation of their production methods, and critics who assume that colorful style impoverishes content are unable to read beyond a narrow template for political cinema.

Thus I propose "pretty" as a polemic intervention into these debates, a way to overthrow assumptions and to put into question the political potential, broadly constituted, of film aesthetics. The overwhelming suspicion of the decorative image suppresses its theoretical elaboration and derails analysis of much contemporary cinema. By paying attention to the surface of the image, its decorative qualities, we can form a different matrix of cinematic texts that map political uses of the pretty.

Pretty's Excluded Bodies

The production of the pretty as a space of rhetorical exclusion depends heavily on its connection to the wrong kinds of bodies. Plato's cosmetics instantiate a connection of the untrustworthy image with the deceptive woman that has dogged the history of Western art, and the devices and tricks of the cinematic pretty oppose an overly fussy feminine mise-en-scène to the grandeur of the masculine exterior. Moreover, the classical binary of Attic authority versus overly flowery Asiatic rhetoric links decorative style both to the non-Western and, in the binary's modern forms, to effeminacy and sexual perversion. The politics of the pretty is therefore always engaged in a critique of gender, sexuality, and race as these terms have been imagined and codified through visual culture. The bodily politics of the pretty, as entirely formal constructions of aesthetic value, are usefully distinct from identitarian categories: the persistent denigration of decorative images in the languages of femininity, perversion, or orientalism enables us to think beyond a politics of representation and to see histories of bodily exclusion instead as underwriting the structuring principles of cinematic value.

Later chapters analyze the operation of this exclusionary move in film theory and criticism, but its effects emerge forcefully in the production of "difficult" films, whose inability to articulate a proper politics frequently stems from a combination of a pretty visual style with a somehow problematic staging of gender, sexuality, race, or all three. *Madame Satã*, for example, narrates the life of João Francisco dos Santos, a 1930s Afro-Brazilian pop cultural icon who was a famous criminal, drag performer, and queer outlaw. The film's use of lush cinematography and staging for João's erotic and criminal lives as well as its presentation of his "exotic" drag performances as "Madame Satã" or "the Negress of the Bulacoche" tie a recuperative queer politics to a sometimes uncomfortable aestheticization of sexual and racial stereotypes. And yet this excessive stylishness is quite clearly at the heart of the film's historical analysis. The burnished tones of a visual schema that aesthetically marks dark skin, bright costume, and nostalgic period lighting are as much a performative articulation as is the protagonist's drag act. *Madame Satã* performs a new iteration of the Brazilian revolutionary outlaw myth, citing and updating Glauber Rocha's rebellious Antonio das Mortes from *Deus e o diablo na Terra do Sol / Black God, White Devil* (1964). A precursor for this kind of queer image is Pier Paolo Pasolini, whose difficult relationship to Marxism illustrates how the pretty is often in conflict with conventional accounts of leftist film practice. Pasolini's films are not always what we might think of as pretty, but *Il fiore delle mille e una notte / Arabian Nights* (1974) deploys highly aestheticized image design to create its homoerotics of the body and romanticized North African setting. The *Arabian Nights* tale elaborates a flowery narrative style composed of multiple desires and deferred pleasures that sprout recklessly throughout the diegesis. Pasolini's fascination with Africa and the Middle East courts accusations of exoticism, but the film's detailed decorative structure—its self-conscious deployment of Asiatic rhetoric—demands that we take this refusal of aesthetic austerity seriously rather than imagine it to be artless.

The gendered qualities of the pretty are even more nakedly disprized. Alan Parker famously called British costume dramas "the Laura Ashley school of filmmaking,"[33] and this disdain for the feminine decorative runs throughout anti-pretty discourse. Sofia Coppola's *Marie Antoinette* (2006) addresses precisely the relationships among rococo style, radical politics, and gender, but its deconstructive deployment of the Versailles decorative regime prompted critical response to view the film as equally clueless as its protagonist. If we regard the film as something other than a discourse on girly frivolity, it is possible to read its emphasis on the decorative as precisely the location of its political intervention. Its young Marie Antoinette is stripped of subjectivity and rendered as a (political) object in a way that is remarkably similar to that of Roberto Rossellini's account of another young monarch in *La prise de pouvoir par Louis XIV / The Rise of Louis XIV* (1966). But whereas the latter film deploys distantiating effects to narrate the alienation of the royal body, *Marie Antoinette* stages the fetishistic status of the royal body as a question of production design. The film connects a feminized world of objects (for instance, a deliberately anachronistic discourse on the shoe as commodity fetish) with the class and gender politics within which Marie's body can be owned first by the state and then violently by the people. Unlike much writing on decorative commodity cultures, this discourse on the historical objecthood of the female body strikingly refuses to blame the woman for her out-of-control consumption. Coppola's revisionism may not be to the taste of every French historian, but her linkage of the politically rejected female body with the disprized decorative image astutely diagnoses the stakes of contemporary film style. But perhaps the most influential contemporary example of the gendered pretty is Jean-Pierre Jeunet's film *Le fabuleux destin d'Amélie Poulain / Amelie* (2001), which vividly brings into focus the centrality of prettiness as a critical issue in contemporary international cinema.

Amelie was a huge success, one of the year's top-grossing foreign films in the United States and elsewhere and a crossover hit for the previously art house director. However, it provoked as much hatred as love: many critics, including those at *Cahiers du Cinéma*, dismissed it out of hand.[34] Negative assessments of the film drew on two charges. First, there is a claim that the film's aesthetic was too composed, overly decorative, and lacking in spontaneous life. Second, a media debate ensued in France (and, to some extent, in the United States and Great Britain) over whether the film whitewashed Paris, presenting an ethnically cleansed vision of an all-white nation. Serge Kaganski wrote in a furious article, "But where are the Caribbeans, the North Africans, the Turks, the Chinese, the Pakistanis etc.? Where are those who live a different sexuality? . . . If [Jean-Marie Le Pen] were looking for a film to illustrate his ideas, to promote his vision of the French people and his idea of France, it seems to me that *Amélie Poulain* would be the ideal candidate."[35] These critiques were connected in the form of the film's carefully orchestrated mise-en-scène: the figure of postproduction alteration of the image signaled both a fraudulent prettification of a gritty real space and an ominous erasure of nonwhite bodies from the image (figure 3).

I argue that the racial critique made here is a symptom—and not a random one—of the aesthetic critique. In other words, the way in which the rejection of prettiness occurs is by linking it to accusations of racism at the level of content. But the dismissal of pretty form is in itself a legacy of patriarchal and racist aesthetics. My aim here is not to defend *Amelie*'s representation of Paris. A film that contains only two nonwhite secondary characters (both Algerian) is clearly no paragon of multicultural representation, and we might legitimately ask why a fantasmatic, romanticized Paris must be so overwhelmingly white. But such a distribution of cast members is not atypical in contemporary film, and most films are not castigated so publicly. Moreover, demanding greater casting diversity is no guarantee of approbation. Many critics slated the most successful

FIGURE 3 *Le fabuleux destin d'Amélie Poulain / Amelie* (Jeunet, 2001)
Postproduction modifications prettify the Paris Métro with matching posters.

multiracial French film of the period, *La haine / Hate* (Kassovitz, 1995), with its neat black-beur-blanc casting, for its overly aesthetic style. When even films with a large black cast and a documentary style such as Laurence Cantet's *Entre les murs / The Class* (2008) construct an incipiently smug white perspective on French race politics, it seems inadequate at best to link casting decisions directly to racial progressiveness. Why, then, was *Amelie* singled out for such vitriolic attack?

To answer this question, we must consider the seemingly apolitical question of the film's aesthetic, its closely controlled images that unfold the colors and lines of narrative space with the same gleeful precision as Amelie's do-gooding plans unspool in the narrative. Dudley Andrew's insightful analysis of the film isolates its careful visual composition as exactly where it goes wrong.[36] He contrasts Jeunet's control with the opening to hazard in the French New Wave: where *Jules et Jim / Jules and Jim* (Truffaut, 1962) is ambiguous, *Amelie* lacks mystery. And for Andrew, this problem can be summed up in Jeunet's statement that "every shot should be like a painting."[37] As Andrew immediately makes clear, we cannot categorize this problem as one of serious art cinema versus frivolous mainstream or postmodern film. He points to Michelangelo Antonioni and Truffaut as earlier examples of the same dichotomy, where Truffaut accused the Italian director of turning his shots into paintings. If painting grass was good enough for Antonioni, we cannot easily reject Jeunet's methods out of hand. And yet Andrew clearly finds Jeunet (and Antonioni) to be less cinematic. Truffaut's "little feeling for fine art" is surely a compliment in this context. Painterly composition, control, and modulations of color are in explicit opposition to cinematic chance, openness to the profilmic, and visual ambiguity. Thus within accounts of *Amelie*'s aesthetic, we find an implicit theory of the cinematic, a claim on what kinds of texts are aesthetically and intellectually valuable as well as proper to the medium.

Kaganski also finds style rather than representation to be at the heart of *Amelie*'s problems; in fact, his polemic accusations spend more time on the film's "artificial" and "lifeless" style than on its racial politics. In a second article on the same subject, he argues that despite the many precedents of designed and composed images in classical Hollywood, art cinema, and the avant-garde, Jeunet's control over the screen is rather comparable to propaganda.[38] He concludes, "This ultraformalist orientation produces a stifling cinema, an animated taxidermy, a moving waxwork museum."[39] These metaphors of suffocated and stuffed lifelessness present a vision of the decorative film as corpse that will recur throughout this study. In his mocking description of its style as "pretty, funny, nice and picturesque," Kaganski demonstrates the patriarchal disdain contained within an attribution of prettiness.[40] *Amelie*'s artificial compositions, he argues, falsify Paris, tell a fraudulent story, and demonstrate how composition and color, like the film's charming but silly and ignorant main character, fail to address the real, material world.

In considering the gendered work of aesthetic critique, it is instructive to compare the reception of Jeunet's earlier films to that of *Amelie*. *Delicatessen* (1991) was equally composed, far from life. In its postapocalyptic Paris, it proposed an equally fantastical diegesis, one with a densely composed mise-en-scène in which each room of an unpleasant boardinghouse mapped its inhabitant's psychic space. Likewise, *Delicatessen* left nothing to chance, constructing a narrative of causal chains so minutely connected that spectatorial pleasure was created largely from anticipating how each suicide attempt would go wrong or how lovemaking on one floor would affect the rhythms of behavior on the others. And yet this film was never criticized as lacking openness or ambiguity. Its aesthetic was not rejected as cosmetic. Rather, the film was lauded for taking an intelligent and original comic-book vision and translating it to moving images. It seems that the more masculine film (black comedy, cannibals, male protagonist) can be praised in terms of a legitimate aesthetic of the surface (the comic book still thought of, if inaccurately, as a male-oriented form), whereas the feminine film (upbeat comedy, romance, female protagonist) with the same stylistic signature is dismissed as cosmetic, fake, solipsistic.[41]

This critical reaction makes *Amelie* a telling case study. But it is not only productive at the level of reception. As Andrew makes plain, the film is actually quite self-aware about how it constructs its own aesthetic of the surface and the pretty. *Cahiers du Cinéma* sees prettiness as a self-evident bad object. For its critic, prettiness is quite clearly gendered: instead of the look of serious film theory, we get the smile, a desire to please, things that are fake and stupid but pretty. Can we list these qualities without thinking of the bimbo? The starlet? Amelie herself? One hesitates to drag out the male gaze, but it seems quite clear here who is doing the looking and who the smiling. But *Amelie* the film understands better than *Cahiers* that aesthetics are both a question of gender and a question of value. When Mathieu Kassovitz's character, Nino, considers his love for Amelie, the photobooth pictures he keeps argue among themselves about how to describe her. Two of them find her beautiful (*belle*), but the others maintain she is pretty (*jolie*). Unlike a conventional aesthetic discourse in which beauty would be self-evidently superior, *Amelie* does not find the pretty to be an inferior form. Although the photographs do not come to any resolution, the film does. For *Amelie*, the *jolie* image contains as much to value as the beautiful or the ugly.

THE GEOPOLITICS OF PRETTY

The pretty derives from Western aesthetics; its foundational influences include Plato's writing on the image, Kant's *Critique of Judgment*, and the impact of neoclassicism on modern aesthetics in Europe and North America. But my study encompasses global cinema both as an object of anti-pretty rhetoric's work of exclusion and as a source of new epistemologies of the pretty. It is therefore important to consider from the outset how non-European or non-Western cinemas engage with the discourse of prettiness and to ensure that Western aesthetics are not simply applied unreflectively to non-Western visual cultures. If, as I argue, the modern form of anti-pretty aesthetic thinking found in film theory draws from colonial-era ideas about artistic value, it is particularly important that any recovery of the pretty should not equally fall into an unthinking Eurocentrism. This book responds to this challenge in two ways: one fairly general and the other quite specific. The general response is to consider film culture as always already global and the aesthetic ideas at stake in anti-pretty discourse as at play across East and West from the beginnings of cinema. Thus Sergei Eisenstein writes on the Japanese theater, and filmmakers such as Wong Kar-wai draw from European as well as Asian sources. The history of how Western aesthetics gains worldwide influence—as with the histories of global Hollywood—are always caught up in the power imbalances of capitalism, but there is no doubt that film cultures around the world have felt the influence of Euro-American aesthetic norms. My focus is on the global influence of Western aesthetic histories, but further research can be done on cinema's intersections with other philosophical systems.

There is also, however, a more particular relationship between the pretty and global transits of aesthetic ideas, and this relationship forms a central thematic of this book. We find Western aesthetic values repeatedly to be constructed in opposition to conjurations of racial and geographical others: colonial "primitives" who elaborately adorn their bodies and possessions (tattoos, jewelry, abstract design); Asian cultures associated with the decorative (Asiatic rhetoric in classical criticism, chinoiserie and japonisme in the modern era); Muslim and Arabic cultures fetishized as exotic orientalism (abstract art and textiles). Thus the very notion of the pretty in Western thought is excluded because it is understood to be racially or geographically inferior. Even where this history is elided in modern cultural criticism and where simplicity is valued in purely aesthetic terms or even valued in the name of radical politics, the geopolitical underpinnings of the exclusion endure. Hence, I argue that the rejection of the pretty is grounded in ideas of geographical difference in the same way as it is structurally contingent on gender regardless of the theme or content of the image.

To propose pretty as a counter to this reactionary aesthetic, then, it is necessary to locate an alternative practice that breaks apart the nexus of "primitive" and "Oriental" as exemplars of decorative inferiority. In film, postcolonial and transnational theory has focused its attention away from Eurocentric models—a necessary move that has nonetheless often left in place the repudiation of the decorative image instantiated by colonial aesthetics. But as the example of Mthethwa indicates, prettiness is not incompatible with a geopolitically resistant reevaluation of the look. To take another example from art practice, Kehinde Wiley's paintings and photographs combine richly patterned textile grounds with figures of black men, layering contemporary styles with historical ones and reinscribing (mostly) African American figures into histories of art (figure 4). For many contemporary artists who have been categorized as neobaroque, turning to adornment is part and parcel of renewing the political work of art. Other examples include Adriana Varejão and Julie Mehretu, both of whom explicitly use decorative forms to engage geopolitical questions. This kind of gesture has not been as prominent in film culture as it has in curatorial circles, but I argue that the same impulses inform the aesthetics of contemporary world cinema.

Many contemporary filmmakers use techniques of prettiness to access the politics of world. Abdherramane Sissako, for instance, presents in *Bamako* (2006) a richly textured map of global economics within the visual and auditory space of an African village. Like Julie Mehretu's

FIGURE 4 Kehinde Wiley, *After Sir Anthony Van Dyck's King Charles I and Henrietta Maria* (2009)
Kehinde Wiley uses decorative patterning as a mode of reinscribing African American figures into histories of art. (Courtesy of the artist and Rhona Hoffman Gallery)

finely patterned visualizations of world space, Sissako uses decorative patterns and colors to form a dynamic social cartography. The rich colors of West African textiles, which the film depicts being dyed and dried in the sun (figure 5), and the sensuous, saturated qualities of the cinematography do not provide an "exotic" distraction to the serious business of putting the World Bank on trial. Rather, this emphasis on the materiality of color and the "wealth of detail" with which the village is staged concretize a resistant discourse to the neoliberal abstractions of the globalized economy. Rey Chow similarly demands that we see the films of Zhang Yimou and Chen Kaige not as orientalist fantasies for the Western spectator, but precisely as engagements with the problem of modern vision from the perspective of the East.[42] *Ju Dou* also features the dyeing and production of cloth (figure 6), and the film's mise-en-scène centers around cloth sheets of pure color that hang in a courtyard. A young woman is married to a violent owner of a dye mill, and the film links aggressive economies of production with patriarchal power. It counterposes the economic functioning of the mill with the female protagonist's resistant vision, in which her desire is aligned with the sheets of color that break up the panoptic order of clear sight lines. Her affair with a younger worker is enabled by these sheets of color, which fill the screen with a formless indulgence of chromatic pleasure at the same time that they function dramatically to shield Ju Dou and her lover from her husband's eye. In both *Ju Dou* and *Bamako*, the dyed sheet articulates an aesthetic and a socially symbolic vision.

Prettiness, then, can be a productive way to counter the Eurocentrism of dominant film aesthetics, but it is not simply one aesthetic choice among many. Rather, the pretty image is strikingly often geopolitically overdetermined. From Zhang's films allegedly aimed at a Western audience to Pasolini's travel to Yemen and Nepal to shoot *Arabian Nights*, the question of the cross-cultural encounter is frequently at the center of controversy over pretty films. I argue that one of the defining features of contemporary world cinema is a deployment of pretty aesthetics to negotiate globality and that we especially find this effect in films whose production histories or narrative themes or both cross regional or continental lines. Such films are often censured: European and American films for exoticizing their subjects and those from East Asia or the global South for playing to a Western audience or aping Western forms. These concerns are real, but what I have found to stand out across my research

FIGURE 5 *Bamako* (Sissako, 2006)
Women's labor dyeing fabrics forms a decorative space in which politics takes place.

FIGURE 6 *Ju Dou* (Zhang, 1990)
Textile production encodes economic, sexual, and graphic spaces.

is how consistently pretty films are interrogated along these lines, whereas films with comparable thematic concerns and production contexts but less pretty style are not met with such hostility.

Vietnamese French director Tran Anh Hung provides an example both of this cross-cultural impetus and its discontents. Born in Vietnam, Tran moved with his parents to France when he was a teenager, and his feature films have combined Vietnamese subjects with Vietnamese, diasporic, and French cast and crew. His two best-known films, *Mùi du du xanh* / *The Scent of Green Papaya* (1993) and *Xích lô* / *Cyclo* (1995), stage space through limited color palettes of greens and blues and place an emphasis on frontal, graphic composition. Although they have fairly conventional art cinematic narratives, plot is often subordinate to the construction of a highly patterned sensory experience. Thus in *Cyclo*, we see a block of flats by night as a grid of illuminated windows, their pale blue squares creating a striking repeat pattern broken up by hanging clothes and human figures (figure 7). There is a certain similarity to Tsai Mingliang in Tran's interest in domestic spaces, cooking, and washing—a desire to tease out compositional beauty in the processes and everyday

FIGURE 7   *Xích lô* / *Cyclo* (Tran, 1995)
The screen as repeat pattern synthesizes urban and surface spaces.

objects of life in the Asian metropolis. And like Tsai's films, *Cyclo* also forms temporal patterns, rhyming variations on a water motif across the narrative. The cyclo drivers must drink water constantly to hydrate, and they suffer from painful urination. The sister is forced to pee for a fetishist, and the cyclo is forced to drink water mixed with gasoline. In happier times, the family has a water gun fight. Each recurrence of the motif binds the film more closely into a compositional system, precisely lacking openness or chance. If pretty films are often accused of fetishism, *Cyclo* materializes the fetish, using the sister's sex work to make explicit the film's metonymic mode of operation.

Although *Cyclo* was internationally successful, Tess Do and Carrie Tarr illustrate the corresponding critical suspicion of the cross-cultural pretty in an article comparing outsider and insider views of Saigon. They write that "director Tran Anh Hung first visited Vietnam as an adult when scouting for locations, in this case for his first award-winning film, *The Scent of Green Papaya*, a nostalgic vision of 1950s Saigon, which, significantly, was ultimately shot in the studio in Paris."[43] There is an insinuation of inauthenticity in this formulation, an implication that by choosing a studio shoot, Tran lacks a properly close relationship to Vietnam. For Do and Tarr, these derogations tie an argument about the inferiority of outsider perspectives to the inferiority of the pretty. They suggest that the film is best read in relation to the heritage of European art cinema as well as of Hong Kong and American popular cinema. This description would fit much postclassical international film, but, as with *City of God*, critics use these reference points to disparage a film as insufficiently indigenous. Likewise, Do and Carr argue that "the casting of the principal protagonists is indicative of the film's outsider perspective" because only the actor who plays the main character is Vietnamese, and his sister is played by a diasporic Vietnamese actor and the gangster by Hong Kong icon Tony Leung Chiu-wai. The positions of outsider and insider are carefully patrolled, and mode of production is directly linked to style where they find the characters to be "depicted from an aestheticized distance."[44] Aestheticization is thus bad because it comes from outside, so that the pretty can be rejected as foreign and proper aesthetics are associated with nativism and an unquestioned sense of cultural authenticity.

I do not mean to dismiss Do and Tarr's analysis; they make a convincing case for a recurrent logic in the films of diasporic Vietnamese filmmakers. My association of the pretty with the cross-cultural encounter tends to support their thesis, and it seems reasonable that films from Vietnam would offer different kinds of representation. However, the assumption that these domestic films will present "a more complex insider view"[45] is where I part company with them. The specificity of the outsider view seems at least as rich with potential geopolitical insight, as has been argued by Hamid Naficy in his account of accented cinema.[46] For Naficy, diasporic film sits alongside exilic and postcolonial modes of response to geopolitical shifts, with filmmakers such as Raúl Ruiz and Atom Egoyan exemplifying an emerging accented aesthetic. The rhetoric of the outsider who makes overly aestheticized films meshes a significant critical strand in contemporary global art cinema with a Eurocentric history of rejecting the Oriental or primitive decorative. Contemporary cinema, by contrast, often deploys the pretty as a way of countering such Eurocentric aesthetics.

A particularly suggestive example is cinematographer and filmmaker Chris Doyle, whose distinctive use of color and light revalues the decorative while elaborating the cross-cultural as a way of cinematic seeing. Doyle is a white Australian who lives in Hong Kong, has worked with many of the most influential Asian directors (Wong Kar-wai, Edward Yang, Pen-Ek Ratanaruang, Chen Kaige), and considers himself to be Asian. In interviews, he explains his style by referring to Chinese color theory and Japanese composition as well as by comparing the street makeup artists in Bangkok to the processes of painting and cinematography.[47] For Doyle, the screen is a cosmetic, but the comparison is a positive one. The decorative culture of contemporary Thai street vendors combines with Asian aesthetic histories to produce a cinematic style that would not be possible without a shift in geopolitical perspective. Doyle's directorial debut, *San tiao ren / Away with Words* (1999), demonstrates this transnational vision. It tells the story of a Japanese man lost in Hong Kong with a drunken English bar owner, and his signature surface light effects articulate directly the disorienting effects of globalized cultural disjuncture. Asano, the protagonist, is synesthetic, and his way of seeing colors as words and memories conjures the very material of cinema as a heady experience of imperfect translation. Following Doyle's example, I explore the usefulness of the pretty for filmmakers working in foreign countries and seeking to produce new—and often radical— accounts of geopolitical exchange. Rather than assuming that distance invariably equals inauthenticity, coloniality, or exoticism, I consider the pretty to broker reimagined looking relations, enabling an outsider (often but not always Western) perspective to look otherwise at the world.

THE HIMALAYAN BLACKBERRY MODEL OF CINEMA

The pretty demands a renegotiation of the historical values attached to visual forms, and it does so in ways that encode geography and sexuality at a structural, not just thematic, level. We can illustrate this process by stepping momentarily from the field of film culture to the nonrepresentational world of horticulture. Poet and essayist Lisa Robertson writes on the decorative properties and modern history of *Rubus armeniacus*, the Himalayan blackberry. Analyzing the significance of a plant categorized as "invasive" and often regarded as a nuisance, Robertson begins, "Illegitimate, superfluous, this difficult genus of frost-tolerant hermaphrodites seems capable of swallowing barns." Unnecessary, voracious, and sexually confused, *Rubus* might remind us of the discursive construction of the pretty. Moreover, Robertson explains, "In late nineteenth-century America, *Rubus* enthusiasm was a faddish adjunct to horticultural orientalism—the identification and importation of Chinese brambles enriched the picturesque aspect of shrubberies, pergolas, and pleasuregrounds."[48] Like the pretty in painting and later cinema, *Rubus* meshes picturesque style with a vague but insistent reference to the non-Western (Armenian? Himalayan? Chinese?). And the nineteenth-century *Rubus* fad is not only coterminous with the development of the modern spectacle, but, located in the American public gardens and pleasure grounds that nurtured cultures of leisurely vision, part of its material history.

For Robertson, *Rubus* instantiates an aesthetic of the surface:

The limitless modification of the skin is different from modernization—surface morphologies, as *Rubus* shows, include decay, blanketing and smothering, shedding, dissolution and penetration, and pendulous swagging and draping, as well as proliferative growth, all in contexts of environmental disturbance and contingency rather than fantasized balance. *Rubus armeniacus* is an exemplary political decoration, a nutritious ornament that clandestinely modifies infrastructural morphology. . . . This is the serious calling of style.[49]

Can the skin of cinema, born from the same aesthetic environment, support such political decoration? A filmic Himalayan blackberry might look like Baz Luhrmann's lush encrustations of antirealist drapery in *Moulin Rouge!* (2001), which proliferates textiles, props, and orientalist tropes in a *mise-en-abyme* of melodramatic gender politics. Or perhaps it can take the form of the snails that proliferate, collect, and distort the surfaces of Peter Greenaway's *A Zed and Two Noughts* (1985). These hermaphroditic, deconstructive organisms take over Greenaway's pictorial screen in time lapse, staging mortality while punning drolly on the process of image making. These films, in their insistence on surface pleasures, perform a kind of aesthetic drag, mimicking and transforming claims on gender, culture, and difference. We might even return to Joachín Jordá, whose films belong to an avant-garde movement, the Barcelona School, which has been largely excluded from Spanish film historiography, in part because the films are too pretty to fit comfortably into a history of modernist countercinema.

These examples only scratch the surface of the pretty, to use a rather inapposite Platonic metaphor. The pretty's rhetorical force consists in its demand that we articulate the supposedly transhistorical discourse of aesthetics with the sociohistorical elaborations of particular images. This book therefore proceeds on two parallel tracks. The first traces the construction of the pretty as a space of exclusion in the history of film theory and criticism, drawing out a rich intellectual history of anti-pretty thinking from its roots in aesthetics and art history to a diverse range of writing on cinema. Chapter 1 analyzes the major concepts and debates in aesthetics and art history that influenced the development of classical film theory, focusing on what is at stake politically in early film theory's adoption of aesthetic concepts. Chapter 3 considers pre–World War II cultural criticism, arguing that the rejection of ornament reveals the racial underpinnings of cinematic modernity's most sacred cow: the inscription of life. Contrasting art nouveau's decorative style with cinema's investment in unstaged reality, it analyzes how the problem of decorative art is intertwined with European cultural criticism in the 1910s and 1920s. Chapter 5 interrogates the iconophobia of postclassical leftist film theory and criticism, proposing that the turn away from aesthetics to ideology theory not only relies on unacknowledged classical aesthetic foundations, but, in doing so, forecloses on the formal potential of postwar film movements. Chapter 7 proceeds from the claim that despite the successes of feminist film theory, we still do not have a model for imagining the radical potential of the image. This is where the pretty offers a profound reordering of aesthetics and politics: if the image has been consistently denigrated as feminine and perverse, then prettiness deconstructs this rhetoric and opens up the productive potential of the aesthetic as feminist form.

Intersecting these chapters is a series of studies of pretty films, organized around different formal qualities of the pretty image. If the critical work of canon formation has tended to sideline prettiness, this strand of the book rethinks the pretty, exploring its productive potential for critique. It asks which filmmakers have been thus criticized and how their films might reveal different ways to read the image. Each analysis responds to a topic in the historical chapter preceding it, although often at a historical or geographical remove. The analyses foreground the visual mechanisms of prettiness, encompassing color, objects, camera movement, spatial relations, and bodies. Chapter 2 considers color in Derek Jarman, taking up the *disegno* versus *colore* debate of chapter 1 and finding his mobilization of prettily decorative colors to be a crucial component of his queer aesthetics. Jarman's films co-opt the logics of art history, and this chapter considers monochromy, filter, and flare as techniques able to articulate historical and political critique. Objects are closely associated with detail, femininity, and the Oriental, and chapter 4 examines Baz Luhrmann's musical *Moulin Rouge* as a way into the operation of mise-en-scène as a function of prettiness. Like the theoretical history that precedes it, this chapter analyzes the racial and sexual implications of the screen diva as well as the material histories of modernity and consumer culture. The reading is organized around two terms that map transnational relations, aesthetics, and gender: *orientalism* and the prop as well as *arabesque* and camera movement. Chapter 6 continues from the study of leftist filmmaking in chapter 5, analyzing the infamous Cuban–Soviet coproduction *Soy Cuba / I Am Cuba* (Kalatozov, 1964). Reviled by many critics as an artistic failure or an exotic fantasy, undistributed in the capitalist world, and finally recovered and restored in the 1990s as a cult classic, *Soy Cuba* is a spectacular example of pretty form and, moreover, a case study of how and why films get accused of formalism. Chapter 8 responds to the investigation of feminism and queer theory in chapter 7: with a sumptuous visual style and a fascination for geographical alterity, Ulrike Ottinger's films have been frequently criticized as bad feminism or ethnographic racism. This case study argues that her lesbian, BDSM-inflected (bondage and discipline, sadism and masochism) visual regime dovetails with her engagement with the "Orient," imagining both perverse femininity and Asian form as integral to a pretty account of the cinematic.

The denigration of the pretty is a constant feature of modern aesthetics, but what styles, films, and movements are so categorized is historically and geographically contingent. The regimes of influence are diverse, but the political imaginary of pretty films shares with my theoretical analysis a deconstructive aesthetic gesture. By counterposing these local and small-scale case studies with a broader historical study of the pretty in film and aesthetics, I hope both to produce a more textured account of the field and, more important, to encourage a dialectical perspective on the pretty. Neither a discursive history of how the pretty is excluded from value nor a transvaluative reading of pretty films is sufficient alone. As in the Benjaminian constellation, it is necessary to amass into a single frame a hitherto unconsidered collection of ideas and objects if one wishes to see history differently. For film studies, the pretty exerts a demand that images be read precisely at the point of their aesthetic exclusion, a practice that might reveal different shapes for the global cinematic body.

FROM AESTHETICS TO FILM AESTHETICS

Or, Beauty and Truth Redux

ALONGSIDE THE EMERGENCE OF CINEMA, THE TURN OF THE twentieth century witnessed a proliferation of scholarship on art history and practical aesthetics. Art historians such as Heinrich Wölfflin and Alois Riegl began to exert a defining influence on the formation of art history as a discipline, and the rise of popular forms of modernism in European and American design created new audiences for domestic and everyday aesthetics in many public spheres.[1] In an analysis of the influence of aesthetics on film theory, it is useful to hold simultaneously an achronological (or, better, a very capaciously historical) view, in which key ideas from throughout aesthetics and art history recur and are reiterated across the century of writing on film, and a closely historicized view, in which the specific moment of film's emergence significantly determined the kinds of aesthetics and the particular histories of art that shaped thinking about the new medium. Thus, for example, the Kantian idea of the beautiful might underlie many accounts of cinematic value from the early twentieth century through to the present day, and contemporary debates on modernist painting might be obvious touchstones for early-twentieth-century film critics reaching to communicate ideas about form to a cultured readership. And although these examples are quite distinct, it is not always so easy or indeed desirable to separate the chronologically localized from the more diffuse causality of discursive fields. The philosophical question of aesthetics can be closely localized, and historically specific art discourses must also be understood philosophically.

This chapter aims to outline this tale of influence, focusing on what is at stake politically in film theory's adoption of aesthetic concepts. It seeks to tease out the formation of the pretty as a (sometimes unspoken) term of exclusion, tracing the ways in which aesthetics and art history form a particular set of foundations, ways of defining aesthetic value and meaning, that are then folded into the development of film-theoretical discourses. This narrative is dauntingly long. Even ancient Greek ideas about art echo in contemporary discourse, and any account of film's relationship to aesthetics must be able to hear these references. However, my project is precisely to strip away the sense of film's aesthetic regime being natural or unconnected to history and ideology. A careful embedding of aesthetic ideas in their social and political contexts is equally required. My resolution to this impasse is, unsurprisingly, dialectical. As much as an ahistorical theory of aesthetic value evades its own political biases, so does the limiting horizon of the traditional historicist. The rejection of the pretty cannot be brought into focus solely by examining the immediate precursors of each discursive moment. Rather, in the manner of Walter Benjamin's constellation, we must amass collections of objects, ideas, and images—collections that demand consideration of the historically punctual as well as the seemingly far flung, collections that arrange history differently and, because they look back from a particular perspective, are able to read history anew.[2]

This particular constellation centers on classical film theory and on how and what it draws from largely modern aesthetics and art history. In its most historically delineated spaces, it considers the debates on art and design that immediately preceded and surrounded writing on the first decades of cinema. But it also looks outward from this rich historical intersection: backward to a history of the visual and plastic arts that classical film theorists consistently referenced in their scholarship and forward to provide a clearer picture of the significance of certain aesthetic problematics for film studies more generally. Questions of line and color, beauty and value, realism and the nature of the cinematic are scarcely limited to classical film theory, but, as I argue, it is in this period that these aesthetic issues were produced as foundational elements of the cinematic. Moreover, I argue that at the core of this construction of the cinematic is an exclusion of the pretty.

LINE AND COLOR

Walter Crane's textbook for artists, *Line and Form* (1900), opens with a fascinating illustration: "The Origin of Outline" (figure 8).[3] In it, a woman sits on a rock, her shadow cast on a wall behind her. Beside her, a man dressed in caveman-style fur toga uses charcoal to draw around

FIGURE 8 Walter Crane, "The Origin of Outline" (1900)
Walter Crane's illustration figures the gendered history of drawing.

her shadow and thus to create the first line drawing. His other hand covers her clasped hands (to reassure her or to keep her still?), while she hunches slightly in an elegant but passive pose. This illustration, although monochromatic, stages vividly the historical and political dynamics of line and color in the early twentieth century as well as the fantasmatic nature of this relationship. The woman's body creates a block of shadow that, like color, forms an unbounded, unintentional mass, while the man turns this raw material into intended meaningful line. In a structure familiar to feminism, passive woman simply is, whereas active man creates. And although Crane's ink drawing poses line against monochromatic shadowing rather than the polychromatic hues of painting, the allegory of the formless feminine shaped by masculine line is vividly evoked. Line and color are never mere formal terms in art historical discourse, but always already gendered, embodied, bound to socially structured hierarchies of power and value.

Moreover, the iconography of Crane's allegorical image suggests the projective fantasy at work in it. Created for the book in 1900, the image nonetheless draws on two distinct levels of historicity. The first is the caveman aesthetic of the couple's shaggy clothing, bare feet, and natural surroundings. It is a prehistoric origin myth, designed to install modern aesthetic values as eternal. (Feminists have long had cause to suspect caveman allegories, which never go terribly well for women.) The second, more subtle level of historicity consists of a medieval aspect to the couple's heads, suggestive of the Arts and Crafts movement, with which Crane was aligned. The woman has long, well-ordered curls; the man, a pageboy-style bob; and both wear a circlet of beads on their heads. This late Victorian, precapitalist retro suggests at once a romanticization of this aesthetic figure and a reflexive awareness of its historical projection. Close on the heels of cinema's invention, we see a projected image imagined not in the more familiar metaphoric terms of Plato's cave, but as the origin of the art historical debate between line and color. And the concretization of woman as formless color in Crane's image moves beyond the transhistorical patriarchy that underwrites this debate to propose, in addition, an ambiguous investment in the premodern within the modern—a desire for a species of modernist primitivism that will recur, along with gender, throughout this story.

Crane's illustration figures the dialectic with which I began: line versus color is at once a long-standing debate in aesthetics and a historically specific question for early film theories. As Jacqueline Lichtenstein argues, a suspicion of the image has dogged Western art since Plato's time, and the separation of *disegno* from *colore* enabled critics to shift from an unhelpful Platonic condemnation *of* painting to a more malleable Platonic schema *in* painting.[4] *Disegno* (drawing) came to figure the masculine and meaningful aspect of reason in art, whereas color was relegated to the secondary role of providing emotion, pleasure, or raw material for the artist. The debate stretches back to antiquity but recurs at various points in the history of Western aesthetics. For example, Kant excluded color from the categories of the beautiful or the sublime, arguing that color might be charming, but it was inherently inferior to both of his central categories. Sir Joshua Reynolds contrasted the "simple, careful, pure, and correct style of Poussin" with the "florid" and "subordinate" style of Rubens. Although Rubens's coloring is skillful, Reynolds finds it "too much of what we call tinted. . . . The richness of his composition, the luxuriant harmony and brilliancy of his colouring, so dazzle the eye, that whilst his works continue before us, we cannot help thinking that all his deficiencies are fully supplied."[5] Both Kant's exclusion of color and Reynolds's tinting and dazzle appear in film discourse, but most important for our current purposes is the nineteenth-century iteration of the debate, with neoclassicists advocating for line against colorists such as Delacroix.

We might not expect this debate to have a great direct impact on early film theory for the simple reason that the first decades of film were not shot in color. Certainly, many black-and-white films used tinting, toning, and other color processes so that audiences did see colors at the movies. Just as silent film was not actually silent, black-and-white film was not actually monochromatic. Iris Barry writes of the problems of using color in film, finding a lack of consideration of tone to be a failing of most color films and looking to the implicit colors seen in black-and-white reproductions of the Old Masters to explain the necessity of subtle shading in cinema.[6] Reiterating Reynolds, she finds "tinted" color to run the risk of tastelessness. Critics of early cinema, then, could consider color as a factor in their experience of film. However, the importance of color to classical film theory is not limited to this possibility: both before and after the introduction of color stock, film critics drew on the debates on line versus color to shape their claims on cinematic value.

In his influential early account *The Film, a Psychological Study*, Hugo Münsterberg broadly opposes color in film, arguing that it detracts from the specificity of the new medium and ultimately reduces the film's artistry. He addresses exactly the type of postproduction effect highlighted by Barry, allowing, "To be sure, many of the prettiest effects in color are even today produced by artificial stencil methods."[7] His compliment here is grudging, and he regards the pretty color effect as attractive but not aesthetically meaningful. We should note his use of the term *pretty*, which appears twice in this book, in both cases in contrast to a more valued aesthetic mode. In this instance, the pretty color effect is in contrast to black-and-white film, which Münsterberg finds to be superior: "We do not want to paint the cheeks of the Venus of Milo: neither do we want to see the coloring of Mary Pickford or Anita Stewart."[8] Just as in Lichtenstein's account of aesthetics, color is supplemental to true art, and as Crane's example suggests, the space of color is structurally understood as feminine, pretty, and passive.

Münsterberg's engagement with the line / color hierarchy extends beyond his explicit critique of color film. In the "Emotions" section of his book, he condemns the excess of gesture and emotion in film in terms of light effects: "The quick marchlike rhythm of the drama of the reel favors this artificial overdoing, too. The rapid alteration of the scenes often seems to demand a jumping from one emotional climax to another, or rather the appearance of such extreme expressions where the content of the play hardly suggests such heights and depths of emotion. The soft lights are lost and the mental eye becomes adjusted to glaring flashes."[9] Here, the excess associated with melodrama (the gestural, the artificial, too much emotion) is imagined in terms of excessive visual effects (lights, glare, flashes) that suggest a dazzling of the spectator. This dazzle may not include color, but it is imbued with another aesthetic critique of color: the Greek notion of *poikiloi*. This term defines color as brightness or effect rather than as essence: "the dazzle that blinds the gaze, the sparkle that obscures vision."[10] For Plato, *poikiloi* implied sophistry, pretty words that hide the truth, and for Lichtenstein it is another variant of the seductive and dangerous feminine. In art historical terms, *poikiloi* implies a distinction between unadulterated color and false sparkle, and so, without referring to actual hues, Münsterberg draws on the aesthetic suspicion of the bright and gaudy.[11]

And it is not only Münsterberg who is suspicious of color. Classical film theorists with views as different as Béla Balázs and Rudolf Arnheim come together in their negative attitude to color film. We might compare their discussions of pictorialism, which Arnheim is broadly in favor of and Balázs entirely against. Despite this conflict, a strikingly similar reading of color emerges in each account. Arnheim, writing in 1935, advocates that film become more composed and painterly, but that it remain monochromatic. He argues that color films look "atrocious" because they remain too close to nature: "Nature is beautiful, but not in the same sense as art. Its color combinations are accidental and hence usually inharmonious. . . . We have become used to seeing a painting as a structure full of meanings; hence our helplessness, our intense shock on seeing the majority of color photographs."[12] Balázs takes an entirely different view on pictorialism, valuing film's ability to move and rejecting anything too painterly. And yet his rejection of the pictorial (a more typical claim for classical film theory) is folded into a critique of color very similar to Arnheim's: "One of the dangers of the color film is the temptation to compose the shots too much with a view to a static pictorial effect, like a painting, thus breaking up the flow of the film into a series of staccato jerks."[13]

In these debates, color centers the larger problem of the cosmetic: meaningless in itself, color bespeaks a veiling or an even more anxiety-provoking lack of reason. David Batchelor has compellingly argued that the opposition to color charts a consistent prejudice in Western thought: "As with all prejudices, its manifest form, its loathing, masks a fear: a fear of contamination and corruption by something that is unknown or appears unknowable. This loathing of color, this fear of corruption through color, needs a name: chromophobia." Batchelor links chromophobia to iconophobia, describing two modes of cultural rhetoric on color: "In the first, color is made out to be the property of some 'foreign' body—usually the feminine, the oriental, the primitive, the infantile, the vulgar, the queer or the pathological. In the second, color is relegated to the realm of the superficial, the supplementary, the inessential or the cosmetic. In one, color is regarded as alien and therefore dangerous; in the other, it is perceived merely as a secondary quality of experience, and thus unworthy of serious consideration. Color is dangerous or it is trivial, or it is both."[14] The aesthetic here is closely linked to ideas about gender, race, and sexuality, and in analyzing discourses such as color in film theory, we can grasp how power is imagined not only in representational politics, but in apparently apolitical questions of form and style. The pretty is not limited to the colorful, but color forms one of its major qualities. Classical film theory's suspicion of color and arguments in favor of limiting its dangerous effects provide insight into cinema's adoption of anti-pretty modes of thought.

As we see in Crane's illustration, color is closely related to gender: the hierarchy of line and color attributes masculine reason to line and feminine emotion to color. Batchelor charts the origins of this hierarchy from Plato's notion of cosmetics to patriarchal anxieties about feminine wiles. Therefore, "if color is a cosmetic, it is also—and again—coded as feminine. Color is a supplement, but it is also, potentially, a seduction."[15] Thus we can locate a gendered logic in critiques of color in film, whether by early theorists who hoped to keep film monochromatic or by more recent critics who have associated color with excess, melodrama, or simple bad taste (later chapters consider the question of feminism in more detail). Indeed, as Dudley Andrew has pointed out, filmmakers and audiences have often been well aware of the connotations of color debates. Describing the process of bringing color film to France, he says, "The French could readily decipher an ideological message in this list of opposing attributes [of competing color processes]. Technicolor had (and promoted) a Hollywood notion of color: purer than reality, needing strong artificial light, aggressive, almost whorish."[16] Even in the moment of Technicolor's ascendance, deep and bright color was read in the language of suspicious, even criminal feminine seduction.

We see the emphasis on this feminizing effect clearly in Siegfried Kracauer's *Theory of Film*, where the uncinematic formative tendency includes among its various aspects the colorful pretty. Thus his description of *The Red Shoes* (Powell and Pressburger, 1948): "Moira Shearer dances, in a somnambulistic trance, through fantastic worlds avowedly intended to project her unconscious mind—agglomerates of landscape-like forms, near-abstract shapes, and luscious color schemes which have all the traits of stage imagery. Disengaged creativity thus drifts away from the basic concerns of the medium" (figure 9).[17] This is a rich passage, containing many of Kracauer's critiques of the formative: fantasy, dreamscape, theatricality, lack of concern for camera reality. We also see color—something that Kracauer, like Münsterberg, avows a lack of interest in, but that erupts, unbidden, in both of their discussions of troublesome films: *colore*, the other of logocentric line. And the word *luscious* hints at a feminizing rhetoric of seduction that has been at play in Kracauer ever since he evoked the wonderfully fetishistic "girl clusters" to exemplify the ideological work of the mass ornament.[18]

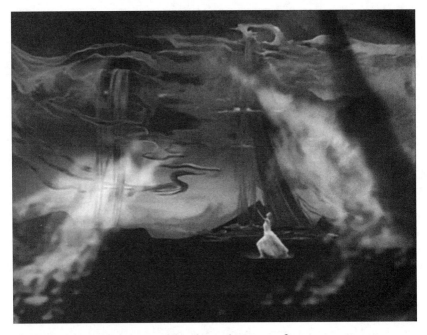

FIGURE 9 *The Red Shoes* (Powell and Pressburger, 1948)
A fantastic and theatrical landscape exemplifies Siegfried Kracauer's concept of the formative.

Color is also used to racialize subjects in modern aesthetics, with various naming strategies of colonialism, primitivism, race, and ethnicity being connected to the consumption of colorful images. Goethe claims in *Theory of Colors* that "savage natives, uneducated people, and children have a great predilection for vivid colors."[19] Although he does not write about race as a question of visible skin color, we can infer that the savage natives are not modern white Europeans. The connection is direct in Johann Joachim Winckelmann, who deploys European encounters with nonwhite peoples to figure aesthetic disgust toward colorful art: "A traveller assures us that daily association with Negroes diminishes the disagreeableness of their color, and displays what is beautiful in them; just as the color of bronze and of the black and greenish basalt does not detract from the beauty of antique heads."[20] The French critic Charles Blanc, writing in 1862, says even more explicitly, "Color, then, is the peculiar characteristic of the lower forms of nature, while drawing becomes the medium of expression, more and more dominant, the higher we rise in the scale of being."[21] Again, the organization of people into lower and higher forms maps aesthetic taste onto emergent modern racialist thinking. Such racist rhetoric can be found imported wholesale in some classical film theory. Thus Arnheim quotes someone named H. Baer, writing in the influential German art journal *Kunstblatt,* in support of his own opposition to color film: "Color invaded the graphic arts as an increased attraction for the eye. Uncivilized man is not as a rule satisfied with black-and-white. Children, peasants and primitive peoples demand the highest degree of bright coloring. It is the primitives of the great cities who congregate before the film screen. Therefore film calls in the aid of bright colors."[22] The logic of primitivism binds colorful films with immigrant and working-class audiences as racialized objects of exclusion.

In addition to this primitivist rhetoric, in which color is directly attributed to the tastes of non-European peoples, aesthetic theories have linked the colorful with the non-European at a structural level. If the colorless line drawing signifies the centered intending subject of Western reason, then color is not only supplementary but also structurally other to meaning or sense. The Latin word *colorem* is connected to *celare* (to conceal), and in art historical terms the notion of the cosmetic claims that painting begins with a colorless field and adds surface material. Thus whereas line is part of the world of meaning (shapes it or even creates it), color can only be the outsider whose entrance detracts from significance. For Batchelor, this structure overlays the cultural construction of whiteness over the absence of color in art: "Here is the problem: not white; not whites; but *generalized* white, because generalized white—whiteness—is abstract, detached and open to contamination by terms like 'pure.' "[23] The absence of color as a pure and meaningful whiteness is enthusiastically taken up by film theory, which is overdetermined (perhaps even more so than art theories) by notions of the cinema as pure light. Richard Dyer has interrogated the racial dynamics of this discourse, whereby moral goodness is connected not only to whiteness as a racial category, but to cinema as light uncontaminated by darkening images. In this way, the white actresses of silent cinema are backlit in order that they might radiate the uncorrupted whiteness of the screen.[24] (In the rhetoric of Hollywood aesthetics, we might draw a distinction between the cinematic beauty of Mary Pickford surrounded by a halo of light and the tawdry prettiness, for Münsterberg, of her colorized image.) In the bodies of Mary Pickford and Lillian Gish, the racial politics of film content is seamlessly matched to the racial dynamics of its dominant aesthetic.

Traces of this discourse continue throughout the history of film theory and criticism, and color recurs as a productive category throughout this book. The filmmaking team central to Kracauer's example, Michael Powell and Emeric Pressburger, have often been read as "flamboyant" and un-British in their dedication to saturated color palettes, suggesting that in Europe, at least, the orientalizing impetus of color remains in force.[25] Likewise, the centrality of semiotics and language in postclassical film theory suggests a hierarchy also based on line over color or on language over expression. This is not to suggest that a semiotics of color is impossible, but that the focus on narrative, editing, and linguistic structures has tended to enclose the scope of film theory in the same ways as *disegno* versus *colore*. Brian Price proposes something similar in regard to David Bordwell's work on the classical Hollywood cinema in which Bordwell's valorization of narrative's perceptual clarity aligns with art historical line. Style, for Bordwell, is like color, something that should be limited and used only in subordination to narrative.[26]

The resilience of this hierarchical structure returns us to Lichtenstein's concept of the moving standard of post-Platonic exclusion. She explains that Aristotle comes to stand as the answer to Plato's rejection of the arts, rescuing painting by positing line as the mark of good painting's truth value: "Removal of the philosophical condemnation of the visual arts does not do away with the dividing line that previously justified their exclusion: it moves this line."[27] This response inaugurates a history of aesthetic goalpost shifting that extends into film theory, saving film as a meaningful art form by excluding the colorful and the pretty. The fungible and historically contingent nature of this line can be demonstrated by contrasting the relatively stable disparagement of color with the reversal of value in regard to formation. In classical aesthetics, the unformed is chaotic and negative, like color, but *formlessness* becomes a valued term in classical film theory—for instance, in Kracauer's idea of endlessness. The problem of being underformed morphs into the problem of being overformed. Hence, the line moves when needed to accommodate new media or new values, but the pretty still finds itself on the wrong side.

Thus although color itself is one important vector of prettiness in film theory, the color / line hierarchy exemplifies a more broadly significant construction of cinematic value from which the pretty is repeatedly barred.

Aesthetic judgment about film, conceived in terms of artistic merit or, increasingly, in terms of medium specificity and cultural importance, consistently proceeds by excluding pretty qualities cognate with supplemental and inferior color. Instead of painting versus no painting (Plato) or line versus color (art history), film theory separates cinematic specificity from uncinematic style and film language from the seductive image. The historical development of this binary clearly requires critique. The rejection of color involves a pernicious patriarchal and racist logic whose operation continues unmarked even in the absence of any thematics of race or gender in a text or critical rubric. But it is also important to trouble the mode of binary valuation, even in reversed form. It does no good, as some feminists and formalists have done, to champion autonomous beauty, the *jouissance* of color, or even the moral good of such pleasure (that is, the idea of beauty as good for the soul). In unsettling the aesthetic assumptions of film theory, we need instead to reconfigure claims on the location of value.

The Aesthetic Language of Film

Classical film theory does not shrink from its roots in art historical and aesthetic debate. Whereas postclassical, Althusserian, and semiotic theories tend to reject aesthetic concepts as part of the problem, and the culturalist turn suspects the aesthetic to be an avoidance of popular taste, the first decades of serious writing on film often aimed to locate the cinema within a long-standing discourse on beauty, art, and value. Thus Vachel Lindsay's *The Art of the Moving Picture* (1915) defines his three main types of film in terms of sculpture, painting, and architecture as well as dramatic, lyric, and epic poetry.[28] Here, earlier art forms sustain a claim on the potential of cinematic art. Arnheim likewise uses painting as a model for cinematic form, although he favors modernist art over Lindsay's more classicist system of value. And, of course, André Bazin's seminal essay, "The Ontology of the Photographic Image," asserts the centrality of photographic reproduction in the history of aesthetic thought.[29] Moreover, it is not simply a case of building up cinema through a comparison with other art forms: classical film theory consistently uses both historical debates in aesthetics and the emergent discipline of art history to ground its attempts to systematize thinking about cinema.

Balázs, for example, repeatedly models his *Theory of the Film* on both formal and historical aesthetics. He argues that "the cut-out of the close-up is a function akin to the composition in painting" and that "the silent film grew less and less 'literary,' following in this respect the trend at that time prevalent in the art of painting."[30] If film's formal mechanisms and historical development can be understood with reference to the other arts, this reference must nonetheless be grounded in medium specificity. Balázs proposes that Gotthold Lessing's *Laocöon* (1766) "should to this day serve as a model for all epic and dramatic art,"[31] a claim that at once links cinema to a broad debate in aesthetic theory and yet cites in Lessing a famous advocate for the inherent and separate qualities of each art.[32] By evoking Lessing, Balázs articulates ideas about cinematic specificity to central questions of aesthetics. He similarly inserts film history into art historical debates about histories of style: "Finally, it is as well to remember what Alois Riegl found more than once in examining changes of style in the course of art history; that a certain phenomenon may be a symptom of decadence in the art of a certain age or class and at the same time be the first manifestation of the form-language of a new class or age."[33] By citing Riegl, Balázs connects cinema to the modern art historical project of theorizing the relationship between social or political histories and the taxonomic history of styles. And by reading this relationship in terms of Lessing, he explicitly connects the history of cinema to that of visual art.

Because the connection between film theory and aesthetics is so direct during this period, we might expect to find art history's hierarchies to be plainly visible, too. The secondary status of the image and the concomitant policing of form and style within the image that Lichtenstein traces in painting should be most apparent during the phase of film criticism in which aesthetic debates and concepts predominate. However, although the influence of aesthetic language is immediately apparent in classical film theory, the latter's central questions of cinematic specificity seem oriented to locating cultural and aesthetic value in the image rather than to denigrating it. This apparent paradox is in fact similar to that of painting, in which, according to Lichtenstein, a problem of the image itself is reimagined as a problem within the image, a question of proper style.[34] In classical film theory and criticism, I argue, questions of aesthetic value get refigured as questions of the truly cinematic, with the category of the pretty linking the two values by way of its mutual exclusion. The crucial theoretical shift from the aesthetic to the cinematic is thus enabled by a discourse on the pretty. We can uncover the mechanisms of this transfer of value by tracing classical film theory's discourse on aesthetics.

BEAUTY, GOOD AND BAD

Beauty holds an ambivalent position in much writing on film, connoting as it does a traditional vision of aesthetic value that might not seem appropriate or useful for exploring the new medium. Nonetheless, many critics construct a category of the beautiful, and as they do so, the pretty also emerges as an operator of judgment. In *The Film, a Psychological Study*, Münsterberg argues that "to imitate the world is a mechanical process; to transform the world so that it becomes a thing of beauty is the purpose of art." The explicit contrast is between the mimetic and the beautiful. However, he immediately supplements beauty with a counterexample of the pretty: "The so-called beautiful landscape may, of course, be material for a beautiful landscape painting, but the chances are great that such a pretty vista will attract the dilettante and not the real artist who knows that the true value of his painting is independent of the prettiness of the model. He knows that a muddy country road or a dirty street or a trivial little pond may be the material for immortal pictures."[35] Here, true value and transformative beauty are located in the modest, the ugly, and the inconsequential, whereas the pretty, by contrast, connotes the vacant, the unserious, and the false.

We see a similar discourse on the picturesque landscape in Jean Epstein's writing on *photogénie*. Epstein complains about landscape films that do not use close-ups. What he wants to see is "shop windows, cafes, quite wretched urchins, a cashier, ordinary gestures made with their full capacity for realization, a fair, the dust of automobiles, an atmosphere."[36] As with Münsterberg's account of cinematic beauty, Epstein desires the small, the ordinary, the unattractive (quite wretched), the dirty. Beauty is understood in contrast to the visually pretty: a lack of visual appeal is necessary to access the true. He continues, "The landscape film is, for the moment, a big zero. People look for the picturesque in them. The picturesque in cinema is zero, nothing, negation. About the same as speaking of colors to a blind man. The film is susceptible only to *photogénie*. Picturesque and photogenic coincide only by chance."[37] *Picturesque* is another key term that intersects with the pretty: denoting a composed landscape, it constructs a pictorial framing of space as less valuable than one that is naturally occurring. Too imagistic an image, the picturesque encloses space and precludes a nobler sense of beauty as value. In a rhetorical turn we will see frequently reiterated, Epstein tethers the valuable and the cinematic by opposing both to the picturesque.

If there is a clear echo of Plato's cosmetics here, there is also a stronger investment in a Kantian notion of beauty as value. Some early film theorists drew explicitly from this aesthetics; Arnheim, for example, calls his work a "Kantian turn of the new doctrine [of gestalt theory]."[38] But even among those for whom an overt claim on beauty would be anathema, the project of defining cinematic specificity sought to map an intellectually autonomous space for film in the same way that Kant's *Critique of Judgment* does for the aesthetic in general.[39] Discourse on beauty can be understood in terms of developing a film-specific aesthetic theory, but to do so it must also draw on the exclusionary scope of Kant's aesthetic schema. As Arthur Danto glosses, "Beauty is the only [aesthetic term] that is a value in addition to being a descriptive predicate. Beauty is a value like goodness or truth, and that distinguishes it from *pretty, delicate,* and so on."[40] The pretty vista is less valuable than the dirty street or the wretched urchins because once these visually unappealing scenes are attached to beauty, they are understood as having inherent goodness, nobility, and truth. To be beautiful is to be good, whereas to be pretty is simply to look good.

Kant invokes the pretty only once in the *Critique of Judgment.* (He uses the German word *hübsch,* which translates as "pretty," "attractive," sometimes with a diminutive and feminizing quality of "cuteness" or "bonniness." It can also become the colloquial phrase *bildhübsch,* or "pretty as a picture.") It is not surprising that the term appears only once because the pretty is far outside Kant's interests in the beautiful and the sublime. However, the instance is nonetheless telling. He writes, "We say of certain products of which we expect that they should at least in part appear as beautiful art, they are without spirit. . . . A poem may be very neat and elegant, but without spirit. A history may be exact and well arranged, but without spirit. . . . [E]ven of a woman we say that she is pretty, an agreeable talker, and courteous, but without spirit."[41] Of all the many iterations of inferior aesthetic qualities, it is the woman who is pretty.[42] Each of these categories continues to resonate in the hierarchies of film theory, which find prettiness, elegance, careful composition, and pleasantness to indicate a lack of soul or, to put it in more modern terms, depth, truth, or essential cinematic value.

A similar structure is at play for Balázs, although he uses the word *beauty* in both cases, distinguishing a good, noble beauty from a debased, picturesque one: "Over-beautiful, picturesque shots are sometimes dangerous even if they are the result of good camera work alone. Their over-perfect composition, their self-sufficient closed harmony may lend them a static, painting-like character and thereby lift them out of the dynamic stream of the action. Such beauty has its own centre of gravity, its own frame and does not reach beyond itself to the preceding and the subsequent."[43] Here the pretty is described as "overbeautiful," an excess of visual harmony that becomes downright dangerous. The picturesque is not to be trusted, for its similarity to the style and composition of painting draws it away from cinematic truth. This figure of the overbeautiful resonates across both film theory and art history. In the image that fails to reach beyond the frame we can catch an echo of Bazin's rejection of the baroque frame, which I discuss later in this chapter. And in the dangerous self-sufficiency of a film that looks inward and is solipsistically concerned with its own beauty, we might glimpse the figure of the beautiful woman regarding herself in the mirror. A fit subject for masculine art, but not a figuration of art itself.

Jacques Aumont locates the appearance of true beauty in Balázs's account of cinema, where he glosses, "If female movie stars must be beautiful . . . it is because, in cinema, appearance is not pure decoration, but already an interiority. The stars' beauty, in film, is simple beauty, that symbol of good hoped for by Kant—because beauty is a physiognomic expression."[44] For Balázs, true and meaningful beauty is exactly a Kantian good, a form of purely cinematic expression that is located not in the surface arrangement of the female star's face, but in an invisible interiority. And we see how important it is for Aumont to separate this effect from "decoration." The star may be female, but her femininity must be curtailed, the surface qualities of makeup, costume, and bodily composition minimized in favor of the close-up that can see through to her interior, disembodied truth. The debate on cinematic specificity depends on locating value in the image, and for this to be done the term *image* must be pried away from its connotations of picturesque, decorative surface and aligned instead with meaning and depth.

This claim is another challenging one for film theory because the screen is precisely a surface, and its images momentary. As Ricciotto Canudo insists, "What is shown above all is the appearance rather than the essence of contemporary life, from sardine fishing in the Mediterranean to the marvel of flying steel and the indomitable human courage of the races at Dieppe or the aviation week at Rheims."[45] Nonetheless, a certain idealist tenor can be found in the repeated connection of cinematic value to depth in the work of the earliest theorists. Victor Freeburg, for example, writing in 1918, exhorted readers, "Let us constantly remember that if our photoplay is to become a classic it must possess beneath the attractive surface which appeals to the crowd the permanent values of illuminating truth, universal meaning, and unfading beauty."[46] Although Laura Marcus points to critics such as Freeburg as constituting a road not taken for film theory, Freeburg's separation of the attractive surface from the meaningful depths of the image retains currency even when the rest of his argument has been largely forgotten.[47] The language of depth is largely abandoned by later theorists, but in the rejection of the pretty surface the association of true meaning with depth retains its explanatory appeal.

Freeburg's association of the attractive surface with what appeals to the crowd suggests a way into this aesthetic structure. Both a classism and a sexism underlie his description of what appeals to whom, with the clear implication that those who can appreciate the classical qualities of film are (elite, white, American) men. Such assumptions are not unusual in discourses on the mass audience for silent cinema, but what is useful in this particular iteration is its Kantian division of aesthetic labor into universal beauty versus the lesser pretty aspects of film, which will be appreciated by certain kinds of people. In other words, the problem with the pretty surface, for Freeburg, is one of interest. To return to Kant's association of beauty with good, we find that although looking good may depend on social particularities, being good should be a universal quality. Münsterberg in particular adopts this model, insisting that art must be "entirely isolated" from the world itself and "sharply set off from the sphere of our practical interests."[48] He argues that "we annihilate beauty when we link the artistic creation with practical interests and transform the spectator into a selfishly interested bystander."[49] The abstracted beholder of universal beauty is without interest, whereas specifically defined bystanders enjoy the less-than-beautiful image.

By reading cinematic specificity through Kantian ideas of autonomous beauty, the pretty emerges as the excluded (and often occluded) term of interest. If we push a little further on the nature of this system, we find that the association of cinematic beauty and value with universality—and the excluded pretty with interest—begins to suggest the political stakes of film's developing discourse on aesthetics. Kant argues that "every interest spoils the judgment of taste and takes from its impartiality, especially if the purposiveness is not, as with the interest of Reason, placed before the feeling of pleasure but grounded on it."[50] Even more clearly than in the cases of reason and ethics, however, constructing universal categories for aesthetic judgment presents problems for Kant. When everyone does not value the same notion of beauty, what criteria can be brought to bear? Kant's beauty unsurprisingly transpires to be bounded in politically significant ways, and, I would suggest, the same structural assumptions underlie the film aesthetics that follow it.

For instance, immediately after outlining the problem of interest, Kant turns to those qualities that must be separated from the consideration of beauty. The gendered nature of the beautiful is visible in this account of "charms and emotions." For Kant, these qualities might be a tolerated complement to the beautiful, but they have no place in its definition or experience: "That taste is always barbaric which needs a mixture of charms and emotions in order that there may be satisfaction, and still more so if it make these the measure of its assent."[51] The language of exclusion here is clearly gendered and raced: both *emotion* and *charms* are highly feminized terms, and a taste for such things is further described as primitive, barbarian. A hint of the pretty also lurks in the word *charms*. Like prettiness, charm implies magic, a form of pleasurable seduction that is outside of reason or agency. To be charmed is to be tricked, and the witchcraft of the charm closely affiliates the inferior unbeautiful aesthetic with the dangerous power of women and primitives.

Many critics have taken issue with Kant's claim on the impartiality of taste, and the political status of what comes to be excluded has been widely interrogated. David J. Getsy, for instance, accounts historically for Kant's relationship to the colonial world: "Scattered throughout Kant's aesthetics, for instance, are counterexamples or comments on cultures *outside* Europe (for instance, the Iroquois). The growing pressure of contact with, and awareness of, non-European cultures contributed to the increasing codification of aesthetic criteria in the Enlightenment."[52]

Probably the most significant rereading is that by Gayatri Chakravorty Spivak, who analyzes Kant's use of the woman and the Aboriginal as counterexamples to subjectivity, unpicking the colonial discourse within which these figures serve as placeholders for that which Kant cannot think of as human.[53] Kant poses the question of why men (humans) should exist and adds parenthetically that this question is hard to answer "if we cast our thoughts by chance on the New Hollanders or the inhabitants of Tierra del Fuego."[54] As Spivak points out, Kant can think of these examples—referring to Australian Aborigines and South American first peoples—only in passing, not as real subjects of inquiry, and she goes on to explain that whether the Aboriginal is human or not was a subject of contemporary European debate. Kant answers in the negative: in order to construct the Western philosophical subject, the Aboriginal must be excluded from humanity. Although the woman is explicitly assigned a lesser place, Spivak argues, the racial other is more thoroughly erased. Their existence casually dismissed as unnecessary, the New Hollander and the Tierra del Fuego native provide evidence that "the subject as such in Kant is geopolitically differentiated."[55]

If Kant's writing expresses at its margins the imprint of the colonial encounter on late-eighteenth-century thought, what happens when a Kantian aesthetics is taken up by film criticism during another era of politically stressed global exchange? In the intervening century of aesthetic thought, Kant's beauty was more explicitly linked to European colonialism. French aesthetician Eugène Véron, for instance, argued that beauty is linked to morality because our ideals of beauty derive from a rejection of the ugliness associated with "inferior races." In describing ugliness, he concludes that "these are precisely the salient characteristics of inferior races, and even of the animals. Physiologically, they result from the inferior development of the intellectual organs, and the predominance of purely physical instincts over moral wants."[56] In post-Kantian thinking, the whiteness of beauty as nobility is made explicit along with an articulation of aesthetic rejection to racial difference. In the first decades of the twentieth century, cinema's ethnographic eye ensured that the likes of the Neuholländer were not only faintly imagined natives, but a major attraction of the medium. Assenka Oksiloff has analyzed the centrality of this ethnographic fascination with "primitive" cultures in early German cinema, and Catherine Russell describes how in Louis Regnault's chronophotographic studies of native bodies, "nonwhite skin color constitutes part of the decorative exoticism of the spectacular body."[57] Across early cinema, the production of a visual regime of race is an enduring issue for scholars of cinematic modernity. Race (or gender) was not the same category for Balázs or Louis Delluc as it had been for Kant, and yet the rhetoric of an uncinematic pretty as a quality defined in terms of interest inevitably conjures the other of aesthetic universality as a structural as well as a representational problem.

One figuration of this problem is the Japanese actor Sessue Hayakawa, a major international star in the silent period and an object of a certain fascination for many European and American film critics of the time (figure 10). Ricciotto Canudo, for instance, saw Hayakawa as exemplary of the vital force of the film star. For him, Hayakawa's performances evoke something other than the bad melodrama of an illustrated story: "He knows that he works with and by light. . . . The art of Sessue Hayakawa consists in creating the oriental atmosphere of the film . . . so that all the literary drama disappears, to leave in front of us

FIGURE 10   *The Cheat* (DeMille, 1915)
In Sessue Hayakawa, early film critics find a racialized figuration of the cinematic apparatus.

something living and with contents torn from life itself."[58] Epstein, meanwhile, regarded Hayakawa as a key example of *photogénie*.[59] Christian Keathley glosses Epstein's interest in Hayakawa's natural movements, pointing out that *"photogénie* results not from what has been aestheticized, but from the real shining through deliberate aestheticization."[60] Mary Ann Doane attributes Hayakawa's importance to Epstein to his "relative restraint as an actor of the silent cinema, rejecting the histrionics usually associated with the era," and, indeed, the subtlety of his expression is positively referenced by several theorists, including Balázs, who claims that because Hayakawa's face does not move, the spectator can see in him something that is not visible in the image.[61] Despite these favorable readings, however, it is easy to see how the valorization of Hayakawa's understated acting style can shade into orientalist stereotypes of impassivity or worse.[62]

In the article "Beauty in the Cinema," Delluc takes Hayakawa and Chaplin as "two expressions of beauty." Here, the two actors represent contrasting modes of beauty: "Hayakawa, through his race and virile style, and Chaplin, through his honest and mathematical naiveté, achieve equally genuine performances. . . . Of Chaplin alone can one say he has talent; of Hayakawa, one can say nothing: he is a phenomenon." In a familiar racist discourse, the white actor's performance is understood in terms of action or agency, whereas that of the racial other displays his ontological nature, simple being. Delluc goes on to invoke all manner of orientalist rhetoric, describing Hayakawa's "cat-like, implacable cruelty" and his "smile of childlike ferocity" and finally dubbing him "this savage Hayakawa."[63] This analysis vividly reviews early-twentieth-century tropes of orientalism, in particular the stereotypes of East Asians that held currency in Euro-American popular culture, but there is more going on here than a racist representational regime. It is significant that Delluc admires Hayakawa and that his racism is closely bundled with his account of cinema's aesthetic value. Hayakawa enables for Delluc a discourse on the cinematic not despite his race, but because of it.

To understand how these ideas are connected, we can turn to what appears to be a counterexample: Vachel Lindsay's more culturally sensitive attempt to read Hayakawa's Asianness. For Lindsay, Hayakawa "looks like all the actors in the old Japanese prints. . . . But he has that atmosphere of pictorial romance which would make him a valuable man for the retelling of the old Japanese legends of Kwannon. . . . The Japanese genius is eminently pictorial. Rightly viewed, every Japanese screen or bit of lacquer is from the Ancient Asia Columbus set sail to find. It would be a noble thing if American experts in the Japanese principles of deco- ration . . . should tell stories of old Japan with the assistance of such men as Sessue Hayakawa."[64] Lindsay's treatment of Hayakawa is less aggres- sive, and, unlike Delluc's, it articulates an awareness of Asian aesthetic traditions outside the Western imaginary. But his description is clearly also indebted to orientalist fantasy, and what Lindsay makes plain is the pictorial nature of this fantasy. Hayakawa looks like a Japanese print: his manifestation of Japaneseness may well help "American experts" to cre- ate valuable art, but he remains on the side of the picture, the prettily composed romantic image of old.

In this way, Hayakawa forces his contemporary critics to reveal their hands, laying out the racial logic of the emerging field of film aesthetics. As Russell and others have outlined, East Asian and Asian American ac- tors in early Hollywood were continually inserted into an orientalist rep- resentational field, and the racial politics of the period's films are well documented.[65] But whereas the stereotypes conjured by *Broken Blossoms* (Griffith, 1919) or by the star personae of Hayakawa and Anna-Mae Wong delineate a specific representational debate around the visual and narra- tive construction of race, the repeated use of Hayakawa in the elaboration of theories of cinema renders visible the underlying centrality of race to the very idea of a film aesthetics. Thus Canudo lauds his performances as having "embroidered for us with the most astonishing luminous silks of his very own Orient," closely binding the cinematic to ideas of decora- tive Asianism.[66] Cinematic concepts of beauty, like Kant's *Critique*, re- quire a non-Western counterweight, and the orientalist pretty is one of its central discourses. The Oriental is conventionally linked to a pictorial, decorative style, but abstracted from this association is the aesthetic struc- ture by which the evaluative move takes place. The pretty is excluded from definitions of beauty and value only by orientalist thinking, such that we should not attribute orientalism to pretty styles, but to the domi- nant aesthetic values that were formed in relation to both of them.

For Keathley, the importance of Hayakawa to the impressionists is his demonstration of how the real shines through in *photogénie*. Here, Hay- akawa represents not Asianism at all, but a wholly Western concept of the meaningful depth and truth of the image. Delluc's racial language not- withstanding, Hayakawa enables for the impressionists a transvaluation of the racial other. And yet this valuable other constructs a field of aesthetic possibility as surely as Kant's natives do. The orientalism of Hayakawa's film roles is replayed in the critics' fetishistic obsession. They find in him whatever it is they are looking for: Canudo, a presentation of modern cinematic life; Balázs, the ineffable truth of the face; Epstein, *photogénie*; and Delluc, beauty. Whereas for Kant the foreigner should remind us that not everyone is a subject whose life has value, classical film theorists seize on Hayakawa not as a human subject at all, but as a figure for the aesthetic apparatus—the nonhuman phenomenon who is able to stand in for the cinema as such.

"THE DAEMON OF PLASTICITY": REALISM AND CINEMATIC VALUE

Münsterberg's rejection of the pretty on the grounds that it is too realistic, too close to the social world, is all but reversed by critics such as Kracauer and Bazin, both of whom equally reject the pretty but locate value precisely in cinema's capacity to capture the real. Even before the postwar heyday of realism, however, film critics deployed ideas of medium specificity to forge theories of value. *Photogénie* is just one concept around which notions of cinematic value coheres, but it demonstrates vividly the impetus away from painterly composition and toward the profilmic real. Delluc, for example, writes, "Since we discovered the possibility of beauty in film, we have done everything possible to complicate it and weigh it down instead of always striving to simplify. Our best films are sometimes very ugly because of a laborious and artificial self-consciousness."[67] For Eugene McCreary, Delluc's opposition to artifice can be read as a neorealism *avant la lettre*: "Certain key words recur again and again in his writings on film: sincere, true, authentic, natural, simple, alive, everyday, interior, modern, sober. Together they trace a conception of film that would emerge twenty-five years later as neo-realism."[68] For writers on film aesthetics, as for the canonical theorists of realism, revelation is to be opposed to any form of overt construction in the image. The true film artist reveals beauty, whereas the dilettante can only construct a pretty scene. In the thread of film theory that centers on the indexical qualities of the medium, then, the pictorial or composed image forms a key element of the pretty and its rhetoric of impurity, secondariness, and untruth.

Classical film theory makes a crucial shift from the aesthetic to the cinematic: medium specificity rather than beauty becomes the dominant mode of judgment. As Dudley Andrew puts it, "Photography and motion pictures initiate new criteria, if not for beauty in visual representation, then at least for appropriateness."[69] Aesthetics almost immediately shades into medium specificity, even if the significance of the latter is not always clear. Of course, aesthetics is itself concerned with medium specificity, as the frequent citation of Lessing in early film criticism demonstrates, but tracing the relationship of cinematic specificity to aesthetic categories enables us to see the central role of the pretty in this developing model of cinema. If, as Andrew's choice of words implies, criteria for appropriateness might not be valued quite so highly as criteria for beauty, some negotiating term is needed to ensure the theoretical place of cinema. *Pretty* serves this function, triangulating the beautiful and the cinematic by being their common enemy.

This process is visualized by writers such as Marcel Gromaire, who in "A Painter's Ideas About the Cinema" complains about the weakness of the current cinema by proposing a tripartite structure: "Light is a first-class actor but our film profiteers only imagine colored picture-postcards for tourists. Look at a Rembrandt, or just throw the windows wide open!"[70] On one side, Gromaire places the studied technique and beautiful aesthetic of "real" art, and on the other the uncomposed, natural potential of profilmic "real" life. Both of these options are positive, for both include beauty (the skillful beauty of the painting and the natural beauty of the landscape) as well as truth (Rembrandt's famous mastery of light and the here-and-now experience outside the window). In the middle, though, are false aesthetics and false reality. The colored picture postcard is too pretty—too picturesque, too attractive—to be either art or life. And in citing the pretty postcard's tourist audience, Gromaire presents it as the heritage film of its time.

Delluc makes a similar claim when he argues that "the cinema is rightly moving toward the suppression of art, which reveals something beyond art, that is, life itself. Otherwise, it would merely be a median term between stylization and transient reality."[71] Here, life is privileged over art, as film theory moves away from older aesthetic models, but Delluc's negative structure, what would happen if film gets it wrong, follows Gromaire's structure exactly. Film would be terribly wrong to find itself in the place of the pretty, the median term between an excess of style and a lack of permanence. The categories are familiar ones, elaborated throughout classical film theory: cinema as access to reality, cinema as life, cinema as the defining experience of modernity. And although these new aesthetic values demand a turn away from prior models (as Delluc finds cinematic life to be beyond art), this turn is frequently enabled by way of a rejected pretty.

Thus Gromaire contrasts the pretty with the beautiful, and Delluc exemplifies the usefulness of contrasting it with the lifelike. *Realism* is a notoriously complex term and one to which we will return frequently, but even before we consider the implications of realism as a historical discourse (for it is by no means the same kind of value as, say, beauty), we will be struck by the similarity in its rhetoric of exclusion. Discussing *La dixième symphonie / The Tenth Symphony* (Gance, 1918), Delluc highlights a striking scene, stylistically quite at odds with the rest of the film, in which a woman dances across a meadow while across the top and bottom of the frame runs a graphic depiction of the muses in silhouette:

> During the first part of the scene, [the dancer's] inner immobility is affecting. Then the daemon of plasticity breathes over her, or rather over Gance, and she opens her wings: in the movement of arms and veils, Gance has had a great vision—a great white bird, a peplos in the wind, or something else. But I saw nothing of all that. Because the appearance of this poetic apparition, so slightly artificial or at least transposed from literature, embarrassed me in a moment that is otherwise true to life. Perhaps this will please spectators. Indeed it's quite pretty to look at. But it's no good; it overlays something fine with something pretty but unnecessary.[72]

The pretty emerges—and, again, the word *pretty* is not found often in Delluc's writing—as a grudging concession of pleasing appearance that is immediately followed by solid devaluation. The pretty is that part of the image that is neither lifelike nor good; not only is it supplementary, but this unnecessary decoration veils that which is fine in cinema.

Delluc goes on to complain of "a calculated disorder, a tendency to substitute for the basic detail, an overabundance of deflecting sensibility which sometimes stands in for sincere human or lyrical intensity. Need I add that the cinema managers present at the Pathé preview the other day preferred these errors. . . . He had understood nothing and would just as easily admire a gaudily colored calendar with the traditional figures of Spring, Summer, Autumn, and Winter."[73] Here, the pretty fails the realist measures of adequating human experience, representing natural disorder, and keeping things in their actual proportions, but these values are articulated almost entirely in aesthetic language. Calculation bespeaks a pictorial or picturesque mode of visual production, the overformed composition of the picture postcard. The clueless cinema manager, a stand-in for the popular audience, likes gaudy colors, rather like Arnheim and Blanc's primitives, and his calendar is both too colorful and too static, counterposing the traditional view against the aesthetic of the modern.

The modern becomes a central term in aligning the cinematic with the anti-pretty. In their overview of the cinematic specificity debates in the 1910s and 1920s, Anton Kaes and David Levin tell us that "already in 1910, one notices the first signs of a shift away from classical-idealist aesthetics."[74] They point to an emerging tendency to write of cinema in terms of the fast pace of modern experience and the rapidity of the city. Well before canonical accounts of cinematic modernity such as Benjamin's, we find an attempt to create a film-specific aesthetics that replaces ideas of beauty and eternal truth with claims on the particular needs of the modern art form. Thus Louis Aragon argues that "the essential 'cinegraphic' is not the beautiful shot. . . . We need a new, audacious aesthetic, a sense of modern beauty. On this understanding the cinema will rid itself of all the old, impure, poisonous alloy that links it to a theater whose indomitable enemy it is."[75] Using the theater as a point of contrast, Aragon aligns cinema with both modernity and nontheatrical life. (We might think here of the feminization of theater in nineteenth-century writing, identified by Andreas Huyssen.)[76] But note how the aesthetic is the real bad object. The composed, artful, painterly is to be expelled, and the language is that of corruption and disease. The aesthetic itself has become a dangerous supplement. Rewriting Kaes and Levin slightly, I argue that there is still a classical–idealist logic at work; modern tropes replace those of eternal beauty, but the aesthetic hierarchy of value remains securely in place.

Delluc's "Beauty in the Cinema" demonstrates precisely how the modern and the cinematic produce a schema of value that is defined against the pretty: "For a long time, I have realized that the cinema was destined to provide us with impressions of evanescent eternal beauty, since it alone offers us the spectacle of nature and sometimes even the spectacle of real human activity. You know, those impressions of grandeur, simplicity, and clarity which suddenly cause you to consider art useless."[77] In an evocation of the aesthetic values of impressionism, Delluc champions the evanescent eternal, a contradictory phrasing reminiscent of Charles Baudelaire's definition of the modern. Delluc's rejection of art places film as other than art, beyond art in its ability to capture life. The modern and cinematic are firmly set on the other side of traditional aesthetics. There is also a hint here of art as artfulness, the uselessness of carefully composed aesthetics over the open qualities of cinematic truth. Citing a documentary on military ships, he says, "There, that's beauty, real beauty—I would say the beauty of chance, but the cameraman must be given his due. . . . After this, how can one indulge in the blunders of a totally new art which the French have shackled with all manner of embellishments?"[78] Cinematic beauty for Delluc makes a claim on the truths of modernity, life, capturing the contingent, but it also demands the rejection of embellishment, the exclusion of a composed pretty.

As contemporary film scholars have returned to questions of modernity, they have explored these theoretical concepts without greatly troubling the hierarchies of value on which they are built. Aumont historicizes the modern cinematic in terms of painting when he maps cinematic vision onto the shift from the picturesque *ébauche*, or composed study, to the nineteenth-century *étude*, the modern glance that captures an impression of reality. For Aumont, the *ébauche* / *étude* binary can be understood in terms of an active / passive hierarchy. Reading Peter Galassi, he "observes the *active mobility* of the visual pyramid that founded the development of the *étude*: at issue is a conception of the world as an interrupted field of potential tableaux, scanned by the gaze of the artist who, exploring as he travels through the world, will suddenly stop in order to cut it up and 'frame' it." The *étude* is active, both in the actions of the artist and in the sense of trapping motion in an image. Thus "never to be retouched, the *étude* remains a work destined to capture a first impression that it fixes in a record of artistic directness." Aumont's language is active, and the *étude* does things (capture, fix). By contrast, consider his account of the *ébauche*: "Canaletto, on the other hand, has used his apparatus to obtain an *ébauche* of a scenographic space, later to be recopied, amplified, and, most importantly, populated with human figures."[79] Note the passive construction throughout. The *ébauche* is obtained; things are done to it. Activity is masculinizing, and the passive scenographic image lacks the dynamism that patriarchal language gives to the modern form of image making. Aumont sets up the terms of this visual taxonomy, but he completely adheres to its ideological givens. This discourse enables a historical claim to underwrite aesthetic judgment: the composed image is not modern and therefore not cinematically valuable.[80]

This historical narrative feeds into much twentieth-century visual theory, with the uncomposed *étude* leading to Bazin's photographic, Roland Barthes's *punctum*, and contemporary phenomenologies of visuality.[81] But if the *étude* represents modern cinematic vision, the exact definition of the rejected *ébauche* is less clear. James Lastra has also linked cinematic modernity to art historical debates, tracing a parallel between Michelangelo's critique of Dutch painting for lacking artistry and the early-twentieth-century shift from lifelike views to the diegetic mode of film. Lastra compares the contingent views of early cinema with the emphasis on real space in Dutch painting, citing Svetlana Alpers's famous description "as if the world came first."[82] For Lastra, the virtue of this comparison is twofold: it links early cinema to a strand of artistic realism in which the modern threatens a pictorial status quo, and it links the cinematic firmly to the contingent and the accidental. But for him, very little of film history can be categorized in this way. He proposes the rapid folding of the modern cinematic into the diegetic mode, with the victory of the Italian form encompassing most film after *L'arroseur arrosé / The Tables Turned on the Gardener* (Lumière, 1895).

If the vast majority of films can be placed in the composed Italian category, then it would be difficult to map Lastra's Dutch image onto Aumont's *étude* or, indeed, onto Delluc's cinematic beauty. The rejected *ébauche* might swell from a way of identifying bad films to a historical category including almost all narrative cinema. My point is not to rationalize this diverse range of theoretical accounts or to suggest that they all value exactly the same qualities in cinema. Indeed, it is significant that the theories do not line up exactly, that very disparate kinds of films are valued in each of these accounts, and yet that it is consistently the composed or pictorial image that is devalued. The close association of the modern, the uncomposed, and the cinematic has nourished many film theories, but it structurally demands that the uncinematic be imagined—and rejected—in the aesthetic terms of a composed, pictorial pretty image.

What does this excluded pretty image look like? Often only defined implicitly in the negative spaces of theories devoted to the cinematic, the modern, and the realistic, it can be hard to make out. We might describe it as something only occasionally glimpsed were not the glimpse a rhetorical trope of the modern anti-pretty. Laura Marcus argues that Vachel Lindsay uses two contrasting forms of beauty: the glimpse and the glitter. She does not find these terms to be perfectly distinguished in Lindsay's writing, but what is clear is that *glimpse* is a positive term, akin to *photogénie*, denoting true and meaningful beauty, whereas *glitter* is a negative result of modernity and is connected to commodification.[83] The glimpse is an obvious cousin to the *étude*, the contingent moment of reality, but glitter is another component of the pretty. Like Plato's *poikiloi*, glitter indicates not just color, but sparkly color beloved by the working classes, women, natives—those who would be distracted by shiny stuff. Le Corbusier also abhorred glitter, posing aesthetic purity against the fashionable patterns beloved of shopgirls.[84] Here, pretty denotes rejection of a popular visual culture, pitting the modernity of true art against the debased modern commodities enjoyed by a feminized and marginalized mass audience.

If the pretty is found in the sparkly aesthetic of the tasteless masses, it can also be located in the stodgy styles of the old-fashioned elites. Paul Willemen writes on style that "there is a form of stylisation in the cinema which is actually the equivalent to academicism in critical discourses. The whole new wave and the discourse of cinephilia, in France at least, was quite specifically against the academic notion of 'the aesthetic,' of what was thought to be a beautiful image, from Autant-Lara to Cayette, the whole *cinéma de papa*. A whole tradition of quite self-consciously aestheticized French cinema was explicitly opposed to the discourse on cinephilia, with its predilection for things which did not appear to be stylized or aestheticized."[85] Theories of cinephilia quite explicitly link composition and style to an old-fashioned aesthetic regime that should be superseded. Delluc praises one film by noting, "Nothing in the film betrays an intention of aestheticism. It is pure life."[86] Those who ignore good taste might produce pretty images for shopgirls, but those whose taste is not modern are similarly consigned to uncinematic death by stylization.

Balázs also addresses stylization, but he seems to find a more positive place for it within the cinematic. He argues that all artworks have a style, derived from the norms of their age, but that stylization describes works that "intentionally deviate from the natural, are deliberately formed and tied," in the way that poetry is stylized and naturalistic dialogue is not. He argues that stylized work can still be realist: "There are plenty of great realists among the poets who write in verse." Moreover, he continues, "We know that the film began seeking possibilities of stylization from the very beginning, photographic technique notwithstanding. The directors strove to achieve the picturesque by composition, light effects, close-ups, soft focus, distortion and especially through the medium of angle and set-up. Swedish films especially sought poetic pictorial effects." Here, the picturesque and the pictorial are not inherently negative qualities. However, his emphasis on the close-up, depth, and movement ultimately forces a step back from this more open position. Seeing human movement as one of the cinematic elements that resist stylization, Balázs concludes, "This explains why the film is so difficult to stylize. The microphysiognomy of the close-up, the intimate play of features, is not susceptible to stylization, and yet it is the very soul of the film. The most beautiful stylized long shots are unmasked by the intimate life of the close-up. The mask slips and the human being peeps out from behind it."[87] The composed and stylized pretty image is revealed in idealist fashion as a mask, behind which we find soul, truth, and life.

Balázs usefully ties the cinematic to specific aesthetic practices. If the close-up demands realism and cinematicity, the composed long shot denies it. Thus "angle and set-up are authentic film instruments because in one way or another they show reality, and their product is after all a photograph. But a director who modifies his objects and tidies up reality before it is shot, robs the film of its claim to authenticity."[88] Balázs is not a Bazinian realist, and yet this contrast of authentically caught reality with kitsch fakery suggests a rather ontological discourse on profilmic truth. Moreover, there is a slight implication of gendering at work, where tidying up the image sounds like housework, prettifying for company. This critique of the director who prettifies the real has been durable: think of Michelangelo Antonioni famously painting his grass greener in *Il deserto rosso / Red Desert* (1964) or Jean-Pierre Jeunet's postproduction cleanup of Paris in *Le fabuleux destin d'Amélie Poulain / Amelie* (2001). The authenticity of the cinematic per se is rapidly co-opted into denigration of films that are too tidied up, too manicured to be real.

The cinematic also opposes the pretty to the pure. We have seen this effect in terms of color, where in Dyer's terms color covers up the pure white body of filmic light and in Batchelor's terms color is a false cosmetic. In art history, Batchelor reminds us, purity has helped construct the white body as transparent, rational, and modern, linking fleshly corruption and racial otherness to excess color. Something very similar occurs in the classical discourse on the cinematic, where the simple, pure qualities of the captured moment place heavily racialized and gendered attributes on the correct or unruly forms of the image. Thus Aragon argues for an avant-garde in terms of bodily purity: "It is time someone slapped the public's face to see if it has blood under its skin. The consecration of catcalls that will gain cinema the respect of people of feeling is still missing. Get it, and the purity that attracts spittle emerges at last! When, before the naked screen lit by the projector's solitary beam, we will have that sense of formidable virginity. *The white awareness of our canvas?* O purity purity!"[89] The virginal woman, enshrining cultural purity in her exposed white body, counterposes the artistic and political value of the pure with the implied colorful / colored slut of inadequate film. As Huyssen's well-known account points out, modern mass culture is imagined as woman, but in this contestation of value, gender, race, and aesthetic history police the boundaries of the properly cinematic.

As Aragon's call for an avant-garde demonstrates, these discourses of cinematic modernity are hardly univocal. Claims on realism may be quite at odds with the more avant-gardist strains of film writing, particularly in the French context. But in opposing their favored cinematic form to the aesthetic and aligning it with the modern, direct, and pure, quite disparate approaches to film construct themselves in opposition to a bad pretty. And the emphasis on modern cinematic vision tends toward a valorization of realism, understood as the medium's ability to capture the real, even in avant-gardist writing.

Realism, then, is frequently produced as a rejection of earlier, impure aesthetic styles. Balázs argues that "the simplification of acting brought about by the close-up changed more than the style of acting. There was also a change in taste accompanying the change of trend which substituted a neo-naturalistic tendency for the neo-romanticism of Rostand and Maeterlinck on the western European stage. After the first world war and the hysterical emotional fantasies of expressionism, a 'documentary,' dry, anti-romantic and anti-emotional style was the fashion in film as in the other arts."[90] The cinematic opposes romanticism and, with it, femininity (hysteria). The new, masculine modern style values the ordinary, profilmic world, but it must also emphasize that this world is pure and lacking feminine excess. Thus Balázs goes on to say that "commonplace faces" in actors came to replace "romantic faces. . . . The decorative, out-of-the-ordinary face now seemed a mask and no longer seemed attractive."[91] The everyday real is valued, but, more important, it is valued in comparison with the false appearance of the hysterical decorative. Realism in cinema moves away from hysteria and emotionalism, revealing instead simplicity, life, the eternal in the evanescent. However, this move is possible only by way of a firm exclusion of the ornamental detail. Whereas the detail enters into value by way of the *étude*, the close-up, and the glimpse, the pretty category of the decorative is feminized and forcibly excluded from value.

ANDRÉ BAZIN: PURITY AND THE FRAME

Bazin's advocacy of realism expands on the modern schema of classical film theory, with the contingency of the profilmic locating cinema's meaningful gesture always away from the composition implied by the ornamental. Perhaps his most famous distinction, between "those who put their faith in the image and those who put their faith in reality," counterposes the image as object of bad faith with a cinematic reality worthy of belief.[92] On Robert Bresson's *Journal d'un curé de campagne / Diary of a Country Priest* (1951), Bazin writes, "Nostalgia for a silence that would be the benign procreator of a visual symbolism unduly confuses the so-called primacy of the image with the true vocation of the cinema—which is the primacy of the object."[93] The language of Christian iconoclasm is here, of course, deliberate, replacing the false god of images with the theological vocation of the meaningful world. Bazin, to be sure, is well aware of the historical weight of his aesthetics. But if we proceed further in this realist iconoclasm, reading with what Spivak has called "constructive complicity,"[94] we begin to glimpse the significant place of the pretty outside of the discourse of the good.

If Bresson allows Bazin to trope realism in theological terms, then the endpoint of this rhetoric is not only the film's final screen, blank except for a graphic cross, but also an appeal to the sublime as a secular category of aesthetic transcendence. For Bazin, "we are experimenting with an irrefutable aesthetic, with a sublime achievement of pure cinema."[95] The sublime, for Kant, is that which interrupts or moves radically beyond the boundaries of imagination, and hence Bazin is able to tie cinematic purity to a screen that refuses the image altogether. The entirely formless image seems like an odd ideal for a realist theory, but the sublime responds to a potential problem in the theoretical valuation of the contingent real. In much aesthetic theory, the formless, contingent, and material signify a lack of beauty or value. In Aristotle, for instance, form is the value associated with line, whereas the formless voices the chaos of color. But the Kantian sublime allows for a redemption of the unformed and, in particular, when it captures a direct experience of nature. The magnificence of ships in stormy weather that Delluc praises is nothing if not a conception of the actuality as enabling a sublime experience. Thus Bazin's invocation of the sublime suggests a spiritual transcendence, but it also realigns the Kantian taxonomy for realist theory: the formless sublime, the formed beautiful, and the overformed pretty.[96]

The contrast of the unformed image with the overformed pretty becomes clear in "Painting and Cinema," where Bazin contrasts the centripetal impulse of the painting, attested to by the "baroque complexity of the traditional frame," with the centrifugal nature of the cinematic screen, "prolonged indefinitely into the universe."[97] Whereas the painting is discontinuous with the world beyond its frame, the film's edges open into reality. Of course, the frame always pulls in both directions, balancing the centrifugal with the centripetal; as much as it points to the endless profilmic, it creates boundaried spaces. For Bazin, however, the quality of the cinematic here is measured by how much a film invokes the off-screen world or by how little it creates internal compositions. We might think of what Bazin calls "the expressionist heresy" as one example of the degree to which he considers a style based on internal screen space as wrong.[98] And when searching for a rhetorical figure for the uncinematic, Bazin turns to art history: the flagrant rejection of aesthetic purity found in baroque ornamentation.

Bazin elaborates the importance of this exclusion in "The Ontology of the Photographic Image," where he avers that "the aesthetic qualities of photography are to be sought in its power to lay bare the realities." Reversing Münsterberg's understanding of cinematic beauty as that which transforms the world, he nonetheless locates images of value in similar places: "a reflection on a damp sidewalk . . . the gesture of a child."[99] The everyday and the ephemeral again locate the cinematic at odds with the decorative or the composed. And this everyday is not simply unposed or inconsequential: it should also be drab and devoid of aesthetic pleasure. Bazin expands this train of thought in "*Farrebique*, or the Paradox of Realism," where he lauds the film's lack of prettiness: "Some people reproach *Farrebique* [Rouquier, 1946] for its ugliness. The men and women in it aren't very good looking. This Rouergue landscape is without grandeur. The houses are dirty and styleless. . . . But, clearly, Rouquier could not have brought his project to a successful end with material whose very beauty would have distorted in some way the chemical reaction of the camera."[100] It is not enough for value to inhere in the overlooked, but beauty must be refigured as a distortion, a perversion of the ontology of the camera.

If beauty is a perversion, where do we find purity? Bazin's theological rhetoric continues in his description of the experience of cinematic seeing, in which the lens strips from the object "that spiritual dust and grime with which my eyes have covered it," presenting it "in all its virginal purity."[101] The religious ramifications of virginity for a gender critique should be all too clear, and the evocation of virginal purity surely reminds us of Aragon, despite the different directions of their criticism. We again find in clarity and purity the rational vision of the Western eye. The transparency of cinematic light inscribes whiteness as both ground and figure, and this mechanical clarity of vision, the objectivity of the camera, connects Bazin's phenomenology of cinema to the clear, white rationality that underwrites both art history and philosophy. In Bazin's dust and grime, the visual supplement is refigured as a degradation of both subject and object.

Dust and grime do not sound terribly pretty, it's true, but it is a measure of Bazin's realist iconoclasm that the decorative or formed can be imagined only as pollution. To tease out the aesthetic implications of this discourse on purity, I offer two canonical counterexamples of Bazin's critique: one positive and the other more ambiguous. The first example is William Wyler, who stands as a key figure in Bazinian realism. I focus here not so much on the formal qualities of Wyler's realism, which are well known, as on the aesthetic language Bazin uses to make his claims. From the beginning, Bazin works to separate what Wyler does from conventional concepts of style or aesthetics. He describes Wyler as having a style but not a manner. Wyler cannot be mannered or mannerist. Bazin speaks of "the aesthetic sense of this kind of asceticism," finding Wyler's mise-en-scène to efface itself.[102] *Asceticism* adds another religious term, connoting a principled refusal of extraneous stuff and more generally a rejection of the unnecessary and worldly. Realism is linked here not only to transparency and purity, but to a historical refusal of the pleasurable and sensual.

Continuing, Bazin says of the design of The Little Foxes (Wyler, 1941), "Nothing picturesque adds to the realism of this somber place, which is as impersonal as the setting of classical tragedy." The real does not need supplementing by the picturesque, and, indeed, its tragedy is increased by stripping bare. For Bazin, this stripping down to the clarity and purity of the cinematic is an aesthetic; he maintains that "nothing is more fallacious and absurd than to contrast 'realism' and 'aestheticism,' as was frequently done in reference to the Russian or the Italian cinema."[103] Thus although Bazin uses aesthetic language, he does so precisely in an attempt to wrest the aesthetic away from aestheticism, demanding a film aesthetic that can be formed in opposition to the decorative image. He dubs Wyler's realism the "Styleless Style": this claim on the moral superiority of style without style (and we should not forget that, for Bazin, Wyler is above all a moral director) provides a provoking contrast with Benjamin's reading of art nouveau as the "stylizing style" (discussed in chapter 3).

The second example is Bazin's reading of Sergei Eisenstein's Ivan Groznyy / Ivan the Terrible (1944), a film he works hard to defend, even though it is clearly in conflict with his aesthetic value system. He points to its richness of historical reference: "The pictorial influences are numerous. The historical period of the action—Donatello has just died (1466), and the Russian court has established relations with the Italian states—allowed Eisenstein to make allusions to the Italian Renaissance, which had always had a strong influence on him. As for the Byzantine references, they are even more numerous."[104] Ivan is textually complex and intelligent, but pictorialism of necessity precludes realism, and Bazin concludes that it works to "deny nature even the briefest of appearances" (figure 11).[105]

So Ivan the Terrible is unnatural and pictorial, closer to the baroque painting than to the purity of the profilmic. Bazin admits that Eisenstein has always privileged composition. "But," he explains, "in his previous films the plastic demands of the image didn't have an effect on the action itself. In Ivan the Terrible, by contrast, it is fair to say that the action is transformed to its very core by the style of the image. From this point of

FIGURE 11 *Ivan Groznyy II / Ivan the Terrible, Part II* (Eisenstein, 1958)
Pictorial aestheticism and Asian excess deny nature in Sergei Eisenstein's late films.

view, one could call *Ivan the Terrible* decadent." He immediately backs
away from this critique, saying that such a judgment would be unfair
and that the film's quality is equal to that of Eisenstein's previous work.
But how easily a rejection of realism shades into an accusation of aesthetic decadence. Bazin does not want to call Eisenstein decadent, but he
cannot stop the word from slipping out, with all its associations of effeminacy, excess, and corruption. By the end of the article, he has damned the
film with faint praise, arguing that "we must make a distinction between
the value of the style as such and the quality of its individual execution."
Thus Eisenstein must be recognized for his skill as a director, but his
chosen style is nonetheless rejected as more or less reprehensible. Bazin
concludes, "One is certainly entitled to consider the path Eisenstein takes
in *Ivan the Terrible* as an offensive return to a dangerous aestheticism,
which everybody believed had been eliminated from all considerations of
cinema's destiny."[106]

Linking *Ivan the Terrible* with a dangerous and retrograde aestheticism is inevitable given Bazin's investment in purity, nature, and the

unformed sublime. And yet Bazin does not want to make quite such a polemical attack on Eisenstein himself, so he attempts to separate the aesthetic from the director. His solution to this slippery problem is a turn to the Asianism we have already seen in earlier film writing. Like Lindsay, Bazin finds in Asian aesthetics a pictorialist heritage that might counter traditional Western style. Thus he defends Eisenstein's unnatural, overly composed film by pointing to the fact that it was shot in Alma-Ata (now Almaty, Kazakhstan): "in spite of the fact that the action takes place in western Russia in the sixteenth century, Eisenstein obviously wanted to make an Asian film. This intention is discernible not only in the preponderantly Asian extravagance of the sets and the costumes, but also in the very conception of the drama and its performance, both of which are so heavily stylized that they border on mime and dance."[107] Asian style is understood in terms of stylization, excess, elaborately composed images, and the unreal, and although this Asianism might, for Bazin, mitigate Eisenstein's aesthetic choices by providing some geographical motivation, the iterative emergence of racial logic as a constitutive element of aesthetic judgment suggests a larger problem for film theory.

TWO

COLORS

Derek Jarman and Queer Aesthetics

As David Batchelor's wide-ranging investigation of chromophobia suggests,[1] the anticolor thinking of classical film theory remains a major force in more recent cinema. To explore the critical potentiality of color as a pretty technique, this chapter focuses on the experimental films of Derek Jarman, whose work offers a fascinating linkage of color theory and queer politics. Jarman was well aware of the chromophobic histories of Western art. In his theoretical meditation on color, *Chroma*, he writes, "As the Roman Empire collapsed, iconoclasts waged war against the graven image. Colour became the fount of impurity. A chasm opened up between the terrestrial and celestial world. The dog chased its own tail to bite it off."[2] He also makes a direct connection between color and queerness: "Leonardo took the first step into light, and Newton, a notorious batchelor, followed him with Opticks. In this century Ludwig Wittgenstein wrote his Remarks on Colour. Colour seems to have a Queer bent!"[3] Jarman's writing on color joins forces with that of critical theorists such as Batchelor and Jacqueline Lichtenstein, discussed in the previous chapter, to produce a modern response to chromophobic (and homophobic) aesthetics.

Jarman was a radical, often troublesome figure in 1980s British art cinema, and scholarship has considered both the queer politics of his feature films and the use of color in his final film, *Blue* (1993).[4] However, his experimental films were for a long time unavailable and perhaps for this reason have not been widely analyzed. Ranging from diaristic home movies to theatrically staged scenes, this substantial corpus beginning in 1971 and continuing throughout his career demonstrates the importance of rich, monochromatic color schemes, image layering, and surface effects to Jarman's aesthetics. And, significantly for the pretty, the films bring together color and queer politics as questions not only of representation but of form. I consider chromophobia not merely as a concept from art history that Jarman's work thematizes, but as a still dominant assumption in film studies that prejudices the critical reception of his colorful films. The richly chromatic visual systems and surface effects of Jarman's Super-8 films are central to his queer politics, articulating a set of formal concerns that also nourish his narrative work. This chapter argues that an attention to the prettiness of Jarman's experimental images gives us a greater insight into his politics of form. By first examining how his aesthetics have been marginalized in avant-garde and British film cultures and then returning to the films and using the concept of the pretty as a tool to look at them anew, we discover therein color's radical refusal of discourses of dominance and alignment with a powerful queer alchemy that opens up utopian spaces for queer life.

Jarman's experimental films deploy color across a range of forms. One strand of his filmmaking engages landscape: *Journey to Avebury* (1972) consists of a series of static shots of fields and ancient standing stones composed in picturesque views and emphasizes the yellow, orange, and green tones of southern England. *Ashden's Walk on Møn* (1973) similarly explores an ancient landscape but also includes startlingly beautiful superimpositions of natural and man-made objects colored in rich blues and pinks. In these films, color and composition stage an intersection of painterly aesthetics with a cinematic experience of profilmic place. Another series of films transforms postindustrial spaces, using theatrical mise-en-scène as well as colorful camera effects. *The Art of Mirrors* (1973), *Death Dance* (1973), and *Arabia* (1974) are largely set on London's docklands, in abandoned industrial spaces transformed by set dressing and costuming into camp tableaux. Recurrent images include figures in ornate historical costumes, bound and naked men, and fires burning in lines along the ground. Filters and postproduction color effects drench the scenes in deep reds and greens, pale yellows and aqua blues. A third set of films is the diary films, including *It Happened by Chance* (1977), which represent accumulated material in a formless flow of images, including scenes from many other films, often projected in communal spaces or, on occasion, in multichannel mode in galleries. These films elaborate a poetics of *colore* rather than *disegno*, and at the time they appeared, they could not have been less legible to an experimental milieu invested in structure over form (much less formlessness).

Thus in addition to providing a corpus attuned to the cultural significance of color, Jarman exemplifies the way in which prettiness can render a filmmaker difficult, illegible, or otherwise troublesome to the critical establishment. In both the film circles that Jarman inhabited—a 1970s experimental film scene dominated by structural film and a critical British film culture beholden to discourses of realism—aesthetic austerity remained strongly preferable to colorful and pretty style. This anti-pretty milieu explains Jarman's difficult position in contemporary film history. Jarman was trained in fine art, and his 8-mm short films demonstrate what many have seen as an overly painterly eye in their emphasis on color and composition. Although Jarman is clearly an important figure and has found acclaim for his uncompromising personal voice, the combination of his radical queer politics and his investment in theatricality, frontal composition, and richly artificial colors has helped prevent his being as widely valued as he might otherwise have been. Tony Rayns calls Jarman "number one in a field of one,"[5] and this sense of him as a misfit figures the institutional effects of prettiness even in a field as accepting of aesthetic difference as experimental film.

One of the earliest scholarly studies of Jarman was a special issue of *Afterimage* dedicated to two "troublesome cases": Jarman and the film *Borderline* (1930). Directed by Kenneth Macpherson and starring Paul Robeson and H. D., *Borderline* represents an earlier iteration of English avant-gardism that, like Jarman's work, can be situated within the artistic and literary cultures of high modernism. But *Borderline*'s representation of bisexuality and miscegenation proved equally indigestible to its contemporaries as Jarman's queer theatrics to his. The *Afterimage* editors see both directors as nurturing their marginal positions, sharing a preoccupation with the borderlines of class, race, and sexuality, and "if they do find a place in the traditions of British cinema, it is with the company of outsiders and intransigents that includes Powell and Pressburger at one end of the production spectrum, Margaret Tait and Jeff Keen at the other."[6] Of course, all these filmmakers might be seen as "national trea-sures" of one kind or another and their outsiderdom and awkwardness as a peculiarly British mixture of romanticism and stubbornness. Cer-tainly, this is the discourse that has nurtured the resurgence in interest in Michael Powell and Emeric Pressburger's films, but even in this popu-lar example we can see how the troubling aspects of color are central to the story. The painted sets and picturesque views of *Black Narcissus* (Powell and Pressburger, 1947) stage an awkward aestheticization of imperial history, and the garish mise-en-scène of *Peeping Tom* (Powell, 1960) is surely part of what made the film so troubling to its contemporary critics in contrast to its successful black-and-white counterpart *Psycho* (Hitch-cock, 1960). We can thus locate Jarman within a history of troublesome cases and, moreover, read in this history a stubborn refusal of aesthetic or political conformity.

This history of a difficult aesthetic of visual plenitude not only is Brit-ish but forms a key strand of postwar European cinema. Jarman's writ-ing on color can be usefully compared with that of Armenian Georgian director Sergei Paradjanov, who makes a similar claim on color's mean-ingful qualities in a 1968 *Film Comment* piece about his film *Tini zabu-tykh predkiv / Shadows of Our Forgotten Ancestors* (1964):

> It seems to me that to refuse to use color now would mean to sign knowingly a confession of your own weakness. Literal colorlessness to some extent means also figurative colorlessness. We filmmakers must learn today from such mentors as Breughel, Arhipov, Nesterov, Korin, Leger, Rivera, from the Primitivists—for them color was not only a mood, a supplementary emotion, but a part of the content. It is essentially a question of all visual culture, which it is silly to re-gard as some kind of dressing up or decoration, but which in itself has content and ideology.[7]

Like Jarman, Paradjanov advocates for the ideological weight of color, but what makes this similarity striking are the resonant echoes in the ca-reers of these apparently quite different filmmakers. Paradjanov, like Jarman, was viewed in many ways as an exceptional case, unassimilable to the dominant aesthetic currents of Soviet cinema. Criticized frequently for ethnographic formalism, he was also imprisoned repeatedly for his Georgian nationalism. Radicals in different areas, both directors wholeheartedly refused to fit into the aesthetico-political molds demanded of them by their respective political film cultures. Moreover, as Steven Dillon points out, both men were influenced by Pier Paolo Pasolini, and this line of aesthetic descent can be traced in both their lyricism and their determinedly awkward politics.[8]

Jarman certainly felt himself to be outside of contemporary avant-garde institutions: he describes using Super-8 film as a way to evade the strictures of the structural film scene.[9] A. L. Rees finds a hostility between Jarman and the London Co-op filmmakers, seeing him rather as a high modernist in the mode of Ken Russell, Lindsay Anderson, and Powell—British filmmakers who "resisted the safer options and who were roundly attacked for their pains."[10] But if Jarman has modernist qualities, his prettiness suggests other art historical categories that might lead to his rejection by the structuralists. A 1975 French introduction to his work defines it as being aestheticist and painterly and as possessing a plastic sensibility.[11] These terms of sensuality are precisely the ones that his British contemporaries sought to expel from the cinematic. Think, for example, of Peter Gidal's aim to minimize film's content "in its over-powering, imagistically seductive sense," his dubbing of people in film as "baroque appendages," and his scathing rejection of the end of Michael Snow's ⟷ / *Back and Forth* (1969) as "rococo rubbish. I am quite happy to admit," he writes, "that I am not interested in Snow's work for the 'beauty.' "[12] Gidal uses the vocabulary of art to promote an austerity of form that strongly rejects the imagistic and the beautiful, the baroque and the rococo. Jarman's sensual colorism was unlikely to be accepted in such a context.

It is not only filmmakers who have rejected Jarman's style. Even some of his most sympathetic and significant interlocutors find prettiness to be troublesome. Michael O'Pray describes *Imagining October* (1984), a film Jarman made in response to a trip to the Soviet Union in 1984, as ambivalent. In an interview with Jarman, he says, "The imagery is Stalinist and yet very beautiful at the same time. You seem to want to criticise certain things, but it's always tempered by beautiful imagery."[13] Making a presumption typical of anti-pretty rhetoric, O'Pray finds that the film's beautiful painted images inevitably work against its political critique rather than forming an integral part of it. Rees goes further, seeing Jarman's experimental film as too theatrical, literary, and symbolic. He finds that "their visual impact was chained rather than liberated by the preordained shooting strategies which they adopted."[14] This description seems odd to me because Rees valorizes filmmakers who make highly arranged films, such as Snow and Gidal. But where the preplanned is also theatrically composed, then both cinematic modernity and art history are called on to explain what is wrong: Rees proposes that the "films don't breathe: every inch of the screen has to be filled, like an academic canvas, but there is still too little work for the eye to do."[15] Academicism is suffocating, and the rhetoric of life evoked by the presence or absence of breath figures a centripetal framed composition, forcefully refusing André Bazin's account of the centrifugal cinematic image. The excess of color, detail, and design is an affront both to the wind in the leaves of cinematic realism and to the austerity of 1970s modernism. If Jarman is, in Rees's words, a "sacred monster" with no children, then this colorful beast is surely a queer creature.

COLOR AS A POLITICS OF FORM(LESSNESS)

If Jarman's experimental work fails according to the formal standards of structural film, his features are more often read as political. Richard Porton argues that "in Jarman's work it is impossible to separate cinematic style from a decidedly undidactic political fervour; formal choices are simultaneously political choices." And although we might respond that they always are, Porton helpfully isolates the way that Jarman's films are not usually thought of in a leftist countercinematic tradition even while they are explicitly activist. Thus, says Porton, Jarman's pantheon of Powell, Pasolini, and Jean Cocteau "are united by their hostility to mainstream naturalism and their radical individualism—an individualism that does not foreclose the cultivation of collective, but non-dogmatic, radical hopes."[16] Whereas many Marxist critics, alongside O'Pray and Gidal, find that prettiness works against political meaning, Jarman's example demonstrates that the opposite is true: to imagine a genuinely radical collective future, he shows us, one needs a decorative eye.

James Tweedie finds a similar potential in Jarman's use of the tableau. For him, "the foundational representational problem for Jarman's filmmaking is how to resolve the formal politics of political modernism and the exigencies of the present, in particular an oppositional queer politics centred on the archaeology of past identity formations and a genealogy of the present."[17] This articulation is particularly fruitful because it identifies a conflict between cinematic modernism and queer politics that is resolved through the tableau vivant—in other words, through the composed surface of the image. I think that a similar representational question hangs over Jarman's colors. Abstraction and politics, the image and the word. Where modernist critics such as Gidal and Rees can see Jarman's colorful films only as inadequately rigorous, reading for the pretty demands that we recalibrate our vision and see the decorative image anew. Politics does not inhere only in formal austerity but can be discerned also in the lush surface of the colorful image. More than this, I argue, it is profligate color, not restrained line, that is necessary to imagine a queer organization of social value. Jarman's final color experiment, *Blue*, uses words centrally to articulate the experience of AIDS, but the early Super-8 films are silent evocations of gay youth. Whereas some critics see *Blue* as a late abjuration of the image, I draw a very different conclusion from that film's immersive color field. Jarman's films demonstrate that we do not have to keep framing the cinematic as a binarized battle between reason and image, *disegno* and *colore*. Color is where Jarman's films make their stand against hetero culture, where they propose utopian spaces, and where they locate a valuable queer life. Just as the tableau in the narrative films negotiates between modernist form and queer politics, so in Jarman's experimental films color is a mobilizing conceptual force.

Jarman's insistence on the queer history of color resonates with Lichtenstein's account of anticolor rhetoric in art history. Describing the *disegno* versus *colore* debates in seventeenth-century France, Lichtenstein outlines the perceived threat of color: "The colorists threatened the mastery of discourse as much as the favor of drawing, the hegemony of a metaphysical conception of the image as well as the primacy of the idea in representation. They attacked the principles of morality and the pedagogical virtues of rules alike. Brash, they defended the purely material qualities of representation. Indecent, they advanced an apology for cosmetics, pleasure, and seduction. Libertine, they praised color for the incomparable effects that its simulacra produced."[18] The practitioners of color trouble moral and sexual as well as aesthetic categories. Indeed, the lesson may be that the aesthetic is bound to the moral and the sexual. As we have seen, something closely comparable happens in film, where color is often regarded as morally suspicious and secondary to the meaningful qualities of linear form. This inheritance from aesthetic history has made Jarman difficult to place within standard canons of value, but it also offers a way to understand his articulation of film aesthetics to sexual politics: Jarman's brash, indecent, libertine style allows us to conceive of him as a film colorist.

INDECENT: QUEER COLOR

Lichtenstein's categories of colorism form a guide for examining the stakes in Jarman's color. Color's indecency speaks most directly to a queering of the image: color as a Platonic cosmetic is effeminate, overly sexual, and duplicitous. It exists on the surface, hiding the true face underneath. For Batchelor, artists such as Andy Warhol use this idea of the cosmetic to evoke drag and sexual indeterminacy in their colored images, "playing with the order of nature and going Against Nature in a very specific way."[19] Jarman, too, plays with this philosophical association, referring to color in *Chroma* as "the bordello of the spectrum."[20] In *The Art of Mirrors*, deeply colored filters are combined with elaborate costuming to stage artifice and cosmetics. In one scene, a woman in a 1920s dress and a feathered hat evokes a historical aestheticism, and the changing monochromatic setting of blues, reds, and greens reminds us, as with Warhol's lino prints, that color is an object in its own right and not a supplement to line. Thus a sea-foam-green shot of burning paper de-emphasizes the fiery qualities of the image's ostensible content, instead demanding that we look at texture, tone, and light. The technique of turning the mirror to the camera in several films further focuses attention on color. Jarman sets the Super-8 camera on automatic exposure, which has the effect, when a mirror flashes light at the camera directly, of closing down the iris entirely for a second. The effect for the spectator is a bright circle of white light rapidly transforming to a black screen and then back out to the shot's bright colors (figure 12). It is an oddly chiasmic effect—the mirror should make us look at a point within the frame, the circle of the mirror flashing, but the point immediately radiates outward to engulf the entire frame, removing and restoring chroma. The mirror and the camera relay light, making us look at the entire colorful surface of the screen, at the tones and textures the mirror light illuminates.

Indecent color implies an erotics, and the immersive quality of these filters is indeed pleasurable. But seduction is also a political question in that dominant anti-aesthetics resist the charms of color, evincing patriar-

FIGURE 12 *The Art of Mirrors* (Jarman, 1973)
A mirror flashes across the bright green screen.

chal fears of overwhelming femininity, formlessness, and the loss of straight male subjectivity. For Lisa Robertson, this borderless cosmetic is precisely a site of political change: "Dangerously pigment smears. Artifice is the disrespect of the propriety of borders. Emotion results. . . . To experience change, we submit ourselves to the affective potential of the surface. This is the *pharmakon*: an indiscrete threshold where our bodies exchange information with an environment."[21] In *Death Dance*, the surface is color itself, filters forming a threshold with the bodies in profilmic space. And that space is changed by its encounter with color, becoming at once a magical mise-en-scène and an immaterial surface. The film depicts a group of naked boys moving slowly around an empty space. Death in white robes and a skull mask dances around, killing them with his touch. The setting is an empty expanse with a concrete wall behind the actors. A frontal camera angle and blue filter render the scene almost depthless, the ground and wall seeming as much a flat color field as a real place (figure 13). It does not look exactly like the abstract field of *Blue*, but there is enough similarity to remind us that Jarman has always

FIGURE 13 *Death Dance* (Jarman, 1973)
The image constitutes a blue field in which color flattens space and denies figuration.

worked with the queer potential of surface color. As Robertson puts it, "For Newton, of course, all colour joined in the pure concept of white-ness, of light. But we are attracted to the weakness and impurity of the bond of pigment, because we can identify with nothing other than insta-bility. This identification is admittedly a style of taste, but it also impro-vises a political alignment."[22]

Tony Rayns offers a fascinating analysis of the Super-8 films in which he reads color as a figuration of sodomy, suggesting that "Derek Jarman's trajectory as a filmmaker demands to be read as a quest for a joyful and fulfilled passivity. This passivity . . . has twin valences: filmic acts and sexual acts. The two sometimes seem indistinguishable." Describing the aesthetic side of this equation, he says, "These were the films of an anti-Eisenstein: languorous, formless reveries in which various theatrical and painterly ideas were subsumed into a never-ending flow of colours and visual textures that was finally pure surface." The formlessness of pure color expresses an anxiety around passivity and the feminine threat of the bodily cavity. As color takes over from form, it operates as a subsuming void, an all-consuming bottom. Rayns sees the films as overly passive, concluding that "for viewer and filmmaker alike, they represent a perpetual state of arousal without the attendant climax."[23] For a reading that proposes sodomy as an organizing metaphor, this analysis exhibits an odd fear of the passive and the formless. If we choose, instead, to value the films' flow of colors and visual textures precisely as a formal articulation of anality, then we begin to see how Jarman's visual style queers aesthetics. The chiasmic effect in *The Art of Mirrors* telescopes this visual mode across production method and text: turning the camera to automatic exposure renders the filmmaker passive in the creation of light effects, and the appearance of the darkened frame repeatedly forces the image into a formless void. In this example, the figures in the image work to create a formless form of color, light, and blackness. Other films elaborate the sensual terrain of passive color in an iconography of naked, masked, and bound men. Thus *Arabia* displays a man chained among lines of fire, a St. Sebastian in a loin cloth, and several naked boys lying on the ground (figure 14). The seductive qualities of bodily passivity and

FIGURE 14 *Arabia* (Jarman, 1974)
The seductive qualities of passivity and masochism propose a visual economy of engulfment.

masochism refute the dominance of masculinist line and instead propose a visual and erotic economy of engulfment.[24]

As Brian Price has argued with regard to Claire Denis's *Beau Travail* (1999), formless color can contain sexually and aesthetically radical potential.[25] The emphasis on ground and figure in Denis's homoerotic visual schema makes a suggestive intertext for Jarman's *Death Dance*. In both films, beautiful young men are placed, naked or semiclothed, against a monochromatic color field, and the value of verticality and masculine action is steadily undermined. *Beau Travail*'s soldiers wait in the African desert, temporality stretched out until abandonment in the endless expanse of dry earth threatens life. In Jarman's short film, Death in a white robe kills young men one by one with his touch. Relations of figure and ground are reversed here, however, as the only active figure is antilife, and all value is to be found in the horizontal compositional space of the men lying still visible on the ground, resisting Death's iconophobic moves. The bright blue tinting of the image also resists Death's efforts, enabling a passive aesthetic of formless saturation to overcome the aggressive temporality of figural violence. *Death Dance* sees queer desire as an engulfment without boundaries—or as a refusal of the fatal boundaries of a politics of linearity. Price's analysis of *Beau Travail* likewise finds a political connection between the film's boundless landscapes and its narrative of queer desire, and he turns to Matisse's *The Joy of Life* (1905–1906) as an example where color dominates line and moralism is replaced with corporeal joy. For Jarman, too, life is joyful, but *Death Dance* insists on a resistance not necessary in Matisse's work. Color's claim on queer life implies something very different from cinematic openness, indecently promising utopic beauties at the same time as it reminds us, melancholically, of the threat of death. Life, here, has a very different implication than it does for cinematic realism.

LIBERTINE: QUEER LIFE

Lichtenstein's colorist libertines praised color for the incomparable effects that its simulacra produced. In other words, they found it a superior means to evoke life. Mimesis is hardly a controversial aim, but problems arise when the life in question is seen as libertine: wantonly sexual or lacking in proper social aims. In this way, queer lives are excluded from the healthy and open discourses of cinematic realism, which emphasize purity and reproduction as opposed to enclosure and death. Modernist architect Adolf Loos describes a "Poor Rich Man" who decorates his house in art nouveau style and, being completely surrounded by ornament, realizes that he has to learn to live with his own corpse.[26] Louis Delluc contrasts cinematic life with the decorative and colorful daemon of plasticity. As Rees says of Jarman, composed spaces do not breathe. Such modernist parables vividly stage what modern aesthetics sees as the wrong kind of life, but they also alert us to the possibilities for transvaluing color's libertine force. Rejecting a realism from which its proponents have consistently excluded the nonreproductive and impure, Jarman turns to color as an improper form. He does, in his later work, have to learn to live with his own death, but his use of color nonetheless celebrates queer life as a *détournement* of aesthetic propriety.

Colin MacCabe says in his introduction to the *Wittgenstein* (Jarman, 1993) scripts that the film's use of bright colors "illuminate[s] a queer life."[27] The same can be said of the Super-8 films, which deploy bright colors to access an contingent experience of time and place. We jump across bodies, locations, and quickly lost scenes in *It Happened by Chance*, one of a series of diary films Jarman made in the 1970s. These films combine the principle of chance encounters with the compositional aesthetic of the short films. Images recognizable from films such as *The Art of Mirrors* and *Arabia* are recontextualized within a rapid-fire tumult of filmmaking life, a temporal flow of queer aesthetics. Punk icon Toyah stands against a pinky red background; red, white, and blue flags hang at a street party; gold light reflects from mirrors; and the pyramids are bathed in deep red. This sensory overload pointedly refuses to follow the rules of the formalist avant-garde, constructing a discourse on colorful life at the same time that it eschews meaningful form. In *Chroma*, Jarman writes, "Red is a moment in time. Blue constant." The book is as much about his experience of AIDS as it is about color, and the two are constantly woven together: "I wrote this book in an absence of time. If I have overlooked something you hold precious—write it in the margin. . . . I had to write quickly as my right eye was put out in August. . . . I wrote the red on a hospital drip."[28] Here we see elaborated a relationship that spans from Jarman's earliest work to his latest: between color and cinematic temporality. The Super-8 films evoke the transient pleasures of life, whereas *Chroma* and *Blue* use color to negotiate the lack of time and the proximity of death. But from the beautiful boys of the eerily prescient *Death Dance* to the blank screen of *Blue*, Jarman insists on the queer potentiality of what has been excluded from the aesthetics of openness: the formless and the engulfing, the nonproductive and the nonreproductive. In the face of figurative homophobia and an inexorable linearity, Jarman's pretty films bond color to the countertemporalities of queer living.

Jarman is interested in color language—in what blue means, for instance. Most theories of color language seem reactionary or naive in their attempts to assign universal cultural associations.[29] However, Jarman does not so much ascribe inherent meanings to colors as engage creatively with a history of inherited associations. In this sense, he expands Sergei Eisenstein's analysis of color in his writing on synesthesia, in which he proposes that filmmakers engage the "anecdotes" or political histories that might make red signify revolution in one context and aristocratic reaction in another.[30] Color's meaning is shaped by historical forces, which exactly dovetails with Jarman's project in his narrative films to construct a queer history. However, as we saw from Bazin's discussion of *Ivan Groznyy* / *Ivan the Terrible* (1944), Eisenstein's "decadence" often creates problems for film theory. This association extends to Jarman's films, in which, for instance, O'Pray writes, not entirely enthusiastically, "his aesthetic saturation of the image through graphic composition, colour and movement is reminiscent of Eisenstein's obsessive aestheticism of the image in films such as *October* and *Ivan the Terrible*."[31] Synchronization of the senses is a *suspicious* style, and Jarman knows well the relationship between aesthetic decadence and the legibility of queer lives. Color marks the artist as deviant, deviating from the aesthetic straight and narrow, and even where the queer filmmaker outs his style as a formal expression of homosexual desire, the problem remains of how to make queer living matter. Eisenstein takes his place in this history as much as Plato, where the theorist's sexuality subtends a revised orientation to color theory itself. What is useful about linking Jarman's project of queer historicity to color is that it demands a meaningful role for what is often seen as mere sensation.

We might compare Jarman's color theory with Henry Adams's notion that each era forms its own color world. Adams discusses the blues in the cathedral of Chartres, which, he claims, we no longer know how to make.[32] For him, color can be the structuring force behind a space (whether a cathedral or, for our purposes, a body of film work), the central organizing principle for how we experience that space, and this force would not be simply an aesthetic choice, but a historical one. In Jarman's films, color also provides a way to create an era or, rather, to create a counter-era. Where the cathedral embodies the dominant site of repressive institutional space, the coercive force of art, Jarman's films elaborate the aesthetic imaginary of queer experience. The vivid chromatic spaces of gay London and the punk appropriation of the postindustrial Docklands conjured in *The Art of Mirrors* and *It Happened by Chance* represent both a counterpresent and a counterreading of aesthetic history. Prettiness deforms form and demands that we find life instead in the richly colored and socially marginal. The somber monochrome of *Blue* speaks to the end of life and the incommensurability of living with AIDS. But by thinking color as a technique across Jarman's career, we read a multiform counter-era. Color is not the surface that prevents deep meaning, but the surface that can dream a queer collective.

Brash: Mineral Histories

The colorists' brashness lies in their defense of the purely material qualities of art, and Jarman equally insists on the significance of film color's visible qualities. *Chroma* narrates the material histories as well as the semiotics of color: "The arrival of indigo in Europe caused consternation. Woad was under threat in 1577 in Germany. A decree prohibited 'the newly invented pernicious and deceitful, eating and corrosive dye called the Devil's Dye.' "[33] Color not only is a question of cultural connotation but is closely intertwined with material politics. What is it made of? Where does it come from? Colors, like most pretty things, are stories of cross-cultural exchange, seen as primitive and exotic, desirable and dangerous. Hence, Jarman tells us, indigo is *indekan* from India; zinc oxide is Chinese white; rose madder "was introduced from the East by the Crusaders to Italy and France"; and the word *red* is from the Sanskrit *rudhira*.[34] Color is materially tied to geopolitical exchange and is a refusal, in the very corpus of art, of cultural purity. As Robertson puts it, "Colour marks exchange. It is border-work. Mixture is our calling."[35] Cinematic color, being composed of light, not pigment, is relatively immaterial, but Jarman employs the physical qualities of 8-mm film to elaborate a mixture of the chemical (effects of light on film stock) with the mineral (the materials of the world). The Super-8 films certainly visualize the kind of Asianism that classical rhetoric associated with colorful style: the pyramids that recur in several films along with hieroglyphics and the cross-cultural religious mish-mash of the tarot. This mystical tendency opens up a crucial discourse on materiality. *Tarot* (1972–1973) introduces the figure of John Dee, an important historical reference point for Jarman because of his association with alchemy. Jarman writes often about his interest in alchemy, and the term *alchemy* provides a rich series of reference points for thinking about his films.[36] Another cross-cultural encounter, of course, the word *alchemy* comes to English from the Arabic and ancient Egyptian, and the practice is associated with a combination of European and Middle Eastern scientific and religious histories. The chemical history of colors promises an alchemical transformation of matter, and it is this juxtaposition of the material and the utopian that grounds Jarman's color theory.

The strongest exploration of materiality is the dialogue between the colorful material of 8-mm film and the remnants of ancient culture that we see in what we might call the landscape films: *Journey to Avebury* and *Ashden's Walk on Møn.* O'Pray finds *Journey to Avebury* dull,[37] but its static compositions of orange and green landscapes and ancient standing stones construct a picturesque view in which the enduring temporality of the ancient stones and the contingent temporality of the spectator are folded into a shared experience of stillness and pastness. We note the difference between this evocation of pastness through mostly empty landscape and the more familiar articulation of domestic pasts in home-movie footage—for instance, the footage included in *The Last of England* (1988).[38] *Journey* does not include the range of colors found in nostalgic family movies. Rather, the monochromatic yellowness of the sky evokes a mystical experience (a journey, not a constant place) such that the off-kilter quality of the standing stones seeps into even the ordinary compositions of English fields. The surface coloration of the image combines forces with the material effects of its profilmic objects to produce in the viewer an unsettling experience akin to the queer temporality of engulfment.

A more exuberantly brash iteration of this dialogue occurs in *Ashden's Walk on Møn.* Another film that leads us to the remnants of long-vanished systems of belief, *Ashden* is set on the Danish island of Møn, which is known for its chalk cliffs and prehistoric burial chambers. The film begins with the sky, superimposing an image of the Milky Way onto shots of nature: moving water, blades of grass, and so on. The blue is darker than *Blue*'s ultramarine, closer to violet. It suggests a night sky, but the images are earthly, projecting a celestial immateriality onto the material world (figure 15). Color takes over line in many shots, where the superim-

FIGURE 15 *Ashden's Walk on Møn* (Jarman, 1973)
Superimposition overlays material nature with the celestial.

position blurs the graphic outlines, leaving us with a sense of color and space (literally space, with stars). After the nature pairings comes a cultural pair, where an old cosmographical drawing of the sun and planets is superimposed over a deserted building, layering histories of observation onto Møn's material space (figure 16). This shot is a paler violet, pinking on the rays of the cosmography's sun. Of course, the film is also a journey—Ashden's walk—and we see glimpses of two men walking through woods and on a chalk cliff beach. Like Prospect Cottage, where Jarman made his garden, Møn illustrates a very particular northern European coastal geography in which a queer counterpresent can draw from a cultural history richly endowed with countercapitalist, even utopian collective spaces.

The final section of the film takes place at a prehistoric site, and superimpositions are replaced by a series of shots of a ground-level landscape of grassy hillocks. The materiality of grass and what looks like ancient structures is combined with a bright green coloration and a lens flare that recurs, dancing across the surface of the screen (figure 17). In

FIGURE 16 *Ashden's Walk on Møn*
Outdated cosmographies meet abandoned buildings in Derek Jarman's utopian spaces.

FIGURE 17 *Ashden's Walk on Møn*
A lens flare stages a momentary meeting of the materials of cinematic light and those of profilmic nature.

these shots, a relationship is forged between the filmic material that does not really exist (light effect, color) and the natural material that is unchanging (grassy hills). Like the "green dreams" of Ulrike Ottinger's *Johanna d'Arc of Mongolia* (1989), discussed in chapter 8, these shots figure an endless expanse of rich green grassland as an auratic experience of both experiential presence and inevitable temporal loss. The exoticism that Ottinger explores in Mongolia is equally available for Jarman in the mineral histories of northern Europe. A mineral history draws from the prettiness of the surface (the chemical qualities of film light and color) but intertwines it with the geographically rooted histories of stone (hard physical reality that is apparently the opposite of ephemeral colors that exist only in the eye). In contrast to Stan Brakhage, who centers the perceiving subject (the straight male filmmaker), Jarman disperses meaning across the surface of the image. Combining the eye and the thing, he stages both a phenomenology and a materialism.

Such an esoteric phenomenology might not seem fertile ground for politics, yet the interrogations of cinematic material by other avant-gardes (the London Co-op, for instance) are understood as political as a matter of course. Jarman's abstractions are too pretty to join this masculinist discourse, and his color work was not admitted to the cultural big time until *Blue*, the only one of his films that critics could redeem as iconoclastic and austere. Conversely, a more realist account of landscape such as Siegfried Kracauer's endlessness or André Bazin's ontology would find social engagement in the transparency of the profilmic. It is Jarman's decorative colors, superimpositions, and light effects that preclude such validatory interpretations, along with a suspicion that ancient relics and standing stones make too hippyish a topic for serious cinema. But it is precisely in this mineral history that Jarman forges a utopian politics: brash color conjures an alchemical relation between pretty form and material content, a negotiation between systems of what you can touch and what you can only imagine.

Karen Pinkus has recently discussed alchemy as a figure of ambivalence, connoting both the transmutations of genius—the artist who can turn meager materials into aesthetic gold—and the hocus-pocus of falsification, linked to fake science and toxic capitalism.[39] Jarman is equally fascinated with both aspects of alchemy. On the positive side, it figures his own artistic process, an *arte povera* that creates something out of not much more than nothing. It also enfolds a queer sense of secret knowledge, of outsiders who trade in occult glances and strange processes. These positive connotations of alchemy are contained in *Ashden's* mysterious images. (Who are these men? Lovers or explorers of the island? What knowledge do the cosmographies and the ancient burial grounds share?) Pinkus's second, more negative sense of alchemy leads us toward Jarman's most direct political critique. In the punk films, he, too, is interested in what goes wrong with capitalism, with what is excluded from the production of wealth, but the mobilization of alchemy as a queer visual technique troubles the stakes of Pinkus's ambivalence. Alchemy is seen as unhealthy, unnatural, and mendacious, just as color and prettiness connote deceptive cosmetics and exclude proper and healthy life. Jarman's refusal of all discourses on aesthetic purity and proper living force a reconfiguration of the politics of alchemy along with those of prettiness. To propose alchemy as a principle of color film is to make a transvaluative—indeed, an alchemical—claim on the politics of color.

We see this distinction most clearly in *Blue*, a film that begins from nothing but a pure pigment and that uses its mineral surface to plumb the depths of life and death. Many critics have placed *Blue* within traditions of iconoclasm, seeing its use of color as a repudiation of visual pleasure. Thus Peter Schwenger finds in the film a sense of image as pandemonium and as a "prison of the soul" from which Jarman desires to be released.[40] Porton aligns it with ascetic traditions of modernism such as that of Loos, and Andrew Moor calls it "creative puritanism: a cinema of denial."[41] These interpretations offer useful insights—Moor, for instance, finds a politics of nonrepresentation in *Blue's* refusal to offer medicalized spectacles of bodies with AIDS—but the deeply hued screen of *Blue* seems to me quite the opposite of the purity Bazin finds in Robert Bresson's denial of the image. A film saturated in deep color, reminiscent of Yves Klein's blue paintings, is sensual, deep, and joyful—not puritan at all. Klein's works accumulate paint rather than writing with it—line is replaced by a solidity of pigment—and it is this experiential density of color that *Blue* evokes. The film's soundtrack offers a plenitude of meaning and emotional resonance, attaching color to a mode of significance aligned with sensual drift—formless but full of content.

In outlining Jarman's iterative reference to Klein, Peter Wollen notes the unique materiality of Klein's invented color, International Klein Blue (IKB): "In essence, IKB is a slab of ultramarine pigment suspended in a clear commercial binder, Rhodopas. The effect is to preserve the granularity of the pigment and to seal it so that a thickness of pure pigment can be hung vertically on the wall, like an upended tray."[42] The materiality of color is literalized in IKB, producing for Klein a double-edged pull between pure color as an escape from the material world and the color itself as material to an unusual extent. This is what happens in *Blue*, where the piece's emotional effect is contained precisely in the impossible dialectic of materiality and formlessness, life and death. Closer to Jean-Luc Nancy's notion of the obvious image than to traditional concepts of representation, the image of *Blue* is a whole encompassed immediately in a process that is entirely other to the question of form. As Nancy puts it, "The image is the obviousness of the invisible. It does not render it visible as an object: it accedes to a knowledge of it. Knowledge of the obvious is not a science, it is the knowledge of the whole as a whole. In a single stroke, which is what makes it striking, the image delivers a totality of sense or a truth."[43] *Blue* does not drain the image of detail and detritus, but fills it with the force of that which is invisible yet material. Schwenger sees in the film a Blochian anticipatory mode of living in which an active conjuring of that which is not yet visible characterizes a transformative political hope.[44] I would argue that we find such an anticipatory hope in the color itself, not just in the refusal of mimetic representation. A force and a knowledge that strike the spectator all at once, the film's rejection of images is not iconophobia, but an experiment in the meaningful potential of intense *colore*.

In his influential account of Kant's aesthetics, Jacques Derrida glosses the concept of the parergon, or frame. If the frame has formal beauty, it can enhance the beauty of the painting, but if the frame's beauty is formless—Kant's example is a golden frame—then it is a mere adornment and will detract from the beauty of the image. What is wrong with the golden frame is the seductive dazzle of its formless color, so, Derrida writes, "what is bad, external to the pure object of taste, is thus what seduces by an attraction; and the example of what leads astray by its force of attraction is a color, the gilding, in as much as it is nonform, content, or sensory matter. The deterioration of the parergon, the perversion, the adornment, is the attraction of sensory matter."[45] Color names the place where aesthetics becomes a perversion for Kant, and Jarman's films work to bring that perverse color from the edge to the center of the image. (Something similar happens in Jarman's late paintings, in which gold is added to the thickly layered canvases along with all kinds of objects, matter, and detritus.) Matter is more important than form: the materials of filmmaking—whether the camera autosetting that produces the dark flashes in *Art of Mirrors* and *Arabia*, the lens flares in *Ashden*, or the invisible profilmic materiality of diseased bodies in *Blue*—all produce a political aesthetic of alchemical color. Both color and the material world are readable as matter rather than form, and thus they can be transmuted as matter can be. Put simply, things can change or be made to change through queer labor. Turning matter into gold is the alchemist's ideal, just as it is the problem for Kant. In Derrida's account, the frame, "in its purity[,] . . . ought to remain colourless,"[46] which echoes the idea that a base metal should, as a matter of nature, stay that way and not be alchemically transformed into gold. Jarman, however, is in favor of transforming matter, and his alchemical transformation of color refigures both the meaningful potential of color itself and, with it, film's ability to encompass queer life.

THREE

ORNAMENT AND MODERNITY

From Decorative Art to Cultural Criticism

IN CONJURING A CINEMATIC PRETTY, WE IMAGINE AN IMAGE that is decorative rather than meaningful and in which the attractive surface of the screen focuses our attention to the detriment of its serious depths. One model for this mode of aesthetic production is ornament, in which the body of the artwork is adorned with surface detail. Ornament forms an important subcategory of the pretty, and *ornament* as an aesthetic term intersects closely with pretty discourse in cinema. The question of ornament is a contentious one in the history of aesthetics and one that has never been able to help speaking about the relationship of the image to gender and geopolitics. Hegel found adornment of the body to be essential to man's nature—an aesthetic impulse to change nature into culture. Thus, for him, "this is the cause of all dressing up, and adornment, even if it be barbaric, tasteless, completely disfiguring, or even pernicious like crushing the feet of Chinese ladies, or slitting the ears or lips."[1] Hegel's sentence moves rapidly from an avowal of ornament's universalist cultural centrality to fantasies of the primitive, invoking both the barbarism of non-Europeans who pierce their bodies and the gendered horror of Chinese foot binding.

Feminist scholars of literature have noted this troubling connection of ornament to primitive bodies. Naomi Schor traces the neoclassical critique of "Asiatic" style in rhetoric, which viewed visual and linguistic detail as "degraded, effeminate, ornamental."[2] And Rae Beth Gordon, writing on nineteenth-century French literature, argues that "the linking of ornament and evil with the operative intermediaries of excess and seduction is as old as ornament itself. One only has to think of the valorization of plainness in manner and attire in the Amish and Mennonite communities, or the seductive and even treacherous ways of femmes fatales like Salomé or Helen of Troy, depicted . . . dripping with ornament."[3] *Ornament*, clearly, is one word for the excessive investment in the cosmetic that classical aesthetics associates with the feminine. Like the woman, ornament is a supplement, secondary and maybe surplus to masculine requirements. It likewise connotes the geopolitical outsider, the primitive whose absence regulates the central place of the European cultural order. In European aesthetics, non-Europeans and women are projected as loving ornament because these groups are viewed as a decorative supplement to that aesthetics. Thus the political quality of the ornament: it may be tolerated, but only if it knows its place.

And yet Hegel does claim that adornment is central to human nature, an originary impulse of art. Gordon considers this contradiction: "First, ornament not only is at the origin of art, it also includes its most essential principles. (Already, the profile of a paradox is glimpsed: if ornament is defined as the inessential aspect of form, how can it contain the essential aesthetic qualities of form?)." For Gordon, ornament's paradoxical status as that which is essential and yet inessential in art leads to a unique potential for critique. She argues that "one of the primary functions of ornament is to carry meaning and intent that have been suppressed or excluded from the central field."[4] In a transvaluative move, she finds in ornament a structure, built into art, where the exclusions of dominant aesthetics might be found. Building on this reading of the ornament, we can locate the same structure in the cinematic image. The ornament can express meanings that have been excluded from the central field and hence can comment on what is missing from those central meanings. Although it is seemingly inessential, it provides an essential critical quality of the cinematic image. If the ornament provides a theoretical space in which the question of aesthetic meaning can be thought in cinema, it also links that question in its historical origins to a politics of bodies and spaces. The value of ornament comes under particular debate in the nineteenth century, directly influencing the emergence of film aesthetics at the opening of the twentieth.

In this chapter, I follow the trajectory of the ornament from art into film, arguing that ornament's paradoxical structure and modern rejection have shaped cinema's engagement with aesthetic and cultural modernity. I begin by analyzing the circulation of ornament as a discourse in late-nineteenth-century European culture, considering how cinema emerged into debates on fine versus decorative art. Questions of mass production and the commodity as well as of the place of mimesis outside of fine art were central to thinking ornament's role in modernity before they became key terms for theorists of film and mass culture in the 1920s and 1930s. These debates, I argue, shaped the ways in which cinema could be understood and valued as a new art form. The second section moves on to the early twentieth century's rejection of ornament, taking Viennese architect Adolf Loos as a central figure. I argue that Loos was widely engaged by European cultural critics and that we can track an important anti-ornamental strain in interwar European film culture by examining the trajectory of his polemic against ornament. Not merely a question of "influence," Loos's critique of ornament is an unspoken aesthetic support to cinematic modernity. Thus we read Loos against Siegfried Kracauer, whose politics were quite different but who also wrote famously on the (mass) ornament. Next, I consider how the gendered and primitivist rhetoric of the ornament—which Loos enthusiastically advanced—enters modern film culture, taking Josephine Baker and Greta Garbo as examples. The ambivalent reception of these stars concretizes the corporeal politics of the ornament. Finally, we turn to Walter Benjamin, who provides a complicating rereading of the Loosian ornament. One of the few contemporary critics to address Loos directly, Benjamin also wrote extensively on both cinema and the ornamental styles of nineteenth- and twentieth-century material cultures. By bringing these aspects of his work into conversation, I argue, we locate in Benjamin a method for thinking of ornament as an essential—and potentially radical—quality of the cinematic image.

ORNAMENT IN AND OUT OF PLACE

The conditions of ornament's rise in nineteenth-century Europe take in industrialization; the development of mass-market interior furnishings, consumer goods, and clothing; the growth of archaeological and historical

discourse on foreign cultures; the exhibitions and worlds fairs that engaged public interest in manufacture, colonial products, and fashion;
and the mid-Victorian series of historicist and orientalist styles. Much of
this narrative is familiar to film studies insofar as it speaks to histories
and theories of visuality, mass culture, and international capitalism. What
has not been brought out, though, is the contested place of the ornament
in this matrix of conditions into which cinema would emerge. Debates
over the proper place of ornamentation in art and design are symptomatic
of a series of tensions: between tradition and modern style, between form
and function, and between industrial design and artisanal production.
These tensions, in other words, pose the questions of the nature, purpose,
and mode of production of art that would become central to modern cultural critique. This discursive trajectory underpins classical film theory's
aesthetic concern with the nature of the cinematic, but it also leads us to
the Marxist criticism of the Frankfurt School and, circling back to its origin, to Benjamin's analysis of nineteenth-century decorative style.

To understand cinema's ornamental rhetoric, then, we must first examine its aesthetic antecedents. In the latter half of the nineteenth century, a rash of books was published offering histories of, guides to, and
most of all taxonomies of ornament. The cataloging urge—what Ernest
Gellner called "world-levelling, unificatory epistemologies"—that under-
wrote the scientific, naturalistic, and cartographic projects of the period
as well as the surveillance of bodies manifested in fingerprinting and
phrenology also brought forth an ordering discourse on the ornament.[5]
In France, Charles Blanc published his highly influential *Grammaire des
arts du dessin* (1862) and *Grammaire des arts décoratifs* (1882), which constructed histories of the arabesque, palm, leaf, and other decorative
shapes as well as patterns for tiles and borders.[6] In 1883, Jules Bourgoin's
Théorie de l'ornement followed Hegel's claim on the universality of ornament, arguing that the desire to embellish and ornament the fruits of
one's labors is instinctive to humanity.[7] In the United Kingdom, too, both
the taxonomic and the evaluative aspects of this discourse exercised
major figures in architecture and design: Owen Jones's *The Grammar of
Ornament* (1856) took a stand on ornament's value, and practitioners from
Augustus Pugin in midcentury through to John Ruskin at its end responded with various degrees of enthusiasm for the decorative. Similar
taxonomies can be found in Germany, such as Franz Sales Meyer's populist *A Handbook of Ornament* (1898) (figure 18).[8]

FIGURE 18 Palmette bands in Franz Sales Meyer's *A Handbook of Ornament* (1898).

Germany's most significant theorist of ornament, though, is Alois Riegl, whose *Problems of Style: Foundations for a History of Ornament* (1893) provides a polemical claim on the autonomous nature of ornament. A foundational figure in the discipline of art history, Riegl's concept of *Kunstwollen*—a worldview that Benjamin later found productive— brought a complexity to accounts of the relationship between art and social history. This engagement with ideas about the autonomy of art as well as his influential concepts of haptic and optical painting have led to a return to Riegl on the part of film and visual culture scholars such as Angela Dalle Vacche. However, in this context I am more interested in the fact that although Riegl is one of the forefathers of art history, his foundational research is not on fine art at all, but on textiles and decorative art. And no doubt as a result of this positioning, he places the ornament at the heart of his aesthetics. Opposing Gottfried Semper's materialism, Riegl argues that ornament is not secondary to basic function but should be considered a meaningful element of art in its own right: "It will become evident, namely, that the human desire to adorn the body is far more elementary than the desire to cover it with woven garments, and that the decorative motifs that satisfy the simple desire for adornment, such as linear, geometric configurations, surely existed long before textiles were used for physical protection." Riegl gives ornament a primacy that undermines the conventional rhetoric of supplementarity. And in a phrase that resonates deeply with my own project, he speaks of the "enormous resistance to making 'mere ornament' the basic theme of a more ambitious historical study."[9]

How, then, does this contentious historical emergence of "mere ornament" as a fit object for scholarship find its way into the film theories of the twentieth century? I suggest two major strands of influence. The first centers on the opposition between fine art and decorative or applied art, which exercised many of the aestheticians who considered ornament. Eugène Véron, for example, argues that we must clearly separate decorative from expressive art, and in a rhetorical move that we find repeated again and again across the theories of ornament, he attempts to delimit the proper place of the decorative. For him, "as long as it stays within its proper limits, which are the gracious, the pretty [*le joli*], the beautiful, and as long as it doesn't propel itself, under the pretext of novelty or distinctiveness, into the strange, the retro or the false, decorative art is a perfectly legitimate art, which responds to a most natural need and which we cannot encourage enough."[10] In a typical damning-with-faint-praise claim, Véron says that decorative art is fine as long as it knows its place. We might hear a gendering note in the structure of this argument, which purports an equality that depends on an obviously subordinating limitation of movement. We must certainly hear it in the condescending language of "*perfectly* legitimate," "*most* natural," and "cannot encourage enough" (by whom?) as well as in the feminized terms allowed to the decorative: *gracious, beautiful,* and, of course, *pretty.*

In the face of this feminizing rhetoric, it should come as no surprise that classical film theorists as well as early film enthusiasts of all kinds should have been keen to locate cinema as a fine art rather than as an applied or decorative art. Talking about film within the discursive terms of fine art was not necessarily a claim motivated by elitist desires for high culture so much as a choice between locating film as masculine and expressive or as feminine and decorative. The aesthetic language of the decades immediately before cinema's emergence overdetermined the categories available for thinking about new visual forms such that any claim on the significance, meaning, and value of cinema had to find a way to include it within fine art, not, as is often thought, as opposed to a non-art category such as "popular culture," but as opposed to the inferior and feminine decorative.

In theory, it made perfect sense to locate cinema within fine art rather than within decorative art because the latter was widely perceived as inferior. In practice, however, cinema had much in common with the applied arts, which in the late nineteenth century had transitioned from artisanal production of luxury goods to industrially mass-produced products. Cinema is, of course, an example of industrial, mass-produced culture, and its push-me / pull-me between art and commerce is a structuring tension of film theory. The impulse to sequester ornament is an excellent symptom of this tension, evoking patriarchal and colonialist disgust at the same time that it raises class-oriented questions of taste and economic ones of mass production. Nineteenth-century debates over ornament addressed the difficulty of including detailed ornamentation in mass-produced goods so that arguments over ornament inevitably interrogated the place of modern industrial and reproductive technologies in the decorative or even fine arts. Benjamin's aura applies to hand-sewn embroidery as much it does to the religious icon, and the ornament presses into close proximity the ideological structures of aesthetic theory and those of the commodity fetish. As Sianne Ngai suggests, minor taste concepts are especially apt for unpicking the stitching of modern capitalist culture, and the ornament is here an entry point to the political economy of the pretty.[11] By comparing the discourse on ornament as a feature of material culture in the late nineteenth century with the discourse on film aesthetics in the early decades of the twentieth, we can discern the significance of the decorative for cinema's negotiation of art and mass culture. In the first decades of cinema, a refusal of ornament enabled critics to define film as meaningful in the exact terms that aesthetics used to separate fine art from decorative art.

Decorative art is first of all abstract, as opposed to fine art's mimeticism. Ralph N. Wornum, in *Analysis of Ornament* (1882), distinguishes picture from ornament: "Any picture, whatever the subject, which is composed merely on principles of symmetry and contrast, becomes an ornament, and any ornamental design in which these two principles have been made subservient to imitation or natural arrangement has departed from the province of ornament into that of the picture or the model, whichever it may be."[12] For Wornum and most of his contemporaries, art was valued for its ability to depict nature, and this representational binding to life itself takes on central importance in film's anti-ornamental realism.[13] For example, Béla Balázs lauds Greta Garbo's ability to express psychological truth: "Garbo's beauty is not just a harmony of lines, it is not merely ornamental."[14] Cinema, like art, aligns itself with life and hence with value via mimesis. For Wornum, the decorative should not stray into the territory of mimesis, for this ability is proper only to fine art. He goes on to give negative examples of decorative art that is mimetic of nature, such as a bell formed of leaves or a gas jet of flowers. These works he rejects in the language of deformed bodies, finding them to be "aesthetic monstrosities, ornamental abominations."[15] This idea of a morality of ornament—that it ought to reveal rather than obscure function—ultimately rejects any attempt at autonomous meaning in ornamentation.[16]

There is a twofold structure at play here: mimetic art is superior, but even in the lesser realm of the decorative only certain kinds of ornament are acceptable *in their place*. This structure is echoed in Balázs's appraisal of decorative editing, which he describes as editing that is done not for narrative reasons, but with "merely formal, musical, decorative significance."[17] The association of the decorative with abstract forms, including music, follows theorists of ornament such as Jean D'Udine, who links ornament to dance, and Jules Bourgoin, who lists "la cinématique" as one of the decorative's affiliations.[18] Like these aestheticians, Balázs is happy for decorative editing to exist, but only in its proper place. When it is raised to become the entire aim of a film, as in the avant-garde, he finds it unsuccessful: "The avant-gardistes and futurists made the mistake of thinking that such rhythms can become independent artistic means of expression of a special kind." He concludes, "Such a system of editing is only concerned with decorative features and nothing else; it shows the world depicted as a mobile ornament."[19] That the ornament can be mobile demonstrates an important development of its rhetoric in film theory: not limited to the pictorial plane, the ornament can be constituted as temporal by the rhythms of editing. Cinema kineticizes the ornament, linking the mimetic qualities of fine art to narrative and, as a corollary, the anti-narrative temporal structures of the avant-garde to meaningless decoration. Thus the mimetic possibilities of the world define cinema in terms of both fine art and narrative, and a mobile ornament can only suborn this representative value.

When decorative art is separated from naturalistic representation of the world, this graphic abstraction is also linked to geographical alterity. Although the emerging discipline of art history focused on western European art, the history of ornament was enabled by research on Asian cultures and by the work of archaeologists in Egypt, Iran, and Mesopotamia. For example, Riegl tells us that "from the time it first fell under the influence of the more refined culture and art of Greece, the Orient resisted the naturalizing tendencies of Western art epitomized in the development of acanthus motifs and the like."[20] Realism is attributed to Western aesthetic values, whereas symmetry, stylization, and the decorative are linked to the Orient. Thus in thinking ornament, we find a colonial and orientalizing logic at work from the beginning. Whereas beauty might be perceived as a Greek concept, based on clean lines and simple forms, ornament begins with a taint of foreignness. Of course, many critics advocated for non-European styles. Jones took the Alhambra as his example of the best of ornamental art and argued that we should learn from the tattooed heads of native New Zealanders.[21] Riegl likewise found Maori spiral tattoos to be an example of pure creativity, not copied from any real-world source.[22] Chinoiserie and japonisme underwent a resurgence in late-nineteenth-century Europe, greatly influencing impressionism and art nouveau.[23] But we nonetheless see an inevitable inequality in ornament's geographical origins. In Bourgoin's taxonomy, ornament is sourced from geometry, art, and nature. Geometry is exemplified by Arab design ("a bit dry and abstract"), nature by Japanese design ("spiritual and animated"), and art by Greek design ("the most artistic of all men").[24] Faint praise characterizes the description of non-Western forms, and the scientific-sounding language of taxonomy is quickly seen to depend on geopolitical clichés.

This discourse of decorative versus fine art sets up geopolitics as an institutional inheritance for cinema. Walter Crane perceptively analyzes the transnational nature of ornament, pointing out the Eastern origin of the Chinese peony, Egyptian lotus, Indian palmette, and others. He continues, "They were capable, too, of infinite variation in treatment, a variation which has been continued ever since, as by importation to different countries (the movement going on from east to west) the same forms were treated by designers of different races, and became mixed with other native elements, or consciously imitated as they are now by Manchester designers and manufacturers, to be sold again in textile form to their original owners, as it were, in the far East."[25] Here, ornament is structurally and historically transnational, written into histories of modernity, colonialism, and mass production. It opposes the unique genius of art with the modern mass-cultural product. This inheritance is something that cinema has sometimes shied away from as it asserts its European origins and its artistry, but such an inheritance is a key aspect of cinema, a history and a form that bind film and ornament as global products.

This geopolitical logic enters film criticism in many overt ways, but for now I want to give a purely rhetorical example in order to emphasize not the obviously racist logic of primitivist representation, but the extent to which ornament always carries a faint whiff of geographical difference. In 1918, Emile Vuillermoz assessed Abel Gance's La dixième symphonie / The Tenth Symphony by means of an extended metaphor of weaving that aimed to show how Gance is good at adding decoration, but not at creating the basic material of art: "Yet for reasons which are hardly mysterious, the producers among us are not accustomed to supplying their embroiderers with the costly materials on which to design their arabesques. Instead, the embroiderer must manufacture the material himself. Abel Gance, who is a subtle embroidery craftsman, has not yet found on his loom enough sumptuous brocade worthy of being accentuated with filigrees of gold, glass beads, satin, and twisted silver thread. Thus he himself has been forced to weave his own canvas, in order to be able to execute his work."[26] Gance, for Vuillermoz, is adept at adding ornamental visual touches to his cinematic style but lacks the basic talents of, we surmise, storytelling, content, and structure. Vuillermoz's rhetoric imagines filmmaking in terms of exotic richness—"arabesques," "sumptuous brocade," "filigrees," and so on. He does not quite say that these ornaments are bad; he certainly seems to compliment Gance's abilities as a craftsman, but it becomes clear that the craftsman is not an artist, and the ability to weave beads onto a canvas is less important than the ability to make a good canvas. Embroidery is secondary, a feminized craft that requires technical skill but no animating genius, as does art. The surface sparkle of silver and gold presents half-hearted praise in the language of the feminine and the Oriental.

This rhetoric of exoticism also demonstrates an opposition between richness and purity—an opposition that we have seen in regard to cinematic realism and that also draws from a critique of decorative art. Rousseau says that ornament is foreign to virtue, and as E. H. Gombrich glosses, this sense of ornament as sexually dangerous dominates the artistic discourse of the fin de siècle, particularly in the work of art nouveau figures such as Gustav Klimt.[27] The fin de siècle also figures in film criticism as an excessively aesthetic style. For example, in her account of the film criticism of the British journal *Close Up*, Laura Marcus describes Kenneth Macpherson's complaint about Film Society programming in similar terms: "Macpherson suggested that the Society was promoting a dilettantism and outmoded aestheticism—a 'fin de siècle snigger'—in which 'hair tidies, samplers, tortoise-shell inlay and early Chaplin comedies became in the twinkling of an eye rare objets d'art.' "[28] Macpherson converts eroticism into a more down-at-heel clutter, but aestheticism and an inappropriate accumulation of objects present excessive and exotic detail in terms of bad ornament. Ornament is thus associated with an old-fashioned and oddly valueless richness, in which excess stuff is the opposite of cinematic art.

This opposition of bad ornament to pure cinematic mimesis presents a variant of the discourse on realism that I outlined in chapter 1. Germaine Dulac, albeit not a fan of narrative cinema, still presents her critique in the language of decoration. She poses that "early filmmakers believed themselves skillful in containing cinematic action in an embellished [*agrémentée*] narrative form of trivial reconstructions, and those who encouraged them were guilty of a shameful error. A train arriving at the station gave a visual and physical sensation. In composed films, nothing like it."[29] Even discussing narrative, Dulac uses the language of decorative visual style to make her point. Just as an image can be composed or raw, so can a film's temporal organization be prettily narrated or rough and truthful. In both cases, embellishment and composition are the enemies of cinematic specificity and meaning. The antidecorative polemic was perhaps most strongly stated in 1946 by Roberto Rossellini: "For my part, I don't like décor [les décors], I hate makeup and I prefer to do without actors. . . . All it needs is a sheer foundation to distort the true appearance of the skin and the features of a face."[30] Rossellini's term décor seems to imply both production design and a more conceptual meaning of decoration that leads back to a Platonic cosmetics. Here, décor leads from the specific filmic area of mise-en-scène to a broader philosophical notion of decorative supplementarity.

The second way that ornament enters into filmic discourse is, paradoxically, via its banishment at the end of the nineteenth century. If the parade of historicist, highly decorative styles that characterized mid-Victorian interior design led to the extremes of art for art's sake aestheticism, then the turn of the new century brought a dramatic rejection of ornament in favor of austere modernity. In his canonical survey of the period, Gombrich diagnoses an apologetic tone in later texts on decorative art. For instance, he cites Richard G. Hatton's 1902 confession that "there is at present a strong desire among persons of taste for plain objects."[31] Véron said much the same thing a little earlier, concluding that although decorative art may be valuable, "modern art has no tendency in this . . . direction. Beauty no longer suffices for us."[32] And in a recent attempt to rehabilitate ornament, Brent Brolin considers that "barring the occasional sumptuary law, the nearly ornamentless, modern design of the twentieth century is an aberration. For perhaps the first time in the history of humankind, the surroundings of the most sophisticated and elegant classes of society have been characterized by a consciously celebrated poverty of ornament."[33] This backlash against ornament gains momentum exactly during the period of cinema's emergence. It should come as no surprise that as dominant discourses of taste and aesthetic value turn strongly against the decorative, film theory closely associates cinematic specificity and its relation to modern experience with a lack of ornamentation.

ART NOUVEAU, ADOLF LOOS, AND CINEMA

To follow the influence of decorative art discourse on cinema, I look to the critical literature on the architectural and decorative art movement known as art nouveau or, in its Viennese context, Jugendstil. Klaus-Jurgen Sembach begins an account of the art nouveau movement with this claim on historical synchronicity: "The 1890s gave the world two innovations: cinema and Art Nouveau."[34] The coincident emergence of these forms speaks, for Sembach, of art nouveau's significance, but what seems striking from the perspective of film studies is the rapid divergence in the successes met by each. Whereas cinema became in a few short years the dominant form of popular visual culture, art nouveau not only was quickly displaced as a "new" style, but under pressure from architectural and aesthetic modernism came to seem actively old-fashioned. As Hal Foster puts it, "As the aesthetics of the machine became dominant in the 1920s, Art Nouveau was no longer *nouveau*, and in the next decades it slowly passed from an outmoded style to a campy one, and it has lingered in this limbo ever since."[35] It might seem, therefore, that the discourse on art nouveau would have little to say to film theory, whose earliest proponents had already moved past the *Gesamtkunstwerk* and embraced the fragmentary experience of the modern. Nevertheless, in cinema's distinct trajectory away from art nouveau's decorative style, we can find both a profound influence and an overlooked model for critique.

Turn-of-the-century European critics of art and architecture elaborated a discourse on modernity in which ornament and the decorative arts stood in regressive opposition to the clean lines and functional beauties of the modern. This opposition to ornament was nowhere more boldly articulated than in Vienna, where highly decorated late Austro-Hungarian culture clashed with a modernizing strain of architectural theory. Architect Otto Wagner exemplifies the way in which Viennese Jugendstil straddled both sides of the battle, for although his buildings include colorfully patterned walls and neobaroque detail (figure 19), he wrote in 1896 that "our feelings tell us already today that . . . the greatest simplicity and an energetic emphasis on construction and material are going to dominate the forms to be developed or created in future."[36] Presciently describing the eclipse of his own school, Wagner's words demonstrate how art nouveau presented itself as forward looking, even though it would soon be rejected as decadent and retrograde.

FIGURE 19 Otto Wagner, Majolikahaus (1898)
This apartment building in Vienna, with its facade of ceramic tiles, illustrates the decorative modernity of art nouveau. (Photograph by B. Welleschik; Creative Commons Attribution–Share Alike license)

The figure most closely associated with this outright rejection of art nouveau is architect and cultural critic Adolf Loos, who admired Wagner but famously claimed that "the evolution of culture is synonymous with the removal of ornamentation from objects of everyday use."[37] For Loos, art nouveau was the enemy of modernity, and he located ornament as the aesthetic antagonist. Loos had broken from the Vienna Secession as early as 1898, when he published the article "Potemkin City" in *Ver Sacrum*, the Secession journal. He asked: "Who does not know of Potemkin's villages, the ones that Catherine's cunning favorite built in the Ukraine? They were villages of canvas and pasteboard, villages intended to transform a visual desert into a flowering landscape for the eyes of Her Imperial Majesty. . . . But the Potemkin city of which I wish to speak here is none other than our dear Vienna."[38] In this early polemic, Loos attacked the sacred cow of Viennese architecture, arguing that buildings with ornate and aristocratic facades but split into apartments constructed from cheaper materials constituted a fraud. His analogy to Potemkin's political fraud already presents ornament as crime, tying surface decoration to a lack of moral as well as architectural integrity.

In 1908, Loos wrote "Ornament and Crime," an essay that has been called "one of the most radical polemics of design criticism of the twentieth century."[39] In it, Loos not only rejects categorically the dominant mode of Jugendstil but ties his excoriation to a sweeping claim on progress and value in which ornament is defined as primitive. The decoration of buildings and everyday objects, he claims, is akin to children smearing walls or to Papuan tattoos. He maintains that although it is natural for primitive peoples to decorate their bodies and artifacts, "a person of our times who gives way to the urge to daub the walls with erotic symbols is a criminal or a degenerate. What is natural in the Papuan or the child is a sign of degeneracy in a modern adult." In contrast to the primitivism of ornament, modern style is conjured in quasi-biblical language: "Behold, the time is at hand, fulfillment awaits us. Soon the streets of the cities will shine like white walls! Like Zion, the Holy City, Heaven's capital. . . . But there were hobgoblins who refused to accept it. They wanted mankind to strain under the yoke of ornament."[40] If the decorative arts revivify primal urges, then white walls open up a revelation to come. As with the white walls of architecture, so with the shimmering screens of the cinema. In Loos's claim on the unornamented future, I suggest, we find the kernel of cinema's aesthetic modernity.

Loos is not usually considered in terms of cinema, for he did not write about film except for brief passing comments. However, I find his writings on ornament and modernity to be essential to understanding the prominent place of the decorative image in the work of cultural critics such as Kracauer, Theodor Adorno, and Benjamin, whose work is foundational to ideas of cinematic modernity. His impact on architectural modernism is undoubted. Le Corbusier cites him as a major influence on his own work, and Nikolaus Pevsner describes him as the person "most responsible for introducing the principles of abstract, austere, orthogonal design into numerous pre–World War I Viennese buildings. . . . Loos's written and built works generally are credited with inventing the forms and inspired countless modernist architects to embrace abstraction and the International Style of the 1920s."[41] I return later to the question of how architectural theory might intersect with notions of the cinematic, but more immediately significant is Loos's location within a broad terrain of central and western European modernisms, whose cultural trajectories suggest a richer field of influence than has been previously considered.

Although Loos published two collections of essays (*Ins Leere Gesprochen / Spoken into the Void* [1921] and *Trotzdem / Nevertheless* [1931]), the majority of his criticism was first published in feuilleton form for the *Neue Freie Presse*, a Viennese liberal paper. He was therefore a part of the emergence of a social and cultural criticism in the first decades of the twentieth century that centered on the German writings of Kracauer, Benjamin, Georg Simmel, and others. Janet Stewart has pointed to the connections between Loos and these German critics: both Loos and Simmel published in the Viennese paper *Die Zeit*, and, more generally, Loos engaged a comparable methodology, writing short essays that attempt to interrogate a culture through the analysis of its everyday objects and experiences.[42] Thus Loos wrote on topics such as "Men's Fashion" and "Chairs," titles that could easily have been essays by Benjamin or Kracauer. Probably because Loos did not write on cinema, film scholars have not much noted his connection to German cultural criticism, but Loos's writing was read by some of the major film theorists of the early twentieth century, and it played a formative role in the European discourse on modernity.[43]

We find traces of Loos's opposition to ornament across twentieth-century writings on modernism and aesthetics. Adorno cites Loos directly in his account of formalism, locating him within a larger critical rejection of the decorative: "Based on a language stemming from the realm of materials, what this language defines as necessary can later become superfluous, even terribly ornamental, as soon as it can no longer be legitimated in a second kind of language, which is commonly called style. . . . Loos was thoroughly aware of this historical dynamic contained in the concept of ornament." For Adorno, Loos is part of a post-Kantian trajectory of aesthetic theory, and by linking Loos explicitly to his own work on music, Adorno assigns him an important place in the politics of modern art. Thus "modern music and architecture, by concentrating strictly on expression and construction, both strive together with equal rigour to efface all such ornament."[44] Here, the rejection of ornamental beauty and pleasure in Schoenberg and Loos is doing something similar, not only emphasizing construction but doing so via an explicit eradication of the ornamental. For Adorno, it is in this overt act of destruction that the significance of the modern can be articulated.

Indeed, for Adorno, ornament is precisely where the emergence of modernity becomes visible. He argues that "criticism of ornament means no more than criticism of that which has lost its functional and symbolic signification. Ornament becomes then a mere decaying and poisonous organic vestige."[45] Here, ornament is defined as that which is not modern, a residue of the past. It is also unhealthy, echoing Max Nordau's idea of the degenerate (a term Loos used in a previous quote).[46] Although Adorno is critical of Loos's puritanism, this discourse of diseased bodies indexes a prevalent use of ornament in early-twentieth-century writing to signify not just the primitive, but also the feminine, the effeminate, and the perverse. Art nouveau was often viewed as a feminine form, and because of its connections to artists such as Aubrey Beardsley and Oscar Wilde, critiques often shaded into attacks on the unhealthy and queer body.[47] Contemporary critic Siegfried Giedion called Viennese taste "effeminate," and Mark Wigley argues that Giedion regarded ornament as sexual degeneration.[48] Recent critics have often maintained this feminizing and effeminizing discourse. Umberto Eco, for example, says, "We might even talk of a narcissistic Beauty: just as Narcissus, on looking at his reflection on the water, projected his own image outside himself, so did the inner Beauty of Art Nouveau project itself on to the external object and appropriate it, enveloping it with its lines."[49] Wendy Steiner criticizes the gendering of ornament in modernist writing: "In modernism, just as woman was banished and yet not banished, so ornament was prohibited and yet constantly at issue. Manifesto after manifesto vilifies artistic ornament: from Pound's Imagist manifesto to Hemingway's writings on artistic honesty, from Adolf Loos to Le Corbusier in architecture, and in virtually every visual movement from Futurism to Dadaism to Surrealism." As she goes onto make clear, the paralleling of ornament and femininity is no coincidence. She concludes that "a good deal of the history of misogyny and anti-art puritanism can be summed up in the use of the word *ornamental*."[50]

However, this view of ornament as decadent and unhealthy was not universally accepted in Loos's time. Ernst Bloch, for one, pointedly glosses the Loosian argument: "Indeed, every ornament became suspect, was condemned for being scabrous and cancerous."[51] As well as referencing the idea of ornament as criminal, Bloch puts his finger on the rhetoric of disease and decay in which depraved ornamentation stains the healthy surface of the aesthetic object. Although he does not address particular bodies, he certainly engages the ideological implications of the "poisonous organic vestige." Thus he critiques precisely the functionalism that Adorno lauds, arguing that "an unquestionably high price has been paid by this kind of clarity for its dissociation from the patchwork of decorative kitsch of the *Gründerzeit*; geometrical monotony, alienated from purpose, together with an undernourishment of the imagination and extreme self-alienation, all represented by this coldness, this vacuous non-aura."[52] Bloch's critique of austere modernist style and defense of ornament bespeak a desire to transcend the binary in which luxurious objects can represent only an obsolete preindustrial order, while the modern industrial commodity reflects the alienation and aesthetic desolation of an oppressive factory system. In *The Spirit of Utopia*, Bloch imagines a modern craft object that might go beyond the dubious contemporary charms of "brightly painted concrete" to form a utopia of "Expressionistic, linear, arabesque ornament."[53] As with the anticipatory mode of living that Peter Schwenger sees in Derek Jarman's *Blue* (1993), Bloch offers a hope for political transformation through a pretty aesthetic. Bloch's critique was ultimately unable to sway the discourse of unhealthy ornament, and we can see the unquestioned status of the disease rhetoric in, for example, Pevsner's description of Loos's readership as "open to the infection from Art Nouveau."[54] Nonetheless, it is important that hostility to ornament is not monolithic in the writing of critics associated with the Frankfurt School.

One major area in which anti-ornament ideas entered into theories of the cinematic image was through positive terms such as *openness* and *life*, which were mobilized by the exclusion of the ornament and the corpse. Because I do not believe that ornament is a crime, I aim to use this historical analysis to make visible the sexed and raced logic whereby the valuable modern is counterposed with excluded figures such as the feminine and the primitive.

ORNAMENT AND LIFE

In his essay "The Story of a Poor Rich Man," Loos tells a satirical fairy tale about a man who furnishes his house in Jugendstil. The story charts how design takes over the rich man's entire life. First, the objects that bear family memories must be discarded because they do not fit into the décor. And he cannot buy anything new because it would not match the design scheme. He must inhabit the house exactly in the way the designers had planned once it is completed: for instance, he cannot wear his bedroom slippers in the living room because the colors would clash. Rather than creating a pleasing artistic environment, the Jugendstil house becomes his prison. Loos concludes, "He was excluded for the future from living and striving, becoming and wishing. He felt: Now I have to learn to live with my own corpse."[55] As a parable of modernity, "The Story of a Poor Rich Man" could not be clearer: architectural simplicity opens onto life, whereas ornament literalizes the fetish by turning the unfortunate subject into a dead object. Like the cinematic image in its temporal invocation of mortality, ornament confronts the subject with an image of himself as corpse. Ornament is not merely a crime, but a synonym for death.

This association of modernity with life and its exclusion of the ornamental corpse run through theories of cinematic specificity. Jean Epstein declaims that "to things and beings in their most frigid semblance, the cinema thus grants the greatest gift unto death: life."[56] Ricciotto Canudo describes film as "those mysterious reels impressed by life itself."[57] Vachel Lindsay goes further, declaring that "the photoplay imagination which is able to impart vital individuality to furniture will not stop there. Let the buildings emanate conscious life."[58] Cinema does not merely impress life on celluloid images but imparts consciousness to furniture and buildings. Décor comes alive at the hands of cinema, in the manner of Marx's famous dancing table. This vitalism of classical film theory is well known and, as Laura Marcus argues, can be connected both to the broader modernist aesthetic of motion and speed as well as to a Bergsonian temporal philosophy.[59] (Henry-Louis Bergson himself wielded a double-edged sword regarding cinema. As Martin Jay points out, Bergson's "vitalist bias for life" implicitly links visuality to rigor mortis such that even if the cinema can be read in terms of Bergsonian temporality, its imagistic qualities are in the same move folded back into an incipient deathlike state.)[60] However, modernist thought is not the only discursive context to shape cinematic life. The nineteenth-century taxonomy of the decorative also drew on vitalism to attribute to fine art a closer relationship to life. Thus Véron can claim that "the presence of lively and sincere emotion [*émotion vive*] is fatal to decorative character; it constitutes both the superiority and the distinguishing feature of expressive art."[61] The accumulation of life-based metaphors that we see in modernist film theory cannot be understood merely as a modish enthusiasm for *vitesse*, but derives from the historical rejection of ornament as a cultural value.

Of particular relevance to this binary of cinematic life versus ornamental death is the writing of Siegfried Kracauer. Like Loos, Kracauer was a trained architect who frequently wrote on exterior and interior design. For both men, questions of everyday aesthetics were crucial to any theory of modern experience. Just as Loos proposes the significance of "objects of everyday use" in assessing cultural progress, so Kracauer argues that "the position that an epoch occupies in the historical process can be determined more strikingly from an analysis of its inconspicuous surface-level expressions than from that epoch's judgments about itself."[62] Of course, there are equally important differences in their methods: Kracauer's Marxism is more complex and consistent than Loos's oblique and sometimes conservative politics. If Loos valorizes an aristocratic and oddly traditional model of modernity (the Poor Rich Man is nothing if not a clueless nouveau riche), Kracauer's class analyses overthrow such bourgeois fantasies. For Kracauer, the surface detail speaks simultaneously of the capitalist regime and of its potential negation. Despite these differences, both critics understand surface as a site of cultural contestation, and both locate ornament and life as central terms in this struggle.

Kracauer's best-known essay is "The Mass Ornament," in which the decorative patterns of Tiller girls stage the aesthetics of Taylorist rationality in terms of mass culture. Here, "the mass ornament is the aesthetic reflex of the rationality to which the prevailing economic system aspires."[63] The Marxism of Kracauer's critique—the *mass* in *mass ornament*—has tended to overshadow its aesthetic element. However, it is striking that Kracauer not only selects the same central term as Loos but also mobilizes a similar rhetoric on ornament. Thus he finds the ornament to be self-enclosed, claiming that "the ornament is an end in itself." And he goes on to describe it as opposed to life, where he finds that "both the proliferations of organic forms and the emanations of spiritual life remain excluded."[64] Ornament is that which excludes and is excluded from life. Just as Adorno rejects ornament as "lifeless, reified repetition,"[65] so Kracauer constructs the mass ornament as animated corpse.

This discourse on ornament as death is taken up in Kracauer's work on the visual, and, indeed, it forms a point of continuity between the early and later periods of his writing. In his influential essay "Photography" (1927), Kracauer theorizes the temporal and ontological specificity of the photographic image, deploying ornamentation as a significant figure. He describes the effect of viewing an old photograph:

> The grandmother dissolves into fashionably old-fashioned details before the very eyes of the grandchildren. They are amused by the traditional costume, which, following the disappearance of its bearer, remains alone on the battlefield—an external decoration that has become autonomous. They are irrelevant, and today young girls dress differently. They laugh, and at the same time they shudder. For through the ornamentation of the costume from which the grandmother has disappeared, they think they glimpse a moment of time past, a time that passes without return.[66]

As for Adorno, for Kracauer ornament renders visible the inscription of time, and if the explicit rhetoric is of pastness and irrelevance, the grandchildren's shudder is surely a response to the ornament's trace of death.

Ornament as a trace of death makes us shudder again in *Theory of Film*, Kracauer's major post–World War II work of film theory. In the book's epilogue, he shifts from a seemingly ahistorical account of film aesthetics to mention briefly the Shoah. Films of the death camps, he suggests, might function like Perseus's shield, allowing us "to look at [the Shoah's] reflection in the shield."[67] Several critics, including Miriam Hansen, have interpreted the "Head of Medusa" section as "the epistemic and ethical vanishing point of *Theory of Film*," the material truth so impossible to speak that it must be almost entirely repressed.[68] Hansen and others have noted that the Shoah enters unannounced into a discussion of Georges Franju's *Les sang des bêtes / Blood of the Beasts* (1949). Kracauer reads Franju's images of calves heads in a Paris slaughterhouse as not comparable but contiguous to images from the camps: "In experiencing the rows of calves' heads or the litter of tortured human bodies in the films made of Nazi concentration camps, we redeem horror from its invisibility behind the veils of panic and imagination."[69] But what of the image of the calves' heads itself? This image is at once obviously a metaphor for mass death and yet at the same time a powerfully exerted demand that we experience it beyond such banal correspondence.[70] And in the description of this image—the central one of Kracauer's entire theory, if Hansen is to be believed—Kracauer returns to the language of death and ornament: "[A] saw dismembers animal bodies still warm with life; and there is the unfathomable shot of the calves' heads being arranged into a rustic pattern which breathes the peace of a geometrical ornament."[71] If the Shoah appears at the traumatic heart of Kracauer's theory, the unfathomable appearance of pattern, geometry, and peace in this place of death locates ornament as the linchpin of the theory's unspeakable aesthetic.

By contrast, outside of the "Head of Medusa" section, the articulation of the anti-ornamental image to life is central to *Theory of Film*. Here, the exclusion of the old-fashioned and the ornamental enables Kracauer to propose a definition of the cinematic that associates film with modernity, openness, and life. Thus he defines the "inherent affinities" of the photographic image as the unstaged, the fortuitous, the indeterminate, and endlessness. These affinities are shared by photography and film, but only film has an affinity for "the flow of life."[72] In each of these characteristics, cinematic specificity is opposed to the careful composition associated with the art nouveau interior and is linked instead to the meaningful and the open. Kracauer makes clear the stakes of this theoretical model when he outlines the realist and formative tendencies in which real-world landscapes are preferable to decorated sets and unplanned events to pictorial mise-en-scènes. The decorative formative tendency is inevitably less able to "record and reveal physical reality"[73] and hence is further from the cinematic. The aesthetic value of the medium is thus closely linked to the opposition of ornament to life.

Kracauer's claim on cinematic specificity has been both attacked for lacking a critique of realism's ideology and rediscovered as a philosophical engagement with modernity, but in either case his basic assumption that the endless, uncomposed "flow of life" is superior to the ornamental or formative tends to remain unquestioned.[74] But whose life is this, and whose ornamental death? We have already seen how Loos connects ornament to the primitive and the criminal and how anti-ornamental discourse ties into rhetorics of misogyny and heteronormativity. It seems that the image itself is not untouched by political histories. If we fold back Kracauer's film aesthetic onto Loos's writings, the ideological formations become apparent.

In "The Plumbers," Loos indexes modernity to a culture's level of cleanliness. Thus "when the Roman view of life still reigned supreme . . . one did not become dirty, but one did not wash either. Only the common people washed. The aristocrats were painted."[75] Painted cosmetics on top of a dirty, decaying body suggest a rhetoric of sin and supplement, where cleanliness is clearly next to godliness. The geopolitical nature of this contrast is revealed in "Culture," where Loos argues that "the cultural ideal of the Latins is the cat. The cat is quite a filthy animal. Of all animals it hates water the most. All day it licks off the dirt which collects on its fur, and therefore it fearfully avoids any dirt. But the Englishman, the representative of Germanic culture, always gets himself dirty, in the stables, on horseback, in the field, in the forest, the meadows, in the mountains and on yachts."[76] The experience of open space, real nature, and "healthy" modernity is a northern European quality as well as a masculine one, to be contrasted to the decadent and effeminate south. The endlessness of landscape in Kracauer's view of cinema and the contrasting enclosure of the decorated set map disturbingly onto Loos's healthy Englishman riding across the fields and dirty, preening Latin or painted aristocrat.

The confluence of Loos's and Kracauer's writings on ornament and life becomes most clear in their respective discussions of the historical. Loos is unsurprisingly horrified by the resurgence of historicism in design. He laments: "Our schools have lost contact with life. The students are being prejudiced against the present: 'Oh, how beautiful were the Middle Ages. And the Renaissance, how even more beautiful. The brocades flounced and the silks rustled and nude women marched in procession to meet the king. And jewellery, and colour and waving feathers. And today? It is horrible. Checked suits, telephone wires, trams tinkling. What have we to do with that? Down with the telephone. Let us encase it in Rococo ornament. Or Gothic, Or Baroque.'"[77] Not only is historicism a category error for Loos (the rococo telephone), but its willful refusal of life is channeled through a perverse and primitive femininity.

Kracauer offers no such blatant disdain, and yet his account of historical spectacle in Eisenstein's *Alexander Nevsky* (1938) depends on the

FIGURE 20   *Alexander Nevsky* (Eisenstein, 1938)
A composed framing at the beginning of the ice-battle sequence emphasizes the posture and patterning of bodies.

same rhetoric. He finds historical representation in general to be suspicious and suggests that an alternative practice might "lure the spectator out of the closed cosmos of poster-like tableaux vivants into an open universe."[78] As with the Poor Rich Man's house, the historical film is overly planned, dependent on sets and props, closed to the life of camera reality. For this reason, Kracauer feels unable to laud the famous ice-battle scene in *Nevsky* (figure 20): "Far from reflecting transitory life, the imagery affects you as a (re-)construction meant to be life; each shot seems predetermined; none breathes the allusive indeterminacy of the Potemkin pictures. . . . Hence, even assuming that the Battle on the Ice were cinematically on a par with the episode of the Odessa steps, these patterns which spread octopus-like would nevertheless corrode its substance, turning it from a suggestive rendering of physical events into a luxuriant adornment."[79] In this final phrase, we discover the foundation of Kracauer's argument: a luxurious adornment—feminine, baroque, even orientalizing. Like the Papuan who adorns his body with tattoos or the naked women who are covered with jewelry and color and waving feathers or even the decadent dandy, a patterned image is corrosive and unnecessary. The octopus figures the art nouveau ornament of multiplying arabesque curves that, even though natural, can be read only as decadent and suffocating. Despite his political commitments (including his postwar attempt to face the horror of mass death), Kracauer's cinematic life, like Loos's modern aesthetic, depends on the expulsion of all the ornamented bodies who trouble the modern European self.

ADOLF, JOSEPHINE, HILDA, AND GRETA

The primitivism of Loos's argument on ornament is unavoidable. He returns to the metaphor of the Papuan compulsively, inscribing more and more iterations of geographical otherness. In addition to the discourse on such "savage" races, Loos conjures orientalist horrors such as the unpleasant fate of the simple craftsman in "Architecture": "And because the craftsman did not have or need the knowledge to draw ornament, because he was a modern, cultivated man, special schools were established in which healthy young people were unnaturally remoulded until they were able to do so, just as in China children are put into vases and fed for years until they burst out of their cages as horrifying monsters."[80] But if China and Papua are the absolute negation of modernity, the example of the clean-living English and the dirty Latins implies that this organization of cultural purity is ultimately aimed at regulating Europe itself.

Many contemporary readers of Loos find this primitivist strand of his work to be embarrassing and probably best avoided. For John Maciuika, for instance, the racism is a side issue, an understandable historical weakness that in no way alters the basic argument. He contends that "Loos advances a fairly sophisticated theory of culture—though one admittedly riddled with . . . cultural biases."[81] In order to take Loos seriously, he implies, it is necessary to disavow race as itself a decorative supplement. Some critics have recently addressed Loos's racial politics directly, in general by situating him more carefully in the field of nineteenth-century thought that influenced him. For example, Mitchell Schwartzer traces Loos's relation to Darwin and anthropology, pointing out that Loos's writings on race echo contemporary social scientists' dominant understanding.[82] However, I suggest that rather than either ignoring or contextualizing what seems unsavory in Loos, we look directly at how his racialized writing crystallizes a primitivism that is central to cinema's anti-ornamental project.

The visual structure of Loos's primitivism appears in a very early essay, "The Luxury Vehicle" (1898):

> The lower the cultural level of a people, the more extravagant it is with its ornament, its decoration. The Indian covers every object, every boat, every oar, every arrow with layer upon later of ornament. To see decoration as a sign of superiority means to stand at the level of the Indians. But we must overcome the Indian in us. The Indian says, "This woman is beautiful because she wears gold rings in her nose and ears." The man of high culture says, "This woman is beautiful because she does not wear rings in her nose and ears." To seek beauty in form and not in ornament is the goal to which all of humanity is striving.[83]

In a logic that becomes familiar in cinema, the privileged position of the Western man of culture depends on the proper installation of a regime of visual pleasure. One must look at an image of beauty and recognize the correct image of beauty in order to take one's place in modern civilization. As Mary Ann Doane has insisted, the cinematic inscription of visual pleasure depends not only on the superior position of the white man who looks, but also on the relative positions of the white woman and the black woman as spectacular objects of that look.[84] Loos's comparison of the adorned Indian woman and the aesthetically pure white woman demonstrates, first, that the gendered and raced body is the locus of the problem of decoration and, second, that this problem is precisely about spectacle, desire, and images that might trouble the senses of the modern man.

As it happens, a desirable image of decorated black femininity connects Adolf Loos and cinema. In 1928, he designed a house for the American actress and dancer Josephine Baker in Paris (figure 21).[85] The house was never built, but Loos's desire to design a living space for a black film star illustrates an investment that goes beyond the typical European modernist preoccupation with the exotic. Farès el-Dahdah has argued that Loos's design symptomatizes the structure of racial and sexual fantasy at the heart of his work. Surviving documents are unclear on why the building remained on paper, but for el-Dahdah the plan represents

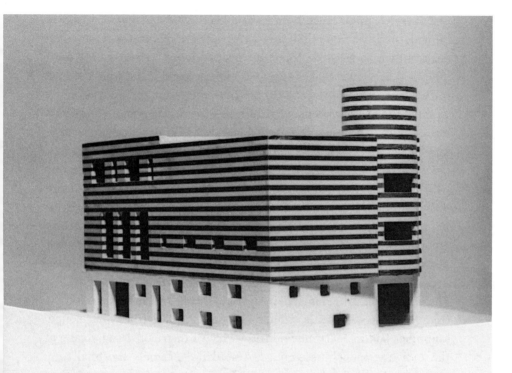

FIGURE 21 Adolf Loos, House Josephine Baker (1927)
A model of the house that Adolf Loos designed for Josephine Baker, its bold stripes encoding
a racial and sexual fetish. (Courtesy of the Albertina, Vienna)

"the principal document of this longing, shared by an entire generation,
for the famous American dancer."[86] The design is intriguing to Loos
scholars because it seems to contradict completely his demand for unadorned exteriors. The house is boldly striped in bands of black and white
that extend around the exterior. For el-Dahdah, these stripes resemble
nothing more than Papuan tattoos, a visual signifier of the primitive fetish. He calls them "the marks of a repressed and savage desire: the flagrant script of Josephine's body, the horizontal *tracé* as woman. . . . By
[Loos's] own definition, this horizontal tattoo results from an untamed
desire now confronted with a vertical line: the standing architect who
seeks to penetrate, 'touch' Baker's body."[87] Not only is Baker the physical
embodiment of ornament, but the modernist fetishist cannot resist his
desire for this forbidden body.

Loos's design for Baker overlays architectural and cinematic histories of modernity, but more than this it lays bare the regimes of ornamental desire in which these aesthetic modes developed. A year before Loos imagined her house, Baker appeared in her second motion picture role, in *La sirène des tropiques* / *Siren of the Tropics* (Étiévant and Nalpas, 1927). In this film, she plays a native Antillean woman, Papitou, embodying a black and Indian racial makeup that both reflected Baker's own heritage and figured the exotic and mobile primitive that would define her star persona. Baker's physical performance as Papitou dovetails the exotic with the erotic in a manner that proposes her body as a site of dangerously primitive desire. This primitivism, moreover, is founded on an ornamental aesthetic; the interleaving of the non-European primitive, the erotic body, and the decorative detail became a mainstay of Baker's star persona. As she herself described her part in *Princesse Tam Tam* (Gréville, 1934), "Again and again we rehearsed a flamboyant number about the French colonies, which included Algerian drums, Indian bells, tom-toms from Madagascar, coconuts from the Congo, cha-chas from Guadeloupe, a number laid in Martinique during which I distributed sugar cane to the audience, Indochinese gongs, Arab dances, camels and finally my appearance as the Empress of Jazz."[88] Baker's star persona plays with the signifiers of ethnographic otherness, but these games are frustratingly unavailable to the modernist critic. For Loos, Baker is the silent and absent fetish figure who refuses to respond to her architect's advances. But in her own performed image—whether dancing in a skirt made of bananas or synthesizing musical traditions from across the non-European world—Baker embodies the aesthetic of the ornament.

I suggest that Baker is a particularly significant figure because she makes visible (and, indeed, actively plays with) the close association of modernism's anti-ornamental aesthetics and its racial and colonial politics. Fatimah Tobing Rony has assessed the importance of ethnographic vision to cinema, focusing both on "the masses' voracious appetite for . . . images of peoples of color" and on the construction of exotic spectacle as a colonial aesthetic.[89] The popularity of non-European bodies on film— especially in cinema's first decades—demonstrates a dynamic market for an image that could be enjoyed as colorful (in all senses), sensual, and foreign, but that was clearly marked off from the nobility and beauty that was reserved for the white subject. Baker exemplifies this kind of figure: massively popular and lauded for her style and modernity, Baker was nonetheless widely evaluated in terms of physicality rather than talent and was viewed as fascinating rather than beautiful.[90] Terry Francis finds that critics read Baker as either cute or savage, and this recourse to minor taste concepts illustrates the racial inflections of the ornamental pretty.[91] Aesthetic and cinematic regimes of looking install the white woman as the proper object of the gaze, and so the black woman must be enjoyed under a different (infantilizing or exclusionary) aesthetic rubric. In her biography of Baker, Phyllis Rose writes, "The cross-eyed, goofy, stereotypically blackface grin would become a kind of signature, even when—most effectively when—she was glamorously dressed, so that it seemed a parodic comment on her own beauty, on conventions of beauty, on the culture that had made her famous."[92] Baker could be glamorous, beautiful even, but her access to beauty came at the cost of parodying her own blackness (figure 22).

It is not hard to locate or condemn the racism of critics who could imagine Baker as only a "lovely animal" or a primitive child, but more subtle, perhaps, is the influence of this aesthetic model across the visual field.[93] The denigration of marked and nonwhite bodies is not simply a representational politics within the image (in the sense of "images of" criticism), but a structural exclusion from the pure and valuable image itself. As with classical film theory's inheritance of an implicit Kantian structure of geopolitical value, discourse on Baker exists within an aesthetic field that rejects the decorative as a formal extension of its explicitly racializing rhetoric. Elizabeth Ezra writes that "Josephine Baker is usually considered part of the décor of interwar French culture but hardly ever the main attraction,"[94] and in this figuration of Baker's supplementarity as decoration Ezra pinpoints the way that the rhetoric of décor correlates at the level of form to the raced quality of the image.

We can triangulate this effect by calling on a quite different example. H. D.'s writing on cinema for the journal *Close Up* brings a literary approach to the aesthetic and, as Jean Gallacher tells us, insists on a lesbian look within the structures of modern vision.[95] We might expect H. D.'s perspective to differ substantially from that of Loos. However, in the essay series "Cinema and the Classics," written the same year *Siren of the Tropics* came out and Kracauer's "Mass Ornament" was published, H. D.'s impression of two encounters with Greta Garbo deploys familiar ideas on the ornamental: "Greta Garbo in Montreux, Switzerland, trailing with frail, very young feet through perhaps the most astonishingly

FIGURE 22 Josephine Baker's famous banana skirt parodies the racialized aesthetic of the ornament.

consistently lovely film I have ever seen ('Joyless Street') could not be, but by some fluke of evil magic, the same creature I saw, with sewed-in, black lashes, with waist-lined, svelte, obvious contours, with gowns and gowns, all of them almost (by some anachronism) trailing on the floor, with black-dyed wig, obscuring her own nordic [sic] nimbus, in the later a 'Torrent.'"[96] Here, H. D. sets up an opposition between natural beauty and ornamented artifice. The wig, the eyelashes, the dresses are surface cosmetics that obscure the true aesthetic form of the body. And, like Kracauer, she finds theatricality and historicism to oppress cinematic life. Garbo in *Die freudlose Gasse / Joyless Street* (Pabst, 1925) is plainly dressed, whereas in *Torrent* (Ibáñez, 1926) she transforms from country girl to glamorous singer. Her cloche hats and graphic-patterned dresses signify modern independent femininity, but it is surely the decorative sparkle of her stage Spanish costume that upsets H. D. so much (figure 23).

That Garbo's changed appearance indicts Hollywood fakery is clear, but there is something else at play in H. D.'s rhetoric: "Something has been imposed, a blatant, tinsel and paper-flower and paste-jewel exterior,

FIGURE 23 *Torrent* (Ibáñez, 1926)
Greta Garbo in the sparkly Spanish costume that, for H. D., obscures her "nordic nimbus."

yet it doesn't quite dominate this nordic ice-flower."[97] Like the Potemkin village, ornament is a fraud, a paste-jewel exterior, and, like Loos's male spectator, H. D. knows the difference between a fake, bedecked beauty and a true, undecorated one. Her affirmative structure of same-sex desire might contest the homophobia or at least the heteronormativity implied by Loos, but her implication of a pure, androgynous Garbo as superior to the straightened-out and prettified Hollywood version recapitulates the logic of the feminized and inferior ornament. What is particularly telling about this example is the cultural location of the body chosen to define the limits of proper representation: the female body, of course, but also a white European body. Greta Garbo, with her Nordic nimbus and northern skin, can guarantee the purity and truth of cinematic beauty.

I do not intend to suggest that H. D. harbored the same racism as Loos or the critics who saw Baker as a savage, but it is nonetheless significant that the problem of ornament enters classical film theory in terms so similar to Loos's sexualized metaphors of the primitive. The manifestoes of modernity that enabled theories of cinema aligned to realism, purity, and life also determined that "gilt decoration and precious stones are the work of the tamed savage who is still alive in us."[98] From Kracauer's "girl clusters" to Rudolf Arnheim's association of bright colors with "the primitives of the great cities," ornament codes as a sexed and raced supplement to the cinematic image. It is no coincidence that "colored" bodies and "colorful" décor (what Le Corbusier calls "the distracting din of colors and ornaments")[99] should be excluded from true beauty in the same gesture: primitivism and ornament depend on the same racializing gestures, and the anti-pretty discourse of modern film aesthetics both derives from and depends on a logic of raced bodies. Garbo's decorated woman in *Torrent* precisely figures this visual logic: dressed in a boldly patterned coat and shiny dress, she makes a spectacle of herself by talking publicly to a black singer whose performance she enjoys. Primitivism is not a supplement to modernist thinking in cinema but rather a central determinant of its aesthetic of unadorned "life."

To read ornament's primitivist history formally is both to build on and to revise Tobing Rony's sense of the ethnographic spectacle. On the one hand, we can see how modernist aesthetics uses racialized discourse to justify the superiority of clean lines. Loos links ornament with the Indian woman, who is not beautiful because she is adorned. In uncovering the racial implications of what might seem like a purely formal question, we extend our critique of cinema's ethnographic gaze. And yet by focusing on the ornament, we also uncover a problem in that model. In rejecting the spectacular, colorful, or picturesque image, Tobing Rony takes up the very aesthetic logic that her analysis works to defeat. For Loos, the decorated image is bad because it is primitive; for Tobing Rony, it is bad because it is primitiv*ist*. The political imperative turns 180 degrees, but the aesthetic judgment does not shift an inch. In revealing the formal rejection of the ornament to be racially and sexually grounded, we might be able to open up a space in which the cinematic ornament can say something else. Unlike the art nouveau objects that exhibited "the curves of a nervous feminism" and were rapidly obliterated by the masculinist modern style, cinema has offered greater possibilities for the ornamental fetish to speak for herself.[100] Baker exhibited an almost Baudrillardian silence in the face of Loos's architectural seduction, and, of course, Garbo is famous for the rarity of her voice. But this is not a banal question of agency. Rather, both iconic film stars perform an excessive, ornamented femininity that is at once a function of and a troubling presence for cinematic modernity.

JUGENDSTIL AND EXPERIENCE

If modernism's rejection of ornamental style and interwar film theory's engagement with directness and life seem to run on parallel tracks, their relationship implicit and elusive, there is one place where they intersect quite explicitly. Not only is Walter Benjamin a central figure in the Frankfurt School's thinking on cinema, but in *The Arcades Project* he places both Jugendstil and nineteenth-century ornamental style at the heart of his political and philosophical project. He is also, not coincidentally, the only major critic of the period to engage with Loos's work directly. In 1930, he wrote to Adorno about having received a collection of Loos's writings from Franz Glück (probably an early copy of *Trotzdem*, which Glück edited), and in a letter to Glück himself he discusses Loos's relevance for his current work.[101] Given Loos's interest in Jugendstil, modernity, and the surface manifestations of history, it makes sense that Benjamin took an interest in him, and, indeed, Loos turns up sporadically in Benjamin's later writings, including *The Arcades Project*, where Jugendstil is a central object of inquiry. Benjamin references Loos in both canonical and fairly obscure essays, and, as I hope to show, his intersection with

Loos has a significant impact on his thinking about film. In teasing out what Benjamin does with Loos and using this thread to counterpose Benjamin's reading of cinema with his analysis of decorative style, we will find a more ambiguous and complex account of the ornament than most versions of modernist cultural criticism might suggest.

Among the things that Benjamin was working on while reading Loos's *Trotzdem* was "Little History of Photography" (1931), an essay that evokes anxieties around ornament in its descriptions of nineteenth-century bourgeois photography; its costumes, its faux-classical pillars and drapes, and its tacky albums with gilt pages remind us of Loos's overstuffed interiors and his horror at modern objects decked out with rococo stylings. The essay does not mention Loos by name, yet we need the context of his anti-ornamental thought to understand the essay's opposition of photography to interiority. We see traces of Loos in Benjamin's horrified response to a photograph of Franz Kafka as a child, "dressed in a humiliatingly tight child's suit overloaded with trimming, in a sort of greenhouse landscape. The background is thick with palm fronds. And as if to make these upholstered tropics even stuffier and more oppressive, the subject holds in his left hand an inordinately large broad-brimmed hat, such as Spaniards wear."[102] The problem with this image is entirely in concert with Loos's Poor Rich Man: the space is too full; the background, thick; the costume, overloaded; the hat, inordinately large. There is too much decoration and therefore not enough space for the life of the subject to breathe. Worse, the subject is overrun by primitive and exotic objects, such as tropical palm leaves and Spanish hats. In this essay, then, Benjamin seems to concur with Loos's critique of ornament, and he goes on to relate this oppressive style to art nouveau, which added artificial photographic techniques to this old-fashioned style.[103]

What makes this example suggestive for film theory, of course, is that "Little History of Photography" outlines many of Benjamin's key ideas on the photographic image. Here we find the optical unconscious, the "tiny spark of contingency,"[104] within each photograph and the emancipation of the object from the aura in the work of Eugène Atget. Benjamin's claim that Atget "set about removing the makeup from reality"[105] seems to echo Kracauer's opposition of the photographic to the ornamental in his essay "Photography," presenting props, sets, and cosmetics as an oppressive impediment to the objective openness of the apparatus. Kafka's geographically distant costuming rhymes with the temporal distance of the grandmother's clothing in Kracauer's article, producing a physical response, a shudder, in the viewer. In this setting, the anti-ornament aspect of Benjamin's account gets in on the ground floor, as it were, of a strand of visual theory that leads to Roland Barthes's *Camera Lucida*, Bazinian ontology, and contemporary work on cinematic realisms.[106]

However, although Benjamin is engaged with some of the same ideas as Kracauer on cinema and photography, when we look at the work where he actually cites Loos, a more ambiguous picture emerges. In "Experience and Poverty" (1933), Benjamin analyzes the radical and destructive force of modernity, famously describing "a generation that had gone to school in horse-drawn streetcars now stood in the open air, amid a landscape in which nothing was the same except the clouds and, at its centre, in a force field of destructive torrents and explosions, the tiny, fragile human body."[107] In elaborating the revolutionary potential of this destruction, he makes this claim:

> A total absence of illusion about the age and at the same time an unlimited commitment to it—this is its hallmark. It makes no difference whether the poet Bert Brecht declares that Communism is the just distributor of poverty, not of wealth, or whether Adolf Loos, the forerunner of modern architecture, states, "I write only for people who possess a modern sensibility. . . . I do not write for people consumed by nostalgia for the Renaissance or the Rococo." A complex artist like the painter Klee and a programmatic one like Loos—both reject the traditional, solemn, noble image of man, festooned with all the sacrificial offerings of the past.[108]

Here, Loos is included in the radical charge of modern experience, but his writing is programmatic—symptomatic rather than truly revolutionary. Modern architecture is part of the destruction of the aura—Benjamin contrasts the use of glass in buildings to the ornamented stone of previous generations—but as Miriam Hansen has explained in relation to cinema, this process is profoundly ambivalent for Benjamin and cannot be reduced to a simplistic mapping of form onto politics.[109] The auratic remains a powerful category for Benjamin, capable of mediating temporality, mortality, and the image. Thus the pure, transparent, hard surface of the glass building can map onto the transparent screen of cinematic realism as well as onto Atget's anti-cosmetic images, but if Benjamin's take on the aura is ambivalent, so too is his reading of Loos. Just as Benjamin does not simply celebrate the loss of the aura, so he should not be viewed as rejecting ornament wholesale. We begin to see how his encounter with Loos might open up possibilities for rethinking his film theory. The ornament cannot stand simply as a bad object.

Ornament is first marked in Benjamin's work in "Karl Kraus," written in the same year as "Little History of Photography." In this essay, as Patrizia McBride points out, "Walter Benjamin was among the first to draw a connection between Kraus's uncompromising rejection of Austria as a macrosignifer of corrupt modernity, on the one hand, and Loos's indefatigable crusade against the inauthenticity of Viennese ornamental culture, on the other."[110] Benjamin compares Loos's separation of the object of use from art with Kraus's separation of information from art. Thus "the hack journalist is, in his heart, at one with the ornamentalist. Kraus did not tire of denouncing Heine as an ornamentalist, as one who blurred the boundary between journalism and literature, as the creator of the feuilleton in poetry and prose; indeed he later placed even Nietzsche beside Heine as the betrayer of the aphorism to the impression."[111] With the claim on Heine bracketed, what stands out here is how ornament is the currency of this exchange. We can tell that Kraus and Loos make similar arguments because they both reject ornamentalist aesthetics, and, indeed, Benjamin gives their use of the rhetoric of ornament as evidence for his comparison of the two men. Ornament, therefore, cannot be a style whose meaning goes without saying in Benjamin: its saying is marked, evidentiary, a sign pointing toward a historical analysis.[112]

Benjamin's political ambivalence regarding Loos also becomes more explicit in this essay. Loos figures again as an avatar of destructive modernity ("One must have followed Loos in his struggle with the dragon 'ornament,' heard the stellar Esperanto of Scheerbart's creations, or seen Klee's *New Angel* . . . to understand a humanity that proves itself by destruction"), but he is also implicated in what Benjamin dubs "the strange interplay between reactionary theory and revolutionary practice that we find everywhere in Kraus."[113] Loos's buildings take part in a radicalization of modern experience, but Loos, like Kraus, is fatally compromised by a conservative relationship to history. Thus Benjamin concludes that Kraus is far from being "on the threshold of a new age," as Loos described him, but is rather unhistorically "on the threshold of the Last Judgment."[114] Predating Benjamin's elaboration of a dialectical philosophy of history and his writing of Klee's Angel as a figure of historical destruction, "Karl Kraus" nonetheless finds him anxious about a radicalism that looks backward but yet cannot think historically. As Werner Oechslin succinctly puts it, "For Loos, it was no longer history that was decisive, but tradition."[115]

The significance of Loos for Benjamin's political and aesthetic thought becomes clear in a late essay, "The Regression of Poetry, by Carl Gustav Jochmann," written in 1939, just a year before "On the Concept of History." As a scholarly essayist with interests in both political and cultural questions, Jochmann, writing in the early part of the nineteenth century, makes an interesting comparison with his early-twentieth-century counterparts. Benjamin connects the two men by claiming that "Loos was an outsider, as Jochmann had been. . . . It is no accident that [Loos's] dictum 'ornamentation is crime' sounds like a résumé of Jochmann's commands on tattooing."[116] Indeed, Jochmann closely prefigures Loos's use of bodily adornment as an index of relative cultural value: "The first care the savage takes of his body consists in its superstitious embellishment; he thinks he is adorning himself by torturing himself, beautifying himself by self-mutilation. Just as he burns and cuts limbs that are exposed to the hostile attacks of all the elements, and that he can neither nourish nor clothe, he likewise, with the same complacency, distorts and poisons his spiritual image with vices and prejudices he takes to be pure merit and wisdom, long before he knows how to protect and preserve that image."[117] As we have seen, anti-adornment discourse is founded in primitivist rhetoric, and tattooing recurs as a privileged figure for ornament's uncivilized regime of desire and display.[118] In this rhetoric, the primitive bodies who decorate themselves infect the decoration itself so that no matter how far ornament travels and how it abstracts and refines itself, it can only ever speak of those bodies against whose exclusion the European aesthetic subject is formed. Benjamin himself exemplifies this tendency later in "The Regression of Poetry," where he writes approvingly, "Jochmann does not adorn future society with the bright colors of the utopian. Rather, he delineates it with the clear, classical line used by Flaxman to render the contours of the gods."[119] The claim on Jochmann is not thematically concerned with primitivism, but the iteration of adornment and color refers Benjamin's formal point back to Jochmann's savage. As in "Karl Kraus," in this essay the rhetoric of adornment emerges precisely when the political implications of form are at stake.

Benjamin brings this issue to the surface when he uses the comparison of Loos and Jochmann to illuminate the transition from a desire for eternal values in the nineteenth century to the presentism of the contemporary. Constructing a dialectical movement away from both historicism and ornament, he inserts Loos firmly into debates on aesthetics and politics:

> Loos's work prepares the way for an awareness of the problematic side of art—an awareness that opposes the aesthetic imperialism of the nineteenth century, the gold-fever pursuit of "eternal" values in art. From Loos, light falls on Jochmann. The former wrote in order to eradicate a deeply rooted infestation; the latter offered remedies for a malaise that was just at its outset. After World War I, the debate entered its decisive stage: the question had to be either worked through in theory or modishly glossed over. Both solutions had their political equivalents. The first coincides with recent attempts to formulate a materialist theory of art. . . . The second has been favored by totalitarian regimes and has appropriated the reactionary elements of Futurism, Expressionism, and to some extent Surrealism.[120]

This passage is useful in tracing what Benjamin's reading does with Loos. Loos may be a reactionary thinker in many ways and programmatic rather than original, but by insisting so vehemently on a particular correlation between aesthetics and politics, he makes their historical mechanisms visible. Loos's progressive view of history could hardly be further from Benjamin's dialectics. But, intentionally or not, Loos functions to clarify for Benjamin the necessity of a materialist theory of art, and as the editors of Benjamin's *Collected Writings* point out, this theory is to be found in "The Work of Art in the Age of Its Technological Reproducibility."[121] Of course, versions of this essay were written before "The Regression of Poetry"; Benjamin worked over the ideas in it repeatedly throughout the 1930s. But what the previous passage demonstrates is the intimate proximity of Benjamin's thinking on ornament and his development of a materialist theory of art. It seems that Loos's rejection of art nouveau ornament speaks directly to Benjamin's most influential account of cinema and politics.

Loos is important to Benjamin because he symptomatically narrates key questions of aesthetics and politics. He is therefore important to theorizing the pretty because he allows us to think the ornament together with Benjamin's theories of cinema. Moreover, mobilizing Loos as a way into Benjamin's aesthetics demonstrates how central the ornament is to Benjamin's thinking, not only in relation to Jugendstil and the Second Empire interior, but as a more widely applicable question of how we read historical significance in the forms of everyday cultural artifacts. Like the exhortations to a destructive modernity, "The Work of Art" appears to validate Loos's anti-ornamentalism decisively. Although the exact form of an aestheticized politics or a politicized art has been subject to debate in postwar cultural theory, materialist theories of art are almost without fail opposed to the ornamental pretty. And yet Benjamin's ambivalence regarding Loos is also an ambivalence regarding ornament. Hansen has drawn out the complexity of Benjamin's attitude toward the loss of the aura, and in his engagement with ornament we find an entry point to a similar complexity with respect to the politics of aesthetic form. Far from simply rejecting decorative styles, as does Loos, Benjamin accords them a uniquely important place in the elaboration of his philosophy of knowledge.

In *The Arcades Project,* Convolute S deals with "painting, Jugendstil, novelty," and it offers a certain Loosian critique of Jugendstil's decorative style. Benjamin even refers to Loos while proposing that Jugendstil used technological motifs as part of an "effort to sterilize them ornamentally."[122] He also quotes Salvador Dalí's depiction of the style as evidence of a "childhood neurosis" and Dolf Sternberger's complaint that "it is by means of the rich and powerful contour that . . . the figure of the soul becomes ornament."[123] As Hal Foster maintains, art nouveau rapidly went out of style when the machine aesthetic and various avant-garde forms became dominant in the 1920s. However, Benjamin does not entirely agree with Sternberger, characterizing his view as "very problematic." At the very least, he finds Jugendstil's out-of-time quality to be significant, attributing to it an attempt at awakening that places it productively at odds with bourgeois historical progression: "When we have to get up early on a day of departure, it can sometimes happen that, unwilling to tear ourselves away from sleep, we dream that we are out of bed and getting dressed. Such a dream was dreamed in Jugendstil by the bourgeoisie, fifteen years before history woke them with a bang."[124] If only in its failure, then, Jugendstil might voice political truths.

But ornamentation, for Benjamin, not only speaks in an untimely fashion through Jugendstil but also articulates suggestive disjunctures of place and subjectivity. Of the nineteenth-century domestic interior, he writes, "The space disguises itself—puts on, like an alluring creature, the costumes of moods."[125] The room, here, evokes a familiar feminization; decoration as disguise, the untrustworthy woman whose cosmetics hide her true self. The "alluring creature" is also dehumanized, less than a subject, a rhetorical cousin to Josephine Baker's lovely animal. The feminizing (delegitimizing) rhetoric is echoed in Siegfried Giedion's account of the 1867 exhibition, quoted by Benjamin: "As was usual with rooms at this period, attempts were made—through furniture-like installations—to prettify these twenty-five-meter-high galleries and to relieve the austerity of their design. One stood in fear of one's own magnitude."[126] Prettiness is an attempt to remove austerity—not an aim that Giedion approves. Indeed, he mocks the fear of one's own size that such prettifying implies, proposing a masculinist discourse of height and vertical power as superior to any attempt to cover up the high galleries via decoration. As is often the case in *The Arcades Project*, Benjamin's response to this passage is unknown. But the inclusion of the quotation suggests that, for Benjamin, the ornamental pretty speaks. Counter to aesthetic orthodoxy, he never finds it to be meaningless. Indeed, in the same Convolute, he even attributes to it a form of political action: "Against the armature of glass and iron, upholstery offers resistance with its textiles."[127]

If ornamental style is feminized for Benjamin, it is also closely tied to sexual and racial otherness. He points to "[Giovanni] Segantini's *Unnatural Mothers* as a motif of Jugendstil, closely related to *Les Lesbiennes*," and continues, "The depraved woman stays clear of fertility, as the priest stays clear of it."[128] The lesbian is a recurring trope in *The Arcades Project*, often in relation to Baudelaire (*Les Lesbiennes* was Baudelaire's original title for what became *Les fleurs du mal*). What interests me here is the explicit linkage of the depraved woman with both Jugendstil and the refusal of fertility as a reproductive aim. As Benjamin concludes a few pages later, "The fundamental motif of Jugendstil is the transfiguration of infertility."[129] Here, Benjamin does not mean infertility in the contemporary sense of an inability to become pregnant, but as a transvaluative claim on a life without reproduction. We should notice in this claim a response to Loos's and Kracauer's opposition of (cinematic) life to ornamental death. For Benjamin, Jugendstil's perversity is tied to in- or nonfertility (often via the lesbian as nonreproductive woman) and hence to the refusal to create life—that is, death. The fin-de-siècle examples of perversity that Benjamin includes, such as Baudelaire and Aubrey Beardsley, are ornamental not only because of their decorative style, but also in their queer rejection of reproduction as an aim. Life is given a secondary level of connotation here. Where infertility binds ornament to perverse sexuality and a refusal of life, fertility comes into view as the unspoken middle term that works to associate an aesthetic of liveliness with the reproduction of the heterosexual family. Cinema's discourse of life is equally implicated in this aesthetic demand for family values. The language of vitalism often touches on masculinist metaphors of life giving, and its rejection of the decorative imbues ornament with both perversity and death.

Benjamin's reading of infertile ornament thus enables a queer response to cinematic vitalism in which ornamental style nourishes a different mode of living. The cinematic has been associated with a limited masculinist vitalism, as where Epstein writes of film as a gift of life that rescues beings from frigidity,[130] but cinema also offers the potential of a queerly prosthetic life. The infertile ornament suggests one way of expanding our notions of cinematicity beyond the regime of reproductive life versus frigid decorative death. It proposes the aesthetic potential of a queer and ornamental vitality that purposefully rejects masculinist aesthetic aims. As with Jarman's color experiments, the materials of cinema offer the possibility of figuring a decorative queer life, but to theorize this life we cannot depend on the conventional aesthetics of cinematic realism. This issue also focuses the problem in H. D.'s critique of Garbo as prettified and straightened out by Hollywood. Although H. D. looks for a lesbian account of Garbo's beauty, she can read her as valuable only in the context of a liveliness that enters into a reproductive cinematicity. As I elaborate in chapter 5, feminist and queer critics have often been tangled in the double bind of trying to use a patriarchal theory of the image as a weapon against patriarchy. H. D. wants to write against dominant Hollywood femininity, but she has to invoke a heterocentrist aesthetic hierarchy to do so. Benjamin's writing on the ornament escapes from this double bind and allows us a portable means to articulate queer life to the radical potential of cinematicity.

Racial otherness also appears in what Benjamin calls "the dreamy and, if possible, oriental interior."[131] I discuss orientalism more in the next chapter, but from Charles Blanc's colorists to art nouveau's infatuation with chinoiserie, the decorative interior style that Benjamin studies in

The Arcades Project is consistently associated with foreignness. To take just one telling example, Benjamin quotes Jules Lecomte on the interior of Alphonse Karr's apartment: "He lives like no one else. . . . His walls are decorated with various old things. . . . Chinese vases, death-heads, fencer's foils, and tobacco pipes ornament every corner. For a servant, he has a mulatto whom he outfits in scarlet from head to toe."[132] In common with many accounts of the exotic pretty, Lecomte turns to the list form to depict the piling up of diverse objects that constitutes Karr's interior décor. And what is included is not only decorative or ornamental but also defined in terms of exotic and foreign *objets*, including the mulatto servant who is described in terms of both racial "color" and the bright color of his costume. Benjamin collects precisely the political logics of ornamental form that I have been teasing out: prettiness, femininity, perverse sexuality, orientalism, and primitivism. In each case, from the exotic and feminine interiors of the nineteenth century to the infertile women of Jugendstil, Benjamin does not find ornament's political salience to go without saying. Quite the reverse: ornament speaks and speaks, and its disjunctive expressions encode something that is hard to find in the more straightforward voices of critique. The phantasmagoria of commodity capitalism is certainly susceptible to a symptomatic reading, but the constellation crystallized into vision by the ornament is never quite so clear-cut for Benjamin as it is for Loos or even for Kracauer or H. D.

Benjamin's discourse on ornament enables a more nuanced engagement with aesthetics. Hansen contends that "granting film dimensions of figurative difference and mimetic experience that Horkheimer and Adorno reserved only for works of high art, Benjamin could envision a cinema that would be more than a medium of illusionist presence, a cinema that would release its archaic dream into a practice of profane illumination."[133] Benjamin opens up the same potential in ornament, and we should recall here Susan Buck-Morss's insistence that Benjamin returns the term *aesthetics* to its full reference to social and perceptual experience.[134] As surely as the aesthetic is a political question for Benjamin, categories such as the decorative and the ornamental must be refigured and even redeemed for political transformation.

It is for this reason that Benjamin deploys the decorative image as a central rhetorical figure. He claims that "the eternal is more like lace trimmings on a dress than like an idea," an example that for Ackbar Abbas demonstrates the potential of fascination with images as a mode of critique. He argues that "Benjamin's use of the image tends neither toward mysticism [as Gershom Scholem argues], nor toward demystificatory political critique as developed by the Frankfurt School, but toward a mode of critical reflection that I call fascination."[135] Fascination moves reading away from the masculinist iconophobia that characterizes antiornamental thought, and it understands the image—in its iconicity—as offering the potential for a unique form of engagement. We might add that Benjamin's images *of* ornament are embedded in a prose style that itself refuses rhetorical purity. One of the many fascinating qualities of *The Arcades Project* is a form, albeit unfinished, that replaces linearity with a baroque and lace-trimmed style. This construction of ornament as both object and figure is political. For Benjamin, the phantasmagoria of material culture and interior design is not simply an outmoded form to be overcome, and in *The Arcades Project* he mobilizes the archaic dreams of art nouveau dialectically.

Benjamin concludes that "Jugendstil forces the auratic,"[136] an idea that ties the ornament to the status of the aura in mass culture. What does it mean to "force the auratic"? Hansen has pointed out Benjamin's ambivalence regarding the decline of the aura, and she finds in essays such as "The Storyteller" a sense of belatedness that plays an active role in modernity's reconstruction of perception. If the aura, even in its decline, can produce dialectical images, then an aura forced by ornament might take part in the aesthetic transformation of modern experience. The fascination of the ornamented image can be separated from its traditional ideological structures of religion or bourgeois taste in much the same way as the aura itself must produce new experiences for the modern sensorium. Like Benjamin's lace trimmings that produce fascination for Abbas, the ornament can mobilize political awakening, its disjunctive times, spaces, and subjects, enabling a vision that directness cannot achieve. This belated, disjunctive image counters the sense of cinematic modernity as engaged only with representing the (almost) present. Thinking form dialectically demands an aesthetic that moves beyond a simple binary of decorated versus plain, savage adornment versus white walls. Whereas dominant discourses of immediacy and the capturing of life impel an antidecorative version of cinematic specificity, both Benjamin's belated aura and its potential to create dialectical images hold out promise for a different kind of political aesthetics. In turn, such an aesthetics can fold into cinematic vision a figuration of different modes of living in which fascinating, ornamental, and, above all, pretty images speak of lives otherwise excluded from European aesthetic value.

Benjamin calls Jugendstil "the stylizing style par excellence,"[137] and this repetition figures ornament's mode of critique. It is the style that makes style, that thinks about style, that articulates the question of style. It is never unspoken, simple, or taken for granted. It redoubles style upon style, producing excess at the same moment that it promises a discourse on iteration. To imagine a politics of ornamental style, we must break apart the Loosian structure in which only visual austerity can adequately depict European civilization and reproductive life. Eduardo Cadava says that "the home of the photographed is the cemetery," but this is not the death that results from poisonous ornament's disease.[138] For Cadava, as for Benjamin, this death is not a simple sign of negativity, a lack of proper and healthy life, but a refusal of the progressive narrative of history, a claim on the dialectical potential of the image. Like the photograph and, indeed, like cinema itself, the art nouveau interior forces immediacy up against finitude. Cadava quotes Benjamin's *The Origin of German Tragic Drama*: "[I]t is only thus, as corpses, that [characters] can enter the homeland of allegory."[139] Under this sign, ornament enters into a dialectical relationship with the image, and Benjamin's fascinated critique suggests a reimagining of Loos's "Story of a Poor Rich Man" in which living with one's own corpse might instead produce a revolutionary transformation.

FOUR

OBJECTS

Oriental Style and the Arabesques of *Moulin Rouge!*

BAZ LUHRMANN'S FILM *MOULIN ROUGE!* (2001), SET AMONG the decadent and decorative interiors of turn-of-the-century Paris, seems precisely designed to appall Adolf Loos. Writing almost in the year that Luhrmann's narrative is set, Loos warns, "And so the domination by the upholsterers began; it was a reign of terror that we can all still feel in our bones. Velvet and silk, silk and velvet, Makart bouquets, dust, suffocating air and lack of light, portières, carpets, and 'arrangements'—thank God, we are done with all that now!"[1] But we are not done with all that, and a century later *Moulin Rouge* returns to the overstuffed interiors and curvilinear forms that the modernizers had imagined swept away with the cinematic street and the wind in the leaves. The film is structured by excessive decoration: Luhrmann and his production designer partner Catherine Martin use an overwhelming accumulation of costume, sets, props, and color to hold realism at bay. In *The Arcades Project*, Walter Benjamin also investigates the political implications of dust, upholstery, and the interior, but, unlike Loos, he imagines the interior as a space of cultural transformation, or at least of possibility. In the words of his suggestive notation in *The Arcades Project*: "Development of 'The Interior' chapter: entry of the prop into film."[2] This chapter follows Benjamin's direction, considering the prop or, more broadly, mise-en-scène not as a function of design history, but as a technique of the pretty in cinema. Where the previous chapter interrogated the political implications of modernism's refusal of decorative forms, this chapter builds on those foundations to trace a cinematic pretty in décor and camera movement. Centering on *Moulin Rouge* as an exemplary text, it asks how Loos's horror of decorated interiors and feminine lines reappears in postclassical cinema and, conversely, how the decorative can figure geopolitics, gender, and sexuality.

Luhrmann's films suggest themselves as examples of the pretty as an entry point for questions of detail, ornamentation, and excess. But their critical reception also points out the odd status that often accrues to pretty films. *Moulin Rouge*, like Luhrmann's earlier films *Romeo + Juliet* (1996) and *Strictly Ballroom* (1992), was a commercial success. Although the musical was not a typical blockbuster genre in the early 2000s, the film's budget, star casting of Nicole Kidman and Ewan McGregor, summer release, and international distribution placed it squarely in the category of popular cinema. But this popular success was not matched either by critical approbation or by scholarly interest. On its release, Luhrmann's status as popular auteur and the film's bold attempt to retune the musical for contemporary audiences guaranteed that it would garner the attention of serious film journalism. Viewed as "artier" than the average summer film, it was widely featured in film and culture magazines. Although there were some positive reviews, most concurred with José Arroyo in *Sight and Sound* that it was an honorable failure. Arroyo admitted that it was "gorgeous to look at" and that "one does feel ravished," but his damning summary is of "textbook postmodernism at its worst, a relentless pastiche of pop-cultural sounds and representations sutured into the service of a cliché."[3]

Arroyo's review is noteworthy because it exemplifies a faint-praise structure that recurs across the various critical institutions, lauding *Moulin Rouge*'s visual style but ultimately finding this very strength to reveal a weakness in real meaning. Thus the film won Academy Awards for production design and costume design—high praise from Hollywood—but one cannot help reading in the limitation of the awards to the field of mise-en-scène a slight implication of all style and no content. We might consider in this context how little scholarship there is on Baz Luhrmann, despite his international profile and potentially useful place in debates on postclassical genre.[4] This absence of critical engagement may not be unconnected to the prettiness of his films: unlike other proponents of the contemporary melodrama (Todd Haynes) or musical (Lars von Trier), Luhrmann is simply not taken seriously.[5] Too arty to fit easily into popular industrial rubrics, his aesthetic is nonetheless too pretty to be included in the critical canon of serious filmmakers. As Marsha Kinder notes, the tension between sentiment and irony that animates the musical becomes, for viewers of *Moulin Rouge*, a tension between loving and loathing the film.[6] *Moulin Rouge*, then, demonstrates a commercial version of the pretty film, more popular by definition than a corresponding experimental or art film, but nonetheless fitting uneasily into its generic, industrial, and critical settings.

My focus in this analysis is the pretty technique of the decorative interior—or how *Moulin Rouge*'s objects, props, and scenographic spaces enable the articulation of geopolitical and sexual discourse. Such an analysis obviously descends in some measure from histories of the melodrama that focus on mise-en-scène as a spatial counter to the dominant ideologies of narrative. It is indebted, likewise, to criticism of the musical, which accounts for the spectacular breaks of the production number and the queer pleasures of the genre. These histories are important, not least because *Moulin Rouge* is so aware of them. Its referential structure points to *The Red Shoes* (Powell and Pressburger, 1948) and Vicente Minnelli, *Lola Montès* (Ophüls, 1955), and *China Gate* (Santoshi, 1998), among many others, and Luhrmann himself has spoken about the political advantages of eschewing realism. However, my aim is neither to add another film to the canon of progressive texts nor, conversely, to condemn this film's underlying heterocentrism or racial shortcomings. Instead, I am interested in how the film's mobilization of objects might be legible in terms of the pretty—how the elements of mise-en-scène (props, sets, costumes, camera movement) can work on embedded histories of gendered and raced representation *at the formal level* rather than as a supplement to or a resistant pull against narrative. Unlike Kristin Thompson's idea of excess, which views style as that which exceeds meaning, I aim to read decorative forms as independently meaningful systems that elaborate a politics as much as a poetics.[7] I draw out what the object says in *Moulin Rouge*, what its place in a historical system of aesthetic judgment enables in the present, and in particular how the pretty object engages the aesthetic categories of exclusion.

To explore this geopolitics of the decorative, I read the film through two critical terms, both of which map transnational relationships, aesthetics and gender, and both of which encode a geographical relation at the lexical level. The first term is *orientalism*, which immediately conjures the difficulties of the film, its appropriation of the exotic other in its representations of an Asian-influenced Paris, and its internal narrative of a Hindi-themed bohemian musical. But orientalism, I argue, is useful here not to undergird a fairly obvious critique of the film's magpie aesthetic, but as an entrance into a politics of stuff. Orientalism describes specific histories of both fine and decorative art and traces with them the ideological stakes of Oriental objects for thinking gender, sexuality, and the ways that these terms might be inflected by geographical place. *Moulin Rouge* takes up the threads of these histories in its Asian- and Middle Eastern–inflected sets and costumes as well as in the sheer material weight of its decorative objects. The Oriental object, for *Moulin Rouge*, does not simply repeat a colonialist gesture but gives us access to a different looking relation. The second term is *arabesque*, a concept at once more abstract and more concrete. It is concrete because it defines a particular technique of Islamic art and a specific pose in classical dance and thus presents a much more closely aesthetic question regarding its use in film. But the arabesque is also definitionally abstract: a line, a shape, a principle of nonrepresentational art, it forces us to think about the gendered and geopolitical qualities of form. The curving line of the arabesque articulates the woman's body or an Arabic inscription of space or both, but without representing anything directly. As such, it provides a way to analyze camera movement, that part of mise-en-scène that shapes scenic space without ever being seen onscreen. In reading *Moulin Rouge*'s dramatic cranes and tracking shots as arabesque, we can open out feminist critique of the suffering beauty to the multiple aesthetic and geopolitical implications of the sinuous line.

ORIENTALIST OBJECTS

Orientalism is closely associated with an excess of objects: nineteenth-century orientalist paintings (such as those by Eugène Delacroix [figure 24] and Jean-Léon Gérôme [see figure 30]) featured harem and court scenes stuffed full of decorative props to create a sense of luxurious exoticism. Aesthetician Charles Blanc, whom we have encountered as an in-

FIGURE 24 Eugène Delacroix, *Femmes d'Alger dans leur appartement* (1834)
Eugène Delacroix's painting depicts a panoply of decorative surfaces in orientalist mode.

fluential critic of ornament and color, explicitly connects color in art to the feminine, the decorative, and the Oriental.[8] The evocation of *disegno* over *colore* is familiar, but more telling is the geographical rhetoric of the decorative supplement. Blanc complains that "our colorists go to the Orient, to Egypt, Morocco, Spain, to bring back a whole arsenal of brilliant objects; cushions, slippers, nargilehs, turbans, burnous, caftans, mats, parasols."[9] In addition to making visible an anxiety of seduction and infiltration, this orientalist litany of accessories is reminiscent of the lines from Heine that Freud famously appropriates in his essay "Femininity."[10] The Orient, like the feminine, is associated with an excess of pleasure in material things, particularly decorative, sensual, pretty things. To undermine the value of these things, critics such as Blanc frequently present them in list form and thus, as Thomas Kim points out, "[commit] them to a homogeneity of presentation via their enunciated serialization."[11]

Moulin Rouge's mise-en-scène is strongly inspired by these nineteenth-century orientalist fantasies, especially in Satine's chamber, a luxurious

FIGURE 25 *Moulin Rouge!* (Luhrmann, 2001)
Satine's elephant-shaped chamber is reminiscent of orientalist painting in its excess of decorative styles.

edifice shaped like an elephant and combining the styles of a French bordello, an Algerian harem, and an Indian palace (figure 25). Indeed, it would be impossible to describe the space without resorting to the listing of exotic objects. In it, we find Arabic latticework, Gothic arches, Moroccan lamps, a Persian rug, Indian flower garlands, a North African tea tray, and a series of harem-style paintings of female nudes. The chamber promiscuously and in great detail mixes European furnishings with objects and architectural features indicative of a range of orientalist representational histories, focusing particularly on the Middle East and South Asia. But the extreme semiotic overload of the space prevents it from reading simply as another orientalist list. The elephant room announces itself as a set, separate from the rest of the Moulin Rouge and bearing more than a little resemblance to an early classical Hollywood iteration of exotic glamour—say, the sets in Cecil B. DeMille's *Cleopatra* (1934) or the *shoji* room in *The Cheat* (DeMille, 1915). Staged at one remove, not as a supposedly authentic representation of the Orient but as a fantasy space within a "real" place, the elephant room proposes the excess of Oriental objects as the language in which the film can articulate the value of what is or is not real.

That objects are at the heart of *Moulin Rouge* is made clear when the Duke, in a jealous fit over his exclusive contract with Satine, exclaims,

"I just don't like other people touching my things!" The plot centers on courtesan Satine, who is loved by artist Christian but has been sold to the Duke in an attempt to finance the conversion of the Moulin Rouge into a proper theater. Satine's status as an object of exchange provides the central conflict in the narrative so that objects are not merely a feature of the mise-en-scène but provide a structuring component in the melodrama. Satine is a thing among things. We see the interpenetration of background objects and narrative ones in the pitch scene, set in the elephant room, where Christian and Satine are caught in a compromising position by the Duke and to save themselves extemporize a plot for the play that they pretend to have been rehearsing. Christian decides that the show is set in India after seeing a giant statue of Ganesha in the corner and likewise makes the hero a penniless sitar player when he glimpses a sitar. Here, props move out of their background role and begin to effect changes in the main story. In fact, objects save the day by allowing Christian to hide his love for Satine behind a "prop" story, in which the bohemian lover becomes a penniless sitar player. The sitar props him up, saves his bacon, and also props up the bohemians by persuading the Duke to fund their play. Most of all, the objects temporarily save Satine, one of their own.

That Oriental objects provide the visible means of negotiating the exchange of sexual and other commodities in *Moulin Rouge*'s turn-of-the-century diegesis should come as no historical surprise: at this exact historical juncture, Oriental objects took on a unique role in Western consumer capitalism. Having long been associated with luxury, exoticism, and the decorative, at the time that *Moulin Rouge* is set Oriental objects were also beginning to circulate as markers of a modern cosmopolitanism that offered desirable mass-market access to cultural capital and fashionable design. Sarah Cheang notes the resurgence of chinoiserie in both Europe and the United States around 1900 as well as its association with both femininity and modernity.[12] Likewise, Kim argues (albeit in the specifically American context) that the rise in the status of the Oriental object brought with it contradictions in which "the Orient (as object and concept) acts both as an agent for and a palliative against the contradictions activated by modern consumption."[13] Often seen as a repository of timeless aesthetic values in contrast to modern Western fashions, the "ahistorical" Oriental object nonetheless circulated precisely because of processes of modernization in both West and East. Enthusiasm for modern access to exotic styles was similarly countered with a projection of raced and gendered suspicion onto the insidious and primitive object (and subject) of consumption.[14] As Victoria de Grazia puts it, consumption has long been associated with "out-of-control femininity" and "carnivalesque excess," and in the consumerist fervor of the new century the Oriental object was peculiarly able to figure both the fears and the desires of the modern.[15]

If, as Kim concludes, the Oriental object "can indeed produce a new modern sensibility . . . making legible the contradictions that mass culture presents to the consumer,"[16] then *Moulin Rouge*'s mobilization of orientalism is the ideal form with which to reflect on the historical imbrication of spectacle, modern consumerism, and pleasure embedded in the mythic structures of popular cinema. The film was made a hundred years after its narrative is set, and its bricolage style, although arguably a "typical postmodern" pastiche, surely enfolds in its many references a century's worth of cinematic props, generic conventions, and objects of popular exchange. Where theorists of the object such as Bill Brown ask us to "find . . . not just the physical determinants of our imaginative life but also the congealed facts and fantasies of a culture, the surface phenomena that disclose the logic or illogic of industrial society,"[17] *Moulin Rouge* stages the Oriental object as a formal distillation of the relationship between film aesthetics and social relations. In this sense, the strange and excessive elephant room is like the baroque ornament, an element that, as Iain Chambers puts it, "seemingly auxiliary[,] . . . reveal[s] [itself] to be obligatory. As if a jewel, the ornament or 'grace note' is not an afterthought, a subsequent embellishment added to the finished work, but is rather the essential point towards which the work strives."[18] Like the baroque ornament, the elephant room seems to be a thoroughly unnecessary flourish inside the spatial design of the film, but in fact its intertwined display of sexual, racial, and decorative commodities reveals the film's essence.

Three elements are woven together here: gender, aesthetics, and the geographical or racial other. Although they cannot be entirely unthreaded because each discourse implies the others, we can bring each to the surface in turn. Beginning with gender, we have seen how Satine's elephant boudoir centers sexual exchange as a narrative and visual problem. I argue that the film elaborates ideas of the Oriental style as feminine but transvalues the historical denigration of the feminine Oriental object into a more positive claim on an antirealist and antipatriarchal decorative aesthetic. Orientalist decorative art has long been associated with femininity—for example, chinoiserie has traditionally been used in bedrooms and drawing rooms instead of in more masculine public spaces. And although certain aspects of Asian art such as diagonal composition and lack of perspective were imported into European artistic modernism, the feminine qualities of decorative style were instead channeled into an emergent mass culture that has itself been famously characterized as womanly. Thus, for example, Sumiko Higashi links the problems presented by the New Woman in consumer culture to the threat of Japaneseness in *The Cheat,* and Cheang points out that modern Oriental interior design was closely linked to the independent woman of the Jazz Age.[19] Needless to say, this independent woman was commonly demonized as sexually loose: think of the City Woman in *Sunrise* (Murnau, 1927), another of *Moulin Rouge's* reference points, or the white woman who prostitutes herself to Sessue Hayakawa's art dealer in *The Cheat.* In a telling example, Cheang describes the publicity of Clara Bow's Chinese living room, which her fans viewed as a sign of her status as a glamorous liberated woman and her detractors as evidence of her immorality (figure 26). In the first decades of Hollywood, female stars were often posed against chinoiserie backgrounds to emphasize their glamour. An Oriental interior poses its female inhabitant as both modern and sexually loose, and it is this double bind that animates Satine's double construction as a mythic courtesan who also wants to parlay prostitution into becoming a "real actress."

The film narrativizes this problem in the Duke's gift of a necklace to Satine, accompanied by the words "I will make you a star." The supposed gift is of course not freely given but designates both the necklace and Satine as objects of sexual currency: props are again not simply background, but a significant term in the narrative of sexual and artistic commerce. The jewelry itself resembles a giant collar, clearly signifying ownership of Satine, but it also connotes the exotic adornment of the non-European native (figure 27). Jewelry is a recurrent figure in orientalist representation: we might think of Loos's bejeweled Indian woman whose excess ornamentation proves that she is less beautiful than the pure white woman. The ornamented native woman appears in orientalist painting, and Malek Alloula critiques the widespread popularity of this figure in his canonical analysis of colonial-era Algerian postcards in *The Colonial Harem.*

FIGURE 26 A publicity image of Clara Bow exemplifies the use of chinoiserie backdrops to emphasize a female star's glamour.

Placing these popular images within histories of the violent colonial gaze, Alloula pays particular attention to their use of jewelry and bodily adornment: "Bedecked in this manner, decorated so to speak, these Algerian women in full regalia bear some resemblance to the Virgins carried in Spanish processions. And that is indeed the impression they all give: they are ecstatic icons, passively submitting to their cosmetic make-

FIGURE 27 *Moulin Rouge!*
Satine's adornment with headdress and collar necklace evokes both Hindi musicals and orientalist art.

over, readied for the other scene, for a feast of the phantasm, whose secret is known only to the photographer. The model and what she signifies . . . are effaced to become no more than the purport of a carnivalesque orgy."[20] In describing this pornographic regime of vision, Alloula's critique resonates with, for instance, the way that Eadweard Muybridge's photographs staged women with clothes and props to emphasize their gendered bodies. There is certainly a sexual and colonial inscription of power at work here, not least in, as Alloula contends, how these props fake an exotic authenticity that is ungrounded (figure 28). In actuality, the women pictured, he argues, are poor, sometimes prostitutes, wearing (and removing) ethnic costumes for money. But what interests me is the intersection of this material history of sexual exchange with a discursive construction of adornment as the signifier of obscenity. For Alloula, the women's bodies are "painted up," their jewels and clothes representing "degradation through excess."[21] But if the association of (available) women with adornment is a patriarchal and colonial production, it is not the fault of the jewelry. The fetishistic blame of visual ornament for colonial regimes of vision both shifts focus back onto the female image and fantasizes an authentic, pure native woman underneath the cosmetics. *Moulin Rouge* considers what it might mean to reconfigure that regime of vision, neither to blame the objects of exchange (necklace or

Maure, phot., Biskra 140

Biskra — Ouleds Naïls.

FIGURE 28 Marius Maure, postcard of Algerian women (1900)
This postcard is typical of those that circulated in the early twentieth century.

courtesan) nor to locate aesthetic truth in the "pure" image beneath the decoration.

For although the Duke's necklace is an ornament that signifies capitalist duplicity and masculine violence, the decorative object is not in and of itself a bad object for the film. Indeed, it centers the film's formal regime. What is wrong with the necklace is the form of its exchange, not the semiotics of its style. Given its interest in the exchange of women, *Moulin Rouge* seems to be in sympathy with feminist analyses of orientalism as a discourse constituted through gender at its most basic level. Meyda Yegenoglu, for instance, has persuasively argued that gender is not a subfield of orientalism, but a defining element of it.[22] For her, however, the decorative imperative of orientalist representation is centered by the veiled woman—that which cannot be seen, the emptiness at the heart of colonial vision. Yegenoglu, too, finds the decorative to be a problem because she reads it as a dispersal of violence against women's bodies across the visual field. But what if we started not from the perspective of colonial patriarchal vision, but from a postcolonial and feminist viewpoint that does not believe in purity, veiling, or the shibboleths of Western aesthetics? *Moulin Rouge* transvalues the feminine, impure Oriental style, cheerfully co-opting Asian decorative styles while simultaneously rejecting puritanical visual codes from East and West.

There is a truth at stake in *Moulin Rouge*: its postmodern pastiche would be as unbearable as its detractors find it if there really were nothing at stake. But its truth is crucially not to be found underneath or despite the ornamental style, but fully within it. Harold Zidler, the owner of the Moulin Rouge theater, describes the show in hyperbolic language for the Duke as "magnificent, opulent, tremendous, stupendous, gargantuan, bedazzling, a sensual ravishment." Clearly, this is showmanship, Zidler's character ensuring that his words are understood as excessive advertising. And yet his association of spectacle, femininity, and orientalist opulence is also an accurate account of the film's pleasures. Mike Sell has argued that the campiness of the performances in the show-within-the-film contrast with the authentic heterosexual romance at the core of the narrative, but I think exactly the opposite is happening.[23] The mythic story of true love is indeed partially coded through the actors recording their singing live. The close linkage of body and voice (the sound and visual appearance of vocal effort as well as the imperfections of the actors' singing voices) grounds the love story in material bodies. But this truth is not the purity that gives the lie to the film's dazzling spectacle. Rather, the real love story is articulated by and through pretty objects, from the morsels of pop songs that Satine and Christian sing to each other through the appropriated costumes and props of the *Spectacular Spectacular* show in which they rehearse their amour.[24]

Oddly, because this film is nothing if not a straight love story, one way to consider Luhrmann's use of orientalism is as a queer appropriation. Just as orientalism has always contained within it a logic of feminization, it has also been considered to be overly effeminate. Joseph Boone finds homoeroticism to be a major topos in the construction of orientalism, despite the resolute straightness of commentators such as Edward Said and Alloula,[25] and we certainly find effeminizing rhetoric in the historical literature. For instance, a nineteenth-century design journal uses the coded language of effeminacy in warning that an Oriental interior is suitable only for men "of delicate make and silky constitution."[26] Similarly, Reina Lewis quotes an 1861 *Art Journal* piece that critiques Gérôme's paintings for displaying "a finished effeminacy" of style and "a culpable lasciviousness" of object.[27] We see here the close association of orientalist art with effeminacy and perversion as well as the extension of this rhetoric of disdain to the artist. Even Lewis's modern analysis seems to concur that Henriette Browne's more restrained and less "luscious" paintings are ideologically superior to Gérôme's sexually perverse ones. Antisex ideas of purity and virtue imbue this whole discourse, where an orientalist image can be less politically troubling if it is less sexually spectacular.

It is this idea that Luhrmann rejects most clearly, celebrating the feminine and queer aspects of the orientalist image as a means of leveraging a pretty politics of style. We can certainly find narrative instances of this refusal. The Moulin Rouge is built on a world of sexual spectacle, and it stakes its claim to bohemianism in a rejection of dominant sexual mores. In one musical number, straight white men dance in an opposing bloc to the sexually and racially diverse Moulin Rouge performers, forming a tuxedoed monochrome phalanx whose homogeneity is marked as such. More broadly, Luhrmann's structuration of looking relations consistently eroticizes the bodies of his male stars (Ewan McGregor in *Moulin Rouge*, Leonardo di Caprio in *Romeo + Juliet*, and Hugh Jackman in *Australia* [2008]) but represents the female leads as beautiful but oddly desexualized (Nicole Kidman's performance is stiff and statuesque, despite the fact that the character is a courtesan, and her body is rarely fetishized in framing). Heterosexuality—as a form of capitalist exchange—is put in question throughout, whereas love is firmly located on the side of bohemian scenographic space per se, whichever bodies choose to occupy it. Kim's enunciated serialization returns not as a list of foreign objects, but as a principle of perverse multiplicity able to counter the monocular perspective of the monocled Parisian clients. Instead of rejecting the exotic, feminine, and queer decorations that orientalism associates with the geographical other in favor of the aesthetic purity of the veiled object, Luhrmann throws out the colonial and patriarchal logic of the veil and returns the exotic decoration and the lascivious object to the realm of meaning and truth.

This strategy is hard to read not only because the representational politics of the film itself is not particularly radical, but also because the approach flies in the face of most accounts of orientalism and aesthetics. In the colonial era, use of the decorative object was seen as Oriental (and hence aesthetically inferior), and in postcolonial criticism it is seen as oriental*ist* (and hence politically problematic). Luhrmann's visual style not only embraces the decorative but also emphasizes the gendered and sexualized qualities of the Oriental object that have redoubled or complicated its historical status. Unwilling to take for granted the chain of associations that have made the Oriental object a particular critical fetish, Luhrmann's excessive mise-en-scènes make a point of their visual richness, demanding that the spectator engage the style in both a historical and a contemporary context. If, as Kim and Cheang suggest, the Oriental object has a history of negotiating modern consumer subjectivities, then Luhrmann's evocation of this history makes visible the relationships between orientalism's subjects and the aesthetics of cinematic spectacle.

The second aspect of the film's orientalist style is aesthetics, and, as we have seen, this aesthetic is steeped in the politics of gender, sexuality, and racial otherness. What does it mean visually to privilege the very terms that aesthetic history has excluded as too feminine, effeminate, or foreign? *Moulin Rouge* makes a decisive claim on exactly those aesthetic elements of the Oriental that, as we have seen in chapters 1 and 3, have been repeatedly rejected in film theory and criticism: interior décor, theatricality, visual richness. One of the major critiques of early film critics was theatricality: ideas of cinematic specificity demanded a sharp distinction between film and other art forms, and theatricality in particular was usually read as a sign of an insufficiently worked out cinematic form. It makes sense that cinema would need to separate itself decisively from the other form of popular culture with which it was so closely entwined, but the historical connotations of theater include not only the play form, but also the Oriental. John M. Mackenzie describes the appeal of the Orient in the nineteenth century in terms of its theatricality, and the associations of display, decoration, and exoticism produce a discourse of seductive yet fake sets that might be proper to the theater, but that suggest a lack of reality and truth when applied to the cinema and the Orient.[28] Luhrmann plays on this ambivalence in his Red Curtain films, which draw attention to their theatricality with an opening shot of a proscenium. *Moulin Rouge*'s theater setting, combined with Oriental sets, links a refusal to define cinematicity through exterior space with a constant reminder that the rejection of theatricality as anticinematic also contains a rejection of the Oriental.

In the terms that became dominant through the nineteenth century and into the discourse of film criticism, to present an object as Oriental is similarly to locate it as decorative rather than fine art and hence as aesthetically inferior. The previous chapter examined how film scholarship took up the decorative / fine art binary, and an important part of this division was between Western and Eastern artworks. Although successive waves of Asian art were imported to Europe and the United States, influencing chinoiserie and orientalist styles from at least the seventeenth century on, this influence for the most part was contained within the decorative sphere. As Mackenzie succinctly puts it, "While Europeans were prepared to acknowledge the influence of 'crafts' and of the decorative arts from the earliest days of commercial contact with the East, they always maintained the outright superiority of western sculpture and painting."[29] Asian aesthetics represented a discourse of craft and commercial beauty rather than Western notions of artistic genius. By constructing *Moulin Rouge* as an Oriental object itself, Luhrmann troubles this engrained aesthetic hierarchy. We might attribute to this critical orientalism the paucity of scholarship on Luhrmann as well as the limitation of the film's Academy Awards to the feminized craft areas of production design and costume.

Oriental style is also closely associated with detail and visual complexity. *Moulin Rouge* makes the excess of detail one of its central formal mechanisms—for example, in the Lady Marmalade cancan number, which early on defines the film's musical style (figure 29). In this scene, the

FIGURE 29 *Moulin Rouge!*
Cancan dancers layer color, fabric, movement, and tattoos in an overwhelming spectacle.

dancers' skirts layer many different fabrics, colors, and patterns, creating a more chaotic and visually overwhelming spectacle than even the typical cancan. Their jewelry includes Indian gold chains, and, in another Loosian adornment, two heavily tattooed men dance together. The mixture of styles includes the music, which mashes up various pop and rock songs, including Nirvana's "Smells Like Teen Spirit." This stuffing of the mise-en-scène and soundscape with as much detail as it can hold pinpoints exactly what many critics disliked about the film: its pace in this establishing scene is frenetic, with no song properly finished, and the scenographic space is fragmented by rapid editing, step-printing, and abrupt changes of film speed. The refusal of openness and realism is extreme here, even by the standards of the Hollywood musical. Not allowing any song to *take place*, to be performed in its entirety in a coherent space and time, might be seen as a doubled refusal of Siegfried Kracauer's realism, lacking openness even in the already formative terms of the musical. And, indeed, the film clearly articulates its refusal of the values of life, realism, and openness in the character of Christian's Scottish Presbyterian father, who voices a thin, puritan life that sees Montmartre as sin and death—which it is, of course—but *Moulin Rouge* defiantly mobilizes the queer aesthetic of living with one's own corpse.

Naomi Schor has recuperated detail from a feminist perspective, critiquing the association of detail with decadence: "Of all the arguments enlisted against the detail, none was to receive more attention in the mid-nineteenth century than the ancient association of details and decadence, which runs in an unbroken continuity from the critique of realism to the critique of modernism."[30] Schor points out how, in a structure that is familiar for the pretty, the rejection of the decadent detail remains stubbornly in place despite the shift in mode from realism to modernism. The Oriental detail is similarly rejected across time, with even less possibility of politically engaged recuperation. Thus, in a canonical critique of orientalist painting, Linda Nochlin argues that the detailed surface of Gérôme's *The Snake Charmer* (ca. 1870) inoculates the Western viewer, using Roland Barthes's reality effect to secure a sense of legitimacy that covers up the salacious nature of the image's voyeuristic spectacle. The "insistent richness of the visual diet Gérôme offers," for Nochlin, allows the spectator to take pleasure in the detailed tiles and carpets at the same time as gazing at the charmer's "rosy buttocks" (figure 30).[31] To be clear, I do not doubt that structures of colonial visuality are at work

FIGURE 30 Jean-Léon Gérôme, *The Snake Charmer* (ca. 1870)
Jean-Léon Gérôme's mid-nineteenth-century painting demonstrates the sexual perversity of the decorative scene.

in the painting, commodifying sexual and racial exploitation just as they do in Alloula's harem postcards, but it is the underlying resilience of antidecorative rhetoric that I want to get at.

Lewis's gloss on Nochlin is telling in this regard: "As Nochlin points out, luscious detail allows the eye to feast on the beauty of the painting as a whole and reduces the Oriental figures to just one more interesting, exotic and potentially dehumanized detail, effectively distancing us from them, their context and the power relations of the picture."[32] For Lewis, simplicity would allow us to have a more critical relationship to the Orient, whereas detail and lusciousness prevent us from seeing social relations. This critique of detail is part of the feminizing discourse that Schor traces, and the seductive power of the patterned luscious image is a familiar anti-pretty trope. *Moulin Rouge* transvalues the Oriental scene of decorative carpets and rosy buttocks, proposing that it is *through* such detail that we can see and indeed potentially transform social relations. Indeed, the social relations in which the film is interested are those that flourish in a world of luscious detail. Tattooed queer couples and the sexual commerce of spectacle are understood better in the bohemian world of the Moulin Rouge than they are in the ascetic and sin-averse world outside.

But this transvaluation of the sexual and aesthetic qualities of orientalism might seem to ignore its third and central feature, the representation of the Orient. The biggest challenge in reinscribing the aesthetics of orientalism must surely be to overcome the racist underpinnings of the whole enterprise. *Moulin Rouge* is scarcely a case study of what used to be called a progressive text: despite its appropriation of sexual and geographical otherness, its plot centers on a white heterosexual couple. In this vein, Sell has critiqued the film for whitewashing its Parisian history, evacuating the figure of the Roma from its bohemia. He sees Satine as a white replacement for the gypsy dancer, arguing that "of course, Satine's beauty is entirely denuded of the gypsy's 'blackness,' and, rather than coins, Satine wears diamonds. In the case of both ethnicity and value, Satine is a second-order displacement of the Roma: just as Kidman's paleness displaces the metaphorical blackness that displaces the Roma, the diamonds Satine celebrates displace the coin that displaces the material acts of production and exchange."[33] We note in passing that Sell, too, finds jewelry and clothes to be more than mere surface decoration in that Satine's diamonds, like Kidman's skin, signify a raced regime of visual desire and exchange. If *Moulin Rouge* offers a potential for real voices, it surely does not open that potential to real Oriental voices.

But I think we can exert some pressure on this refusal of authentic voice or representation. Sell himself extends his analysis into a fascinating account of the intercultural origins of the European avant-garde, arguing that "the concept of the avantgarde developed over a long-enduring process of hybridization with Islam that began with the Crusades and reached its first fruits in the intercourse among Western European romantics, orientalists, and critical tendencies in Islam, particularly Sufism."[34] Thus, for him, the cultural politics of the avant-garde are bound up in its persistent interest in geographical and ethnic alterity. The use and appropriation of non-Western forms, as he sees them, are not a subsidiary aspect of avant-gardism, but a central motor of its formation. In this respect, *Moulin Rouge* again makes plain across its surface a structuring logic of modern culture. Its Parisian artists can easily be seen as colonialist cultural poachers, misappropriating Roma bohemianism, Hindi musicals, and so on. The film's postmodern defense, of course, is that it is self-aware in its appropriations. But beyond self-reflexivity, *Moulin Rouge* makes visible an articulation of orientalism, cinema, and transnationality that has, like the Oriental object, an ambivalent role in modern capitalist subjectivity.

The film's major geographical references are Paris and India, the actual setting of the bohemian club and the fictional setting of the *Spectacular Spectacular* musical. Both places are conjured in an antirealist manner, with Parisian clichés including distressed old photographs of Montmartre, the *chambres à la journée* sign on Christian's building, and the joking reference to little frogs. Like Benjamin's critique of artificially aged art nouveau photographs, *Moulin Rouge* replaces historicism with historical fantasy. Where Paris is represented as a fantasy version of a historical place, India is not represented directly at all but invoked constantly across the objects of the mise-en-scène and the soundscape. In the pitch sequence, in addition to the Ganesha and sitar already mentioned, Satine is wrapped in sari material and dances in a faux-Indian fashion. By the big finale of *Spectacular Spectacular*, an entire Bollywood-style show has been elaborated, with detailed costuming and jewelry, the song "Chamma Chamma" from the Hindi film *China Gate* and dancers posing in the forms of Hindu gods and goddesses (the black dancer Chocolat, for example, poses as Krishna). To be sure, there is no authentic representation here, but to expect such a thing is surely to miss the point of elaborating such inauthentic self-constructions as bohemian Montmartre and the Bollywood production number. Rather, these geographical references produce a lopsided cosmopolitanism in which Paris evokes a fantastical but influential history, and India joins Anglo-American popular music as the stuff of the anachronistic present.

Indeed, Luhrmann's insistence on the fantasmatic nature of both Eastern and Western fantasies constitutes a return to one of the more interesting aspects of earlier orientalist style.[35] Most scholars of chinoiserie and orientalist décor agree that, despite the seeming specificity of these names, many countries were the origins of production and aesthetic influence. The term *chinoiserie* was applied to Japanese, Indian, and Persian styles as well as to authentically Chinese ones, in part because objects tended to be named for the port from which they left for

Europe, which often was not the place where they were produced.[36] One interpretation of this confusion is that consumers in the West could not distinguish or did not care about the differences among Asian aesthetic traditions. But as Oliver Impey points out, this process of influence did not simply go one way. Just as western Europeans copied Asian styles, so Indian artists and artisans borrowed ideas from Japan and China, and British styles fed into East Asian manufacture.[37] This aesthetic and commercial exchange was shaped and determined by the politics and economics of colonial trade, but in a crucially complex way. For example, the major decline of Asian style in Britain in the mid-nineteenth century derived in part from the aggressive cultural politics of the Opium Wars. As Patrick Conner explains, "The evangelical movement encouraged the notion that conflict between East and West was inevitable and, ultimately, to be welcomed."[38] Rejection of Oriental style was linked to colonial nationalism and conservative religion, whereas cross-cultural aesthetic fantasy refused this reactionary rhetoric of purity. In Impey's apposite phrasing, "By the eighteenth century most people using chinoiserie styles for any form of decoration were well aware of its mixed parentage, but they did not care. What did it matter if it were a mixture of Chinese, Indian and gothick as long as it was pretty? Correctness is a nineteenth- and twentieth-century phenomenon."[39]

Moulin Rouge takes up this impurity as a pretty, aesthetico-political stance, refusing contemporary iterations of authenticity that can function to reinstate the inevitability of East–West conflict. Thus the *Spectacular Spectacular* number borrows from Bollywood, but not in any authentic manner. The dancers are Indian themed, and Hindi pop music is used, but the staging is more Busby Berkeley than Ganesh Acharya. Marsha Kinder gets at this impetus in *Moulin Rouge* when she describes the film's genre mobility in terms of "daring transcultural dialogue and exchange" and likewise when she lauds the racial, sexual, and bodily diversity at play in the Diamond Dog dancers.[40] Prettiness stages the penetration of diverse subjectivities into the limited spaces of Western visual culture. No longer as troubling a presence as Josephine Baker's French colonial drag, Luhrmann's orientalism plays on the contemporary cultural and political problematic of East–West circulation. As befits a product of international consumer culture, it is the object that speaks the loudest about its material histories. The film's emphasis on the encounter of Eastern and Western decorative objects suggest a modern appropriation of geopolitical fantasy in which an impure and pretty mixture enables a different visual regime. The pretty, it seems, is particularly useful for thinking about ambivalent and unstable cultural meeting points and for articulating cross-cultural desire rather than for expressing authentic racial or national identities

In contrast to postcolonialist claims, such as those made by Alloula and Lewis, that the pretty is orientalist, *Moulin Rouge* reminds us that the austere preference for realism and simplicity is itself built on a foundation of orientalist thought. The pretty (and, in particular, a style based on excessive objects) is excluded by orientalist thinking that finds it to be decorative, foreign, and inferior. At work here is the critical double bind that we see repeated across the terrain of the pretty: colonialist thinkers such as Loos rejected the decorative object because it is primitive to find it desirable, whereas postcolonial scholars reject it because it is colonialist to find it desirable. Despite the total reversal of ideological position, the aesthetic conclusion remains almost entirely static. The fetishization of the Oriental object is always matched by its exclusion; indeed, this relation of overvaluation and dismissal defines the erotics of the colonial image. Conventional wisdom has held that to counter this colonial logic, one should avoid any of the forms or styles associated with orientalism. We can compare this approach with feminist theory, which in some of its more radical moments suggested that the only way to oppose the simultaneous overvaluation/punishment of women in the image was to strip the image of visual pleasure or, indeed, of women. The logic underlying this politics is that the pristine image is more truthful, but although the rhetoric of the true voice is appealing, that logic is exactly the one that consigned racial and gendered others to the lesser realm of the pretty in the first place. *Moulin Rouge* attempts to mobilize the prettiness of the Oriental object as a tool to articulate the object's own history, drawing out the geopolitical, economic, and cinematic stakes of its cross-cultural encounter.

ARABESQUE MOVEMENTS

Moulin Rouge's opening shot across the Paris skyline sets the stage for excess with several layers of superimposition, and the introductory scene in the eponymous club, as I have described, piles on decorative excess in the mise-en-scène. But between these shots of highly visible plenitude is another form of excessive mise-en-scène: a long, sinuous, and impossible camera movement that carries the spectator from a distant overview of the city, down into the streets, through the gates of Montmartre, and in through the window of Christian's boardinghouse to end in a medium shot of the hero slumped over his typewriter. This fluid, curving movement, drawing on digital effects and cranes to sculpt and delineate scenographic space, forms another mode of prettiness in the mise-en-scène.[41] Along with objects in the image, camera movement forms a vector in cinema's engagement with the decorative. The static camera, although presenting a consistent frame for pictorial space, is not itself decorative and indeed tends to create minimal, stripped-down effects. The mobile camera offers many possibilities, but the most distinctive, perhaps, is the long take as a signifier of aesthetic or political rigor. Jean-Luc Godard's epic tracking shots in *Weekend* (1967) and *Tout va bien* (1972) are the most obvious example. Beyond the linear track, we could point to Béla Tarr and Miklós Jancsó, whose aleatory camera movements are folded into an unsparing Euro-modernity that refuses decoupage and hence establishes a purer aesthetic challenge. The pretty is forced out at both ends of this conceptual spectrum. A realist aesthetic subordinates camera to event and thus avoids composed lines of movement, whereas modernist claims often emphasize duration, perspective, and linearity over shape and style. In between, we find the ambiguous ground of the pretty, where the elegant mobility of the camera in *Lola Montès* is feted within a limited auteurist response, but the swooping postclassical camera style of *Moulin Rouge* or of *Sweeney Todd: The Demon Barber of Fleet Street* (Burton, 2007) is rejected as overly aestheticized, lacking either realist transparency or modernist rigor.

I want to think about these prettily curvilinear camera movement in terms of the arabesque, a concept that is used in everyday language to mean an elegant curve, but that opens onto a rich aesthetic and political history. André Bazin, in "An Aesthetic of Reality," discusses the necessity of the camera's being as ready to move as to stay still and gives as one example "the slow motion in the documentary on Matisse which allows us to observe, beneath the continuous and uniform arabesques of the stroke, the varying hesitations of the artist's hand."[42] In this instance, the arabesque is in Matisse's lines, not the camera's, and the example articulates an important distinction for Bazin. Matisse's arabesque brushstrokes are like the smooth cranes of Hollywood or the third-person effects shots of *Moulin Rouge*, whereas the neorealist point-of-view shot reveals its own place and time, documenting the hesitations of the artist's hand. Viewed in this light, the arabesque describes a deliberate foregrounding of form over the integrity of profilmic space, a preference for abstract line that evokes the Islamic arabesque's transformation of nature-based representation into purely geometric forms. This taxonomy is appealing but ultimately a little too neat, for, as we shall see, the cinematic arabesque is more plastic than Bazin's example suggests.

To analyze the significance of the arabesque in *Moulin Rouge*, we must look not only at its camera movements, but also at its interwoven references to film history, dance, and the non-European art forms that the term *arabesque* evokes. *Moulin Rouge* is an intensely referential film, and its deployment of the arabesque links abstract shape to more material forms of cultural citation. The analysis is thus itself structured like an arabesque, aiming not toward a picture of a thing but toward a pattern of lines and figures, endlessly connected, one growing out of another. It exchanges the clarity of a linear argument for a pattern form that values the aesthetic shapes and historical interconnections of the decorative. Not unlike Benjamin's constellation, the arabesque allows us to weave a more complex vision, incorporating images, moments, and objects from different times and places. Markus Brüderlin finds that the arabesque "made visible the spaces in between things,"[43] and this equalizing of positive and negative space suggests the historical potential of the form.

Not so much an analysis of *Moulin Rouge* as an arabesque constellation departing from it, this reading searches for decoration's aesthetics and politics in the moving camera's tendril lines and the prop's leaf and flower objects. In *Moulin Rouge*'s intertwining references, we can mediate theories of aesthetic abstraction with the material traces of film history. The arabesque does not provide a constant aesthetic or political meaning, as Bazin's description might imply, but it does offer a figure for thinking the gendered and geopolitical implications of abstract form.

First, a definition. The term *arabesque* originally refers to a diverse class of Islamic ornament, emerging in the eleventh century although deriving from classical antiquity, that abstracts vegetal forms into a pattern of swooping and spiraling lines and shapes.[44] First theorized in this way by Alois Riegl, the arabesque was an important part of his argument that ornament has a history and is not simply a response to material conditions. Riegl argued that the arcuated lines and motifs of the arabesque can be traced back to classical representations of acanthus, pomegranate, and palmette and that its lines and shapes are really tendrils, flowers, and leaves. Thus abstraction can "still refer to actual models in reality" and, importantly for us, can be historicized.[45] Several aspects of the arabesque's history and form present themselves as relevant. Eva Baer describes the style's cross-cultural formation, pointing out that it not only traveled across the Islamic world and into Europe but was influenced by Chinese motifs such as the peony.[46] As with orientalist art, Western appropriation is complicated by non-European crossings. Also significant is arabesque's nonnaturalistic patterning. Richard Ettinghausen, Oleg Grabar, and Marilyn Jenkins-Madina define it thus: "Quintessentially Islamic, the formalization known as the arabesque is created when a vegetal design consisting of full palmettes and half palmettes becomes an unending continuous pattern—which seems to have neither a beginning nor an end—in which each leaf grows out of the tip of another."[47] The leaves and tendrils of the arabesque are stylized rather than mimetic, tending to the anti-naturalistic (figure 31). This patterning has affiliations for a nonrealist aesthetic, refusing the mimetic imperative of European aesthetics as well as suggesting an eccentric, unnatural perspective that offers formal possibilities for those image makers invested in articulating a position that is, in Riegl's words, "entirely counter to nature."[48]

No doubt because of its anti-mimetic and unnatural form, the arabesque first entered into European aesthetic debate in a largely negative light. In the latter half of the eighteenth century, Johan Joachim Winckelmann critiqued the rococo arabesque as meaningless; Goethe called it a "subordinated form of art"; and Adolf Riem—anticipating Loos—described it as an aesthetic crime.[49] Carsten Strathausen makes plain the feminizing and orientalizing logic of the opposition to the arabesque when he glosses that these German scholars "condemn [it] precisely because it cannot be subsumed under the structuring principle of rational thought and philosophical language."[50] The arabesque could enter into European aesthetic discourse only if it could be drawn into a Western model of aesthetic value, and this is exactly what happened with Friedrich Schlegel's rehabilitation of the term *arabesque* to indicate a movement of the parergon into the ergon, an ironic and reflexive principle of poetry.[51] Winfried Minninghaus argues that the arabesque emerged at a crucial point for German aesthetics, with Goethe's "On the Arabesque" in 1788 moving the debate from interior design to philosophy. Thus she

FIGURE 31 A column in the Alhambra exemplifies the pattern forms and the unending qualities of the Islamic arabesque. (Photograph by Yves Remedios; Creative Commons Attribution 2.0 Generic license)

points out that "the spreading of the arabesque through various fields and disciplines is both temporally and in essence coextensive with the foundation of modern aesthetics in Kant's *Critique of Judgment* and in early Romantic poetics."[52] The intricacies of the debate are beyond the scope of this study, but it is suggestive that the arabesque emerged into European aesthetics at such a crucial moment, placing an ambivalence about decorative form at the heart of discourse on value and beauty.

Modern appropriation of the Islamic arabesque continued the same demand that it be configured within a Western model of aesthetic value. In a mode similar to orientalism and chinoiserie, Islamic art became increasingly popular in late-nineteenth-century Europe. The first scholarly study of it, in French, came in 1877, and in 1910 a highly influential exhibition of Islamic art was mounted in Munich.[53] Laura Marks has traced this influence, finding that "undoubtedly the many techniques of abstraction, algorithmic construction, tactile surface qualities, meditative repetition and other qualities found in various Islamic arts influenced the rise of Western modernism."[54] A major study of the influence of Islamic ornament on Euro-American modernism came out of the 2001 "Ornament and Abstraction" exhibition in Basel. The catalog traces a history of Western ornament from Otto Runge through Henry van de Velde and from art nouveau to modernist abstraction. Van de Velde— Adolf Loos's bête noire—called for a "new ornament" using a "pure arabesque," and this pretty use of the arabesque was part of modernism's rejection of earlier ornamental forms.[55] As Ernst Beyeler says, "In the 1920s and 1930s an artist would have been deeply insulted if his works were described as 'decorative,' probably because he wanted to avoid any association with salon painting and Art Nouveau. But after the breakthrough to abstraction it was soon no longer possible to manage without the forms of ornamentation."[56] And Brüderlin argues that categories of ornament moved from Islamic art to Western abstraction—the arabesque to organic artists such as Matisse and Pollock and the geometric to linear artists such as Mondrian.[57]

The "Ornament and Abstraction" catalog is not unaware of the geopolitical problems of its narrative. Viola Weigel writes of the Western imperialism that underlay the exhibition in Munich in 1910 and problematizes the notion of non-Western traditions as so many ideas to be plundered by modern art.[58] But this moment of self-reflection far from exhausts the political implications of the show, which ultimately limits Islamic ornament's significance to a particular trajectory of modernism. Art historian Jenny Anger critiques the exhibition's elision of gender as a constitutive question of the decorative and points out the patriarchal logic of folding Islamic art history into the form of the Western agonistic artist and revaluing the decorative by rescuing it from feminization.[59] Following this critique, I suggest that the arabesque is uniquely able to figure the intersection of gender and geography in aesthetic abstraction. The word *arabesque* was coined in the Italian Renaissance and then adopted by German aestheticians.[60] Thus although the arabesque form is Islamic, the term's perspective is European. Bound up in the histories of modern European thought, the arabesque nonetheless derives from an encounter with the East. A form alternately feminized and recuperated for patriarchal art, it figures both a sexual ambivalence and a geopolitical encounter.

The tango sequence in *Moulin Rouge* perfectly captures the aesthetic potential of such a form. Moving among three spaces—the tango dancers narrating a story of doomed love, Christian's anguish at Satine's rendez-vous with the Duke, and the scene of sexual violence that he cannot save her from—the scene appears to emphasize cross-cutting as its central formal mechanism. But just as the music draws equally from the emotions of Argentine tango and the Police's song "Roxanne," the visual track counterpoints its rhythmic editing with sinuous camera arabesques that follow both Christian's pacing and the bohemians' dancing. The tango provides a rich, expressive form for this movement: not only is it a dance traditionally composed of elegant curving movements of the body, but it also encodes geopolitical encounters in its history and contexts. The tango developed in the mixing of African slaves with poor Argentineans in the nineteenth century, a colonial history shared by many popular dances. But it also traveled to Paris in the early twentieth century, where, according to Clare Parfitt, it produced a new form of exoticized looking that meshes with cinema's orientalizing gaze.[61] In this scene, the tension between the camera's curving movements and the cuts between spaces formally stages the disparity in power between the prostitutes, bohemians, and narcoleptic Argentinean on one side and the rapacious Duke on the other.

I find the arabesque uniquely suited to expressing both East–West intersections and the gendered qualities of the curved and decorative line. Ella Shohat articulates the shifting status of the arabesque in her analysis of a 1939 *National Geographic* photograph of young Turkish women drawing a nude model in a life-drawing class. She sees the picture as "a site of syncretism between Greek mimesis and Islamic arabesque," celebrating the newfound liberation and modernity of Turkish women, instantiated in their ability to take part in Western art forms. The arabesque represents tradition, whereas representational art figures the same secular cultural modernity that allows the women Westernized gender roles. Changes in aesthetics map onto changes in global politics and feminism, but, as Shohat continues, things are not so simple: "In this strange rendezvous between 'East' and 'West,' realistic aesthetics signified modernity, while non-figurative art was implicitly cast as past times. Yet such an encounter generates some fascinating paradoxes. During the same period that the 'Orient' was learning realism, the 'Occident,' partly inspired by the non-West, was unlearning it."[62] In the move from traditional Islamic art to modern abstraction, the pretty arabesque is a way of figuring the decorative feminine that must be rejected for patriarchal value to be retained.

So what does this feminine, cross-cultural arabesque look like in cinema? A particularly vivid example, Marie Menken's *Arabesque for Kenneth Anger* (1961), emerges from another urban bohemia, this time New York's experimental film, art, and poetry scene of the 1950s and 1960s. *Moulin Rouge* evokes a history of mobile camera work as well as the bohemian avant-garde, and the trails of its historical reference suggest a constellation extending beyond those films it cites directly. Menken's film is shot at the Alhambra palace in Spain, exploring in feminine and lyric form the major expression of Islamic architecture in Europe. The film begins with shots of a pigeon flying into the sky in an arabesque curve. P. Adams Sitney says, "The spiraling flight of a pigeon among the rooftops of the Alhambra provides her with an initial rhythmical figure and a metaphor for her wildly eccentric camera movements."[63] The film continues by exploring the relationship between the arabesque patterns visible on the building's surface ornament and the mobile arabesques of the camera that swings through profilmic space. In some shots, Menken's camera follows architectural shapes closely, as when the camera tilts around an archway, retracing the archway's material line with the implicit one of the camera, mapping temporal movement onto scenic space. In other shots, the camera produces contrasting lines, as when it zigzags over a classical leaf and star arabesque pattern or when the movement is too rapid for the spectator to make out any pattern in the image and the cinematographic arabesque dominates. *Arabesque*'s exploration of camera movement and architectural object juxtaposes Islamic decorative form with the Western lyric form of the New American Cinema.

Melissa Ragona argues for the influence of Menken's characteristic arabesque camera work on the New American Cinema, citing Stan Brakhage's positive assessment of her "free, swinging, swooping handheld pans."[64] For Ragona, this camera style is a central quality of the personal, lyrical, and radically low-tech aesthetic of the postwar American avantgarde, and in Menken she finds an overlooked female instigator. Menken's work has often been read only in the context of that of her poet husband, Willard Maas, and even in the context of her fellow filmmakers she has been viewed as a minor and unimportant figure within the boys' club of the New American Cinema.[65] Where lyricism could signify a romantic seriousness in filmmakers such as Brakhage and Jonas Mekas, it bespoke only a diminutive sweetness or charm in Menken, according to the critics. The arabesque as a form of Islamic art provides a useful interlocutor for both of these contexts for Menken's film because they both speak at the intersection of abstraction and historical representation, women's embodied speech and silencing.

This example illustrates the centrality of gender for thinking the arabesque. The idea of a curved and elegant line is strongly associated with the female body, as in William Hogarth's famous lines of beauty and grace.[66] As Menken demonstrates, the abstraction of the arabesque can voice both the rhetoric of femininity and the material female body, yet without representing it directly. Her camera movements are pretty arabesques that are very much about the filmmaker's embodied point of view. Moreover, Menken's marginalization in the New American Cinema suggests how the feminine arabesque has been masculinized by modern avant-garde practice, just as the Islamic one was westernized and formed by patriarchal aesthetics in the eighteenth century and reformulated by modernism in the twentieth. We should pay close attention, therefore, to how and to what end the arabesque line figures the female body. Hogarth finds his line of grace perfected in the shape of whalebone stays, a classically patriarchal synecdoche for the restrained beautiful woman.[67] In a cinematic example, Jacques Rancière describes Pina's death in *Roma, città aperta / Rome, Open City* (Rossellini, 1945) in terms of the arabesque: "Never have the weight of a falling body and the lightness of grace been better joined than in this body whose gentle curve vanquishes from the outset all pain and disorder. This line that closes in on itself (it wasn't so long ago that Jacques Rivette turned to Matisse, the painter of swooping birds, to talk about arabesques) is the happiness of this image that condenses the relationships and tensions of the film without symbolizing them, without identifying them with something other than the interplay of black and white that defines the filmic image."[68] For Rancière, aesthetics here does not refuse meaning but creates it. He finds that the curve of Pina's fall produces at once "an ethical upsurge and an aesthetic trace," the arabesque speaking ethics through aesthetics, articulating meaning in the image without symbolization. This aim is surely laudable, yet we hesitate because, as with Hogarth's stays, this expression of grace comes at the expense of female bodily disfiguration, pain, and even death. What is at stake for women in the abstract potential of the arabesque?

We can address this question by considering the second main use of the term *arabesque*, which is a pose in classical dance. In another iteration of the graceful line, "the pose or body attitude called arabesque is executed in supporting the body on one leg while the other leg is held backward in the air."[69] In the words of the choreographer who first defined the pose, "Nothing can be more agreeable to the eye than those charming positions which we call arabesques."[70] The arabesque is charming and pleasing to the eye in a way that is repeatedly associated with the pretty. Moreover, although the classical dance developed the arabesque pose that is familiar today, an earlier form was influenced by painting and was formed by "a group of dancers in a harmonious and picturesque attitude on stage."[71] The arabesque is pictorial, frontal, developed to emphasize the elegant lines of neoclassical form as well as the femininity of the dancers' bodies. According to Francesca Falcone, the pictorial arabesque was a strongly compositional form, creating a balanced whole through the addition of props such as garlands, flowers, and crowns to the dancers' forms.[72] Like the pretty mise-en-scène of *Moulin Rouge*, the dance arabesque is highly composed, molding scenographic space out of props, decoration, and feminine movement. It similarly draws from non-European decorative principles not only in the impetus toward detailed props, but in the "intensive exchanges with the East" to which Falcone attributes the naming of the arabesque.[73]

The arabesque, therefore, is a highly feminized pose that binds femininity to the abstraction of the body. It is also a stopping of movement and hence in some ways the opposite to the idea of a mobile camera. In the body, an arabesque demands stillness (because a person cannot move very much on one leg), whereas in film it implies a multidirectional, potentially endless motion. The juxtaposition of implied movement and actual stillness as well as the contrast between elegance of line and difficulty of bodily extension have been interrogated by feminism, pertinently in Sally Potter's *Thriller* (1979). *Thriller* uses the arabesque pose to center its feminist critique of *La Bohème*'s familiar narrative of artistic bohemians and dead women. Mimi in *La Bohème*, like Satine in *Moulin Rouge* and, indeed, Pina in *Rome, Open City*, has to die for the story to work. The film contrasts still photographs from a performance of *La Bohème* with moving images of a different Mimi investigating her death and posing in a repeated arabesque. Corinn Columpar has described Potter's use of dance as a feminist deconstructive tool,[74] and in *Thriller* we find a materialist critique linked to a narrative one. Potter makes the spectator see how the arabesque form contorts the dancer's body, how her elegance is borne of pain, and, moreover, how this abstract line relates to the narrative of Mimi's pain and death, which are required for the romantic textual effect of *La Bohème*. Here, the arabesque's abstraction covers up its representational work, contorting the body to hide the patriarchal narrative that we might otherwise see.

However, this reading of the arabesque, accurate as it is, threatens to limit the form's potential. The ability to speak about gender through form is important for feminism, as E. Ann Kaplan's early account of *Thriller* makes clear.[75] For Kaplan, the second Mimi's arabesque both repeats and undoes the first Mimi's death; in other words, the abstract form offers a multivalent staging of feminine formation, as able to reverse as to reiterate the terms of beauty's oppression. And this multiplicity points to the pretty potential of the arabesque line to reveal the codings and structures of gender. The idea of the sinuous and excessively curved line as graceful and feminine and yet also contorted or meaningless sets the arabesque against Western classicism and realist representation. The arabesque refuses to represent in a natural way, and its arcuated form refuses straight lines and mimetic logic. Like other aspects of the pretty, it is associated with the feminine and the foreign. Feminist critique of the arabesque's significance in classical dance needs to be complicated by an engagement with the potential of the figure to speak from and about the position of the aesthetic other.

We can see this potential in a final example of the cinematic arabesque: Max Ophüls's famously sinuous camera work in *Lola Montès*. Even more than *Moulin Rouge*, *Lola Montès* has had an awkward relationship to critical and popular success. Made at tremendous expense in three different language versions, the film was, in Susan White's words, "both a terrific flop and a critical bone of contention when it came out in 1955."[76] Most critics viewed it as a failure, and Ophüls died soon after its completion. Its running time cut drastically in response to negative reactions, *Lola* has circulated in truncated versions for decades and was fully restored only in 2008. For all its failures, however, *Lola* was also named by Andrew Sarris as the best film ever made,[77] and if that judgment has not really sustained over the years, the film is nonetheless widely understood as a flawed classic. In other words, *Lola Montès* follows the reception pattern of many pretty films, which, no matter how feted their directors, seem to find it hard to fit into their supposed place in the film canon.

In another parallel to Baz Luhrmann, Max Ophüls is often character-ized as a decorative director, an auteur whose films might be beautiful but are suspected of overprivileging visual style. Mary Ann Doane says that "accusations against the emptiness of technique abound in Ophuls criticism," and this sense of faint praise resonates with the criticism of *Moulin Rouge*.[78] For example, Virginia Wright-Wexman says that Ophüls's style "combines lyrical movements of incandescent emotion with end-lessly repetitive patterns that only signify within the private space of memory, never as part of a larger historical reality."[79] According to this clearly anti-pretty logic, Ophüls's decorative qualities—note the endless pattern of the arabesque—signify a loss of history and a rejection of real meaning. But for critics who take Ophüls's pretty style seriously, mean-ing is to be found precisely in the arabesque form of his camera move-ments. For Chris Wisniewski, "his is a cinema of elegant, precise camera movement, where tracking shots reveal and negotiate complex chronolo-gies and social hierarchies, particularly as they relate to questions of gender and femininity."[80] In Riegl's terms, these camera movements are "tendril lines," the curves that circle around in the arabesque, support-ing and connecting the motifs.[81] It is this articulation of the camera's tendril lines to both visible objects and social relations that I want to consider in the context of *Moulin Rouge*.

Lola Montès is a key intertext for *Moulin Rouge*: both tell stories of fallen women whose ambitions extend beyond the limited freedoms of their historical situation and who end up as courtesans and showgirls, objects of specular and sexual exchange. Both films are set in debased theatrical spaces—the circus and the club—and both begin with a shot of a theater proscenium. *Lola's* curtains are not red, but they are deco-rated with rows of subframes, rectangular depictions of events from the story that redouble in *mise-en-abyme* to form an excess of scenographic space. And, most strikingly, *Moulin Rouge's* opening crane shot echoes a yet more excessive use of the mobile camera in *Lola*. After the opening of the proscenium curtains in *Lola*, a smooth camera movement slides first upward and then back and around to the left, drawing the spectator past the stage, its lights, and then through a gauntlet of jugglers in red dresses. Once it reaches a new "view" with the lines of performers centered, it be-gins to move back and forth, tracking the compere as he weaves between them. The camera's excessive movement (this is all one long take) plays against a similarly spectacular movement of people and objects in the frame. Once all the girls start juggling, a suspended crown rises and falls into the frame in the foreground, while in the background plates are being spun and snowflakes and other prop objects are rising and falling. As the ringmaster promises "the most sensational act of the century," the sensory space of the mise-en-scène is being overloaded with spectacular stuff. Finally, on the introduction of Lola's name, we cut.

The object supported by these tendril lines is Lola, who is brought onstage in a sparkly, shiny costume and then circled in a full 360-degree track by the camera (figure 32). Feminist critics have tied this formal mechanism to the structures of the gaze, whereby, as Kaja Silverman puts it, the film "quite literally circles around Lola-as-spectacle."[82] Lola is the object of all gazes, and for Silverman the film is a self-conscious deployment of Mulveyan modes of investigation and display. Lola is trapped in the circus as a public spectacle, and she is likewise pinned down by the camera that circles and exposes, forcing the spectator's reluctant complicity in her humiliation. On stage, Silverman argues, Lola "does not so much move as submit to movement," as we contrast her stillness with the huge apparatus of performance and camera movement that circles her.[83] The camera arabesque works to articulate Lola's imprisonment in the image with a structure quite as richly ambiguous as the deconstructive arabesque in *Thriller*. Just as in Potter's film, *Lola Montès* presents a female

FIGURE 32 *Lola Montès* (Ophüls, 1955)
Lola is circled constantly by the camera and trapped by objects in the mise-en-scène.

performer, onstage, who turns her place as spectacular object into an occasion for feminist revision. For Doane, the film interrogates the relationship of woman, image, and spectacle, whereas for White the impassive and reviled Lola is "the queerest of all Ophuls' characters—a veritable cipher of possible gendered and sexual identifications."[84] The arabesque tendril form, as Riegl points out, tends to work against nature.

Much of *Lola Montès* takes place in flashback, tracing the romantic adventures that have led to Lola's present-day display in the circus. Throughout the narrative, however, we see Lola trapped in the mise-en-scène, caught between the moving camera and her settings. There is a recurrence of complex architectural spaces with columns, caryatids, archways, and staircases, in relation to which Lola is often dwarfed. She is frequently filmed through screens—lace curtains or cast-iron grillwork placed between the camera and its supposed subject. Objects constantly protrude into the frame, demanding to be looked at—whether a cupid detail on a wall close to the camera, a chandelier hanging into the frame, or a rope swinging back and forth, crossing the frame in a theater set. In some shots, Lola is completely surrounded by decorative objects that threaten to overwhelm the frame. In an arabesque logic, there is no real distinction between ground and figure, tendril and blossom. Meaning happens through the movement of objects in the frame, and it is by no means certain that Lola is the most significant of these objects. As Wisniewski says, "These camera movements give Ophuls an opportunity to show off the extraordinary production design by Jean d'Eaubonne and to subvert the human element of his story. Given the flatness of her characterization and the loveliness of her physical presence, [actress Martine] Carol herself becomes another aspect of this spectacular mise-en-scène, and the camera, by ceaselessly following her in her movement through these elaborate spaces, comes to confine her within them, as much as it traces a literal and figurative rise and fall."[85] In other words, the film deemphasizes the human qualities of its protagonist, rejects classical psychologization, and instead constructs meaning out of space and things. We return to the world of the orientalist object, and Lola, like Satine, becomes an object among objects.

Both Lola and Satine perform on a trapeze, creating arabesques in the air, and when each woman falls, it signifies the fatality of the spectacular exchange in which she is trapped. Satine faints from consumption, the disease that will kill her by the end of the film, and Lola lives to continue falling, her death only deferred in the cruel logic of the circus. She ends the film literally caged, exchanging kisses for money in a scene that strips bare the logic of sexual commerce that has structured the narrative. In these harsh conclusions, we find that the arabesque movement and the orientalist object are not purely decorative, but the form in which these films articulate the troubling intersections of gender, consumer culture, and capitalism. If the arabesque encodes female suffering, it does so from the perspective of a pattern that speaks from outside the dominant modes of patriarchal and Western aesthetics.

I have been using the arabesque as a conceptual tool, a way of prizing the pretty away from engrained notions of meaningless decoration in order to enable a new model of formal analysis. The sinuous camera movements of *Moulin Rouge* map a feminized and transnational scenic space in exactly the same way that the Oriental objects in the mise-en-scène do. And because the arabesque is inherently abstract, it demands that we think about "pure" form as having the potential to activate critical discourses of both gender and geography. Annemarie Schimmel relates the arabesque to a kind of Islamic idealism, a sense of the "wonderful construction of the world" in which the image of the tendril always refers to the gardens of paradise.[86] In this view, the arabesque might refer to an enchanted world, relevant to the New American Cinema directors whose investment in the abstract has often been seen as having a spiritual or sublime dimension. John Whitney's *Arabesque* (1975) can be read this way, as indeed might Derek Jarman's more mystical films. But Menken's response to Kenneth Anger's masculinist aesthetic and the queer itineraries of *Lola Montès* and *Moulin Rouge* argue against such a depoliticized version of the curvilinear. The pretty certainly opens up the possibility of an aesthetic experience that is not wholly rational and meaningful in the sense that it refutes the limiting masculine rationality of *disegno*. But religious transcendence and a Kantian sublime are not the only ways to construct such an experience. Drawing from a critical engagement with romanticism, the quotidian yet enveloping experience of decorative art in the domestic space, and the complex development of the object in modernity, the arabesque extends an aesthetic category that abstracts, sensualizes, and scatters across the surface the tensions and pleasures of geopolitical being.

FIVE

AT THE CROSSROADS

Iconoclasm and the Anti-aesthetic in Postwar Film and Theory

THE POST–WORLD WAR II ERA SOLIDIFIED AND EXPANDED FILM culture's suspicion of the pretty. In the wake of Italian neorealism's assertion of uncomposed immediacy as the aesthetic mode ethically appropriate for the postwar world stage, its effects of artless visual contingency were increasingly adopted as signifiers of political radicality and communal self-determination.[1] The European and Asian new waves, Third Cinema, and later the new Hollywood put faith in an anti-aesthetic visual openness that required as a founding rhetorical gesture a negation of studio perfection, stultifying formalism, or bourgeois aesthetic pleasures. This gesture is repeated in postclassical film theory, which is often assumed to have overcome the problem of the aesthetic, but which in fact merely submerges its denigration of the decorative image in the language of ideology and form. The dominance of anti-aesthetic modes of thought in postwar film and cultural theories depends on an excluded pretty that nonetheless makes its presence felt in some of the period's most important cinemas. In European art film, composed and self-consciously stylish images make claims on the political and the cinematic, and in Latin America *beauty* becomes a key term for revolutionary cinema. This chapter seeks to shift the terms of debate for postwar film aesthetics, forcing the iconoclasm of Marxist-influenced film theory up against the unacknowl-edged and complex discourse on visual style elaborated by international cinemas.

Bringing suspicion of the decorative into the postwar era, Roland Barthes writes in *Mythologies* that he wants "to track down, in the decora-tive display of *what-goes-without-saying*, the ideological abuse which, in my view, is hidden there."[2] The decorative image here meshes with the veil of false consciousness—a smoothly self-evident surface that hides the inner workings of ideology. Although Barthes had a complex relation-ship to Marxism, this formulation perfectly encapsulates the engrained inclination of postwar leftist thought to associate the aesthetic image with ideological corruption. Thus a major strand of postwar Marxist cul-tural criticism aimed to problematize the entire category of aesthetics: Raymond Williams, for instance, claims that the idea of aesthetics de-rives from an alienating division between artist and artisan and that aesthetic theory can work only to separate art from its social processes.[3] Where cultural studies emerges precisely in opposition to aesthetics as a field, postclassical film theory rather transforms the aesthetic into a privi-leged site of contestation. In contrast to classical theory, post-1968 cine-Marxism deliberately refuses the language of beauty but nonetheless rig-orously engages cinematic form and style. Its aim is to replace aesthetic judgment with an analysis of ideology, and the pretty image therefore becomes a central object of attack.

So striking is this assault on the aesthetic image as a synecdoche for ideology itself that if there is an originary impetus for this book, an *ur-sprung* of my thinking about the pretty, it is probably to be found in the anti-aesthetic claims of this postclassical film theory. The lionization of countercinematic, avant-gardist, or sometimes art cinematic forms that is common in post-1968 Marxist-derived scholarship also installs a regime of aesthetico-political judgment that comes to dominate modern film stud-ies. In this influential theoretical field, an image that is ugly, sparse, or imperfect performs a formal critique of ideology that is in many accounts precluded or actively undermined by spectacle, beauty, or visual plea-sure. This structure is vibrantly staged in the debate over Jean-Luc Go-dard's *Vent d'Est* (1970), in which, as James Roy MacBean describes it, critics argued over "whether or not *Vent d'Est* can be considered a 'visu-ally beautiful film' and whether or not 'visual beauty' is an attribute or a liability given Godard's revolutionary aims."[4] Godard himself says that "if

Vent d'Est succeeds at all, it's because it isn't beautifully made at all."[5] However, in an assessment illustrative of post-1968 Marxist film discourse, MacBean finds the "lush colour" in the film to be questionable but defends Godard's use of beauty as a self-reflexive critique of bourgeois aesthetic values.[6] Thus only in speaking against itself can the colorful or well-made image be permissible.

For Godard and MacBean, beauty is a technique of ideology, creating only false realities, and this chapter charts this intersection of ideology theory with particular aesthetic values. However, there is another factor at stake in both *Vent d'Est* and postclassical cine-Marxism, and that is the relationship of Latin American to European Marxists—or, to put it another way, of Third Cinema to art cinema. *Vent d'Est* narrativizes this encounter by casting Glauber Rocha as a figure at a crossroads, pointing out alternative paths to revolution through formal experiment or Third World aesthetics (figure 33). After the film was completed, Rocha criticized

FIGURE 33 *Vent d'Est* (Godard / Gorin / Dziga Vertov Group, 1970)
Glauber Rocha stands at the crossroads between European Marxist countercinema and Latin American Third Cinema aesthetics.

Godard for trying to destroy aesthetics, seeing Godard's emphasis on formal experiment as evidence of a bankrupt European experience of politics and arguing that only Third World filmmakers retained a positive faith in art and could create a genuinely new cinema.[7] MacBean has little time for Rocha, though, suggesting implausibly that he wanted to make bourgeois films about revolution. In this controversy in miniature, however, we find the historical nexus of Marxist criticism, geopolitics, and film form that this chapter explores.

The first section investigates Euro-American Marxist film criticism's opposition of ideological critique to the aesthetic image, foregrounding both the iconophobia at the heart of postclassical film theory and the contradiction the theory encounters in reconciling this rejection of the image with a determining interest in formal analysis. In the second section, this tension becomes fully visible in the discourse on 1960s and 1970s art cinema, where authorial style and a claim on the meaningful potential of the cinematic image demand a reading of visual composition and aesthetic form that anti-pretty theories simply cannot admit. Art cinema, I argue, thus has a central place in negotiating the problem of valuable form in postwar visual cultures. The final section of the chapter moves from Godard to Rocha, engaging the significant differences voiced by contemporaneous Latin American film theory on questions of beauty. Breaking away from the modernist inheritance of iconoclasm, this chapter proposes that the postclassical anti-aesthetic model is Eurocentric and that to understand the potential of the pretty we must read aesthetics geopolitically.

ICONOCLASM AFTER PLATO

I begin, though, by looping back to the Platonic denigration of the image, discussed in chapter 1 with regard to color, which underwrites in large measure the secondariness of the image in Marxist film theory.[8] In his *Symposium*, Plato separates the idea from the image, arguing that the (philosophical) idea is primary, whereas the (aesthetic) image is merely a sensible impression or copy. Moreover, he does not use the usual term *eikon* for "image" but instead chooses *eidolon*, a word that connotes false appearance, and adds to this connotation references to phantom, apparition, and even magic.[9] In the classical basis for our language of imagery, we already find both an explicit claim on the inferiority of the image for socially engaged thought and a strong implication of its propensity for trickery. As with the etymology of the term *pretty*, when one deviates from the nobility of masculine meaning, witchcraft is never far behind.

When Plato turns to the question of beauty, he has harsh words for those he calls sight-lovers (*philotheamones*), consumers of culture who privilege images, colors, and fine things over philosophical knowledge.[10] He wonders what it would mean "if it were given to man to gaze on beauty's very self—unsullied, unalloyed, and freed from the mortal taint that haunts the frailer loveliness of flesh and blood."[11] Purity in divine beauty is opposed to the mongrel and sullied images of the world. The image is closely related to the superficial and ungrounded, the sensual and trivial, and is opposed to the abstract truths of linguistic reason. In this model of the image, Plato lays the foundations for an iconoclasm that grounds much modern image theory. (As well as laying out clearly the terms of what becomes an influential structure of iconoclasm, this notion of the beautiful illustrates the problem of taxonomizing aesthetic categories at all. The process and desire for such categorization demands an exclusionary logic that is inherently troubling for a radical aesthetics. This is why I resist thinking of the pretty as a new aesthetic category to be added to the more familiar terms *beautiful, sublime,* and so on.)

Moreover, even though Plato's main interest is not aesthetics itself, his writing on beauty and knowledge formulates modes of discrimination that are highly suggestive for approaching the pretty. He distinguishes between what is fine (*kalos*) and what is merely pleasant (*hedone*).[12] His concept of *kalos* is not exactly equitable with beauty because it encompasses the morally good or admirable as much as the aesthetic and applies to social things rather than to just artworks. Nonetheless, in defining the beautiful in terms of the noble and the good, Plato constructs a corresponding secondary category of the pleasant, sensual, or charming. And if the pleasant seems to indicate the faint praise of prettiness *in nuce,* we also find in the Platonic image a strong sense of surface ornamentation as unnecessary and undesirable. Central to this critique is the idea of cosmetics (*kosmètikè*), in which the surface nature of the image determines its dissembling form and proves its inability to equal the good. This cosmetic, devious surface clearly has much in common with the dangerous power of the feminine. Jacqueline Lichtenstein writes that "Plato knew very well, too well surely, that ornament was never simply ornament, a supplement added to the thing, whose excesses could be avoided by control of its use. He thought of it rather as a principle of perversion that held the germ of all dissolution since it wiped out all the differences upon which philosophy established the authority of its realm."[13] The cosmetic here is not only a surface effect, an aesthetic choice to be condemned or ignored, but also a structural component of the image and one whose significance is its corrupting force. If Lichtenstein is correct, and I think she is, then Plato's aesthetics gave rise both to iconoclasm and to a long-standing critical aversion to the feminine, the colorful, and the surface in the aesthetics of the image.

This issue has been examined more rigorously in art history than in film studies. For instance, Arthur Danto has argued that Plato is at least honest in defining philosophy as superior to art, whereas later aestheticians more underhandedly used the structure of philosophical aesthetics to disparage art as a danger to philosophy. Moreover, Danto sees clearly the imbrication of the pretty in modern art's response to this problem: quoting Marcel Duchamp's assertion that "the danger to be avoided lies in aesthetic delectation," Danto says, "I owe to Duchamp the thought that from the perspective of art aesthetics is a danger, since from the perspective of philosophy art is a danger and aesthetics the agency for dealing with it. But then what should art be if it throws off the bondage to prettiness?"[14] Where prettiness puts art in bondage (an overdetermined term that I examine more closely in chapter 7), Danto presents Duchamp's rejection of aesthetic delectation as a gesture of liberation. Here, prettiness is installed as the primary problem of an aesthetic modernity that leads from Duchamp and the avant-garde to conceptualism and much of the anti-aesthetic thrust of postwar visual cultures.

In twentieth-century Marxist visual theory, the question of iconoclasm is a discursive constant. Writing in the late 1980s, W. J. T. Mitchell describes a "growing collection of iconoclastic polemics" in modern criticism, locating the source of this "rhetoric of iconoclasm" in interpretations of Karl Marx's description of ideology as a camera obscura, or false image.[15] Although Mitchell is careful to separate out vulgar Marxist ideas of false consciousness from more refined accounts of historical materialism, he traces a pejorative association of the image with what he calls "modern idolatry" from Walter Benjamin through Barthes to Susan Sontag and Bill Nichols.[16] The invocation of idolatry reminds us that iconoclasm also has a religious history, and the Judeo-Christian rejection of the image has had an equal influence, especially on constructing the false image as sexual. John Peters notes that "for the Hebrew prophets, the worship of idols is always figured as adultery, a wandering from the father-spouse, and for iconoclasts since, a similar rhetoric of sexual abomination persists in attacks on the image."[17] We see echoes of this rhetoric everywhere that Marxist critics address visuality, from Guy Debord's *Society of the Spectacle* to Fredric Jameson's dig at the visual as "essentially pornographic."[18] And as this word choice implies, even twentieth-century iconoclasm echoes its religious predecessors by figuring the false idol as feminine, fetishistic, and sexually perverse.

These examples illustrate the centrality of iconophobia to modern thought, even or indeed especially after aesthetics as such is forcefully expelled. If art history has a closer disciplinary connection to the complications of classical aesthetics, postwar film studies has not entirely ignored the philosophical inheritance of iconoclasm. Dudley Andrew points to Marxist and feminist film scholarship as iconoclastic and finds that "the Western tradition—consolidated and culminating in Hegel—maintains a tender but often patronizing affection for images as part of the prehistory of philosophy. Images seem to embody thought sensuously, immediately, and engagingly, but in a childish and uncritical manner."[19] Although Andrew's "image in dispute" has become an influential rubric for film studies, the iconophobia he flags has perhaps not yet received the attention it deserves. I argue that these echoes of Platonic and religious iconoclasm suffuse postclassical film theory, tethering visual austerity to radicality just as surely as the iconoclasts bonded it to philosophical and sexual purity. A structure develops in leftist film theory akin to the *disegno–colore* debates in painting, in which a problem with the image itself is transmogrified into a problem within images. Certain images are endowed with the potential to speak philosophically or socially, whereas other, lesser images represent the troublesome sensuality of the image itself. Even as Marxist-derived film theory rejects aesthetic valuation, it requires aesthetic judgment in order to make claims on the workings of ideology. Moreover, it needs a negative category of the deceptive pretty that can contain the problematic qualities of the image itself, albeit one rewritten in terms of political rather than aesthetic value.

IDEOLOGY AND APPEARANCE

In the degree zero of ideology critique, Jean-Luc Comolli and Jean Narboni's *Cahiers du Cinéma* manifesto "Cinema, Ideology, Criticism," we find a central association of bourgeois humanism with "depiction." Although the narrative economy of classical Hollywood is certainly at stake, the "whole conservative box of tricks" is summed up in terms of picturing—the process of rendering the world in images.[20] Comolli and Narboni's claim, like Georg Lukács's, is ostensibly on mimesis, the illusionism on which both commercial cinema and bourgeois ideology depend. Nonetheless, this claim contains within it an assumption about aesthetics, an implication of what kind of ideological work certain images might perform. Their canonical location in opposition to realism neatly illustrates how we cannot collapse the various anti-pretty positions onto one another: what is valued in anti-illusionism has little in common with what is valued by André Bazin or even Hugo Münsterberg. But if we bracket momentarily the evaluative binaries set up by these theories, we can discern their strange aesthetic proximity. According to ideology critique, the composed images of classical Hollywood link aesthetic smoothness to dominant discourse, and when outlining the ideological forms that political filmmakers might attempt to strip away, Comolli and Narboni cite, along with traditional narrative, an "emphasis on formal beauty."[21] Here, beauty is not a Kantian value but codes an excessive formalism, an overly pleasing construction that produces aesthetic drowsiness. This line of reasoning leads to these authors' famous taxonomy in which modernist countercinema such as *Vent d'Est* is taken as exemplary of cinema's potential for political critique.

It is important to note here that Comolli and Narboni's text does not make political critique dependent on a rejection of the aesthetic image. It merely demands that the political film work on the signifier as well as on the signified, and it goes on to assume that only modernist strategies of unpleasure can do this work. However, retaining a Marxist approach while attending to the work of the excluded, pretty image is quite possible. Indeed, we might read the tensions inevitably created by the Marxist rejection of the pretty in the enormous popularity of the category "e" film in general and Douglas Sirk's work in particular, despite Comolli and Narboni's spectacularly unsuccessful attempt to persuade their readers that this category was a minor one.[22] What emerges in the category "e" film is the crucial importance of thinking the image ideologically, and in both Marxist and feminist readings of Sirk's visual plenitude is precisely the site of critique. (In *All That Heaven Allows* [1955], Jane Wyman's characteristically American home is filled with Asian decorative objects, a

FIGURE 34 *All That Heaven Allows* (Sirk, 1955)
Asian decorative objects hint at domestic captivity as well as bourgeois style.

collection that pinpoints her bourgeois taste but also hints at her lack of access to feminine glamour or mobility [figure 34].) Sirk's highly constructed and color-saturated images are ideologically significant in these Marxist and feminist analyses precisely because he has no other way to speak; like his housewife protagonists, he is trapped in an American bourgeois prison. Sirk becomes the exceptional case because of his political background, as does Rainer Werner Fassbinder. But, as we shall see, the colorful and composed mise-en-scènes of other filmmakers are rarely so well received.

Marxist film theory is thus built on a structuring ambivalence: a claim on the work of the signifier should not a priori exclude any formal strategy, and yet the aesthetic discourse that silently props ideology critique demands exactly this gesture of exclusion. Comolli and Narboni rehearse this ambivalence, and their interlocutors have identified the problem of purity that lies within iconoclasm. Colin MacCabe sums up the logic of anti-aesthetic documentary: "If cinéma verité opposed Hollywood, this opposition was in terms of the effacement of style, where a pristine representation, an authentic relation between film and fact, was contaminated by arrangement and conscious intervention."[23] MacCabe opposes this faith in the truthfulness of vérité, of course, for its attempt to deny the work of mediation. What is striking, though, is his language, which forcefully condenses the rhetoric of sin, deception, and untruth that iconoclastic theory depends on. Film must be pristine (not sinful) and authentic (not false), and its pretty Hollywood other is arranged (by trickery or sophistry) and contaminated (by disease or sin, figuring ornament itself as a rash on the smooth white skin of representation's body). This brief assessment encompasses a whole corporeal lexicon of film aesthetics.

As Peter Wollen has pointed out with regard to Godard and, in particular, *Vent d'Est*, the post-1968 attack on narrative has its roots as much in a philosophy of the dissembling nature of appearances as in Marxist thought per se. What Wollen describes as "the impossibility of reading an essence from a phenomenal surface, of seeing a soul through and within a body or telling a lie from a truth,"[24] produces a slippage from the critique of realist narrative to a critique of the cinematic image as such. For Wollen, this claim both underlies and tends to contradict Godard's Marxism. The notion that realism produces the mystifications of bourgeois ideology creates a Marxist analysis of visual form, and yet the image must be capable of political labor for countercinema to be possible. For *Vent d'Est* to work as a political film, there must be a form of image that does not lie, a possibility that Godard's iconoclastic subtext would deny. The pretty is required to cover over this potential gap—a scapegoat image whose pleasurable excess of visibility stands in for the dissembling appearance and thus enables the countercinematic image, by contrast, to signify something other than its own nature.

Gertrud Koch articulates this idea in her discussion of mimesis and *Bilderverbot*, where she describes the secularized version of the Jewish *Bilderverbot* (prohibition of images) to be found in the Frankfurt School theorists.[25] Thus in *Negative Dialectics*, Theodor Adorno writes, "The materialist longing to grasp the thing aims at the opposite: it is only in the absence of images that the full object could be conceived. Such absence concurs with the theological ban on images. Materialism brought that ban into secular form by not permitting Utopia to be positively pictured; this is the substance of its negativity. At its most materialistic, materialism comes to agree with theology."[26] Koch argues that this structure is, paradoxically, what allows Adorno to find some positive value in cinema.

In her reading, the only way out for Marxist film theory after the damning negativity of Adorno's essay "The Culture Industry: Enlightenment as Mass Deception" (1944) is to foreclose on mimesis—that is, the image as a representational form. Alexander Kluge is her example of how this idea could enable a modernist film aesthetics. He describes the potential of montage, in which "a third image emerges which is latent in the cut and is not itself material." Koch affirms that, for Kluge, "the third image is the utopia which follows the *bilderverbot.*"[27] Thus for Kluge as for Godard, countercinema provides a model of the good image as the one that can somehow speak against the image itself.

Something similar happens in Stephen Heath's work, where both the image and aesthetics as categories are tied to bourgeois ideology, and thus his close analysis of film form finds little space for what I am calling "pretty images." Arguing against surface / depth models of ideology (and hence, of course, purportedly against the rhetoric of the deceptive surface), Heath says that "ideology is not a kind of cloud of ideas hanging over the economic base and which analysis can 'dispel' to reveal the coherent image of a simple truth."[28] This account is fairly basic, but what interests me is that in conjuring what ideology is not, Heath pointedly does not make the false surface an image, but a cloud, and it is the simple truth underneath that can be imaged. This model is set up to be rejected, and thus it places the image in the "wrong" place: this version of ideology cannot hold because the terms *simple*, *truth*, and *image* just do not belong together. Heath does not go so far as to say that the image *is* a deceptive surface, but the cloud metaphor oddly avoids disavowing that claim.

In a similar way, Heath does not explicitly reject aesthetics or the aesthetic image, but articulates the field only in negative contrast to ideological critique. Considering film in its specificity "does not entail pulling film as specific signifying practice towards some aesthetic idea of a pure cinematicity," as in Russian formalism, because this would be a way of avoiding ideology.[29] Heath's seminal essay "Narrative Space" examines the cohering work of classical narrative in terms of a Marxist critique of quattrocento perspective. Narration is apparently the mechanism at stake, but the essay has frequent recourse to spectacle as a mechanism of ideological centering. The imagistic quality of the image, its seductive visual power, is a recurring bad object. "Like fetishism," Heath writes, "narrative film is the structure of a *memory-spectacle*," and he later quotes Hélène Cixous's determination that "I look elsewhere and differently, there where there is no spectacle."[30] The concept of spectacle—here and elsewhere in postclassical film theory—defines this kind of image as exceeding its proper bounds, overtaking meaning and reason, as an oppressive operation of ideology and something to be escaped from. The spectacle is not coextensive with the pretty, but it figures an intersecting concept of an overly imagistic image that should be restrained, a bad image that helps turn the Platonic rejection of the image into a scapegoat category within the image. Even in Heath's deconstruction of surface / depth binaries, the cinematic image, it seems, can be understood *only* through the filter of this suspicion.

Heath does read the excessive image as productive in his textual analyses, though, and we see this apparent contradiction most clearly in "The Question Oshima." In this essay, Heath posits *Ai no corrida / Empire of the Senses* (Oshima, 1976) as a film that poses critical questions to cinema about "the articulation of the sexual, the political and the cinematic," a set of concerns that shares much with what I consider the potential of the pretty. He describes color in the film as a point of excess, a place in which the film invokes a purely aesthetic mode of political articulation: "No tease of erotic suspense: everything has been seen but there is something else to be seen, nothing, a more than seen . . . perhaps to be there as a colour (the red that makes the surface of the film, colour is always potentially in excess of 'the seen,' a threat to the 'objective' image and its clear subject)."[31] Formal excess—bright color here—works against dominant spectacle, breaking apart processes of suture, identification, and ideological coherence. But it can do so only by becoming something other than a visible image, something other than an aesthetic experience. This example demonstrates where a concept of the pretty might intervene differently in formal analysis, for Heath exactly gestures toward the work of the pretty in articulating the sexual, the political, and the cinematic: Nagisa Oshima's colors and the shapes and compositions of the image in *Empire of the Senses* articulate an erotics of power that radically confounds patriarchal reason. But because Heath has already excluded the pretty from the field of politics, he can connect the film's color only to a radical nothingness in excess of the seen. Thus to make an aesthetic, colorful image into a positive term, Heath has to remove it from the visible field altogether.

Comolli explicitly addresses this question in "Machines of the Visible," where he performs an ideological analysis of visuality, engaging the imbrication of Enlightenment subjectivity, light, and vision. Here, again, there is also an older rhetoric of vision at play. Discussing the "frenzy of the visible" at the end of the nineteenth century, he adopts an anti-spectacular logic, figuring the image as out of control and excessive. Realism is problematic for Comolli, but so, too, is the spectacular image that "fully gratifies the spectator's taste for delusion." Reiterating the idea of the dissembling image, he reminds us of its feminine wiles when he refers to visual spectacle as the "magic of the visible." The article concludes: "Yet it is also, of course, this structuring disillusion which offers the offensive strength of cinematic representation and allows it to work against the completing, reassuring, mystifying representations of ideology. It is that strength that is needed, and that work of disillusion, if cinematic representation is to do something other than pile visible on visible, if it is, in certain rare flashes, to produce in our sight the very blindness which is at the heart of the visible."[32] Like Heath and Godard, Comolli sees the anti-aesthetic or countercinematic as the ugly image capable of redeeming cinematic vision. Illusion is the category of ideological vision, and disillusion its repair; we must split apart the seductive surface, combat the rhetorical excess of visible piled on visible. We must slice, we must cut, we must reach the film body's blind, avisual core.

Comolli's attempt to excise the visual altogether and to locate cinematic value only beyond the surface of the image is, according to Martin Jay, part of a denigration of vision that stretches from classical to modern thought. For Jay, Christian iconoclasm is only one part of "a much wider antivisual discourse that extends beyond the boundaries of religious thought. This discourse . . . is a pervasive but generally ignored phenomenon of twentieth-century Western thought." His account addresses a somewhat different object of study than the pretty because Jay is interested in vision as a mode of understanding, not necessarily in the aesthetics of the image as such. Nonetheless, there is useful overlap between a rejection of vision and a rejection of certain types of image as too visual. Speaking of Comolli's frenzy of the visible, Jay finds that he "writes from within the antiocularcentric discourse we are examining in this study, so his generalizations may seem extreme."[33] To argue that cinema gains insight only when it reveals it own blindness is certainly a limit point, but the antivisual discourse that Jay finds in, for example, modern art theory finds close parallel in contemporaneous cinematic modernisms. Just as Marcel Duchamp becomes a key artist for the theorists of the journal *October*, so film theorists such as Comolli and Heath prefer the institutional critique of the avant-garde to the aesthetic practice of art cinema (which is compromised by its aestheticized visuality, just as high modernism is in art). Jay quotes Duchamp's assertion that he selected his ready-mades for their "visual indifference" and his claim that "one had to defend oneself against the 'look.'"[34] Like Joachín Jordá (whose Barcelona School had a distinct Dadaist component), Duchamp finds the aesthetic appeal of an object to be a danger against which one must guard.

However, if antivisual thought could be articulated to institutional critique, it was far from certain that such a discourse would guarantee a progressive ideology. Mikhail Iampolski argues that the anti-mimetic image culture in prerevolutionary Russia also saw cinema in Platonic terms. For him, "this is a fundamentally Platonic attitude characteristic of a pre-modern world: it is based on the quasi-religious conviction that the world has a meaning hidden behind the empty gaudiness of the visible, so that the visible world needs to be transcended in order to reach its truth."[35] This is exactly what Comolli thinks: the visual is gaudy, illusory, and empty, and yet he would presumably balk at any religious sense of transcendence and hidden meanings. The danger, therefore, in importing Platonic iconoclasm is that one can slide too easily into idealist modes of interpreting the visual. Indeed, the complexity of historical materialism often seems undercut in film theory by this reinsertion of a form of false consciousness in the bad surface of the aesthetic image. Some Marxist film theorists have taken on this exact problem, attempting explicitly to reconcile iconoclasm with a nuanced analysis of the cinematic image.

For example, Fredric Jameson considers the immolation of the house in Andrei Tarkovsky's *Nostalghia* (1983), seeking to reconcile the aesthetic appeal of the image of death with its emotional gravity:

> The image remains beautiful and false unless that Kantian disinterested viewer's body can be somehow tricked back inside of it, to lend it truth: an uncertain matter, which the "ban on graven images" was meant to solve, too simply and peremptorily, by removing the problem. If, however, film is given in advance and here to stay, then what arises for a Tarkovsky is the rather different, but no less delicate problem of the relationship between aesceticism and

visual pleasure, between a life-denying fascination with sacrifice and the wide-screen libido of a created world that gorges the eyes rather than putting them out.[36]

We can see here a recurrent Marxist rhetoric of the image as a libidinous excess of sensuality, gorging the eyes with a visual pleasure that is likened to gluttony. And yet Jameson also counterposes this model of feminized overenjoyment with a Kantian disinterest that raises its own problems: a lack of genuine engagement from a spectator who is unwilling to "pay the price" of experiencing historical suffering. He rejects the *Bilderverbot* as a supposed solution that actually just begs the question. We cannot just get rid of images: film is given in advance, and we must instead find a mode of aesthetics that takes the image into account. Jameson here sets out a key problematic for leftist film critics: how to reconcile a disdain for the image with analysis of cinematic images or, more productively, how to retain the philosophical inheritance of iconoclasm without limiting one's object of study to versions of the *Bilderverbot* (or its anti-aesthetic descendents). But why must we work so hard to retain iconoclastic concepts of the image, even at the expense of finding meaning in the capabilities of the cinematic? The concept of the pretty allows for a less constricted model of cinematic vision: by recognizing iconoclasm's legacy as fully bound up in the reproduction of dominant structures of power, the pretty names types of image with the potential to evoke countermeanings. Pretty images have the potential to speak politics in, rather than against, the cinematic. And if Marxist film theory has often foreclosed on this possibility, the cinemas that surrounded it insistently put the aesthetic image back into question. In the sections that follow, we will see this tension played out across the critical literature on 1960s and 1970s political and art cinemas.

ART CINEMA, CRITICISM, AND THE PRETTINESS DEBATE

As the filmic examples used by the theorists discussed in the previous section demonstrate, art cinema of the 1960s and 1970s provides a crucible for postclassical theorization of aesthetics and politics. Filmmakers such as Godard, Rocha, and Pier Paolo Pasolini played an active role in debating the ideological implications of film form, and film critics found in the work of Kluge, Oshima, and Tarkovsky a rich seam of textual practice that might counteract the hegemonic aesthetics of Hollywood. This is also a period in which many of the significant film journals were established, developing a progressive film culture in western Europe and the United States. These journals' emphasis on contemporary filmmaking helped focus critical debate on new practices so that the theoretical accounts addressed previously drew strongly from critical discourse on art cinema and countercinemas, European auteurs versus American cinemas (both New American Cinema and New Latin American Cinema), and the increasingly global reach of the film festival. Thus the period provides a unique imbrication of film production with criticism in which filmmakers and critics as well as the international audience for art cinema that developed after World War II sustained a highly self-conscious discourse on film aesthetics and politics from certainly an engaged, if not always radical, perspective.

This ferment of writing on new cinemas offers a productive place to look for the pretty for two reasons. First, we find in critical writing on art cinema something of a practical application of Marxist theory's disdain for the image. Cinema's anti-aesthetic finds a strong foundation in the discourse on postwar art cinema, where modernist aesthetic discrimination already has a strong toehold, and, in the wake of neorealism, the question of how to balance social engagement with aesthetic propriety becomes determining for leftist criticism. In the valorization of the postneorealist art film, visual asceticism often seems to be the mediator between humanistic realism and radical modernism. And yet art cinema also provides a space in which the aesthetic is valued, where the cinematic image itself, with all its expressive potential, is of central importance. Given art cinema's definitional interest in the artistic qualities of the medium, we might expect to find in its critical discourse a complicating rejection of modernist austerity. Directors such as Bernardo Bertolucci and Michelangelo Antonioni are canonical auteurs precisely because of their explorations of color, composition, and detail—features that seem entirely consonant with the pretty. We might think, for example, of the grass that Antonioni had painted the exact shade of green that he wanted in *Il deserto rosso / Red Desert* (1964) or the graphic construction of historical spaces in Bertolucci's *Il conformista / The Conformist* (1971). Cinematographers and production designers can become famous in art cinema because critics and audiences are invested in the surface qualities of the image. Thus art cinema criticism is also a useful place to look for the pretty because it promises to value it. Between anti-aesthetic austerity and the richly designed image, prettiness is at stake in art cinema and in the terms of its critical contestation.

The concept of art cinema prompts an anxiety about the competing claims of aesthetics and meaning. Thus, despite its inherent interest in the aesthetic qualities of film, art cinema is often described in terms of and even defined by anti-pretty language. Where the very critics who helped usher "art cinema" into existence via taste-making journals use the term *art cinema* or *art film*, they often do so in a derogatory way that pits aesthetic surface against meaningful depth. Nigel Andrews exemplifies this tendency in a *Monthly Film Bulletin* review of *Hrst plná vody / Adrift* (Kadár, 1969): "Despite all the eulogies that attended its showing in the States and at last year's London Film Festival, Ján Kadár's *Adrift* seems a disappointingly pretentious work, transparently determined to be an 'art film,' full of superficially ingenious linking of motifs and images (the river, the oil lamp) and some eloquent camera work (the sinuous lateral motion of the camera constantly evoking the movement of water), but remaining at centre hollow and lifeless."[37] For Andrews, being an art film is about pretension—a clichéd label but here given a specific rationale—in which the aesthetic surface stakes claim to a seriousness that it does not really possess. The surface is a Platonic false appearance, and the hollow, lifeless center returns to vitalist discourse through which the composed screen comes to signify the Loosian corpse. Describing this surface form in terms of eloquence evokes the sneaky persuasiveness of Asiatic rhetoric, and sinuous camera movement reminds us of the arabesque. In a familiar faint-praise structure, what is well done prompts suspicion of unwholesome trickery, a patina of aesthetic meaning that draws attention away from the missing "dramatic truth."

Andrews presents his critique in purely evaluative terms, but the sense of a tension between formal elaboration and ideological clarity is also often explicit in the film journals. In a 1962 issue of *Film Comment*, Edith Laurie reports on the Karlovy Vary International Film Festival:

> Most of the delegates find much to criticize in the pessimism, the decadence, the empty experiments with form in work by Resnais, Antonioni, Malle, and others, However, even in the hard-driving, anti-aesthetic arguments, there seems to be less rigidity. Brazilian delegate Walter de Silveira may say—"Abstract art is impossible in

a socialist country because it can't reflect the people"—but his statement sounds curiously dogmatic. Soviet director G. M. Kozintsaev strikes a truer tone. After paying tribute to Fellini and *La Dolce Vita*, he says: "But Cuba could not use the art being used by Fellini."[38]

Here, the politics of form is a keen object of discussion, and the intersection of global Marxist aesthetics with European art cinema provides a focus for thinking theory and praxis. The pretty is always implicitly at issue in this debate because the decadent or decorative style of Alain Resnais and Louis Malle might go too far. In this regard, it is perhaps a neat coincidence that, as Laurie tells us, the festival was held under the art nouveau glass ceiling of the Florentina building. Karlovy Vary is not so far from Adolf Loos's Vienna, and its heated debates on modern aesthetics and political art are overwritten on the architectural spaces of central Europe's 1920s modernisms.

Laurie continued to report on international film festivals for *Film Comment* through the 1960s, and at Venice in 1963 she cites Godard's claim that Roberto Rossellini is his favorite film director and Antonioni and Federico Fellini are his least favorites.[39] Describing contemporary cinema in terms of two camps articulates a central binary in the denigration of the art cinematic pretty: the good realist, pure, or austere film against the bad formalist, excessive, or decadent one. As we move across this critical terrain, some directors such as Antonioni will flip alarmingly from one camp to the other, depending on who is talking and when. It matters less that we track exactly who is in what category and more that we can use the process of categorization to focus our attention on what values are being upheld or dismissed. The same binary is in place in Italian film journals such as *Cinema Nuovo*, which address explicitly the political implications of style. Hence, Carlo Lizzani asks Pasolini whether historical films can avoid falling into either naturalism or decadence.[40] Neither option is positive for Lizzani, and there is a strong sense in the piece that he suspects Pasolini of both sins at once, but naturalism nonetheless carries a great deal more positive connotative weight than decadence. Lizzani thinks there must be another option, but the dilemma of inadequate realism or retrograde decoration, for him, still shapes the debate.

Whereas Italian directors such as Pasolini and Antonioni are evaluated differently depending on the context, praise for Rossellini is something of a constant in the field. Moving from neorealism to the stringency of his later work, he provides a way for art cinema criticism to articulate a shift from realist to modernist aesthetics without falling prey to decorative prettiness en route. Thus John Hughes in *Film Comment* describes the historical films as "didactic and severely beautiful," a formulation that neatly recuperates beauty as something serious and difficult—far from any sensual visual pleasures. Indeed, Hughes restates the difference between this beauty and a lesser prettiness by contrasting *Le prise de pouvoir de Louis XIV / The Rise of Louis XIV* (Rossellini, 1966) with Jean Renoir's *French Cancan* (1954). Both deploy "ravishing color pictorialism" and "prolix historical theatricality," but whereas Renoir's film is spectacular, Rossellini brings "terrifying objectivity" to his critique of spectacle.[41]

Valuation of austere beauty reminds us of the more overtly aesthetic concerns of classical film theory discussed in chapter 1, where beauty is a Kantian value, able to discriminate between true cinematicity and false glitter. Indeed, art films are one of the few places in postclassical cinema in which beauty can be proffered as a quality, and any such valuation of the aesthetic is almost always justified with a rhetoric of formal purity or truth. For example, just a year after his rejection of Antonioni, Godard had apparently gotten over his dislike and interviewed him for *Cahiers du Cinéma*. He asks whether Antonioni creates abstract compositions out of a pictorial spirit, and Antonioni responds rather that he attempts to stage reality in terms that are not realist, that begin not from life, but from things.[42] This exchange hints at a double bind that haunts the two filmmakers' conversation, in which the aesthetic material of film is of paramount importance, and yet there is a constant danger of sliding into aestheticism. A pictorial spirit is clearly not a good thing, and Antonioni does not take the bait. But he does give attention to line, shape, and color, explaining the abstract compositions and color design of *Red Desert*.

In a similar back-and-forth argument, Miklós Jancsó is praised in *Monthly Film Bulletin* for the "surprising and beautiful images" of *Még kér a nép / Red Psalm* (1972), but even with such an impeccably unpretty style Jancsó is susceptible to criticism for letting his aesthetic dominate. The same review that lauds the film's abstraction worries that "the medium risks eclipsing the message" and that the climactic tracking shot might be "just another gesture in a film made up of beautiful, yet crushingly formalised gestures."[43] In this context, beauty does not signify a positive value to be contrasted with an inferior prettiness but stands alone as an aesthetic disparagement. Although the word *pretty* appears relatively infrequently and almost always in a negative context, *beautiful* is such a common word that we must carefully parse its connotations in each utterance. In art cinema discourse, to describe a film as "beautiful" often hints at the backhanded compliment of Godard's pictorial spirit or the outright anxiety expressed by *Monthly Film Bulletin* about Jancsó's formalism. Critics may laud Antonioni's or Jancsó's distinctive styles or praise the "splendid beauty of the images," as a 1963 *Film Comment* article does of Luchino Visconti,[44] but even in such art cinematic approbation beauty is closely monitored.

If we examine the rhetoric on art cinema that emerged across some of the influential European and American film culture journals of the 1960s and 1970s, we discover a litany of anti-pretty concepts. Checking back in on *Vent d'Est*, the go-to text for rejections of the aesthetic, Joan Mellen's review approvingly singles out the scene in which the voice-over asks, "Where are we now?" and we cut to a makeup artist painting multicolored stripes onto the face of an actor.[45] What is wrong with contemporary cinema, as Mellen reads Godard, can be envisioned as a Platonic cosmetics, a deceptive act of painting on the surface and, worse, painting over the true skin of man. Moving forward in art historical reference, the Italian directors are consistently dismissed in the language of excessive painterly style. The picturesque appears in several negative reviews: *Zabriskie Point* (Antonioni, 1970) is dismissed as "a picturesque display of nihilism," and Fellini is described as having an "omnivorous appetite for the dramatic and the picturesque."[46] Fellini is also accused of decadence and, in another nod to art historical excess, of "baroque delirium." In case the relationship between such rich images and lack of meaning is unclear, this review of *Fellini–Satyricon* (Fellini, 1969) adds that "the first and most striking aspect of the film is its extraordinary visual power," but "much of this power is lost . . . in the sheer decadence of the imagery."[47]

Fellini is an obvious target for those critics ill disposed to excessive imagery, but the same language recurs across the critical discourse. In a 1963 article addressing the general state of non-Hollywood cinema, Marcel Marën complains of a "totally cinematized universe" in which filmmakers can automatically harness rhetoric and refinement in order to engage their audience in the spectacle: "Henceforth, it will suffice to assemble all the banalities and all the clichés, to blend in assorted out-of-date situations involving the most grotesque characters, and to dress the whole in color and noise in order that the critics nod in admiration, thus affirming that they are incapable of reflection and of escaping the spell."[48] Marën conjures in Platonic terms all that is wrong with the pretty spectacle. It is colorful and shouty in the manner of *poikiloi* or dazzle and like the *poikiloi* is a false glitter that prevents reflection. Moreover, the spell that is thus placed on the viewer implies both the deceptive lure of cosmetics and the sense of witchcraft carried in the pretty. That this sense of art cinematic deception gained scholarly influence can be demonstrated by comparing Marën's assessment with that of Thomas Guback, who writes in his 1969 industrial account of European cinema that "so many of the new international films border on dehumanization by brutalizing sensitivity, often deflecting attention from reality. They count on developing audience response with synthetic, machine-made images. Their shallowness and cardboard characters are camouflaged with dazzling colors, wide screens, and directorial slickness."[49] *Dazzle* and *surface impression* become key terms with which international film and in particular European art cinema are divided into good and bad groupings.

In the post-1968 years, this anti-pretty rhetoric solidifies into a more explicitly Marxist counterposing of the aesthetic image to political value. Philip Strick, reviewing *Zabriskie Point*, complains that the film places too much emphasis on the sensual and the surface:

> Even the steely-eyed Mrs. Eldridge Cleaver, conducting the debate as an authentic high priestess of revolution, is studiedly an object of admirable splendour, her ear-rings, eyelashes, jutting chin, and astonishing turban of hair infinitely more important than the words she utters. From the landscape of faces, Antonioni moves to the equally entrancing landscape of the city with its enormous glowing jungle of colours. . . . Antonioni never having been able to resist improving the appearance of his environment, one may suspect with considerable justification that a fair share of MGM's millions went on poster-paint, his artistry leaving his Marxism far behind.[50]

For Strick, the film's framing of Kathleen Cleaver's facial features and jewelry is of a piece with Antonioni's indulgent control over the objects in his mise-en-scène: an image constructed with artistry is in direct opposition to any Marxist critique. Thus, for Strick, the image of Cleaver provides a perfect example of form undoing content as Antonioni "re-turns repeatedly to the images Mrs. Cleaver would surely have preferred him to loathe."[51] It seems more likely to me that Cleaver would have loathed Strick's insidious primitivist metaphor in which she signifies as a splendid high priestess, her fetishized features (a turban of hair, no less!) part of a landscape that, of course, turns out to be a colorful jungle. We see here the twisting reversal of anti-pretty discourse in which the image of the black woman, despite herself, provides the troublesome ex-ample of too much image, too much decorative splendor for real politics to occur.

But if Antonioni falls afoul of the critics with the ill-received *Zabriskie Point*, it is Bertolucci's post-1968 films that produce the most sustained illustration of this critical response. Critics reviewing *The Conformist* and *Strategia del ragno / The Spider's Stratagem* (1970) repeatedly find the relationship of aesthetics to politics to be problematic. Bill Nichols, writ-ing on *The Conformist* in *Cineaste*, argues that "in fact, his artistry seems capable of absorbing the most intense emotions and stylizing them into patterns of consummate aesthetic design that, from a Marxist, world-transforming viewpoint, have a strangely self-enclosed feel about them." Like art nouveau, Bertolucci's stylizing style is overly enclosing (figure 35), and Nichols binds the artistry of art cinema to the interiority of the decorative so that the more the film elaborates a cohesive style, the less it can speak of the world. Nichols continues, "The complement to the film's political sentiment is the lyrical, enveloping style, source of its own plea-sure, creator of its own milieu. . . . It is a highly seductive operation and one that undercuts the film's political force."[52] Here, the gendering un-dercurrent of the critique surfaces, with the Platonic suspicion of the se-ductive image wedded to an account of the film's style as "enveloping" and the phrase "source of its own pleasure" presenting an almost stereo-typical evocation of Irigarayan femininity. The inward-looking, smother-ing aesthetic of *The Conformist*'s decorative compositions produces a fa-miliar anxiety around the pleasurable, feminine image.

Bertolucci's films fared no better in European journals. Jean-Pierre Oudart, analyzing in *Cahiers du Cinéma* the political and theoretical im-plications of the new European cinema, cites *The Conformist* as part of a retrograde category of film that draws on ideas of radical rupture but makes formal radicality into a mere aesthetic signature. Oudart accuses the film of having only "a semblance of political discourse," thus neatly

FIGURE 35 *Il conformista / The Conformist* (Bertolucci, 1971)
Stylized compositions produce a critical anxiety about the enveloping and seductive image.

expressing Marxist criticism's dependence on categories of false appearance.[53] And in *Cinema Nuovo*, Gianfranco Corbucci contrasts Bertolucci's appeal to fascination to the depth that would be found in a more mature vision of life.[54] Corbucci claims that in *The Spider's Stratagem*, Bertolucci constructs politics as an alibi that allows him to justify his interest in the purely personal. Instead of the detailed filling in of the social spaces (*tratteggio ambientale*) of fascism and antifascism that would mark a genuine political discourse, the film provides only an agreeableness (*gradevolezza*) that keeps attention on the surface and turns history into myth. This argument—that a pleasant or an agreeable aesthetic precludes historical critique—is one that recurs in much subsequent scholarship on historical films and, in particular, the more popular types of art film such as the heritage drama and the nostalgic melodrama.

What stands out here is the choice of *gradevolezza* as an aesthetic failing: pleasantness or agreeableness has a long history within hierarchies of aesthetic value. Plato's notion of the pleasant proposes it as a lesser form than the good, and Kant locates the agreeable as a secondary taste category, structurally excluded from the purity of the beautiful: "Aesthetic . . . judgements, are divisible into empirical and pure. The first are those by which agreeableness or disagreeableness, the second those by which beauty, is predicated of an object or its mode of representation. . . . A judgement of taste, therefore, is only pure so far as its determining ground is tainted with no merely empirical delight. But such a taint is always present where charm or emotion have a share in the judgement by which something is to be described as beautiful."[55] Charm and emotion are also removed from the ambit of aesthetic value in art films: the agreeable is a form of prettiness that must be excluded in order for regimes of value to emerge. Moreover, Corbucci directs us to think about larger aesthetic categories in his use of a painterly metaphor to express this problem. The term *tratteggio* means "drawing" or "hatching in," and later in his article on *The Spider's Stratagem* he compares Bertolucci's bright and naive color scheme with the work of primitivist painter Luciano Ligabue.[56] Thus, for art cinema's Marxist critics, line versus color is still at the root of representational politics.

Aestheticism—another word for "stylizing style"—thus emerges as a way to express the contradiction of pretty form and political content in Bertolucci. British critic Rosalind Delmar presents the problem as one of "visual self-indulgence," and in New York, Amos Vogel asks Bertolucci in an interview if he feels that aestheticism is always a bad thing.[57] Vogel is much more willing to grant a positivity to aestheticism than Bertolucci is (Bertolucci retreats rapidly from the term, evidently understanding only too well that it is a losing proposition for him), praising his filmmaking as having "a profound feeling for a tactile, sensuous, pictorial cinema of (radical) form, décor, texture, color and composition." But even with his eye for radical and poetic film form, Vogel sees in this structure a contradiction: "It is abundantly clear that Bertolucci's entire work is permeated by a profound, continuing and as yet unresolved tension between a luxuriant, vibrant aestheticism and a possibly artificial endeavor to simultaneously create a radical, politically committed cinema."[58] Vogel wants to value both aspects of the equation at once, but he finds it hard to do so. Leonard Quart rehearses this same structure in an article a few years later on *Novecento / 1900* (Bertolucci, 1976). After describing Bertolucci's style in terms of opulence and the baroque, Quart complains that "his sense of style and aesthetic form is so confident that at times it seems to exist independent of (sometimes even subverting) his moral and political vision." He continues, "In another director (e.g. Von Sternberg) Berto-lucci's aestheticism would provide little difficulty. But in a director who views *1900* as a film based on class dialectics and as a film which tries 'to give a face, many faces, to the word communism,' the exquisite sense of beauty causes problems." Here we see clearly mapped out a refusal to al-low the aesthetic any part in articulating politics. Moreover, Quart speci-fies, the "surfaces are too aesthetically beautiful," and the "voluptuous compositions distract from, or even jar with, his political perspective."[59] Quart's discomfort with *1900* draws the conclusion that was all along inherent in the leftist response to art cinema: politics is in direct contra-diction to the aesthetic image.

Ultimately, the pretty is perceived as positive in art cinema criticism only where it can be read as speaking against itself. *Monthly Film Bulletin* provides several instances of this rhetorical move, including one in refer-ence to *The Conformist*. Jan Dawson makes the case that the film's use of aesthetic images should not be read as prettiness, but as a critique of prettiness: "And what Bertolucci offers his audience—visually and, to some extent, viscerally—is a demonstration of how style, architectural and rhetorical, seduces intelligence." The image is still seductive but can be harnessed to render visible the political dangers of seduction. Style is here mobilized to warn against style. She concludes, "Far from undercut-ting the film's ironic indictment of attempted conformity, the set-pieces . . . bring home to the spectator through their very stylisation the danger of mistaking beauty for truth or shadow for substance."[60] In another twist-ing reversal, the film's tendency, in the eyes of leftist criticism, to privi-lege beauty over truth can be redeemed by attributing a self-conscious and perhaps self-flagellating quality to its shadowy invocation of beauty.

Whereas Bertolucci can be rehabilitated only by reading his aesthetics against the grain (and we might make a similar case for Visconti), Fass-binder offers a much clearer potential for an autocritique of the pretty. His mise-en-scène is so frequently framed as referential or ironic that there is less critical suspicion of his motives, and his images, although often beautifully composed, are too heavy, too excessive, too deliberately ugly to fall entirely into what most critics would view as the realm of the agreeable (figure 36). Thus Richard Combs calls Petra's world in *Die bit-teren Träner der Petra von Kant / The Bitter Tears of Petra von Kant* (Fass-binder, 1972) "a supremely stylised region" that is repudiated from within when the mundane intervenes "to give the lie to the whole baroque

FIGURE 36 *Die bitteren Tränen der Petra von Kant / The Bitter Tears of Petra von Kant*
(Fassbinder, 1972)
Rainer Werner Fassbinder's crowded frame is critically redeemed as a satirical uglification of
film décor.

edifice." Note that Fassbinder is just as baroque as the Italian directors,
but here "the lush textures of light and shadow emphasise both the opulence of the setting and the emotional deviance which relegates Marlene
to the dark corners of the room."[61] If the film is seen to be criticizing deviance and perversion, then the aesthetic figures associated with it are
acceptable. Reviewing *Angst essen Seele auf / Fear Eats the Soul* (Fassbinder,
1974), Combs spells out this structure: "Fassbinder in general uses décor
(like the plushness of the Douglas Sirk movies he admires) as so much
rich, encrusted detail to both characterise and satirise the stereotypes of
social milieux." Décor can be legitimately used to satirize its own social
meanings, but not to speak the truth directly. Thus Combs must offer
the caveat that "while Fassbinder shows off the tragi-comedy in florid
details and extravagant effects, he delineates its underlying mechanism
with utmost simplicity."[62] The baroque image is acceptable when it speaks
against itself in this way (it is just about okay: the words *florid* and *ex-*

travagant still suggest a slight moue of distaste), but to express the deep mechanisms of truth we need simplicity.

Fassbinder's uglification of art film aesthetics leads us to an important distinction in the critical demarcation of the pretty. Uncomposed or deliberately austere films propose an anti-aesthetic refusal of the image, but travel far enough in the other direction and excessively aesthetic films become ugly, camp, or deliberately transgressive. Fassbinder's heavy interiors crystallize his Marxist irony, and in an entirely different register Jack Smith's sensory overload threatens to annihilate rather than to engage the decorative image. The pretty is therefore not an exact fit for *excess* (a term with a crucial history in thinking film genre and politics) because it refers only to a certain level of aesthetic overload. Although the mise-en-scènes of Bertolucci (or Baz Luhrmann or Wong Kar-wai) are excessive in comparison with rigorous, naturalistic, or streamlined classical forms, they are carefully controlled. The pretty composition is not sublime or edgy; it, unlike an underground film, does not offend good taste. As in the much maligned heritage film, the pretty aesthetic ensures that not a thing is out of place. This complaint becomes commonplace in post-1970s European cinema—for instance, in Carlos Losilla's description of *La colmena / The Beehive* (Camus, 1982) as "a pretty [*bonito*] film, refined, pleasing [*agradable*] to the eye and to the ear even though it deals with the harshest subjects." Sally Faulkner challenges his dismissal of the film, but we see in Losilla's vocabulary a continuation of the terms used to undermine prettiness in the art films of the previous decades.[63]

This neatness presents an in-between aesthetic that is rejected on both sides—"prettiness" denotes a style that does not go far enough as much as it is describes one that goes too far. When a style does go too far, it get remasculinized: camp is too much to be taken straight, but therein lies its redemption. The same can be said of exploitation's reverse-macho charms. Going too far gets you back into the aesthetic and political good books. Thus the pretty is dismissed for its excessive style, but it is important that its critics separate this excess from any implications of radicality. This in-between style resonates somewhat with the despised taste category of the middlebrow but is not quite the same thing. Whereas the term *middlebrow* describes a fairly coherent body of accessible art films or "quality" popular films, appealing to a specific kind of audience, prettiness is to be found in films ranging from the avant-garde to art cinema to popular genres. Not a taste category in itself, it crystallizes the formation of taste regimes across the spectrum of cinematic forms. Art cinema is a particularly useful place to look for the effect of anti-pretty thinking precisely because it brings this question of style to the forefront, demanding that we value the sensory pleasures and artistic labor of its image. Outside the underground economy of aesthetic revulsion as much as the mainstream demand for invisible style, art cinema forces us to confront the consumption of aesthetic images as a fundamental cinematic activity. The debate around prettiness in art cinema thus foregrounds something that is otherwise hard to discern: that the problem of the aesthetic image is not a question of genre, but a grounding element of the cinematic.

THIRD CINEMA AND THE THEORY OF BEAUTY

If the issue of beautiful form is an implicit, if troublesome discourse in Euro-American criticism, it becomes an explicit and indeed central problematic in Latin American cine-Marxism. The Latin American theorists of Third Cinema have often been treated separately from post-1968 Marxist film theory in part because of the field's narrow North American and European perspective and in part because of the position that Mac-Bean exemplified at the beginning of this chapter. For many theorists oriented to European film history, Godard's countercinema provides the only possible form of political engagement, and the films of someone like Rocha are therefore illegible. Third Cinema theorists, by contrast, reject outright the avant-gardism of European political cinema as just another facet of Second Cinema, which is to say the bourgeois art cinema. Fernando Solanas and Octavio Getino's manifesto "Towards a Third Cinema" (1969) dismisses art cinema as merely the commodification of revolutionary fashions: "Virulence, nonconformism, plain rebelliousness, and discontent are just so many more products on the capitalist market; they are consumer goods. . . . Examples are . . . plays full of anger and avant-gardism which are noisily applauded by the ruling classes . . . and the cinema of 'challenge' and 'argument,' promoted by the distribution monopolies and launched by the big commercial outlets."[64] For them, art cinema might be radical in form and critical in content, but these effects are simply the permitted—and impotent—rebellions built into the capitalist market. Their refusal of art cinematic forms might seem to subtend an inevitable rejection of the pretty, and, indeed, we will see forcible anti-pretty arguments in Latin American theorists. However, in rejecting the conclusions of European cine-Marxism, the theorists of Third Cinema also permit the possibility of thinking politics and aesthetics differently.

At first glance, the commonalities between the European and Latin American versions of Marxist film theory are more striking than their differences. Most relevant to our purposes, the two are closely related in their understanding of the deceptive and dangerous image. Glauber Rocha writes, "We know—since we made those ugly, sad films, those screaming, desperate films in which reason has not always prevailed— that this hunger will not be assuaged by moderate government reforms and that the cloak of [T]echnicolor cannot hide, but rather only aggravates, its tumours."[65] The colorful image is a veil, hiding the diseased body underneath. This rhetoric returns to Loosian notions of bodily corruption, the pure and healthy body eaten from within (or without) by the cancer of ornament. Here, this aesthetic idea is linked to the political one of bourgeois progressivism, which papers over problems with superficial policies and distracting images. Solanas and Getino use the same rhetoric when they argue that "imperialism and capitalism, whether in the consumer society or in the neocolonialized country, veil everything behind a screen of images and appearances. The image of reality is more important than reality itself. It is a world peopled with fantasies and phantoms in which what is hideous is clothed in beauty, while beauty is disguised as the hideous."[66] Like the false woman, the image deceives with its clothing, its *veil*, and the critique of neocolonialism draws on a Debordian society of the spectacle, where the screen of appearances thwarts true social exchange. The image versus reality binary recapitulates not only Marxism's iconoclasm, but also the realist aesthetics of classical film theory: "The cinema of revolution is at the same time one of destruction and construction: destruction of the image that neocolonialism has created of itself and of us, and construction of a throbbing, living reality which recaptures truth in any of its expressions."[67] The desire to destroy the image and recapture truth in living reality rhymes neatly with Siegfried Kracauer or even Louis Delluc.

Julio García Espinosa, founder of the Instituto Cubano de Arte e Industria Cinematográficos and leading theorist of Cuban cinema (and therefore part of the institutional film culture in which *Soy Cuba / I Am Cuba* [Kalatozov, 1964], examined in chapter 6, was spurned), articulates a

rejection of technical perfection that has much in common with Comolli
and Narboni's ideological critique of dominant film style:

> Hollywood films are not only reactionary because of their content.
> They are reactionary above all because of their form and structure.
> Form is neither decoration nor ornament. . . . The form judges the
> theme, or the content, if you like. "This film is pompous (or reac-
> tionary), but it's so well done." It is not the quality that is important
> but the cultural instance which sustains it. Between Maria Antonieta
> Pons and Jeanne Moreau, between Fellini and Juan Orol, the most
> important thing is not the quality which separates them but the pos-
> sible cultural instance which could bring them together.[68]

As in Comolli and Jean Narboni's "Cinema, Ideology, Criticism," it does
not matter whether films are good or bad or whether their stories are
progressive or reactionary. What matters is the structure encoded in
dominant media, the "cultural instance" of capitalism. We note here that
García Espinosa uses the terms *decoration* and *ornament* in their architectural sense, as something superfluous to a built structure, and yet
there is a lingering association of the ornament with the superficial and
reactionary qualities of Hollywood film.

In his most influential article, "For an Imperfect Cinema," García Espinosa uses the idea of the perfect to pinpoint the exact suspicion of the
pretty in Latin American Marxism. Perfect cinema, whether Hollywood
or art film, is well made, composed, "masterful." It is, he suggests, "almost
always reactionary cinema." Such suspicion of the perfect image resonates
with the iconoclasm of cine-Marxism at large. In the place of this too composed, too pristine commercial cinema, García Espinosa proposes an
imperfect cinema, one that is "no longer interested in quality or technique."[69] And this investment in roughness, in working against the technical polish and complex formal mechanisms of first-world production,
repeats across the manifestoes of New Latin American Cinema. Rocha,
for example, says, "Wherever there is a film-maker prepared to stand up
against commercialism, exploitation, pornography and the tyranny of
technique, there is to be found the living spirit of Cinema Nôvo."[70] Perfection of technique, an investment in cinematic style, is for him equivalent to all that is bad in the image—tellingly, not only neocolonial and
capitalist exploitation, but also pornography. The perfect image, like the

pretty image, harbors anxieties about sexual perversion. García Espinosa is similarly resistant to style, arguing that "maximum austerity in forms of expression is not only a way of creating resistance to contemporary cinema, but it is also our own present way of making films."[71] Austerity in the image confronts plenitude, pitting righteous poverty against decadent richness. Metaphors of excess are folded into a materialist politics of production.

However, although the discourse on perfection performs some of the same work for Rocha and García Espinosa as the discourse on prettiness does for the European Marxists, the two are not exactly coextensive. Imperfection is not, for García Espinosa, a theory of the image as such, but a practical response to historical conditions. Imperfect cinema is necessary in the period of struggle, but this is part of what makes it imperfect. A true popular cinema, made by the people, would look quite different. So there is a slippage in the way that a well-formed style comes automatically to connote reaction for some of García Espinosa's readers in the same way that a rough documentary style connotes authenticity for some audiences of realism. As with Zwelethu Mthethwa's turn away from the monochromatic codes of documentary photography, the charitable gaze of postwar realisms is, if anything, more problematic than overly decorative composition. Style, in this respect, is not to be trusted as a simple marker of ideology, and although that lesson seems painfully obvious in the case of documentary roughness (every undergraduate knows this "authenticity" is cheaply bought), it remains unlearned with the composed mechanisms of the pretty. The complexity of imperfect cinema as an aesthetico-political concept exceeds any simple sense of aesthetically impoverished films as revolutionary.

Thus although anti-pretty rhetoric abounds in Third Cinema's demands for an imperfect cinema, an aesthetics of hunger, the Latin American theorists of the 1960s and 1970s also at the same time carve out a place for cinematic beauty in a way entirely foreign to European Marxists. García Espinosa, echoing Kant, calls art "one of mankind's 'impartial' or 'uncommitted' activities [una actividad desinteresada]."[72] Even in the midst of outlining a theory of revolutionary cinema, he is engaged in thinking the aesthetic. Indeed, the importance of cinema comes not from its potential for communication or national culture, but from its potential to reconfigure the aesthetic within the material and quotidian world. Arguing for an end to the false prestige of elite culture, he proposes that "we should understand from here on in that the body and the things of the body are also elegant, and that material life is beautiful as well. We should understand that, in fact, the soul is contained in the body just as the spirit is contained in material life, just as—to speak in strictly artistic terms—the essence is contained in the surface and the content in the form."[73] Beauty becomes a key term in constructing materialist culture, and surface form is defended against the false privileging of essence and content. This argument radically overturns the surface / depth model of the Platonic false image as well as the iconophobic turn in Marxism. Materialism, for García Espinosa, involves rediscovering the beauties of life's surface, not its elitist spiritual depths.

This engagement with the aesthetic as a space for revolutionary change is echoed by Solanas and Getino, who argue that the separation of "the privilege of beauty" from revolutionary politics is a misunderstanding and that beauty must have a role to play in political art.[74] Rejecting the conventional aesthetic values of European art cinema, or Second Cinema, they attempt to rethink the relationship of aesthetics and politics by advancing another beauty as a legitimate and indeed necessary mode of political art. Instead of the beauty that enforces relations of exploitation and oppression, they argue, there is an urgent need for culture, films, and beauty to "become *our culture, our films, and our sense of beauty.*"[75] Bolivian director and writer Jorge Sanjinés even more clearly expresses this notion of a different beauty, whose political potential derives from its cultural specificity, in a 1977 interview pointedly entitled "Political Cinema Must Not Abandon Its Interest in Beauty": "We reiterate that a beautiful film can be more revolutionarily effective, because it won't stay at the level of the pamphlet. A cinema like a gun, as the cinematic expression of a people without cinema, must be preoccupied with beauty because beauty is an indispensible element. For we are fighting for the beauty of our people, this beauty that imperialism today tries to destroy, to degrade, to overwhelm. . . . The fight for beauty is the fight for culture, it is the fight for revolution."[76] Rather than associating beauty with imperialism, Sanjinés situates the aesthetic as a locus for revolutionary resistance. The aesthetic, for Latin American film theorists, is not in opposition to the political but must be its mode of articulation.

Of course, as Solanas and Getino emphasize, political beauty must be carefully constructed. They caution that "ideas such as 'beauty in itself is revolutionary' and 'all new cinema is revolutionary' are idealistic aspirations that do not touch the neocolonial condition, since they continue to conceive of cinema, art, and beauty as universal abstractions and not as an integral part of the national process of decolonization."[77] They warn against the dangers of beauty, certainly, but they equally warn against assuming that New Latin American Cinema is revolutionary. The aesthetic does not have a privileged (or, rather, a deprivileged) position as the place whence error will likely come. What matters is concretizing the forms and techniques of any cinema in terms of history and geography. The locational integrity of any claim on beauty is what counts. Sanjinés expands this point in "Problems of Form and Content in Revolutionary Cinema," where he dismisses films that deploy beauty for its own sake, "with some revolutionary theme as its pretext."[78] There is a strong resemblance here to Comolli and Narboni's category "d" films, which "have an explicitly political content . . . but which do not effectively criticize the ideological system in which they are embedded because they unquestioningly adopt its language and its imagery."[79] For Sanjinés, these films reveal their dominant structure when they are showed to the people whom they take as their subject in that the people find nothing of value in them.

Despite linking an ideology critique of form for its own sake to a politics of the indigenous audience, however, Sanjinés is not so quick to foreclose on beauty, even beauty derived from Europe. As Dennis Hanlon has indicated, Sanjinés purposefully drew stylistic influence from canonical European art filmmakers such as Theo Angelopolous.[80] For Sanjinés, cinema's cross-cultural encounter is enabling rather than exoticizing, and formal techniques that mean one thing in a European context might take on more radical purposes for an indigenous audience. Writing for the journal *Cine Cubano*, Sanjinés makes an argument that the sequence shot (borrowed in part from Angelopolous and other European art film directors such as Jancsó) is better attuned to the worldview and storytelling traditions of his Aymara–Quechuan audiences. But unlike those European directors who view long takes and austerely distancing camera movements as anti-aesthetic techniques, he does not see this kind of operation as a "falling out" with beauty: "On the contrary. We are concerned in parallel to communicate the cultural vision of our people, and the film, in situating itself through those internal rhythms of our Andean culture, communicates its beauty."[81]

This sense of beauty as not only culturally specific but also political in its material forms provides an unexpected linkage between Sanjinés's

Andean aesthetic and the secondary qualities of the pretty within art discourse. Stating a case for beauty's dialectical value in his book *Teoría y práctica de un cine junto al pueblo*, he argues:

> Political cinema, to be effective, must not abandon its concern for beauty, because beauty, in revolutionary terms and in our understanding, must be a method and not an objective, just like the artist. The artist in a revolutionary society must be a means and not an end, and beauty should play the same role. Beauty should have the same function as it has in indigenous communities, where everyone has the capacity to create beautiful objects, each person makes cloth and this cloth, which serves them for clothing, is at the same time an artwork that expresses the spirituality of the community. And this is what we want, that our film represents another mode of spirituality and the conception of beauty of our people.[82]

The clothes woven by the Andean villagers are decorative rather than fine art: crafted and composed, designed with both pattern and function in mind. They are the type of artwork rejected by nineteenth-century aesthetic theory, by Loos's colonial modernism, and, in turn, by film theory. The colorful patterns of Andean textiles are worlds away from the sense that the pretty can speak only against itself, as it does in Sirkian melodrama. In the latter, the lovely surface bespeaks repression below, but the Andean cloth articulates its use-value and its cultural meaning in the beauty of its surface, with both aesthetic and material production available to all. Just as Rocha turned his back on Godard's films for lacking positive or constructive values, so Sanjinés rejects notions of beauty as deception, asserting that cinematic beauty can perform a significant communal function. Imperfection does not close off the possibility of beauty because poor cultures are nonetheless nourished at the quotidian level by beautiful things. In one move, Sanjinés accounts for the value of aesthetics in Third Cinema politics and more audaciously implies that the aesthetic is not only allowable, but definitional. The political film, like the Andean textile, is well made, decorative, and attractive, and the worldview it expresses merges political thought with aesthetic pleasure.

The trope of the Andean textile, of course, invokes the distinction between popular and mass culture that is most famously addressed in Max

Horkheimer and Theodor Adorno's *Dialectic of Enlightenment*.[83] And the popular is a key concept for Third Cinema theorists, who locate political art within the quotidian sphere of a genuinely popular culture. For García Espinosa, too, popular cinema precisely means a cinema in which the people are producers as well as consumers, and he opposes this model to the bourgeois aim of allowing wider entrance to the halls of elite culture. Thus "popular art preserved another even more important cultural characteristic: it is carried out as but another life activity. With cultivated art, the reverse is true; it is pursued as a unique, specific activity, as a personal achievement."[84] The mode of production in such popular art is a familiar topic for scholarship, but the decorative potential of artisanal production has not previously been addressed. Decorative art emphasizes craft and skill, beauty without auteurism, pleasing designs without the agonistic artist's oppressive perspective. By the most stringent standards of the Marxist popular, most instances of pretty film would be thrown out as bourgeois and elitist, but then again so might Sanjinés's or Solanas and Getino's distinctive films.

Although Sanjinés's commitment to indigenous cinema demands a more radical mode of production and distribution than most art cinema (or even Third Cinema) can attain, his theorization of cinematic beauty offers a more expansive way to think aesthetics and politics than many left-oriented theories allow. The figure of the Andean textile provokes comparisons with Abel Gance's woven film style and with the modernist discourse on art nouveau and decorative art. With the help of Latin American film theory, we can think the rhetoric of the decorative in parallel with the popular creation of beautiful objects (both "folk art" and interior décor). This move allows us to tease out a distinction between the beautiful and the pretty in Latin American cinema, even where the same word, *belleza*, is often used for both concepts. The aesthetic that Third Cinema theorists critique is the Eurocentric beauty that I have argued dominates cinema's aesthetic inheritance: a hierarchizing marker of patriarchal and colonial value conditioned by ideas of European purity and nobility. By contrast, the beauty that Sanjinés outlines is much closer to my concept of the pretty. Like the Bolivian textile, it is decorative, sensual, feminized in its valorization of everyday crafts over masculinist high art. Moreover, it is geographically distinct, trading the universalizing rhetoric of Western beauty for an investment in the materiality of place and space. Where Le Corbusier and Loos rejected unnecessary pattern in objects of everyday use, Sanjinés finds in these pretty patterns the expressive force of Andean communities.

This distinction has implications beyond New Latin American Cinema. Indeed, I would argue that only the Eurocentric inheritance of aesthetics in film theory has prevented Latin American accounts of beauty from finding a stronger influence in the field. To locate ideas of an indigenous pretty outside of the revolutionary context, we might turn to the artisanal side of the avant-garde, to the radical aspirations of microcinemas, and to the grassroots groups that form a symbiotic culture of makers and viewers. Naomi Uman's film *Leche* (1998), for instance, emphasizes the hand-made techniques of its own production in dialogue with the farming practices of the Mexican family with whom she lived while filming. Film that was hand processed in buckets depicts the making of tortillas by hand, and the two women's labor creates something both sensually pleasing and politically astute. Uman's work can be contrasted with the romanticist high-art aesthetics of a filmmaker such as Stan Brakhage, whose abstract and colorful films are certainly beautiful, but too wrapped up in the patriarchal fantasy of the agonistic male artist to be easily seen as pretty. Where Brakhage presents himself, alone, as masculine figure in a natural landscape and continues the woman-as-muse trope by filming his wife giving birth, Uman's films are communitarian, materialist, and feminist. *Leche* (and its sister film, *Mala leche* [1998]) traverses cultural spaces, demanding the filmmaker's participation and using the decorative aesthetics of hand-processed film to articulate women's labor and U.S.–Mexican relations. In her films, as in those of Sanjinés, it is cinema's ability to intervene materially in communities' life practices that situates a radical "beauty" outside the confines of Eurocentric aesthetic purity.

SIX

FORMS

Soy Cuba and Revolutionary Beauty

THE PERCEIVED INCOMMENSURABILITY OF PRETTINESS AND political radicality as well as the conflict of Latin American and European models of cinematic Marxism are given concrete shape in the difficult history of *Soy Cuba / I Am Cuba* (1964). The film was directed by Mikhail Kalatozov, cowritten by poet Yevgeny Yevtushenko, and shot by iconic director of photography Sergei Urusevsky, all of whom traveled to Cuba in 1961 and spent the best part of three years researching and producing a poetic account of the cusp of revolution. In a portmanteau structure of four separate stories, *Soy Cuba* builds toward the moment of revolution through the experiences of a prostitute in a Havana full of playboy Americans, the life of an impoverished sugarcane farmer who is about to lose his land, the brutal suppression of student protests, and the revolutionaries' movement from the mountains toward Havana. The first Cuban–Soviet coproduction, *Soy Cuba* was not popular upon release in those countries, was unseen in the capitalist world, and was largely forgotten until screenings in 1992 and 1993 at the Telluride and San Francisco international film festivals and a subsequent restoration and release on DVD supported by Martin Scorsese and Francis Ford Coppola. The film now has something of a cult reputation as a *film maudit*, misunderstood by its original audience, but also, in the words of popular critic Jonathan Rosenbaum, "undeniably monstrous and breathtakingly beautiful . . . a delirious, lyrical, epic piece of communist propaganda . . . simply too campy and grotesque to qualify as a 'masterpiece.'"[1] Rosenbaum's designation of committed cinema as propaganda speaks to a post-1989 critical milieu that is far from the leftist reception context of Jean-Luc Godard and Glauber Rocha, but it is also telling that for him it is a lyrical and grotesque beauty that leads to both aesthetic and political monstrosity. The phenomenon of the rediscovered film depended on its being both aesthetically stunning and, as a consequence, politically disastrous. In this chapter, I question this received wisdom that the film is a misbegotten monster, arguing that anti-pretty discourse has constrained our historical perspective. Reexamining the film's reception makes clear the geopolitical stakes of this misreading, and an attention to its articulation of decorative space enables us to read its revolutionary aesthetic anew. As far from Jorge Sanjinés's indigenous filmmaking as an intercontinental coproduction can be, *Soy Cuba* nonetheless weaves a revolutionary vision out of the cloth of beautiful cinematic form.

Soy o No Soy Cuba?

The idea of *Soy Cuba* as an oddity is enshrined in its Milestone re-release, which appeals to audiences with an array of positive reviews ("Spectacular! Visually stunning," "Exquisite," and "Dazzling" are among the pull-quotes), yet the back cover blurb describes the film as "an epic poem to Communist kitsch." Reviews praising the film's beauty are undercut with a belittling judgment of tastelessness, and even in the pull-quotes we might hear the negative connotations of *poikiloi* and Le Corbusier's "dazzle" as well as the Marxist suspicion of spectacle. The DVD back cover suggests that the film is sensorily exciting but lacks proper restraint. It is too extreme, both politically and aesthetically. This undermining impetus extends beyond the packaging. *The Siberian Mammoth* (Ferraz, 2005), a documentary on the film's production and history, is included in the DVD extras of *Soy Cuba* and perfectly sums up the faint-praise structure within which the film was rehabilitated. The documentary begins from the premise that the film was a complete failure in Cuba, and although it certainly interviews many of those involved who did not like it much, it also makes a number of unfounded assertions and rather one-sided critical assumptions. For instance, the voice-over narrates that "each photo and newsreel that Enrique [Pineda, the Cuban screenwriter] showed to Kalatozov and Urusevsky later became a new reality, idealized and completely stylized by the Soviets." Just like Rosenbaum, the documentary makers read style in opposition to truth and, moreover, attribute photographic truth value to the Cubans and distorting visuality to the Soviets. They later present as propagandist deception the fairly routine narrative film technique of postsynchronizing a singer's voice. For a documentary about a supposedly valuable text, *The Siberian Mammoth* is oddly determined to make its subject look bad.

But why consider this short documentary at all? The answer is that *The Siberian Mammoth* not only encapsulates the conventional wisdom on the film (after all, the DVD producers were the film's greatest advocates, and even they selected this highly partisan extra) but, since its inclusion on the DVD, has been cited by many scholars and critics as evidence of the film's unpopularity. Several articles on *Soy Cuba* refer to the *Mammoth*'s interviewees as proof that Cubans hated the film, and almost all cite its claim that the film played for only one week in Cuban cinemas. However, there is a problem here: this claim is not true. In fact, *Soy Cuba* played for two weeks in Havana alone and at several theaters.[2] Two weeks might not sound very different from one week, but the implication of the claim of a one-week run is that the film was disastrously unpopular and was pulled from theaters as soon as possible. In fact, Cuban film culture in the early 1960s was incredibly rich, and turnover was often rapid. Of the films playing in Havana alongside *Soy Cuba* in the first week of July 1964, the only ones still on screens a month later were the major international art films *Jungfrukällan / The Virgin Spring* (Bergman, 1960) and *Plein soleil / Purple Noon* (Clément, 1960) and popular hits such as *Pinocchio* (Disney, 1940). Other films such as *Crónica cubana* (Ulive, 1963), *Valčík pro milión / Vals para un millón* (Mach, 1960), and *Harakiri* (Kobayashi, 1962) played for between one and three weeks. Perhaps the film was publicized as such a major event that it failed to meet high expectations, but in the week of its Havana release one could also have gone to George Cukor's *Les Girls* (1957), Andrzej Wajda's *Lotna / Speed* (1959), Roman Polanski's *Nóz w wodzie / Knife in the Water* (1962), Kurt Maetzig's *Preludio 11* (1964), Mauro Bolognini's *La viaccia / The Lovemakers* (1961) with Jean Paul Belmondo and Claudia Cardinale, as well as several other new releases. If *Soy Cuba* underperformed, it did so in a highly

competitive market. Moreover, its two-week booking was a fair run—
not a notable success but not the abject failure that the documentary describes either.

The documentary's claim that Cubans hated *Soy Cuba* similarly vocal-
izes a critical and scholarly hegemony on this point. Michael Chanan
cites in his recent account of Cuban cinema Ugo Ulive's negative opinion
and then adds that "no one in Cuba thought much of these films [copro-
ductions with European Communist countries] either" (Ulive's own film
was competing for the same screens and seemingly performed poorly, so
he may not have been the most independent witness).[3] Rob Stone argues
that "Cubans responded to this film with great scepticism," but he cites
only Cecelia Lawless's reference to a single bad review as evidence that
contemporary Cuban journals rejected the film.[4] Lúcia Nagib, in an interesting article I address more fully later, cites the documentary as her
source on the film's unpopularity.[5] These claims raise red flags for me
because they seem to speak confidently of the film's reception without
offering much, if any, direct evidence of audience reaction and because
they jump too easily from what journalists and critics thought of the film
to whether audiences liked it. Moreover, scholars of Latin American cinema do not think very highly of the film, and there seems to be a slippage from the claim that contemporary Cuban commentators rejected it
to an assertion of the film's (lack of) quality and historical value. I want
to exert some pressure on this chain that moves so seamlessly from
claiming that Cuban critics hated *Soy Cuba* to projecting that audiences
must have therefore hated it, too, and finally to concluding that the film
is in fact aesthetically and politically worthless.

The first element in this hegemonic view of *Soy Cuba* is the contention that Cuban critics despised it from the beginning. Oddly, considering that this empirically verifiable claim is the easiest one to document,
none of the scholarly literature really spends any time in doing so. Most
of the writing on *Soy Cuba* simply cites prior scholarship so that the entire edifice, the common knowledge of its bad reception, is based almost
entirely on a single written review. The fact is, though, that the film received several highly positive reviews from both daily papers and magazines.[6] Josefina Ruiz, writing in the weekly *Verde Oliva*, calls it "a film of
the highest quality," working at "an exceptional standard" and offering
"an overwhelming visual beauty." Refuting what we shall see is a common criticism that the film failed to understand Cuba, Ruiz says that "for

the first time we have seen a real Cuban cinema that has paradoxically been produced by foreigners." She concludes with the categorical exhortation that nobody should miss it.[7] An equal enthusiasm can be found in the daily press. In *Hoy*, the influential critic Alejo Beltrán describes the film as "a real display . . . of cinematic creation," characterized by a "strong lyricism." He does find some elements to be less successful: the script, he says, has moments of melodrama and tackiness. However, he argues, its strengths in acting, its deployment of the poetic as a mode of analysis, and the cinematic qualities of its images outweigh these problems. Moreover, Beltrán makes a fascinating case for the film's aesthetic as working for its revolutionary aims rather than contradicting them. He suggests that *Soy Cuba* mobilizes a kind of *acercamiento* (closeness) instead of using Brechtian distanciation. The spectator is brought closer to the image in order to take part in the film's revolutionary analysis. Whereas the more familiar distanciation effect derives from theater, he argues, the makers of *Soy Cuba* looked to the specificity of cinema to create the same political spark through very different means. And in the manner of a *Variety* reviewer, Beltrán assesses the film's potential with audiences, confidently predicting that "its success in Cuba is guaranteed."[8]

Cine Cubano, the journal of the Cuban film establishment, did not include many film reviews in the postrevolutionary period. It did publish, however, a long interview with Urusevsky a few months before the film's release, the introduction of which describes the cinematographer as one of the best of the age, compliments his stylistic harmony and personal vision, and breathily advises that "Urusevsky is cinema."[9] It can legitimately be argued that all of this positivity came before the critics saw the film, and perhaps they changed their tune on Urusevsky at that point. The dismissive attitude of the head of the Instituto Cubano de Arte e Industria Cinematográficos shown in *The Siberian Mammoth* supports this interpretation, but I can find no direct evidence of this position in the pages of *Cine Cubano*. Moreover, what we find in Eduardo Mane's interview is far from a dismissal of Urusevsky's carefully composed and fluid images, his poetic use of light, and his overall belief in the plasticity of the image. These stylistic qualities were radically different from the formal needs of revolutionary Cuban cinema even in April 1964, when the interview was published, but Mane was apparently not so dogmatic about diverse approaches to film art. Nor was *Cine Cubano* opposed to the film the following year, when Mario Rodriguez Alemán included Kalatozov and Urusevsky, alongside Joris Ivens, Chris Marker, Armand Gattí, and Kurt Maetzig, in an overview of prestigious foreign filmmakers with whom Cuba had made coproductions. In this article, which celebrates the cross-cultural perspective of the coproduction, *Soy Cuba* is described as "a fresco of the heroic feats of the Cuban revolution."[10]

At the same time, although *Soy Cuba* was not released in Europe or the United States, Kalatozov was part of the international art cinema community. His earlier film *Letyat zhuravli / The Cranes Are Flying* (1957) had won the Palme d'Or at Cannes in 1958, and in early 1965 he sat on a jury with Satyajit Ray, Georges Sadoul, Lindsay Anderson, and Andrzej Wajda at the International Film Festival of India.[11] His next film, *Krasnaya palatka / The Red Tent* (1971), was coproduced with Italy and released in Paris.[12] Meanwhile, where *Soy Cuba* was seen, critical response was again enthusiastic. In a 1967 overview of recent Soviet cinema, Steven P. Hill in *Film Quarterly* describes it as "the most brilliant Soviet film since the 1920s," proposing that "Kalatozov and Urusevsky have . . . realized [Sergei] Eisenstein's dream, which he was trying for in his abortive Mexican film—to give an extremely dynamic, emotional, epic picture of the revolutionary struggle of oppressed Latin American masses."[13] Lauding the film's use of crane shots and wide-angle lenses, Hill links the film's formal complexity to an Eisensteinian politics of film form. I return later to both Beltrán's and Hill's specific analyses of *Soy Cuba*'s formal mechanisms, but for now I can conclude simply that in the 1960s the film was rather well received and took its place in an international conversation on Marxist cinema and art film.

Thus the idea that *Soy Cuba* was universally rejected by audiences and critics alike is untenable and not borne out by historical investigation. So what is at stake in the ubiquitous narrative that the film was a flop? I am not interested in performing a dramatic reversal to reveal that the film was actually hugely popular. Many people probably did not like it, and it certainly went against the grain of contemporary Cuban film aesthetics. Audiences apparently did not like *Soy Cuba* in the Soviet Union, where, according to Josephine Woll, viewers voted it among the twelve worst films of the year.[14] But why have scholars—and documentarians—presented such a one-sided, even hostile picture of a film that in fact prompted a range of critical responses? I focus on this question of criticism because I think it is key to unpacking the anti-pretty discourse on *Soy Cuba*. Those who repudiated the film did so from a strongly anti-aesthetic perspective, and more recent film scholarship's determination to see only the negative judgments is symptomatic of the domination of anti-pretty thinking in Latin American film historiography. Moreover, the hostility toward *Soy Cuba* reveals some significant details in the content of this anti-pretty logic. Here we find the second element of the hegemonic reading of the film: a closely woven connection between the wrong kind of aesthetically complex form and the wrong kind of political subject. In this discourse, geographical and sexual alterity become vectors of impropriety, in which a film's aesthetic surface can speak only of its misplaced and monstrous enunciative body. The preeminent example of this rhetoric is the one bad review that is the *only* primary source I have found referenced in any of the critical literature, and it is indeed instructive.[15] Less of a review than a rant, the hyperbolic rhetoric of "No *Soy Cuba*" tells us much about the film's perceived aesthetic threat. In order to unpack the aesthetic and political stakes of this threat and thus to make visible how a pretty reading can view the film differently, it is necessary to read "No *Soy Cuba*" closely.

Luis M. López's review in the weekly magazine *Bohemia* stands out for its vitriol as much as for its opinion. Written in highly intemperate language, the piece does not include any of the characteristic features of the review format. Unlike the reviews cited earlier, for instance, it does not assess the film's commercial potential at home or abroad, nor does it spend much time in weighing up the quality of each technical aspect of the production. Instead, the article angrily denounces the film at length. Calling it "intolerable" and "a monstrous and incredible deformation," López repeatedly frames his critique in a Marxist vocabulary of surface deception. He accuses the film of superficiality, indulgence, and affectation, repeating the critique of art cinema's artiness by referring to "this Dantesque and pretentious film." He explicitly links this overly artistic surface to a lack of truth and depth, deploring the film's false audacity and bluntly stating that "the representation is false."[16] Like the directors of *The Siberian Mammoth*, he conflates the aesthetic image with falsity, which is opposed to a presumed equation between anti-aesthetics and unvarnished truth.

For López, as for many critics influenced by the official aesthetic tenets of a certain brand of midcentury Communism, the problem with surface deception can be named as "formalism." In the review's opening sentence, he calls the film "a total defraudation, a spectacular artistic failure, enmired in a hallucinative and terrible formalism."[17] This critique resonates in the Soviet reception, in which the film journal *Iskusstvo Kino* accused the film of too much emphasis on aesthetics, an art for art's sake approach, and a problematic subjugation of content to form.[18] This problem of formalism is, of course, one of the main ways that Soviet cultural policy enforced socialist realism and challenged the avant-garde. The question of Soviet film policy and state intervention into cinematic practice demands to be understood in its national and regional specificity, but "formalism" as a Marxist bête noir did not develop in a vacuum. There are strong familial relationships among the prohibition of formalism in Communist cultural policy, its denigration in Marxist aesthetics, and left-oriented critiques of art cinematic form in the capitalist West. As Hill comments in reference to a film by another Georgian-born Soviet director, Sergei Paradjanov, "*Shadows* is one of the most unorthodox, colorful, 'formalistic' (in the West read 'arty'), religious-superstitious and sensual-erotic films ever made in the Soviet Union."[19] Films that emphasize form to a degree perceived as excessive are dubbed "arty" in the West and "formalist" in the Communist world, and in both cases the crime is the same. Art film is partly defined by its art, so even when it is lauded, its very definition holds within itself the strong possibility of too much form. For both López and *Iskusstvo Kino*, *Soy Cuba*'s pretty images exemplify art cinema gone wrong, but, more than this, they represent cinema gone wrong. The accusation of formalism is one of the myriad avatars of anti-pretty rejection, in which the image becomes too imagistic, too threatening in its plasticity.

López's repudiation of *Soy Cuba* goes beyond the Marxist rejection of the aesthetically excessive image, revealing in its heightened rhetoric the fantasmatic content of this monstrosity. The film is bad because it is too formalist, but it is too formalist in large measure because it is foreign. Many critics make a point of the novelty of Soviet filmmakers presenting a vision of Cuba: for López, as we see in his title, this representation from outside is a big problem. He adopts an anti-Soviet tone throughout the article, a projective vision of pretentious big-city Russians. López describes Yevtushenko ("without prior credit as a screenwriter," he snidely inserts) as declaiming his verses on the street corners of the big city in Moscow, surrounded by young people who admire the audacity of his concepts.[20] There is a bullying tone in this passage as it dismisses the poet as pretentious and appealing only to foolish youth. Moreover, his

image of Soviet culture as consisting of grand squares and poetic decla-
mation is every bit as exotic a fantasy as the tropical vision of Cuba that
he accuses the film of creating. The review goes on to let all of the Cuban
talent off the hook for the problems with the film, arguing that they either did work that did not make it into the film or, in the case of screenwriter Pineda, were simply not responsible. López wants to blame foreignness for what he dislikes in *Soy Cuba*: the film is bad because it is not
Cuban, not an authentic vision, and if its badness stems from its foreignness, then the Cubans involved must not have been responsible for anything. As a corollary, the audience will not like it because "our spectators,
who have seen a lot of film, intuit that this film's character is foreign to
us."[21] The notions of realist authenticity and the purity of the undecorated artwork are lashed to the authentic voice of the true nation. For
López, *Soy Cuba* is above all a foreign film, foreign to "us," coming from
abroad and therefore not real, authentic, or true.

The same attitude can be found in *The Siberian Mammoth*, where the
interviewees constantly repeat the complaint that the filmmakers present an incorrect image of Cuba. One member of the Cuban crew says
that the film's timing and rhythm are wrong, following a Soviet tempera-
ment rather than a Cuban one. The problem is not that the tempo is un-
pleasing or counterrevolutionary in some way, but simply that it is not
how *they* would have done it. The filmmakers failed to be Cuban; they
did not speak in an authentic native voice. And like López's view of Moscow, *Mammoth*'s assertion that Kalatozov created an exoticized and unre-
alistic vision of Cuba is vocalized through an egregious fantasy of the cold
and uptight Slav. The assertion that *Soy Cuba* produced an exoticized
representation of the Caribbean because its makers were *chilly Slavs* unable to truly experience *the passionate heat of Cuba* is so dissonant and
self-defeating that it would not be worth belaboring its inconsistency if
this view did not remain the dominant one on the film. Nagib cites the
documentary as evidence that *Soy Cuba* flopped because it was "mainly
the vision of foreigners," "a foreign vision of Cuba."[22] What we see in her
article is the domino effect of this originary fantasy of authenticity. She
is not at all invested in this critique, but the hegemonic force of the anti-
pretty discourse on *Soy Cuba* leads her to take the critique as read. Across
the history of the film's reception, foreign vision is linked to failure and
to lack of authentic expression. This view's dependence on an underlying
fantasy of the Slav forms another instance of the recursive exoticism that

I discussed in relation to Baz Luhrmann: Luhrmann is attacked for his orientalism, and Kalatozov is attacked for exoticism. In each case, films are rejected when they speak about elsewhere and do not use realist means so do so. But as López's excessive hostility toward the filmmakers' nationality shows, it is the one who condemns any attempt to speak about elsewhere who actually enforces a politically limiting rhetoric of nativist representational purity.

There is another fantasy at work in "No *Soy Cuba*" that resonates with the pretty's history of rejection. As with the Asiatic rhetoric abhorred by neoclassicist aesthetics, *Soy Cuba*'s formalism presents a sexual threat bundled with its geopolitical alterity. In the film's climactic revolutionary sequence on the steps of the university, a student activist is shot, and a dead dove visualizes this historical turning point figuratively (figure 37). The sequence first links the death of the activist, falling from a window, with the clandestine pamphlets he has been manufacturing that are swirling against the sky as they are released to the crowds below. Later, as the police shoot into the crowd, birds disperse, flocking against the sky in

FIGURE 37 *Soy Cuba / I Am Cuba* (Kalatozov, 1964)
Graphic composition foregrounds the dead dove as a revolutionary symbol.

a similar pattern. Activist Enrique finds a dead dove (shot arbitrarily, we infer) and holds it aloft, a metonym of the police violence that has just killed his comrade. Rallying behind him, the crowd advances down the steps, singing and linking arms. For López, this scene reveals the inadequacies of the film's antirealist form: "Frankly, here the dove didn't mobilize anyone, it was the rebellion, the emphasis on justice, the hatred of tyranny. In contrast to reality, the symbol becomes effeminate."[23] López evinces here a kind of vulgar Marxist claim on the materiality of the struggle as superior to any poetic or rhetorical trope, in which aesthetics can never hope to adequate reality. But the rhetoric of this claim frames the problem of reality versus symbolic representation or truth versus art in terms of masculinity versus effeminacy. As with Cicero's rejection of ornamental and effeminate detail, López finds the film body to be excessively ornamented and far from the ideal of forthright masculine form. For him, staging the dove as a meaningful object makes it too expressive; the affective transformation of the detail becomes an effeminate gesture. We see laid bare here the sexual and geopolitical fantasy that underwrites anti-pretty rhetoric, in which a film such as *Soy Cuba* cannot be politically or aesthetically valuable as long as its images are viewed as formally decorative and hence foreign and unmasculine.

This fantasmatic material continues to shape the critical discourse on *Soy Cuba*; indeed, I find López's article most fascinating for the canonical position it has been accorded as the only contemporary source on the film that scholars ever cite. It is hard not to conclude that this choice speaks volumes about the critics' agendas, not to mention the field's unconscious fantasies. Although few contemporary readers of the film are as vehement as López, the anti-pretty discourses of aesthetic purity and authentic truth continue in more recent scholarship to associate *Soy Cuba* with both "formalism" and a dangerously feminized foreignness.[24] Thus, for example, Paul Julian Smith critiques the film's aestheticization of poverty and reminds us that "from the first shot it is characterised not so much by ideology as by the 'formalism' of which Soviet director Mikhail Kalatozov . . . had been accused in his own country since the 30s."[25] Smith contextualizes the accusation of formalism, but he still appeals to Soviet-era interdictions on aesthetic decadence as a basis for evaluating antirealist film style. Other critics follow the same pattern: Augusto Martínez Torres and Manuel Pérez Estremera condemn the film's "exaggerated rhetoric," and Rob Stone goes further, arguing that "in each episode the politicized recreation of events is overwhelmed by a strident use of expressionist techniques that render the events as spectacle."[26] Politics is not only undermined but overwhelmed by the image: note the feminizing rhetoric of the image that supplants reason as well as the gendered overtones of a "strident" image (an adjective usually applied only to the woman too opinionated for patriarchal comfort). On the subject of foreignness, Michael Chanan argues that "the foreign visitors didn't do their homework properly—not even Yevtushenko, who was especially enthusiastic. Still, even he was unable to get beneath the skin and go beyond the traveler's image of the island that Soviet revolutionary poetry inherited from Mayakovsky's visit in the 1920s."[27] Chanan speaks more temperately than López, but he still sees the view from outside as superficial and a perspective that can at best be transcended. In each of these examples, rejecting the film's form as formalist dovetails with rejecting it as inauthentic: the visually expressive and the view from elsewhere are folded together as self-evident signifiers of failure.

REVOLUTIONARY CLOSENESS / TRANSNATIONAL DISTANCE

Focusing on the pretty allows us to read the beautiful image in *Soy Cuba* differently; where Third Cinema theorists propose a new form of beauty, *Soy Cuba* takes seriously the political potential of the aesthetic. Attending to this beauty is a transvaluative move that finds in the film's formalism a claim on revolutionary cinematicity and in its outsider perspective an aesthetics of the transnational. Above all, this is a film about spaces: the social spaces of the tourist hotel and the shantytown, the university and the sugarcane farm, the street and the mountains. *Soy Cuba* understands Cuban space as the prerequisite for revolution, but it is not interested in a nationalist representational politics. Rather, it mobilizes two other spaces in constellation with the Cuban profilmic: the filmmakers' foreign cultural reservoir and the screen's aesthetic surface. Urusevsky explained that the filmmakers decided not to attempt a novelistic representation of Cuba because, as foreigners, they could not aspire to reflect reality in psychological detail. Instead, they wanted to make a poem dedicated to Cuba, using not the detail of a novel, but some clear images that could penetrate into the imagination.[28] This distinction between the novelistic and the poetic stages a claim on the political value of nonrealist formal strategies. Instead of a realist discourse of endlessness, arbitrary happenstance, and life, poetry conjures a rhetoric of composition, condensation, and metaphor, a heightened use of the materials of cinematic expression. And unlike the antirealism of countercinema, it places the aesthetic at the center of meaning production. Moreover, Urusevsky claimed these modes of expression as especially apt for the cross-cultural encounter, where the tension between one place and another can be encoded as a productive function of enunciative form. The Soviet does not fail to speak as Cuba but rather speaks in relation to Cuba. Form— or "formalism," the bugbear of Marxist aesthetics—becomes in Soy Cuba the means to imagine an exuberant aesthetics of geopolitical transformation.

As Cine Cubano's interview with Urusevsky intimates, cinematography is a central feature of the film's aesthetic. Most critics refer to the film's camera work, with a typical newspaper review of the re-release describing "innovative camerawork . . . [f]ilmed in luscious black and white . . . sweeping languidly through the fields of sugar cane."[29] All these reviews mention the camera's complex mobility and especially the famous shot that moves down from the roof terrace of a hotel to the sun-bathers on the deck below and finally into the swimming pool, ending under water. The shot is indeed memorable, but all this technical virtuosity prompts in critics the faint-praise structure of the decorative and the feminizing rhetoric of lusciousness. But cinematography does more in Soy Cuba than provide bravura technical effects. Urusevsky tellingly spoke of his dislike of shooting that was not planned, saying that he could not imagine getting to a location and improvising.[30] For him, to articulate place is a work requiring choreography, a labor between camera and location that comes to fruition in visible style. He rejected the idea that improvisation somehow enables a profilmic truth, imminent in the place itself, to shine through. Urusevsky here gestures toward an aesthetic of compositional space in which prettiness is a signifier of engagement, of a truth teased out of intersecting visual perspectives rather than one assumed to inhere in the world itself. I want to think about cinematography as a feature of the pretty first in relation to framing and camera movement and second with regard to film stock and visual effects within the frame.

Although the long take that ends in the hotel swimming pool is the most famous camera movement in Soy Cuba, the film's most important shot arguably comes later. In the third, climactic story, a group of students and activists clash with the police around the iconic steps of Havana University. One of the young people, Enrique, is shot by the same policeman whose brutality we have already witnessed on more than one occasion. The mourning sequence that follows his death elaborates a revolutionary aesthetic that depends on both closeness and distance, on the material spaces of Cuba, and on the aesthetic spaces of the cinematic. Hill sees the film as Eisensteinian, and there is an obvious reference to *Bronenosets Potyomkin / Battleship Potemkin* (Eisenstein, 1925) in the location of the university steps. But more than an echo of past revolutionary cinema, the reference to Eisenstein bespeaks an insistence on the political potential of cinematic form. Hill points to *Potemkin*, *Stachka / Strike* (Eisenstein, 1925), and Kalatozov's own *Sol Svanetij / Salt for Svanetia* (1930) for their agitprop insistence on self-conscious form over safe socialist realism.[31] But where Eisensteinian form is often (reductively) understood primarily in terms of montage, *Soy Cuba* proposes the fluidity of the long take as a mechanism for revealing social relations. We can trace this effect through this sequence's mobile and elegant camera movement and its carefully highlighted optical point of view.

After Enrique's death, the next scene begins in a close-up of his face as his comrades pull a Cuban flag over it, then the camera pulls back and reframes the beginnings of a funeral procession. The mourners move through the space of the violent confrontation that we have just watched take place: library steps in the background, we move across ground soaked by water cannons and between burning cars. This lengthy take is curtailed by the church bells that signal a quick cut to a bell tower. The camera pans round each bell in turn as they ring and then looks out beyond the church. As the shot continues, we look vertiginously down to the ground, meeting back up with the funeral procession, which has now grown to quite a crowd (figure 38). The angle at this moment reminds the spectator forcibly of Soviet constructivism, in particular Alexander Rodchenko's photograph "Gathering for a Demonstration" (1928). The shot's composition draws attention to its own constructedness, a self-consciously aesthetic framing that evokes a history of revolutionary and avant-gardist art. But in this version of the image, it is the Cuban flag that draws the eye, directly framed by the high angle and centering the movement of bodies through the frame. The image speaks doubly: of the Soviet Union in the photographic reference of its spatial perspective and of Cuba in its architectural, human, and symbolic objects. Layering Cu-

FIGURE 38 *Soy Cuba*
The first high-angle shot of the funeral procession echoes Alexander Rodchenko and the photographic style of Soviet constructivism.

ban space over Russian space and the immediate history of the Cuban Revolution over the Soviet avant-garde of a generation ago posits an aesthetic and political lineage and points to the differences in time and place that have brought these filmmakers to this scene. In its palimpsestic reference, the shot thus visually encodes the Soviet–Cuban encounter that has brought it into being.

As the sequence continues, though, it is not the still composition of the image that draws our attention but its movement. We cut only occasionally, and the camera is constantly in motion. The next shot begins back at coffin level, surrounded by mourners. The camera tracks backward into the crowd and then cranes several stories up the side of a building as women on balconies throw flowers into the procession below. From roof height, we see a growing throng of mourners stream from all sides of an intersection. Next, the camera slides smoothly across the road (still several floors up), through a window, and into an internal courtyard where men are hard at work making cigars. They seem oblivious to the events in the street, but as the camera dollies forward, one man retrieves a Cuban flag from his desk, and it passes from hand to hand before the camera, until a group of workers unfurl it out of the window that we are fast approaching. For a moment, our view into the street is partially blocked by the waving flag, and then, seemingly impossibly, the camera surges over and past the flag, out of the building entirely, and floats down the street above the procession. Kalatozov and Urusevsky are famous for precisely this kind of bravura camera movement: a similar sequence in *The Cranes Are Flying*—this time in a story of separated lovers— is equally breathtaking. In the context of *Soy Cuba*, however, this impressive crane shot functions to render visible a particular configuration of social space and at the same time to tether sensory awe to a geopolitical poetics.

Across the duration of this shot, the physical spaces of Havana come into detailed view. As the camera outlines the architectural shapes of the city's old residential blocks, we notice cornicing, balconies, and filigree ironwork (figure 39). But this outline is not an inert one of architectural history, but a fascinated exploration of an awakening public space. Residents spill from every window and doorway, witnessing Enrique's death and forming a gathering force for revolutionary action. Like Marie Menken's *Arabesque for Kenneth Anger* (1961), made just a couple of years earlier, *Soy Cuba*'s cinematography employs an embodied camera that traces the shapes of architectural spaces, engendering an encounter between the filmmaker's location and movement, on the one hand, and the film's (physical and cinematic) place, on the other. In both films, a pretty aesthetics mediates this encounter and enables it to speak of geopolitics. For Menken, the patterns of Arabic architectural space promise a spiraling feminine refusal of Eurocentric art practice. For Kalatozov and Urusevsky, the object is more dispersed: the revolutionary imaginary of Cuba can come into visibility only in an alchemical distillation of its spatial energies. Views of women on their balconies, men in cigar factories, and students in the streets provide not just a visual account of revolutionary forces, but a performative mobilization of their spatial relationships. In the funeral sequence, the inheritance of the Soviet avant-garde touches momentarily against the public culture of Habana Vieja, prompting an aesthetics of popular movement. The camera synthesizes the crowd's physical motion and revolutionary emotion, even while it moves independently, an outsider viewing events from an impossibly labile vantage point.

FIGURE 39 *Soy Cuba*
In this long take, bravura camera movement links sensory awe to a close rendering of geopolitical spaces.

We can usefully think of this movement in terms of Beltrán's concept of *acercamiento* (closeness). Just as Brecht's distanciation is a way of staging the political as a relationship between performer and spectator, so *acercamiento* offers to reconfigure politics between the image and the spectator. The key difference is Beltrán's claim that distanciation does not work in cinema as it does in the theater and that in order to create political art the cinematic image must deploy closeness. In this sequence, the viewer is brought close to the action, but not in the classical sense of being offered the best and least obtrusive viewpoint or even in a postclassical sense of spectacular immersion. Instead, we feel moved—physically—by the camera as it lifts us, leads us vertiginously between buildings, and swoops us into open space. We see the funeral from here and now here and yet over here in a sensory transport that at once puts us in the place of the Cuban people and yet demands that we locate our experience elsewhere—in the aesthetic experience of pleasure in the plasticity of the image. Closeness is not identity, and just as Brecht aims to preclude the ideological effects of realist identification, so Kalatozov and Urusevsky's cinematography is more interested in the space between the spectator and the image than in aping an "authentic" Cuban perspective. Rather than distance, though, the film engages closeness to conjure a revolutionary aesthetics formed from the materiality of the cinematic image.

A comparison with Brechtian film aesthetics will allow us to get at the significance of visibility to this formal mechanism. Harun Farocki's *Nicht iöschbares Feuer / Inextinguishable Fire* (1969) uses distanciation to render visible the violent structures of capitalism, laying bare the system in which a Dow Chemical factory might as easily make napalm as vacuum cleaners. The film uses (German) actors reading the roles of American workers so that in place of visual realism we see the equally material but usually invisible logic of the military–industrial complex. Resolutely anti-aesthetic, *Inextinguishable Fire* teaches its viewers to see structures rather than images, making clear the connections between everyday factory workers and the war in Vietnam that they inadvertently and incrementally support. *Soy Cuba* is aesthetically entirely opposed to Farocki's film, but it stands in a dialectical relationship, not a polar opposition. Kalatozov, too, is interested in rendering visible the structuring forces of history, but to make us see how a revolution comes into being, his project is not to strip away the blinkering visuality of ideology, but to figure in image form the affective processes of political transformation. The movement of the camera through the American hotel in the film's first segment describes the sensual pleasures of the imperialist body, and the funeral sequence responds with an equally sensory—but now politicized—cathexis to the Cuban revolutionary body. The camera's exhilarating movements work to make revolution visible, which is to say desirable, attractive, and lovable. For Beltrán, *acercamiento* is more suited to cinema precisely because of the affective draw of the filmed image, and *Soy Cuba* puts that desire for closeness to work to animate the aesthetic potential of political transformation.

In addition to camera mobility, *Soy Cuba* uses highly aestheticized black-and-white cinematography in which film stock, composition, and visual effects elaborate a pretty visual style. Perhaps the most striking element of this formalist form is the use of infrared film stock in several sequences. Urusevsky pointed to the infrared film as a part of his idea of a poetic version of Cuba that could be formally meaningful rather than mimetically authentic.[32] In the story of Pedro the farmer, infrared makes the sugarcane fields stand out in bright whites against a dark sky (figure 40). The monochrome palette becomes unexpected, rich, and vibrant. Unlike the shiny contrast of film noir lighting, for example, the effect of infrared seems internal to the objects filmed. Things glow. A dialectical tension is forged between the profilmic objects in the landscape and the cinematographic, the materiality of the special film stock that draws this effect out of the world. Mimetic realism is abandoned in favor of a decorative realism: the object world can speak differently when it speaks aesthetically.

The visual effect of infrared film on sugarcane fields ties a pretty aesthetic to political allegory. The sugarcane is central to Pedro's life, and the infrared makes it visually central also. The spectator can see as Pedro sees—or, rather, can see social relations made visible. Pedro does not own the land, having signed a contract with the landowner that he could not read. He has worked the fields for years, however, first with his wife

FIGURE 40 *Soy Cuba*
Infrared film stock creates the dramatic effect of bright white sugarcane against a dark sky, using light outside the visible spectrum to figure invisible social relations.

and then, after her death, with his son and daughter. The crop, he tells the children, represents a lot of money. One day Señor Acosta, the landowner, comes to tell Pedro that he has sold the land to United Fruit and that Pedro no longer has any right to his sugarcane crop or even to his house. Sugarcane is the guarantor of Pedro's place in the world, and when Acosta tells him that it has been sold, Pedro becomes literally homeless and worthless. In an act of desperation and refusal, he burns down his fields. The burning of the sugarcane is a political act staged as an aesthetic one, but Pedro's destructive spectacle repeats within the narrative the decorative logic that the infrared cinematography has already established. Realism, for *Soy Cuba*, can articulate only the rationality of Acosta's ownership, the writing in the contract that Pedro had to sign whether he could read it or not. To see through capitalist rationality, one must see more than the visual protocols of realism. Infrared film stock precisely does see more: it responds to light beyond the visible spectrum and thus produces an image outside of what is normally part of human vision. *Soy Cuba* exploits this quality of light to make visible the growing desire for revolution, figuring powerful social forces in aesthetic form. Acosta can see only the legal ownership of the land, its written documentation, but *Soy Cuba* visualizes the affective identification with Cuban space that is raised alongside the sugarcane. Infrared here effects a Benjaminian politicization of aesthetics not as a refusal of the aesthetic image, an anti-aesthetic iconophobia, but as an articulation of political relations in wholly cinematic form.

The sugarcane segment expands on infrared film's antirealist visuality throughout, adding camera and editing effects to its aesthetic expression of revolution's affective roots. Near the beginning of the story is a sequence relating Pedro's memories of the farm, his wife, and his children. After an idyllic few shots of Pedro as a young man, walking in the fields with a woman, there is a montage of their wedding and young family, followed by her death and a scene of an older Pedro signing the fateful contract with a thumbprint. Narratively the sequence is expository, but visually it creates a trancelike effect by using a slight slow motion and by being shot through glass with water running past the lens. The effect is blurry and attenuated, the image legible but precarious, constantly melting toward abstraction. The water effect blurs our vision, but it also visualizes as equal parts beautiful and nightmarish a process that in real time was mystified to its actors. Later in the story, a very different distortion of the image emerges. After Acosta tells Pedro that he is homeless, Pedro charges blindly into the sugarcane, scything it haphazardly in an emotional daze. Now the camera moves rapidly, and quick, rhythmic cutting locates the spectator strongly with Pedro's optical point of view and, more, with his pain. The image becomes abstract, graphic, recognizable only sporadically as leaves of sugarcane. Once again it is the image of the sugarcane, made vocal by the distorting work of film aesthetics, that enables a perspective invisible to oppressive realism. Different distortions of the image figure historical turning points in the process of revolutionary consciousness, but there is no correlation between naturalistic vision and political truth. Blur, abstraction, graphic composition, and camera movement visualize social processes, with the expressive potential of cinematography enabling the affective stakes of Cuban experience to come into view (figure 41).

One recent analysis has located *Soy Cuba* within the context of a political aesthetics: Nagib compares it with Rocha's *Terra em transe / Land in*

FIGURE 41 *Soy Cuba*
The affective stakes of political histories are imagined in distorted and blurred memories.

Trance (1967), thinking about the aesthetics of political crisis as a key feature of New Latin American Cinema.[33] Nagib's main claim is that the two films are similar—exactly the opposite idea from the dominant critique that *Soy Cuba* fails to be the kind of revolutionary text that Rocha's Cinema Novo represents. She makes productive connections between the pretty aesthetic of *Soy Cuba* and the antirealism of the New Latin American Cinema, pointing out comparisons in tempo, acting style, form, and influence, thus making it harder to sustain that conventional critique of *Soy Cuba*. Nagib analyzes the concept of *transe* in Portuguese—which encompasses "danger," "struggle," or "crisis" as well as "trance"—and she argues that in both films poetic and nonrealist form is a way to access this historical condition. Following Ismael Xavier, she finds Rocha's aesthetic to draw on earlier aesthetic movements such as baroque allegory as well as on modernism and the avant-garde.[34] It is a symptom of the poverty of the scholarship on *Soy Cuba* that such important aesthetico-political forebears have scarcely been imagined as interlocutors for the film's antirealist form. As my reference to Rodchenko illustrates, *Soy Cuba* also draws on the historic avant-garde, and, as in *Land in Trance*, its combination of allegorical narrative and heightened visual effects visualizes a moment of crisis, a trance that opens, like Benjamin's baroque allegory, onto a radical transformation of historical time.

From my perspective, it is also striking that Nagib's defense of *Soy Cuba* proceeds by means of a return to Rocha, who provided in *Vent d'Est* (1970) a crystallization of European film theory's rejection of Latin American radical aesthetics. Dismissed by post-1968 Marxists such as James Roy MacBean and even Godard as insufficiently radical in form and then emerging as a canonical figure of Third Cinema's rebuke to European art film, Rocha indexes the changing fortunes of a certain aesthetic impetus in the international discourse on political cinema. The national authenticity of Rocha's *"terra em transe"* has superseded his political internationalism so that his films' intense visual formalism has been welcomed into the world cinema canon at the price of being legible as an expression of purely Brazilian culture.[35] But if Rocha's star has risen as Brazilian and Latin American film scholarship has gained a stronger place in the field, *Soy Cuba* has been lost in the interstices of these geopolitical debates. It is ironic that Third Cinema and New Latin American Cinema, revolutionary models so attuned to internationalism, would exclude so violently an intercontinental vision. Moreover, the film's transnational engagement with the aesthetics of revolution is precisely what has been suppressed in order for the film to be rediscovered, and thus its recent champions have rewritten its expressive visualization of a radical geopolitics as "Communist kitsch." By insisting on *Soy Cuba*'s integration of cinematic and geopolitical spaces, we animate the pretty's potential as a revolutionary aesthetic.

SEVEN

PERVERSE PRETTINESS

Sexuality, Gender, and Aesthetic Exclusion

WHERE THE PREVIOUS CHAPTER EXAMINED THE HISTORY OF iconoclasm that underwrites postclassical leftist film theory, we turn now to the construction of a gendered and sexualized aesthetic that lies at the heart of this anti-pretty rhetoric. Gender is a defining quality of prettiness, and making visible its political nature is a strategy that recurs throughout this book: from the feminizing rhetoric of color and cosmetics to the secondary nature of the decorative and, indeed, the dangers of aesthetic seduction; making the pretty into a critical term is an unequivocally feminist move. But if feminism is always implicit in the proposition of the pretty as a space in which we can see the form and shape of critical abnegation, it is nonetheless crucial to direct our attention to the explicit role of gender and sexuality in forming—and deforming—the pretty. This task is (at least) twofold. First, we must return to the aesthetic histories of modernity, this time with an eye to the formation of regimes of beauty and value at the expense of particularly gendered, sexed, and raced bodies. The pretty always suggests a discourse of bodies, and these bodies are first of all feminine: Plato's Pharmacia was a nymph, and femininity is written into this originary critique of the cosmetic and colorful image.

Closer at hand, though, this chapter addresses how the foundation of modern aesthetics in the mid-eighteenth century builds a hierarchical valuation of simplicity and European masculinity to the detriment of the prettily composed and decorated image. This disprized image, in turn, is rhetorically and materially linked with the feminine, the effeminate, the exotic foreigner, and the colonial subject. This gendered hierarchy is installed in the DNA of the modern image, and cinema inherits its assumptions about seriousness of meaning and aesthetic value. Although feminist film theory has crucially enabled us to engage with the gendering of the image as a question of form, it often retains a suspicion of prettiness that derives from this foundational aesthetic hierarchy. The pretty intervenes in feminist and queer debates on visual culture by deconstructing this rhetoric of purity and perversion. By bringing the gendered prettiness of the modern image into view, I argue that we can reorient the relationship of aesthetics and politics for a queer feminist perspective on visual culture.

In order to view clearly the sexual logic of the rejected pretty, the first section of this chapter examines neoclassical aesthetics, a discourse that forms a key moment in the historical construction of an anti-pretty visuality that has shaped film theory. In neoclassicism, the femininity of the rejected image is overlaid with orientalism and, I argue, with insistent allusions to queerness and sexual perversity. Recall, for instance, the critique of "Asiatic" style, which condemns visual and linguistic detail as "degraded, effeminate, ornamental."[1] Dovetailing this exclusion of Asianism with a contemporaneous disparagement of female ornament as artifice, Naomi Schor concludes that "neo-classical aesthetics is imbued with the residues of the rhetorical imaginary, a sexist imaginary where the ornamental is inevitably bound up with the feminine, when it is not pathological—two notions Western culture has throughout its history had a great deal of trouble distinguishing."[2] The neoclassical rhetoric of form and style continues to police cinematic value. As we know from *Stella Dallas* (Vidor, 1937), feminine adornment and bad taste are archetypal mistakes in film.[3] But it is not only a question of films that narrativize the problem of excessive decoration. Flowery "Asiatic" style is degraded and feminized as such in the canon formations of modern cinema. As with the *disegno* versus *colore* debate, the problem *of* film (its visual language) becomes a problem *in* film, where a rhetoric of indecent adornment performs the work of exclusion. In the intense production design of *Fa yeung nin wa / In the Mood for*

Love (Wong, 2000), we discover a modern iteration of effeminate Asiatic ornament.

The second part of this investigation addresses feminist and queer film theory.[4] Of all the critical models considered in this study, theories of sexuality and gender have most incisively addressed the kinds of denigration that I am gathering together under the heading of the "pretty." Canonical feminist film theorists from Laura Mulvey on changed the terms in which film could be read as gendered, insisting that we read the forms and structures of cinema's seductive charms, not just its representations of women. For instance, the *Stella Dallas* debate articulates a key feminist intersection of melodrama, surface decoration, and femininity, illustrating the critical drive toward finding texts that are valuable (lovable?) for female audiences. Likewise, in searching for value outside of or in opposition to hegemonies, queer theory has sought to value different kinds of images and different aesthetics of the body. The surface / depth binary is deconstructed in theories of drag and gender performativity, in which bodily surface and decoration form a productive source of meaning and political agency. And yet, these crucial pathways of feminist and queer intellectual labor do not overthrow the iconophobia of traditional patriarchal aesthetics. Even while championing radical accounts of the image—and while disagreeing with one another on much else—feminist and queer theorists maintain a remarkably similar exclusion of the decorative image. The chapter's second and third sections explore the contradictions and productive tensions for a feminist and queer critique of film aesthetics. Perhaps there is an opportunity in this apparent contradiction: if theories of gender and sexuality overturn the ideological aims of neoclassical aesthetics while often retaining their formal prejudices, we might find within these entangled tendrils a space to read film aesthetics differently.

The final two sections of the chapter ask what a valorization of the queer pretty might look like, counterposing two models of contemporary iconophilia. Recent scholarship on enchantment has brought aesthetics and the feminine back into the limelight but has often relied on conservative models of heteronormative femininity to do so. In sharp contrast to these mythifying versions of the beautiful feminine image, I propose a perverse iconophilia capable of marshalling and redeploying the rhetoric of sexual perversity that modern aesthetics has attributed to the pretty image. If the hierarchies of neoclassicism install a patriarchal arrangement of aesthetic power, the pretty perverts this dominant structure of domination, forcing open pathways for a kinky revisioning of the erotics of the image. Reading queer and BDSM (bondage and discipline, sadism and masochism) visual culture against aesthetic theory's rhetoric of perversity, this chapter insists on the pretty's ability to reconfigure the sexual anatomy of the modern image.

NEOCLASSICISM'S MANLY CONTOURS

The rise of neoclassicism in the mid-eighteenth century provoked a modern iteration of classical iconoclasm and created the foundations for what would become the enduring anti-pretty rhetoric of modern visual cultures. The discourses on simplicity and masculine form that we find in Johan Joachim Winckelmann, Gotthold Lessing, and their contemporaries installed a value system that influenced both the purity and realism of classical film theory and the anti-effeminate iconophobia of cine-Marxism. E. H. Gombrich, in his magisterial study of decorative art, tells us that "a deliberate rejection of ornamental profusion has always been a sign of classical influence." Moreover, "where this influence becomes a matter of pride, as in the Italian Renaissance and in 18th century neoclassicism, the emphasis on form rather than [on] decoration becomes a sign of self-conscious artistic virtue."[5] Such a privileging of virtuous form over inferior ornament is familiar from the nineteenth-century discourses on decorative art that influenced early film theory, but neoclassicism powerfully imbricates antivisual thought, antidecorative aesthetics, and the creation of value around the image of a white male body. As we shall see, not only the image of woman is at stake in this aesthetic history, but the production of a properly valuable male body. Thus we find in neoclassicism a complex rejection of the effeminate and of the foreign body in addition to an exclusion of the feminine. It is important to maintain a sense of these different bodily regimes—not only as a way of reading the intersections of feminist, queer, and postcolonial image critiques, but also because the pretty is exactly produced by the overlapping nature of these exclusions.

Barbara Stafford has traced the eighteenth-century origins of visual skepticism, arguing that British, German, and French philosophers shared an iconoclasm that associated manipulation of the image with charlatanism and sophistry:

It is not accidental that the critical condemnation of visual quackery—judged to be a sort of empty conjuring or voyeuristic display—coincided with the rise of a neoclassical "methodism" and a romantic "algebraicism." These late eighteenth-century artistic movements, usually conceived as divergent, actually converged in their attack on a Lockean optical epistemology. Their most notable theorists—from Winckelmann to Baudelaire, from Novalis to Coleridge—posited an abstract systematics, that is, an aesthetical logic directed at the demolition of rococo legerdemain. For reformers, conspicuous signs of manufacture signified circus juggling and mountebank trickery. Flamboyant hypervisibility not only deviated from good taste, it served as a counter-example of nondiscriminating gullibility.[6]

Stafford's account of sensory skepticism encompasses neoclassicism's rejection of the rococo as the wrong kind of image with the kind of philosophical antivisuality that Martin Jay analyzes in French thought.[7] Thus eighteenth-century visual theory performs the same slippage as that in Plato's image: from suspicion of the image *as such* as a form of knowledge, we move to an aesthetic strategy of rejecting certain kinds of image as too visual to be trusted. We might hear in accusations of "flamboyant hypervisibility" or audience "gullibility" and bad taste the precursors of the negative reviews of Baz Luhrmann or indeed of many forms of spectacular cinema. And this excessively visual image doubles back onto the problem of the image itself. By defining a kind of image that is both empty and a conjuring trick, a hat without a rabbit that is empty precisely because it promises fullness in the space of the image itself rather than elsewhere, eighteenth-century theory harnesses the problem of the aesthetic image to the feminized pretty logic of trickery and deception.

Let us take a couple of illustrative examples. Friedrich von Schiller, in *Letters Upon the Aesthetic Education of Man*, condemns an aesthetic of "superficial glitter" and "artificial covering that hides truth and replaces reality," and he finds dishonest appearance in "lying colours which mask the face of truth and are bold enough to masquerade as reality."[8] This sense of the deceptive qualities of the aesthetic image where it refuses mimesis and creates a false surface already evokes the feminine witchcraft of the cosmetic. But Schiller extends this figuration beyond the feminine body, warning also of the dangers of effeminacy that beauty often creates. Suggesting that an "energetic beauty"—a healthy aesthetic like that of Adolf Loos's northern European—might help mitigate effeminacy, he argues that "impotence and perversity alone have recourse to false and paltry semblance." He advocates the "beneficent semblance" of objects of "genuine merit," but this proper beauty is separated from the "delight in semblance" and "propensity to ornament" found in the "savage" and in "all races which have emerged from the slavery of the animal condition" as they enter into humanity.[9] It is striking how interlinked the areas of denigration are: in order to produce genuine merit, the artist must avoid glitter and color, impotence and perversity, and savage ornament. The beauty that Schiller conjures is carefully policed to ensure that it is available only to the proper kind of body, with the foreign, the feminine, and the effeminate located firmly on the wrong side of the line.

Winckelmann is perhaps the most significant proponent of neoclassicism, writing in the 1750s and 1760s and providing an important influence on the major German aestheticians such as Lessing and then Kant. Winckelmann helpfully distinguishes noble beauty from the merely sensual pretty, just as Kant uses the example of the attractive face in real life as a counter to artistic value. Thus, says Winckelmann, "the beauties impersonated by art" are "less pleasing to the uninstructed mind than [the] ordinary pretty face which is lively and animated. The cause lies in our passions, which with most men are excited by the first look, and the senses are already gratified, when reason, unsatisfied, is seeking to discover and enjoy the charm of true beauty. It is not, then, beauty which captivates us, but sensuality."[10] Winckelmann clearly sees a certain value in the pretty, and he speaks more positively about the pleasures of a lively face than do many of his successors. Nonetheless, the pretty face that this passage conjures is seductive rather than truly valuable, capturing the attention of the uninstructed mind. True beauty, instead, is pure in a way that strips out the stuff of the senses. Beauty, he says, "should be like the best kind of water, drawn from the spring itself: the less taste it has, the more healthful it is considered, because free from all foreign admixture."[11] In distinct contrast with the pretty, the beautiful is pure, colorless, not foreign or mixed and thus creates a healthy body.

Winckelmann's writings elaborate neoclassicism in terms of an aesthetic and moral linkage between purity of form and the proper masculine body. In "Thoughts on the Imitation of the Painting and Sculpture of the Greeks," he argues that "exercises gave the bodies of the Greeks that great and manly contour which the Greek masters imparted to their statues, with no vague outlines or superfluous accretions."[12] What are these "superfluous accretions" that must be avoided by masterful art? Breasts? Body fat? Decorative clothing or jewelry? In valuing simplicity (*Einfalt*) above all, Winckelmann places the nobility of the healthy male body in direct opposition to the aesthetic accretions of color, ornament, and detail. The male body is characterized by the nature of its contours, such that line's superiority to color can be concretized in specifically masculine lines, which are preferable to feminized curves. Superfluity is a vice of both linear excess and colorful addition. Thus in *The History of Ancient Art*, he argues that "all beauty is heightened by unity and simplicity" and, moreover, that "color . . . should have but little share in our consideration of beauty, because the essence of beauty consists not in color, but in shape, and on this point enlightened minds will agree. As white is the color which reflects the greatest number of rays of light, and consequently is the most easily perceived, a beautiful body will, accordingly, be the more beautiful the whiter it is."[13] Winckelmann's account of neoclassical style makes explicit what becomes occluded in film theory's neoclassicist emphasis on purity, simplicity, and linearity: the extent to which these values depend on the masculine European body and inherently devalue the nonwhite, the nonmasculine, and the female.

In the neoclassical rejection of the baroque and rococo, there is a feminizing rhetoric that associates the expressivity and exuberance of these styles with female frivolity. Winckelmann disapproves of artists such as Bernini and Caravaggio, finding a lack of masculine wisdom and restraint in their "too passionate and uncontrolled" forms (figure 42).[14] Umberto Eco finds that "there is a profound nostalgia in Winckelmann's aspiration to a clear and simple, linear purity, the same sentiment that Rousseau felt for the original purity of natural man. But there is also a sentiment of rebellion against the empty abundance of Rococo constructions, artificial at best and simply against nature at worst."[15] We might hear in Eco's phrasing a suggestion of the discourse on homosexuality that describes it as being against nature or indeed, to the Anglophone ear, of Joris-Karl Huysman's *À rebours* / *Against Nature* (1884). Such echoes resonate with the aestheticism of the fin-de-siècle dandy discussed in chapter 3, perhaps posing a masculine Greek version of queer aesthetics against an effetely decorative one. The rococo is still an impossible aesthetic in the late nineteenth century, when Ralph Wornum describes it as a "final decline—mere love of display, gold and glitter . . .

FIGURE 42 Gianlorenzo Bernini, *The Ecstasy of Saint Teresa* (1647–1652)
Bernini's sculpture exemplifies the "passionate and uncontrolled" forms criticized by Johan
Joachim Winckelmann.

absurd."[16] As the reference to Plato's *poikiloi* suggests, overriding these implications of queerness and aristocratic decadence is a structuring misogyny. Christopher Wren comments on Versailles: "Not an Inch within but is crowded with little Curiosities of Ornament: the women, as they make here the language and Fashions, and meddle with Politicks and Philosophy, so they sway also in Architecture."[17] The measure of aesthetic impurity is thus precisely the entrance of women into public life.

In a feminist analysis of clothing, Kaja Silverman pinpoints this eighteenth-century shift in style from decorative to plain as a crucial turning point in the modern construction of gendered vision.[18] Questioning the association in feminist film theory of the adorned body and self-display with the oppressive male gaze, she argues that for many centuries ornate dress was a signifier of class rather than of gender and operated as an instrument of power rather than a signifier of subjugation. Men wore ornate dress to signify their wealth and power, claiming the gaze of others in a visual regime that could be exemplified by the court of Versailles. In the latter half of the century—in other words, as neoclassicism came to dominate aesthetic thought—male dress became plain, and women became the decorated sex. What had once been a valuable masculine style became a trivial feminine one. Hence, according to Silverman, the relatively unchanging quality of male dress in the past two centuries associates men with stability, constancy, and modern capitalist power. The decorative and fast-moving styles of women's fashion associate women with inconstancy and a merely decorative function, thus leading both to the spectacular quality of the woman in classical cinema and to the semiotic association of ornate style with gendered exclusion from the spaces of power.

Overt decoration is similarly linked to foreign, especially Asian, bodies. Stafford identifies in eighteenth-century aesthetic debate an emergent Protestant geopolitics of purity, rejecting what was seen as an Oriental Catholicism marked as fetishistic, effeminate, and sinful.[19] Arguing for the continuing influence of this aesthetic attitude in contemporary art and scholarship, Stafford claims that "not much has changed since eighteenth-century *philosophes*, echoing Plato's fear of *mimesis*, condemned the 'Oriental despotism' of the eye and the superstitious gaze of pagan idolators."[20] The phrase "Oriental despotism" derives from Nicolas-Antoine Boulanger's book *Despotisme oriental* (1761), which popularized the idea that nondemocratic Western systems such as Catholicism were Asian in style. Thus the Catholic styles of highly decorative art exemplified by Bernini and the baroque could be negatively associated not only with aesthetic excess, but with "false religion," abuse of power, and an orientalist suspicion of the devious East. Schiller, for instance, in describing the triumph of classical art over excessive nature, writes: "The divine monster of the Oriental, which roams about changing the world with the blind force of a beast of prey, dwindles to the charming outline of humanity in Greek fable; the empire of the Titans is crushed, and boundless force is tamed by infinite form."[21] Gottfried Semper, writing a century later in the Victorian era of archaeological discovery, found the Doric to be classical architecture's stage of most beautiful development. By contrast, the Corinthian style "is characterized by a degenerative pomp and Asiatic overcrowding."[22] Although the Asiatic style could sometimes be justified, it, like sexual representation in film, had to be used sparingly and be, as it were, necessary to the plot.

A racializing rhetoric can also be discerned in the neoclassical contrast of classicism to primitive forms. We have already considered the primitivist discourse in eighteenth- and nineteenth-century writing on color: Semper, for example, writes that when early man first decorated his primitive shelters, "his childlike imagination favoured bright colours in motley combinations, as nature around him had done."[23] Semper sets up a historical rather than a geographical distinction, in which early human cultures are childlike and primitive. His examples include Egypt and Nubia, but also the Etruscans. Thus ideas of "primitive man" are not inherently racializing in tenor. However, when brought out of aesthetic history and deployed in arguments about present-day art, "primitive" decoration, like the Maori tattoos considered by Alois Riegl and Owen Jones, is consistently linked to non-European cultures. Where bright colors signify primitive cultures, then colorless beauty should be a standard for modern European civilization. Color as pigment and style bleeds into color as a racializing discourse—thus Winckelmann's startling opinion that the whiter a body, the more beautiful it is.

This perception helped precipitate controversy over polychromatic antiquities in which the discoveries of colorful decoration in Greek and Etruscan architecture led to an anxiety about the whiteness and purity of the European heritage.[24] Until the nineteenth century, it had been widely assumed, despite plenty of evidence to the contrary, that classical architecture was originally white, and the definitive discovery that it had actually been highly colored caused something of a crisis. As Clyde Taylor tartly puts it, "Such sculptures came to function as the very realization of the transcendent Whiteness that preoccupied European intellectual thought. Thus, the knowledge that the Greeks painted their sculptures did not meet with enthusiasm."[25] Semper agreed in his "Preliminary Remarks on Polychromatic Architecture" that color was a significant element of Greek aesthetics, but he still found it to detract from the purity of true beauty.[26] Archaeologist and aesthetician Antoine-Chrysostome Quatremère de Quincy, who discovered early evidence of painted sculptures, found surface color on statues to be monstrous and *foreign* to Greek taste, and historian David Van Zanten tellingly characterizes Quatremère's attitude less as outright rejection and more as a "morbid fascination" with the primitive and exotic.[27] This anxiety about the primitive color found at the heart of Western culture recurs across modern European aesthetics.

Importantly for film's inheritance of neoclassical aesthetics, rejection of the foreign was not limited to associative logic, but also demanded a legible difference in form, visible across the body of the aesthetic object. Neoclassicist aestheticians revived thinkers such as Quintilian, who held that "ornament must, as I have already said, be bold, manly and chaste, free from all effeminate smoothness and false hues derived from artificial dyes, and must glow with health and vigour."[28] The connection of masculinity, purity, and vital energy fits neatly into the neoclassical worldview, but what we also see here is the association of classicism with colorlessness, in which false hues imply both a feminizing artificiality and a primitive imaginary. What I am proposing is not simply a set of related binaries (male / female, white / other, plain / ornamental), but a triangulation of gender, race, and ornament that engenders a much more dynamic account of aesthetic vision and its relationship to the political.

The neoclassical valuation of simple form insists on its abstraction in terms of medium specificity—for instance, in Lessing's *Laocoön*—beauty, or technical skill, but close attention to the period's rhetoric reveals the bodies that must be excluded for this apparent aesthetic purity to be produced. It is therefore troubling that film theory from its earliest days has drawn on neoclassical aesthetic ideas to construct cinematic value. Film theory occasionally takes inspiration from this aesthetic history in a more positive manner (for instance, Christine Buci-Glucksmann's use of the neobaroque as an anti-Platonic and proto-postmodern critique of rationality),[29] but the rarity of such polemics serves to highlight the hegemonic force of neoclassicism's iconophobia and the pervasiveness with which its ideas have seeped into filmic critical discourse. Although neoclassical ideal forms might seem at odds with the modern love for contingency, Peter Galassi connects the growth of photographic vision to "the Neoclassical principle of artistic renewal, which sought to replace the fantasies of the eighteenth century with a more sober art, based in part on careful visual observation."[30] A rejection of frills and frivolity binds the masculine forms of neoclassicism to photography's realist gaze. Look, for example, at Denis Diderot's critique of academic mannerism: "All those stiff, contrived, academic positions . . . what does all this have to do with nature, its positions, its gestures? . . . These men who seem to plead, pray, sleep, reflect or faint with care, what have they in common with the peasant struck down by fatigue, the philosopher meditating by the fireplace, or the man fainting in the crush of a mob? Nothing, my friend, nothing."[31] Anticipating cinematic vitalism, Diderot dismisses composed images and values the violent truths of the modern crowd.

Just as we can see cinematic ideas anticipated in eighteenth-century aesthetics, so film theory pays back this debt, invoking neoclassical ideas directly. Vachel Lindsay aims to bring "Doric restraint" into cinema to replace the "overstrained" and "overloaded" nature of current films.[32] These overloaded images echo Semper's Asiatic overcrowding, conjuring the Doric as a linkage between European purity and cinematic openness. The excesses that Lindsay finds in spectacular films are, for him, precisely comparable to the overly decorated styles of baroque or rococo art. In an even more telling account, André Bazin argues for a Protestantism of cinematic style, even in the making of a Catholic film. In "Cinema and Theology," he finds: "Everything that is exterior, ornamental, liturgical, sacramental, hagiographic, and miraculous in the everyday observance, doctrine, and practice of Catholicism does indeed show specific affinities with the cinema considered as a formidable iconography, but these affinities, which have made for the success of countless films, are also the source of the religious insignificance of most of them." He continues, "To make a long story short, it seems that, although the Protestant sensibility is not indispensable to the making of a good Catholic film, it can nevertheless be a real advantage."[33] For Bazin, even a director aiming to make a religious film from a Catholic perspective would be better served using the plain and unornamented forms of Protestantism.

The fear of Oriental despotism remains in force such that even where the ornamental facets of Catholicism are valued in everyday life, they must be expunged from the image. The engrained influence of neoclassicism demands that cinematic value and communicative power are aligned with antidecorative and antivisual thinking, even if that alignment produces a theological contradiction such as the Protestant Catholic film.

But if neoclassical ideas continue to structure film criticism, contemporary cinema nevertheless turns decisively toward the pretty. Accounts of cinema that esteem Doric simplicity and Protestant style are simply unable to analyze the hypervisibility of Derek Jarman's colorful films or the Asiatic overcrowding of the mise-en-scène in Wong Kar-wai's *In the Mood for Love*. Wong's film meshes a story of emotional reticence with a key historical juncture in modern Chinese history, but both the cheating spouses and History as a representational force remain crucially off-screen. Direct representation is precisely what is impossible, and instead the film disperses emotion and meaning across the detailed patterns of the mise-en-scène. Wallpaper, period objects, and, most notably, 1960s cheongsam fabric produce a feminized historical scene in which spectatorial cathexis depends not on words, but on the Asiatic floweriness of the decorative image. Realist openness is replaced by interiority and limited perspectives, and the logic of the anti-aesthetic is supplanted by a poetics of style.

Wong's prominence as a Hong Kong director suggests an Asian rejection of the Eurocentric discourse of Asiatic style, and we can certainly trace a trend toward elaborated and colorful mise-en-scènes in the films of Hou Hsiao-hsien, Pen-ek Ratanaruang, and even Jia Zhangke. (Jia is often thought of as a neo-neorealist, the opposite of pretty in his underground background and visualization of the gritty realities of Chinese modernization. But his films also evince a fascination with mining the decorative spaces of the provincial everyday; think of the old-fashioned bedroom wallpaper in *Ren xiao yao / Unknown Pleasures* [2002] or the play with color design in *Shijie / The World* [2004].) But rather than link contemporary Asian directors with "Asiatic style," it is more productive to locate an emergent politics of world that resists the Eurocentric strictures of neoclassicism. Thus both Santosh Sivan's *Theeviravaathi / The Terrorist* (1998) and Claire Denis's *Beau Travail* (1999) deploy decorative image design to engage the intersections of gendered and raced bodies in situations of postcolonial trauma. Demanding that we recalibrate our aesthetic expectations, these films, like *In the Mood for Love*, articulate meaningful experiences of gender, politics, and the postcolonial through the screen's aestheticized surface. Lindsay's and Bazin's classicist concerns might seem far removed from the interests of feminism and queer film theory, but drawing from the heritage of neoclassical aesthetic thought necessarily engenders a formal value system based on the white, masculine body. By contrast, modern pretty films invite us to look otherwise at the aesthetic image and to open up the valuable potential of "feminine" forms to political critiques beyond the scope of "representations of women." From a feminist perspective, it is imperative to interrogate the rejection of colorful, foreign, and nonmasculine bodies that underlies neoclassicism's aesthetic of simple and linear forms.

THE DOUBLE BIND OF THE IMAGE IN FEMINIST FILM THEORY

If we agree that the modern denigration of the decorative and pretty image derives from a sexist aesthetic history, then we are led to a particular problem for feminist film theory: of necessity, it builds an antipatriarchal account of film on a fundamentally patriarchal theory of the image. The most influential of examples, Laura Mulvey's "Visual Pleasure and Narrative Cinema," folds a feminist reading of the image that lies (because ideology distorts gender) into an iconophobic one (in which the image lies by definition).[34] This move is troubling because the latter idea is precisely an example of the kind of patriarchal regime that necessitates the former, replacing "image" for "woman" as the object of gendered disdain. In other words, "the woman lies by definition" is always already present inside "the image lies by definition." For this reason, Mulvey's critique of patriarchal film aesthetics proceeds by means of an unspoken patriarchal iconophobia. For example, "The determining male gaze projects its fantasy onto the female figure, which is styled accordingly. . . . Woman displayed as sexual object is the leitmotif of erotic spectacle: from pinups to striptease, from Ziegfeld to Busby Berkeley, she holds the look, plays to and signifies male desire."[35] As with our art historical examples, the decorative, composed, *styled* image is a lie, and these pleasurable aesthetic qualities allow us to recognize it as such. Of course, Mulvey reverses perspective so that a feminist critique of patriarchal ideology—rather than sexist value systems—allows us to see through this fantasy, but the underlying logic that enables the argument to be made is the same. Mulvey writes that "the woman as icon, displayed for the gaze and enjoyment of men[,] . . . always threatens to evoke the anxiety it originally signified."[36] We can take the phrase "woman as" out of this sentence and find that it reads just as well as a statement on the feminine threat of the icon as such. Mulvey's argument and that of much feminist film theory that follows it depend on the gendering of the icon yet attempt to deploy the icon circularly in a critique of itself.

However, despite its polemic qualities, Mulvey's essay is less iconophobic than its interpretation by many subsequent readers. She finds cinematic narrative to be as much of a problem for feminism as spectacle is, two sides of the same patriarchal coin, but in the extensive afterlife of her essay narrative is privileged as a site of potential political engagement, whereas seductive spectacle is emphasized as the problem for feminism. There is a slippery quality to this critical trajectory that the discrepancy between accounts of narrative and spectacle reveals. Although feminist criticism decries specific narratives as patriarchal, it is always necessary to do the labor of ideological analysis in order to understand how narrative works politically in each case. Criticism of spectacle, however, moves in the opposite direction: rather than reading individual films, post-Mulveyan feminist criticism often takes as axiomatic a rejection of spectacle per se, deploying it as a totalizing category that can stand for patriarchal image culture. For instance, Teresa de Lauretis quotes Yann Lardeau, who, writing in *Cahiers du Cinéma*, claims that "it is cinema itself, as a medium, which is pornographic."[37] The image is suspicious in and of itself, and that suspicion is always gendered. Like pornography, cinema provides an image that is not truth. And like pornography, the cinematic image can be figured as a female body that lies about its *jouissance*. It is as if Guy Debord's spectacle were conflated with Mulvey's, letting narrative's sadistic work off the hook and minimizing the extent to which we need to *read* the spectacular and gendered image.

Thus although the engagements of feminist film theorists with sex, gender, and the image are in sympathy with my own politics, I find that both the circularity of Mulvey's political aesthetics and the iconophobia of her readers recur as obstacles in otherwise highly productive critiques. Whereas psychoanalytic theory articulates the political stakes of using the master's tools, the implications of this patriarchal *aesthetic* foundation have not been so rigorously explored. For example, Janet Bergstrom concludes in her 1979 essay "Enunciation and Sexual Difference" that the task of understanding cinema's mechanisms involves "coming to terms with our relationship as spectators and film analysts to it and to the seductiveness of the image in general," and more than a decade later Elspeth Probyn warily writes that "the image is always up to something."[38] Both women articulate the defining struggle that feminists have experienced between the female spectator and the patriarchal image: we are right to be suspicious of an image culture that does not have women's desires and interests at heart. This suspicion endures where feminist theory has questioned the totalizing category of woman. Lack of good faith is complicated but by no means erased where lesbian spectators are concerned, as in Probyn's article. Even though bell hooks's account of black female spectatorship takes white feminist theory to task, she shares a focus on the need not to be "seduced and enchanted" by Hollywood films and on the ambivalent experience of viewing critically.[39] However, articulating feminist ambivalence toward the image in the language of seduction and suspicion has the counterproductive consequence of underwriting the political analysis of patriarchal culture by means of a patriarchal rhetoric of the image.

The problem, then, is how to locate a feminist theory of the image. Feminist critical theory has been consistently leery of endorsing existing regimes of vision and, in fact, has been a major source of contemporary antivisual thought. Thus Luce Irigaray's critique of masculinist philosophy aims to deprivilege the visual, which she sees as one of the baleful inheritances of Greek thought. "Woman," she claims, "takes pleasure more from touching than from looking, and her entry into a dominant scopic economy signifies, again, her consignment to passivity: she is to be the beautiful object of contemplation."[40] *Beauty, passivity, contemplation*— these terms recur in the intersection of feminism and the image. Irigaray does something very similar to Mulvey here, rejecting the regime of to-be-looked-at-ness that women are compelled to enter, but retaining entirely the idea of the image as suspicious. For Irigaray, the image is too masculine rather than too feminine, and she thus aims to reject it for a feminist theory of pleasure. Regardless, the image is still rejected. The emphasis on touch, recently elaborated by theorists of the haptic such as Laura Marks, therefore finds no space for the visual composition of the image.[41] The cinematic image itself structures the same castration problem that the woman's image does for Mulvey: it is the presence that always harks back to absence, the excess that covers a dangerous gap. This double bind may explain the notorious difficulty that feminist film theory has had in locating an alternative to the patriarchal image.

There is an echo of this recursiveness in my own analysis, too: the insights of feminist film theory enable my reading, even where that reading produces a critique of feminist iconophobia. To analyze the image as a site of gendered contestation in its very structures is one of the crucial legacies of Mulveyan theory. Thus much feminist theory post-Mulvey has engaged the gendering of the image as an explicit problem, and significant models of contemporary critical theory have emerged from feminist engagements with the image's "femininity," its association with the superficial, and its pleasurable visual appeal. In important ways, the positive valuation of women's genres and spectatorial practices as well as scholarship on surface, masquerade, and pleasure ground the intellectual formation of this project. The pretty is nothing if not a feminist account of the cinematic image. Consider, for instance, how Mary Ann Doane, when speaking of the veil in cinema, refers to the visible as "a lure, a trap, or a snare."[42] Doane uses this gendered language quite deliberately, ventriloquizing Freud to make visible the relationships among spectacular images, vision, and gendered power. We see a cognate impetus in queer feminisms, as in Probyn's claim that the surface is a mode of belonging: "For the surface is not another metaphor nor yet another fad within intellectual circles: it is a profound reordering of how we conceive of the social."[43] Reading feminism's relationship to anti-pretty aesthetics is a more sensitive and perhaps fraught process than doing the same with Marxist or classical film theory because the latter models have no inherent stake in redeeming the femininity of the cosmetic image. Feminist theory, though, forms the foundation of my defense of the pretty, even while it provides evidence of anti-pretty thinking. Moreover, in the tension between these two forces, we find demonstration of the recursive double bind involved in feminism's critique of the image. To tease out the stakes of prettiness for feminist film theory, then, we must read the discourses of film feminism as, at once, histories of anti-pretty thinking and of its opposite. I focus on three key debates in this history—mass culture, masquerade, and melodrama—before concluding with recent feminist philosophies of the image.

The debate around mass culture as feminine, initiated by Tania Modleski's and Andreas Huyssen's responses to Ann Douglas's book *The Feminization of American Culture*, demonstrates feminism's procedure of revealing the masculinist hierarchies of value that permeate modern culture.[44] Less interested in the image per se, this debate proceeds, like analysis of the pretty, by investigating the rhetorical connections between femininity and devaluation. Modleski points out how the idea of feminization figures the emergence of mass culture and operates as a way of disparaging the popular. Her aim is "to show how our ways of thinking and feeling about mass culture are so intricately bound up with notions of the feminine that the need for a feminist critique becomes obvious at every level of the debate."[45] Thus trivial Victorian novels enjoyed by women were simply a form of consumption, whereas difficult texts read by men demanded a readerly act of production. Huyssen agrees, describing "the notion which gained ground during the nineteenth century that mass culture is somehow associated with woman while real, authentic culture remains the prerogative of men."[46] Expanding the argument into a theory of modernism's relationship to mass culture, Huyssen finds a repeated vocabulary of seduction in which modernist art must avoid the temptation of mass culture: "The autonomy of the modernist art work, after all, is always the result of a resistance, an abstention, and a suppression—resistance to the seductive lure of mass culture. Abstention from the pleasure of trying to please a larger audience, suppression of everything that might be threatening to the rigorous demands of being modern and at the edge of time."[47] Modernism's fear of mass culture closely aligns with the aesthetician's fear of the seductive image. Rey Chow glosses this alignment as a puritanism that opposes feminine culture as a gilded whore, and we see in this metaphor the rhetoric of glitter and duplicity that underwrites aesthetically the discursive formation of a bad feminine culture.[48] Modernity draws on a neoclassical simplicity of line and form in the emergence of classical cinematic economy as much as in Le Corbusier, whereas feminized mass culture is characterized by the superficial detritus of fan culture and the fashion for Oriental objects—in short, the market for pretty things. The pretty does not map directly onto the modernism / mass culture divide because prettiness is found in avant-garde films as easily as in popular ones, but the rhetorical logic of delegitimizing a dangerous femininity is strikingly similar.

Huyssen and Modleski also open up feminist inquiry into image as surface and femininity as mask. Their accounts of mass culture as, respectively, woman and masquerade explicitly counter Marxist valorization of depth, focusing instead on the material histories that consign women to the superficial. Psychoanalytic feminist theory extends this connection of surface to feminine subjectivity, drawing from Joan Rivière's notion of womanliness as masquerade. For Rivière, "women who wish for masculinity may put on a mask of womanliness to avert anxiety and the retribution feared from men." Reading the deceptive surface of femininity as a defense mechanism against patriarchal violence, Rivière contends not only that the mask is a valuable part of feminine subjectivity, but, more significantly, that there is no difference between womanliness and its masquerade: "[W]hether radical or superficial, they are the same thing."[49] This idea has been enabling for film theorists attempting to find a place for women's subjectivity within the constrictive patriarchal apparatus of cinema. Doane argues that because woman *is* the image, the desirable spectacle, the female spectator of conventional cinema is placed by dominant regimes of vision as too close to the image, unable to create a proper mastery and separation.[50] Masquerade becomes a way out of both this infantilizing proximity and the equally undesirable alternative of a masculinized distance—an ability borne of necessity for women to watch cinema differently.

However, neither Rivière nor Doane wholeheartedly values the masquerade: for Rivière, the masquerade describes a patient uncomfortable in a male-dominated profession, and Doane, in her reconsideration of the question, points out that in both her own argument and Rivière's femininity does not actually exist.[51] As Stephen Heath explains, "Collapsing genuine womanliness and the masquerade together, Rivière undermines the integrity of the former with the artifice of the latter."[52] For Heath, the notion that femininity is nothing but the mask worn to create femininity is a radical and useful one that begins to deconstruct the surface / depth binary and thus works toward both an anti-essentialist feminism and a psychoanalytic critique of the centered Cartesian subject. Doane is more skeptical, arguing that even though Rivière's masquerade may not believe in a feminine essence, it is still dependent on an originary masculinity against which the feminine can define itself.[53] Both Doane and Heath, though, are highly aware of the philosophical legacy that has associated femininity with the seductive and deceptive surface, and their examinations of cinematic surface speak in conversation with contemporary feminist philosophy.[54]

It might seem, therefore, that theories of masquerade would lend themselves to a cinematic pretty. Poststructuralist feminist theory has repeatedly attacked the surface / depth logic of patriarchy, unpacking the ways in which femininity has been constructed as a surface, and yet in a typical double bind women's interests have been dismissed as superficial. Prizing gender and sex away from ideas of depth, nature, and truth is certainly an important step in rejecting essentialism and, indeed, in complicating anti-essentialism. Although theories of masquerade form an important precursor for the pretty's politics of surface, they focus on masquerade in filmic texts rather than address superficiality as a vector of the cinematic image itself. Both Heath's and Doane's essays analyze films that thematize masquerade, moving symptomatically from the figural to the structural. Doane reads the melodramatic investment in the woman's gaze in *Now, Voyager* (Rapper, 1942) and *Leave Her to Heaven* (Stahl, 1945), and Heath points to Marlene Dietrich as a figure who uses masquerade knowingly and to Max Ophüls as a director who "develops the masquerade as pure cinema, the hyper-spectacle of fantasy."[55] This hyperspectacle recalls the hypervisibility of the rococo, offering an immediate contrast between feminist attention to Ophüls and Dietrich and neoclassicism's rejection of what Stafford calls conspicuous signs of manufacture. But masquerade theory does not map neatly onto the concerns of the pretty. We must triangulate several critical turns to access both their similarities and their critical differences. Thus critics such as Heath and Doane analyze filmic thematizations of the masquerade as examples of the surface qualities of the feminine. This analysis makes the films useful for feminist critique, but the image itself is significant only insofar as it enables the thematics of gender to be visualized—Dietrich stages the superficiality of gender through costume, for instance, or John Stahl narrates scenarios of impossible feminine vision. What is missing is a reading of the image per se, exterior to its culturally mediated ability to figure scenes of gendered visuality. The pretty responds to the masquerade's sticking point of essentialism versus anti-essentialism by asking how the image is gendered formally and how thematic iterations of gender in film can be read not just against women's historical conditions, but against the gendered aesthetics of cinema itself. Again, the question of gender in the image must be folded back to reveal the underlying problem of the aesthetic gendering of the image.

A particularly potent instance of this type of analysis is found in Linda Williams's oft-cited essay on *Stella Dallas*, which takes up the idea of the masquerade, arguing that Stella's blatant spectacle demands to be read as a produced image: "But the more ruffles, feathers, furs, and clanking jewellery that Stella dons, the more she emphasises her pathetic inadequacy.

Her strategy can only backfire in the eyes of an upper-class restraint that values a streamlined and sleek ideal of femininity. To those eyes, Stella is a travesty, an overdone masquerade of what it means to be a woman."[56] Stella's masquerade takes the form of a list of decorative objects, like Freud's hats that ponder femininity or the nineteenth-century theorists' presentation of orientalist objects. Here, *masquerade* is not a critical deconstruction of the feminine, but a misogynist epithet—it is an ornament, a supplement, a *mise-en-abyme* of prettiness. Stella's outfit might reveal the problem of the image for feminism, but, like the pretty in Marxist film criticism, it can speak only against itself.

Williams looks for a way that this arrangement can benefit the spectator. Following Doane, she suggests that "one way out of the dilemma of female over-identification with the image on the screen is for this image to act out a masquerade of femininity that manufactures a distance between spectator and image."[57] Stella's image is thus so excessive that it breaks apart conventional modes of identification. Although this account of masquerade locates political critique on the surface (of the subject), its underlying logic is still the tearing down of images. We must be distanced (not seduced) by the image, keep our distance, and distance ourselves. The image in its imageness is the problem, a seductive surface that cannot be trusted unless it can be made to speak against itself. Only by keeping our distance can we be rational, make readings, be masculine. The description of the problem of the image therefore reverses the radicality of the feminist gesture and threatens to suck the debate into a losing vortex. Williams recognizes this danger and seeks to avoid it, calling not for a masculinist distance, but rather for a juggling of "all positions at once."[58] But by grounding the discussion in a suspicion of the image per se, this debate allows all orientations except that of being political *in* the image. My account of the feminist pretty seeks to fill this gap by proposing a politics not based in feminine positionality, but in a perverse counteraesthetics of the desirable image.

The example of *Stella Dallas* leads us to the third field in which feminist film theory intersects with the concerns of the pretty: melodrama and the women's picture. Christine Gledhill traces melodrama's association with mass culture, the feminine, and cinema—the last connection contributing to some critics' viewing of cinema as an inferior and feminine art form. Gledhill here adapts Huyssen's and Modleski's readings of mass culture as feminine to the specific historical trajectory of melodrama. Thus she argues that twentieth-century culture was masculinized at the same time that realism became a way to discriminate between high and popular culture: "Realism came to be associated with (masculine) restraint and underplaying."[59] This is the same naturalistic style that Béla Balázs discusses in chapter 1 and that enables early film criticism to oppose cinematic value to the excessive forms of the pretty. Melodrama and the pretty share this historical affiliation with the popular, sensible, feminine, and trivial against the high-cultural, rational, masculine, and serious. And because some defining qualities of melodrama are akin to those of the pretty—excess, a focus on mise-en-scène, a rich visual style—we can see feminist scholars of melodrama as a wellspring for thinking about the pretty.

Sue Harper, for instance, forges a rare positive bond among femininity, racial difference, and the decorative image in her work on Gainsborough melodramas, a low-brow British subgenre that has been critically rediscovered for its romantic and antirealist pleasures. She argues that the films "have a rich visual texture . . . [and] contain female protagonists (usually visually or diegetically coloured by 'gypsiness') who actively seek sexual pleasure." She goes on to describe the eclectic mise-en-scène of *The Wicked Lady* (Arliss, 1945): "A Jacobean door, a Baroque candleholder, an Elizabethan canopied bed, a Puritan bible, a medieval fire-basket are combined to form an unpredictable and dense visual texture. The past is signified not as a causal, linear structure, but as a chaotic amalgam—an opened cache of objects with uncertain meaning but available 'beauty.'"[60] By aligning this detailed décor with both female agency and ethnic difference, Harper demonstrates feminism's recuperative valuation of melodramatic excess and, in particular, its ability to challenge high-cultural norms from a popular-culture perspective. This kind of reading is useful for thinking the pretty, most notably in its reversal and valuation of the orientalist list of objects, which here belong to the badly behaved heroine. However, although Harper's scare-quoted gesture toward beauty is suggestive, we cannot entirely collapse the feminine pleasures of the popular bodice-ripper into the aesthetics of the pretty. As Gledhill explains, feminist work on melodrama is much less interested in mise-en-scène than are Marxist accounts that use it to crack apart ideology. Instead, this work tends to focus on creating feminine spaces around maternity, as in *Stella Dallas*, or sexual agency, as in *The Wicked Lady*. It overturns dominant regimes of cinematic quality by taking low genres and their female audiences seriously, but it skirts the hierarchizing structure of the feminine image itself. By contrast, a reading for the pretty would open out the potential meanings in such a beautiful mise-en-scène, which aligns the Gainsborough house style—a refusal of British restraint and postwar austerity—with an antipatriarchal aesthetics of formal exuberance.

The terms of debate have altered more recently, and feminist inquiry has followed the return of the status of the image as a central area in film studies. Where culturalist readers of melodrama reverse conventional hierarchies to celebrate the popular feminine, contemporary feminist film theory has attempted to reconceptualize the status of the image, turning to philosophy to elaborate a pro-image model. Catherine Constable, for instance, uses Michèle Le Doeuff's writing as a way of breaking apart the logocentric hierarchy: "Le Doeuff's work challenges a long tradition within Western philosophy, beginning with Plato, in which images are viewed as either textual decorations that do not add to the overall argument, or examples that serve to translate complex ideas into a more accessible form. In contrast to these constructions of the image as a more or less useful form of decoration, Le Doeuff argues that imagery is integral to philosophy, serving as the means through which concepts are created and expressed."[61] Constable's project is in this way analogous to mine, for she, too, begins from the gendering involved in the philosophical rejection of the image and from the iconophobia that reaches from Plato into cinema. However, her movement from figurative imagery in philosophical writing to actual visual images in film texts often elides the specificity of the cinematic image. The problem is not that it is impossible to extend ideas about rhetorical "images" in literary texts to an analysis of actual images, but that without enough attention to the politics of the cinematic her readings fall back on a "positive images" model of film feminism. Drawing on various post-Nietzschian theories, she aims to reevaluate the notion of woman as illusory surface, finding that Dietrich's roles offer "positive spins on the figures of the torturess, woman as caprice and the seductress." Thus she mobilizes Nietzsche to read Dietrich's performance in terms of truth within falsity and Baudrillard to find in Dietrich's Shanghai Lily a "hypersimulation of her public role as an image of indecency" that opens up a space to critique dominant values.[62] Although Constable's interrogation of philosophy's potential to think images differently is undoubtedly valuable, her case studies focus on performance and narrative rather than on the labor of the image it-self. Dietrich's rebellious and sexual characters remind us of the femme fatale's power in the image, and they similarly limit the concept of the feminine image to the performance of a strong actress in, against, and despite the image.

By contrast, instead of focusing on the representation of women, the pretty approaches the centrality of gender in reading the image, quite separate from any female characters represented. Refusing to see por-nography in visual plenitude—indeed, recognizing that it is this associa-tion that enforces patriarchal regimes of vision—flips the conventional feminist suspicion of the image and provokes a realignment of aesthetics and politics. How might we read *Rue cases nègres / Sugar Cane Alley* (Palcy, 1983) differently if we were to view the film's richly saturated sepia tones and picturesque compositions as a pointed intervention in the racializa-tion and gendering of the visual rather than as a retreat from Third Cin-ema's more radical forms? If we can read "tinted" and "overcrowded" im-ages as offering refusals of the patriarchal aesthetic experience, we can produce a new account of feminist aesthetics. Moreover, the complex in-terweaving of race, sex, and geography in the exclusion of the pretty might foreclose on feminism's habit of reifying the category of woman. The pretty, I argue, enables us to return to the canonical debates of femi-nist film theory with a fresh eye, revitalizing its foundational questions and reimagining the potential of the feminized image.

QUEERING THE PRETTY BODY

The space between the aesthetics of the image and that of the body in the image is also a problem for queer film studies, which has often fo-cused on identitarian issues and, as a corollary, has rejected aesthetic modes that smack of beauty as a means to refute dominant forms of gay and lesbian representation. Ugliness and the deformation of the image are more common tropes in queer critical theory than are their oppo-sites, and queer film criticism has often focused more on combating the invisibility of gay and lesbian bodies than on the question of style. Thus Barbara Creed outlines masculine, narcissistic, and animalistic les-bian bodies in popular cinema as particularly queer variants of a gro-tesque and abject feminine body that recurs across patriarchal visual culture.[63] In a similar vein, Harry Benshoff discusses "monstrous predatory homosexuals" in horror films as one ambivalent way that queerness was able to become visible in film history.[64] These readings communicate with the pretty insofar as they seek to transvalue cinematic representations that have previously been devalued or gone unnoticed. Moreover, many film critics have drawn on the literary and art historical associations of queerness with aestheticism and decorative decadence. Benshoff links the generic history of monstrous queers to Oscar Wilde and fin-de-siècle aestheticism, and Creed traces her grotesque lesbians to the vampiric fin-de-siècle ladies of early cinema. Cindy Patton has likewise pointed out the connection of lesbianism and decadentism in Anna Nazimova's portrayal of the title role in *Salomé* (Bryant, 1923).[65] Queer film histories seem closely adjacent to the conceptual constellation of the pretty, yet the "horrific" and "grotesque" queer body ultimately rejects concepts of prettiness along with heterocentrist beauty discourse.

I contend, though, that there is a slippage in this logic from the perception of beauty as a property of bodies to the pretty as a mode of cinematic form. The focus on bodily beauty invokes the regime in which the whiter the body, the more beautiful it is (and all the concomitant demands of modern aesthetics on the appropriate shapes and forms of both masculinity and femininity). The pretty body is perhaps even worse, suggesting a submissively heterocentrist kind of gender performance—the kind that H. D. disapproves of in Greta Garbo's American films. In contemporary discourse, the pretty is closely associated with the shallowness and vacuity of celebrity culture, in which young actors are of interest only for their tanned and perfect bodies on the red carpet and in the nightclub. And yet even this most unreconstructed of examples opens up the ideological divisions of the pretty. We would not look to the pretty bodies and faces of Jessica Alba or Zac Efron as locations for radical critique; in fact, in the regime of such celebrity, many critics would see an oppressive use of the pretty to regulate racist and heterosexist norms. But the typical association of this regime with feminizing rhetoric and with a dismissal of mass culture should be enough to remind us that prettiness is less the problem here than the familiar structures of power that demand that only certain bodies get to be called beautiful and that those bodies can be valued only aesthetically.[66] More important, though, the pretty image is not the same thing as the pretty body filmed, and to conflate them is to foreclose on any politics of form. If we turn to queer criticism's formal rhetoric, we will thus be unsurprised to find a devaluation of the pretty image.

Anti-pretty rhetoric is certainly as strong a feature in 1980s and 1990s queer film criticism as it was in the leftist and feminist journals of the 1970s. Influential gay critic Thomas Waugh provides a particularly helpful case study, for his collected writings offer a contemporary gloss on the original articles.[67] His review of Jarman's *Sebastiane* (1976) was famously vitriolic, and he invoked the pretty as a signifier of all that was wrong with the film: "Having removed the religious content of the myth, the director has failed to find anything else of substance to inject into this empty pageant of pretty men in loincloths and armor running around a pretty Mediterranean landscape. The film critic for *Gay Left* has credited Jarman, a former set director for Ken Russell, with the intention of making a statement about sexual repression and violence, but this assessment of a tawdry jumble of s / m formulas seems rather generous to me."[68] The term *pretty* here refers directly to some of the key elements disparaged throughout film criticism's anti-pretty history—bodies, costume, and landscape—and the surrounding sentences add equally common accusations of superficiality, decorative mise-en-scène (pageant), and perversion. Waugh says in his introduction to the reprint of this review that he was "wrong wrong wrong" about the film,[69] so my point is not to take issue with his reading but to show how anti-pretty ideas prevented him from seeing what he later found to be the film's valuable qualities.

A remarkably similar retraction is made regarding his reading of Maria Luisa Bemberg's *Camila* (1984), a film set during Argentina's nineteenth-century dictatorship in which an heiress has a forbidden affair with a priest. For Waugh, "the parallel with repression under a more recent junta is all but explicit, and it's easy to see why this pretty film about doomed sexual passion has been seen as the official cinematic celebration of that country's return to liberalized civilian rule."[70] The critique here is less stringent, but there is a clear implication that the film is of minor interest—an insufficiently radical take on state repression of sexuality that might be compared with the touristic pleasures of the heritage film. But Waugh once again recants in his introduction to the review, telling us that he loves the film more now then he did on first viewing and is "sorry that I called it 'pretty.' "[71] What I find fascinating here is the recurrence of the pretty as a mode of rejecting quite disparate styles of gay filmmaking. Waugh saw *Sebastiane* as inadequately serious, an experimental excuse for erotic games, but *Camila* as, if anything, overly serious, a damped-down official version of history that plays it too straight. Moreover, his revised assessment of *Camila* shows that he has not changed his mind on the value of a pretty aesthetic: rather, if he thinks the film is now lovable, it must therefore no longer be pretty. Different as their styles are, Jarman and Bemberg are examples of the kinds of queer filmmaking that tend to be misunderstood or critically underexposed because of their pretty styles. And Waugh exemplifies the problems that the pretty causes for queer critics who might otherwise be predicted to champion a cinematic pageant of perversion.

When we turn from public criticism to film scholarship, the same iconophobic logic is prevalent. In her reading of *Damned If You Don't* (1987), Su Friedrich's lesbian reimagining of attraction between the nuns in Michael Powell and Emeric Pressburger's *Black Narcissus* (1947), Andrea Weiss finds that "first, the poor quality of the image disturbs rather than creates visual pleasure, and directs the viewer more strongly toward the spoken narration—narration which clearly spells out, and thereby deconstructs, the good nun / bad nun polarization, a process which is further assisted by the film's conversion from its original color to the more oppositional black and white."[72] Weiss proceeds from a Mulveyan linkage of visual pleasure with patriarchal oppression, exaggerating the feminist model so that a deterioration of the image performs the labor of critiquing patriarchy and heterocentrism. Not only a deterioration of picture quality but a removal of color and a redirection of attention to the spoken word are praised: Weiss reiterates both a Platonic valuation of word over image and its visual equivalent of valuing graphic black and white over dangerously lush color. This example is exaggerated—Does anyone really believe that the black-and-white image is oppositional?— but the sense that the surface of the image is the site of ideological danger runs through queer feminisms as strongly as through its straight counterparts. Mandy Merck critiques the "mannered style" of the sex scenes in *Lianna* (Sayles, 1983), finding that art cinematic stylistic pleasures repeat classical constructions of the woman as object of the gaze.[73] Although I see no reason to contest her conclusion, the rhetoric of mannerism signals a critique of visibly dominant style that sits ill at ease with her desire to represent a queer sexuality unencumbered by heteronormative restrictions.

Thus queer film theory is caught in the same double bind as feminism, whereby a political rejection of the sexual regime inherited from classical and modern aesthetics is frequently undermined by a continuation of that tradition's formal account of the image. We have seen an example of this ambivalence in the work of Probyn, who argues for the "surface nature of belonging" and yet finds the image to be an object of suspicion.[74] In the same way, queer scholars and critics reject mannerism, color, and a pleasurable mise-en-scène as signifiers of a film's political failure and find pretty bodies, such as those in *Sebastiane*, to indicate a lack of conceptual depth and substance. As in feminism, in queer theory there is a built-in resistance to any countering valuation of the pretty, a resistance deriving from a belief that politically constituted theoretical models reject the pretty from the side of radicality, as a principled refusal of oppressive aesthetic norms. It is easier to recover the disprized space of the pretty in relation to early-twentieth-century demands for aesthetic austerity than it is to gainsay those theories that overthrow patriarchal and heteronormative cultural standards in order for marginalized bodies to appear. For one thing, a queer aesthetics of aesthetic deformation makes a compelling and direct claim on visual transgression. For another, there is a significant difference between a lesbian's rejecting feminine prettiness and a straight man's decrying it.

Perhaps this resistance explains why influential tropes of queer theory such as drag and the performative seem not to mesh very well with the pretty. In a certain usage commonplace in 1980s and 1990s academic discourse, drag is not at all pretty; typically formed of an excess of femininity, it deliberately distorts the prettiness associated with "real" women. Like camp, drag takes pleasure in perverting, overdoing, and reversing the orthodoxies of straight aesthetics, mocking prettiness for being too close to beauty rather than too far away.[75] Not all practices of drag follow this pattern, but many accounts of its transgressive power focus on its refusal of aesthetic good form. But if drag can seem far removed from prettiness, its major theorization does perform some of the same conceptual work as the pretty. In constructing an antidepth epistemology, Judith Butler's account of gender performativity at least implicitly counters the iconophobic heuristic model that finds the surface to be inferior and deceptive. Butler deconstructs the surface / depth binary of sex and gender, asking us to think differently about the potential value of surface appearance: "The critical potential of 'drag' centrally concerns a critique of a prevailing truth-regime of 'sex,' one that I take to be pervasively hetero-sexist: the distinction between the 'inside' truth of femininity, considered as psychic disposition or ego-core, and the 'outside' truth, considered as appearance or presentation, produces a contradictory formation of gender in which no fixed 'truth' can be established."[76] Butler's dismissal of the feminine core at the heart of heterosexist sex discourse importantly does not entail valorizing surface appearance as a countertruth. Responding to her critics in a discussion of the drag film *Paris Is Burning* (Livingston, 1990), she insists, "Although many readers understood *Gender Trouble* to be arguing for the proliferation of drag performances as a way of subverting dominant gender norms, I want to underscore that there is no necessary relation between drag and subversion, and that drag may well be used in the service of both the denaturalization and reidealization of hyperbolic heterosexual gender norms."[77] The same is true of prettiness, which does not necessarily produce radical outcomes. Just as drag might or might not subvert gender norms, the pretty might or might not subvert the association of the decorative image with the secondary qualities of femininity.

In a wholly structural way, then, reading for the pretty is indebted to Butler's analysis of gender performativity in *Paris Is Burning* and beyond because drag as a hermeneutic mode asks us to rethink the valuation of depth, the political potential of surface, and the bodily inscriptions of gender, sexuality, race, and class. Moreover, some of the many critiques of Butler's position include anti-pretty language in their assertion of the lived (deep, real) materiality of queer lives in contrast to the postmodern (superficial, illusory) transgressions offered by drag performance. Elisa Glick, for instance, suggests that "feminist and queer theorists like [Sue Ellen] Case and Butler efface the histories and contexts of gay lives by glorifying butch / femme roles as performative, surface identities, uncomplicated by race or class and detached from specific communities and interests." Glick contrasts what she sees as a surface politics of style with more genuine histories of social activism and lived queer experience, taking as a privileged example the contrast between Butler's version of drag and mid-twentieth-century lesbian cultures: "Tellingly, these valorizations of the 'new lesbian chic' in both the straight and gay press clearly distinguish 'the new butch / femme' from the unpretty, politicized working-class butches and femmes of the 1950s."[78] Between these unpretty activists and 1990s lipstick lesbians, a connection is forged between theories of the surface and counterfeit pop-cultural representations as well as between materialism and authentic historical experience. Neither Butler nor Glick is talking primarily about aesthetics. For them, films and other cultural texts are examples of broader social and psychic paradigms, and this difference is important. Film aesthetics do not have the hegemonic weight of gender norms, and the pretty is not an identitarian category. Its politics are closely tied to cultural ideas about the body, but these ideas do not map onto any group of people in the world. Thus although the theoretical relationship of drag to the pretty is structural rather than corporeal, we should pay all the more attention to Glick's invocation of unpretty bodies to repudiate Butler. A turn to queer ugliness enables an unspoken reliance on aesthetics to underwrite ideas on sexuality.

Thus despite the apparent undesirability of prettiness for a queer feminism, it bears investigation that queer theory harbors an aesthetic logic imported from patriarchal, colonial, and homophobic modernities. As with feminist film theory, it might prove troubling to base a radical critique of cinema on a reactionary view of the image. A different method might be glimpsed in Sara Ahmed's work on orientation, which sidesteps questions of surface and depth by thinking instead about left and right. Ahmed smoothly engages the raced and gendered histories of orientation that associate left with femininity and wrongness, on the one hand, and right with masculine reason and correctness, on the other, intersecting these cultural histories with orientalism as a geopolitical mode and its devaluative feminization of the East. The Orient is part of the word *orientation*, and our very concepts of directionality and view construct the perspective of a male Westerner facing the feminine East. Ahmed says that "the object function of the Orient, then, is not simply a sign of the presence of the West—of where it 'finds its way'—but also a measure of how the West has 'directed' its time, energy, and resources."[79] We might profitably build orientation into a practice of thinking the pretty, for the pretty also asks us to look, in this case at film aesthetics, from a different place. From this new perspective, the inferiority of prettiness becomes marked rather than obvious. Pretty is a digression from the proper orientation of film, a digression from right, reason, beauty, truth, and so on. And more, it is a digression from the aesthetic propriety of the West to the object world of the East. The Oriental object aesthetic speaks of Western desire, but there is a necessary obverse to this function: not only is decorative stuff devalued because it is connected to the Orient, but it is connected to the Orient because it was already associated with otherness in regard to right-thinking masculine values.

Ahmed is not concerned primarily with aesthetics, but she opens up pathways for a queer pretty film theory when she considers the straightness of straight lines: "To go directly is to follow a line without a detour, without mediation. Within the concept of direction is a concept of 'straightness.' To follow a line might be a way of becoming straight, by not deviating at any point."[80] In this linguistic overlapping of straightness as an orientation and straightness as a formal mechanism of line, we find the logic of modern aesthetic simplicity in which directness speaks more clearly, more rationally than unnecessary decoration, and decoration deviates from the purity of heterocentric aesthetic form. Just as we must deconstruct the *disegno* versus *colore* binary, so we might consider the potential of a line that does not do the work of straightness and patriarchal reason. The unstraight line suggests a queer pretty in which filmmakers might be oriented differently toward aesthetics, the categories of straightness, correctness, and aesthetic deviance. It is perhaps the nature of the pretty's deviance not to offer obvious radicality or a wholesale antiaesthetic refusal. Pretty is not a transgressive or an activist form in any ideologically simplistic manner. This is why it names a space of exclusion that in large measure has been formed by the dismissive moves of radical modes of critique. But it is this ease of exclusion—the way that the pretty comes to stand in for aesthetic exclusion as such—that makes it an interesting case for queer practices.

If we consider how queer filmmakers have deployed prettiness, we find a proliferation of aesthetic practices that cannot be fully understood within an iconoclastic aesthetico-political model. Todd Haynes asserts production design as a primary method of elaborating social relations in his film *Far from Heaven* (2002), for example, and both François Ozon and Tsai Mingliang repurpose camp excess within art cinematic forms. Ozon's *Angel* (2007) turns classical melodramatic techniques such as back projection into visible style, forcing the cinematic image to speak the impossible beauties engendered by the class contradictions of its social-climbing heroine. Tsai's rococo grandeur in *Tian bian yi duo dun / The Wayward Cloud* (2005), meanwhile, uses highly colored musical fantasy as a counterpoint to his ongoing exploration of Taiwanese modernity and globalized urban space (figure 43). Campy costuming and choreography provide bursts of prettiness that are as disjunctive in their way as the film's quasi-

FIGURE 43 *Tian bian yi duo dun / The Wayward Cloud* (Tsai, 2005)
Musical fantasy intersects with political space in Tsai Ming-liang's queer pretty aesthetic.

pornographic scenes of watermelon sex. Each of these films is startlingly pretty, offering their audiences expansive sensory pleasures and demanding that the audience read these visual strategies as both thematically complex and politically productive. If the ugly is a direct reversal of previous modes of value—making desirable what has been thought of as beyond the pale of aesthetics—then the queer pretty is a more complicated mode.

ICONOPHILIC ENCHANTMENT

What does a feminist or queer pretty look like? Although modern aesthetics have formed the pretty as a gendered and sexualized space of exclusion, reversing the Platonic binary and finding value only in the image emphatically does not solve the problem. The humanities have seen an often conservative return to aesthetics in recent years, with feminist scholars at the forefront of the trend, but the pretty does not oppose ideology with regressive models of beauty, femininity, or moral good. Quite the contrary. My insistence on mobilizing a polemic of the pretty is explained by the persistent conservatism of those cultural critics who might at first glance appear aligned with my argument. For instance, in her analysis of neoclassical aesthetics and "contemporary iconoclasm," Stafford acutely diagnoses the historical trajectory of iconophobia, but her critique of Marxist and poststructuralist thought tends to throw the political baby out with the rhetorical bathwater. Her call to reenchant images feeds a reactionary humanist project whose aesthetic centrism worries that art is out of step with mainstream values and lauds reevaluations of Norman Rockwell, which can "fit our limited local perspectives into a bigger picture of humanity." Moreover, she outright condemns as "disturbing" and "debasing" cultural practices that for many critics have nourished lively political debate, such as copyright infringement and pornography.[81] In this section, I argue that the pretty can negotiate between the iconophobia of much modern film theory and the iconophilia of beauty discourse, creating a space for the aesthetic image that troubles rather than accedes to dominant notions of femininity. This queer space counters the enchantment of beauty with the perversity of the pretty.

Several contemporary theorists have revisited Max Weber's notion of the disenchantment of the modern world, calling, like Stafford, for reenchantment with a view to superseding modernist theories or extending the parameters of aesthetic experience. Some of this work shares a critical impetus with my project. W. J. T. Mitchell, for instance, mobilizes the enchanted image as a way out of iconophobia, and Christopher Pinney has associated disenchanted vision with oppressive colonial aesthetics.[82] Yet I find this discourse troubling and not only because of the avowedly conservative critics who claim reenchantment in the name of an antisecular revival.[83]

The advocates of enchantment often present a false choice of two undesirable options: ugly rationality or pseudo-religious magic. Jane Bennett in *The Enchantment of Modern Life* counterposes a particularly joyless version of Theodor Adorno's critique with an ethical generosity and pleasure in the ineffable.[84] Even though she is careful to include the secular in her nonrational space, the connotation of magic is straightforwardly positive as she seeks to reverse dominant terms and value magical enchantment. However, just as I find it impossible to subscribe to a feminism that favors seduction or feminine wiles as a response to patriarchy, I am likewise leery of an ethics that responds to capitalist modernity by seeking to reenchant the world. Many variants of feminist cultural theory prioritize pleasure without returning to mystification as a response to the problems of Enlightenment thought. The pretty inter-

venes in this field by insisting that we read aesthetic exclusions politically rather than swap one oppressive paradigm for another.

That the image of the woman is at stake in these calls to reenchant
culture and to reinstate beauty should not be doubted, and the problem
for feminism is the limited scope of the feminine image proposed. The
affiliation of Stafford's antiporn feminism with this aesthetic resurgence
does not seem to me to be coincidental. Wendy Steiner, another major
humanities scholar to take up the banner of contemporary aesthetics,
valorizes feminine beauty against what she sees as the sexual and political affront of modernism. Her claim is in some important ways coextensive with my own: she identifies gender as the stake in a seemingly un-
fashionable question of aesthetics, and she considers a phobia of the
feminine to be at the heart of the matter. As we saw in chapter 3, Steiner
understands the modern antipathy to ornament to derive from misogyny, and she sums up the history of twentieth-century art discourse in
the qualities of "form, fetish, woman, and ornament."[85] Accusing the
historic avant-garde of a patriarchal formalism, she rereads Kant for a
feminist aesthetics that offers parallels with the pretty. However, when
Steiner unpacks modernism's cultural denigration of the feminine, she
proposes as an alternative a deeply problematic return to a model of feminized value that embraces the woman as muse, the domestic and reproductive spheres, and the heterosexual family.

Steiner petitions for beauty as a positive force that fosters shared values and "our deepest nature,"[86] but she begs the question as to whose
values are being included here and to what ends the "natural" is ex-
tracted. It is not long before the ideological undercurrents of beauty are
rendered clear: she repeatedly returns to the heterosexual couple as one
model for art and the mother and child as the other. She cites approvingly Henry Adams's paean to motherhood and Christian order, in
which "God was a father and nature a mother." And she finds this familial order to be Mary Shelley's ideal, too, seeing in *Frankenstein* a "domestic vision of life made in the image of a loving woman . . . now [in moder-
nity] lost." Instead of modernist formalism, Shelley "offered a metaphor
for artistic creativity in which the artist loves what she creates because
she recognizes herself in it and responds to its beauty, charm, and even
allure."[87] She thus returns us to a Victorian sentimentalism, installing
the angel in the home, the woman who is at the center of the world only
insofar as this position enables man to be God and woman's power to

look is directed narcissistically inward at the child that she loves because it resembles her.

Steiner's valuation of the women's look on her husband and baby constrains aesthetic production to the most clichéd of straight social imaginaries, but it at least provides some form of recognizable agency in the mother-as-artist figures of Shelley and painter Marlene Dumas. Her account of feminist theory, though, is focused on a reading of Manet's *Olympia* (1863) as a strong woman who compels the gaze and thus produces the artist's model as her major figuration of women's stake in the aesthetic. Olympia, she contends, has an agency (both in the image and as a smart and interesting historical personage) that is more significant than the looking relations theorized by feminist film scholars and art historians. We should value women like Olympia, Steiner concludes, because "the female model dominates the aesthetic situation. . . . [T]his idealized real woman becomes the essence of the aesthetic experience. Moreover, insofar as women in our culture participate in both reality and ideality on a daily basis, they are always models—spurs to aesthetic experience. Contemporary culture, in its turn towards beauty, is beginning to recognize the pivotal position the female / model plays."[88] I am trying not to be too visibly horrified at the implications of that slash mark in "female / model," but I think that it is clear that this conception of feminist visual theory will not mesh comfortably with the pretty's aesthetico-political aims. Indeed, Steiner goes out of her way to consign feminist theorists to the same opprobrium held by misogynist modernists: from Mary Wollstonecraft to Laura Mulvey, any critique of how women have been limited by the requirement of beauty is anathema to her project.

This is the core problem with conservative feminist iconophilia. In reversing the Platonic hierarchy of value, it lauds traditionally feminine roles but leaves the constrictive structures of patriarchal and heteronormative visuality unmolested. For Steiner, "the problem is how to imagine female beauty, in art or outside it, without invoking stories of dominance, victimization, and false consciousness."[89] The desire invoked here is to wish away feminism, to be able to look at images of women without any unpleasurable reminder of social inequality. What this desire leads to in practice is an inability to see—or rather to love—any image that does not conform to traditional feminine values. For Steiner as well as for the theorists of enchantment, the aesthetic image and the feminine stand in opposition to politics, modernity, and pornographic vision. But what of sex-positive feminism in this aesthetic regime? What, indeed, of femininities that do not engage the "pure" beauty of heterosexual motherhood? What, that is to say, of the ornamental and the perverse?

ICONOPHILIC PERVERSION

Figures of sexuality and, in particular, images of bodies engaged in perverse, violent, or proscribed acts recur throughout this history. Both the anti-pretty polemics of Charles Blanc and Adolf Loos and the apparently iconophilic revisions of Stafford and Steiner imagine the dangerous misuse of images in terms of sexual representation. The contemporary writers use pornography to figure the politically and aesthetically reprehensible, and more than a century earlier Blanc made a very similar move when he argued that "the taste for color, when it predominates absolutely, costs many sacrifices; often it turns the mind from its course, changes the sentiment, swallows up the thought. The impassioned colorist invents his form for his color, everything is *subordinated* to the brilliancy of his tints. Not only the drawing *bends* to it, but the composition is *dominated, restrained, forced* by the color."[90] His rhetoric proposes a scene of perverse seduction in which color as dominatrix upsets the natural order by restraining masculine line. A few years later, Loos began his campaign for aesthetic plainness by seeking to rationalize male and female dress. I have already discussed the gendering of modernist simplicity, but the perversity of Loos's vision is revealed in a truly bizarre essay titled "Ladies' Fashion," in which he argues that because women have to dress to impress men, women's clothes are thus related to fashions in sexual acts. There is a kind of feminist critique being made here, but what stands out is the astonishing rhetoric of perversion. He begins: "Ladies' fashion! You disgraceful chapter in the history of civilization! You tell of mankind's secret desires. Whenever we peruse your pages, our souls shudder at the dreadful perversions and unbelievable vices."[91] The piece goes on to evoke cracking whips, flagellants, and the writings of Leopold von Sacher-Masoch as influences on voluptuous and feminine styles. Across the modern history of thinking the aesthetic, the decorative and colorful image is not only feminine, but positively kinky.

This curious iteration of perversity limns an important new quality of the pretty. As with the pretty's other qualities, its perversity describes a negative space repeatedly figured as politically suspicious or aesthetically inadequate across otherwise diverse critical positions. Of course, many feminist and queer film theorists have drawn inspiration from the psychoanalytic literature on the perversions, but these accounts focus on structures of spectatorial identification and desire rather than on the sexualized formal qualities of the image itself.[92] When perversity *in* the image or the perversity *of* the image is in question, anti-pretty thinking frequently supersedes Freudian or Lacanian feminisms. In an example from public film culture, B. Ruby Rich describes how the influential lesbian film *She Must Be Seeing Things* (McLaughlin, 1987) was picketed by feminist groups in Great Britain for its BDSM content.[93] In a more recent example, Tanya Krzywinska's book *Sex and the Cinema* condemns Pier Paolo Pasolini's *Salò o le 120 giornate di Sodoma / Salò* (1975) both for the violence of its scenes of torture and for their superficiality. She complains that "even if the viewer is able to actively disavow what they [*sic*] are seeing by focusing intently on the aesthetic glossiness of the carefully-staged images, the capacity of human beings to negate human values is still glaringly apparent."[94] I do not want to suggest that *Salò* is a pretty film— this example should clarify the difference between a critical discourse of prettiness and a category of "pretty" into which films can be placed—but Krzywinska's disapproval of both antihumanist images of sexual depravity and surface aesthetic sheen demonstrates how closely related these seemingly distant qualities can be for both filmmaker and unsympathetic critic.

More progressive accounts of BDSM are to be found in the critical response to Monika Treut's films, especially *Verführung: Die grausame Frau / Seduction: The Cruel Woman* (1985), which reenvisions Sacher-Masoch's *Venus in Furs* in a queer sex club. Andrea Reimann sees the film as "dragging German history" and places its masochistic aesthetics in the same category as Rainer Werner Fassbinder's radical provocations.[95] Other critics have pointed to *Seduction*'s queer appropriation of Sade and Sacher-Masoch as a mode of both historical and psychoanalytic revision. Thus for Barbara Mennel, "*Seduction* recreates and complicates the interrelatedness of perverse desire and heteronormativity; transgression and commodification; traditional accounts of sadism and masochism and current formations of S&M. Furthermore, the film reproduces the aesthetics of perverse desire structured around suspense and fetishization." So far, so positive. However, Mennel discloses the pretty qualities of the fetish image when she describes how "arrested images of the cruel woman, adorned with fetishes represent the permanent delay of sexual gratification to the extent that the investment of pleasure lies in the suspense itself. *Seduction*'s stylization of S&M performances in staged tableaux quotes the stillness and coldness of the construction of the 'original' dominant woman in *Venus in Furs* and creates the suspense that underlies the masochistic aesthetic."[96] This description, of course, reflects Gilles Deleuze's account of masochism and brings to the forefront its reliance on a patriarchal decorative order. Amber Musser has argued that Deleuze's masochism at first seems useful for a queer reader, but that it falls apart both in its project of reconstituting heterosexual male subjectivity and in its dependence on the female dominant as merely a prop to that subjectivity.[97] Adornment, tableau, and the gendered prop recall art nouveau's decorative death, the lack of a healthy and proper cinematic life, as well as Mulvey's masochistic spectacle. The surface composition and cold lifelessness of the film's perverse couples contrast with a dynamic and narrative vanilla relationship such that, even in the context of a positive reading of the film, the heteronormative and patriarchal decorative order of Deleuzian masochism develops parallels between vanilla and perverse, narrative and mise-en-scène, real and pretty. Less sympathetic readers of *Seduction* can easily conclude that the masochistic aesthetic undoes its sexual radicality to the extent that it produces a cinematic pretty. Birgit Hein thus comments that "[*Seduction* is] a very nice film, I like it as a film, but some parts of it are also too picturesque."[98] Perversion can be politically transgressive (that is, valuable), such critiques say, but only if it is aesthetically unappealing.

Returning to Pasolini, Leo Bersani and Ulysse Dutoit elaborate a sophisticated theory of cinematic perversion in their reading of *Salò*, in which, they propose, "it is the very limitlessness of our aestheticism which constitutes the moral perspective on sadism."[99] The linkage of aesthetic seduction and morality is a welcome rebuttal to the politics of anti-aesthetics, but Bersani and Dutoit specifically exclude from relevance what the feminist critics of Treut's work bemoan the lack of—an ethics (and aesthetics) of relationality. Thus they point out that "neither *The 120 Days* nor *Salò* is at all about the complicity between torturers and victims. . . . [I]n none of these cases is it a question of the irresistible appeal of being tortured. This appeal doesn't even have to be denied; it would simply be a superficial point, and in works so profoundly investigative about sadomasochistic sexuality and politics as *The 120 Days* and *Salò*, it can be ignored."[100] What I am interested in following here is Bersani and Dutoit's attribution of superficiality to the desire of the tortured, completely reversing Reimann's and Mennel's investments in a queer masochistic aesthetic. They find any such erotic complicity to be superficial, not profound, and ultimately quite ignorable in a way that uncannily echoes Freud's address to women as themselves the problem.[101] Thus although Bersani and Dutoit's reading of *Salò* is far richer and more compelling than Krzywinska's, the account of cinematic perversion that it entails posits as cosmetic something that a feminist pretty would rather see as central. How, then, might we think about the perverse image—the perversion of aesthetics—not as fascistic alienation from the other, but as an ethical pleasure?

One evocative example, not from cinema but contemporary art practice, is Catherine Opie's photography. Her "Self-Portrait / Pervert" (1994) features a Regency fabric, which cites a history of decorative aesthetics and hangs behind Opie, while Opie herself is elegantly posed wearing a leather mask and with dozens of thick needles arranged symmetrically along her arms and a leaf motif cutting across her bare chest, spelling "Pervert" in an art nouveau style (figure 44). A conventional feminist or queer reading would see the stylized aesthetics as ironic counterpoints to the photograph's confrontational nakedness, gimp mask, and piercings and thus might find it to be either voyeuristic or simply aimed at shock value. We can read differently if we notice that the image is definitively pretty as I have discussed the term and that its deployment of rich color, balanced composition, and art historical reference demands that we do not read its subject in terms of violence, ugliness, or confrontation. Judith Halberstam has made a similar defense of Opie's photographs of BDSM and masculine dykes, arguing that their rich color and stylization—constructing their subjects as "positively regal in their opulent settings," with "colorful displays of tattoos and body markings"—actually prevent what some critics decry as a voyeuristic structure by forcing viewers "to be admiring and appreciative rather than simply objectifying."[102] Tattoos and piercings move from being a primitive sign of exclusion and ugliness in Carl Gustav Jochmann and Loos to become a bodily claim on perverse aesthetics. Opie asks that we find her "perverted" body to be aesthetically pleasing in exactly the same ways that the patterned and colorful fabrics are, and she moreover reminds us that they, too, have a history of aesthetic perversion. "Self-Portrait / Pervert" addresses both

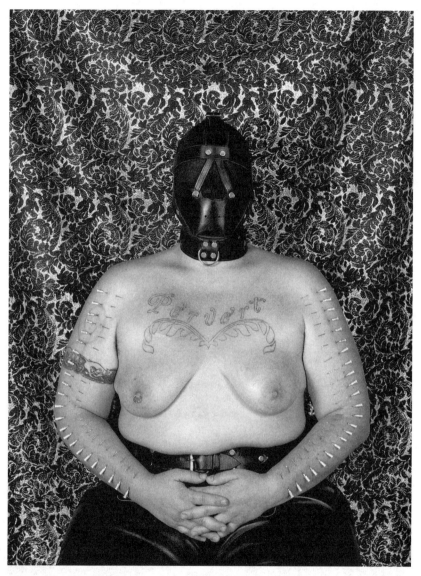

FIGURE 44 Catherine Opie, "Self-Portrait / Pervert" (1994)

A queer / BDSM pretty. (Chromogenic print, 40 × 30 inches [101.6 × 76.2 cm]; Solomon R. Guggenheim Museum, New York; Purchased with funds contributed by the Photography Committee, 2003)

the complicit spectator that Bersani and Dutoit foreclose upon and the critics of *Seduction* who demand that perversion not be picturesque. I find this example important because Opie's photographed bodies are precisely not the ones a patriarchal aesthetics would find pretty. The pretty is decidedly not a polemic for traditional, white, hetero femininity. Color, opulence, excess, and style are aesthetic weapons for queer bodies also.

A cognate example from experimental film is Maria Beatty, whose BDSM shorts bring together 1920s film style, the decorative image, and an erotic ethics of masochism. *Ecstasy in Berlin 1926* (2004) opens with an aestheticized composition of flesh and lace but soon adds a needle piercing the woman's thigh. Like Opie, Beatty takes something that might look violent or shocking and renders it part of a pretty seduction, asking the spectator to find it beautiful (figure 45). And just as Opie draws on the eighteenth- and nineteenth-century traditions of portraiture as the backdrop for her image, Beatty turns to a filmic equivalent: the glamour and romanticism of Weimar culture. *Ecstasy in Berlin*—set

FIGURE 45 *Ecstasy in Berlin 1926* (Beatty, 2004)
A cinematic queer / BDSM pretty also deploys decorative sets as a background to an erotics of sensation.

a year before Siegfried Kracauer's essay "Mass Ornament" and Josephine Baker's first movie—is full of jazz music, tap shoes, and flapper pearls. Beatty emphasizes the drag aspects of 1920s film style, presenting a submissive starlet with platinum blond hair and cupid's bow lips as well as a dominant dressed in a man's suit, white gloves, and slicked back hair. In a scene of boot licking, the top has changed into silent cinema femme fatale makeup, with dark lipstick and a haircut reminiscent of that of the iconic lesbians in *Mädchen in Uniform* (Sagan, 1931). This costume changing continues in *Ecstasy*, with each sexual scene (spanking, cropping, caning, and so on) matched by a different costume worn by the top so that the decoration of the body aligns to its erotic punishment. The theatricality of setting is similar to Opie's tableaux, and although the bodies on screen are less resistant to conventional versions of feminine beauty, the acts of violence and humiliation they undergo certainly are. Body piercings, needles, and whip marks adorn skin in the same way that period costumes and art nouveau décor dress the sets. The pretty style of cinematography and bodily costuming is aligned to and helps articulate the erotics of bodily pain and confinement. By refusing to create a conflict between pretty decoration and perverse sexuality, the film mobilizes the decorative to create a queer cinematic vision.

Katrien Jacobs has argued that the Versailles room of a refined dungeon seems to represent the "stifling code of conduct of the upper-class" but codes something else entirely to the practitioner.[103] This example captures the way that a prettily arranged set or a decorative image or an art nouveau house might not provoke simply living with one's own corpse, but playing (perversely) with it. Jacobs describes "Beatty's trompe l'oeil scenery" in terms of a radical sex politics,[104] and in *Ecstasy in Berlin*'s erotic violence we see both glamorous film style and the 1920s not as restrictive and stifling, but as radically reimaginable. It is noteworthy that Beatty identifies as a submissive and plays one in her films: Beatty's direction "from the bottom" demands that we revise clichéd feminist accounts of agency and power and vitiates Bersani and Dutoit's cathexisless sadism.[105] In an interview, Beatty stated, "I wanted to explore my own sexual universe, to focus on the pleasures and the ecstasy of the submissive position in BDSM, which is in opposition to the clichés of the dominant. I wanted to live that erotic experience in going as far as possible, to show it in a way as beautiful and aesthetic as I perceive it."[106] She tethers both sexual agency and aesthetic pleasure to restriction in a way that offers potential for pretty film. Her BDSM performance reimagines restriction as erotic play, pleasure, and cathexis, indicating how feminist and queer versions of pretty can deploy the restrictive charge of the art nouveau interior as a way to stage the perverse possibilities of cinematic space.

Opie's and Beatty's perverse images pinpoint the difference of reading for the pretty. A feminist mobilization of the pretty as a category does not trope sexuality as that excluded from meaning or value but explores the coincidence of aesthetics, sexual deviance, and the modern image. Beyond *Salò*, Pasolini's films often elaborate pretty bodies and spaces. In the Trilogy of Life's *Il fiore delle mille e una notte / Arabian Nights* (1974), for instance, ornament, excess, and decay trouble art cinematic rhetorics of beautiful form and disturb geopolitical and gendered fixities. Tony Rayns describes locations from Yemen to Nepal as conjuring "an endlessly varied and cosmopolitan world: inconceivable palaces with jewelled and mirrored sanctums, bazaars, deserts, tortuously winding alleys, the high seas."[107] Like Michael Powell's *The Thief of Baghdad* (1940), the film uses the arabesques of its geographical otherness to produce "sensate pleasures"—or, in other words, aesthetics. Plots nest within plots, and both same- and opposite-sex couples intertwine in the gorgeous desert settings. Zumurrud pretends to be a man, donning an elaborate golden beard and costume. Her laughter in the face of Nur-e-Din's perplexed desire produces a pleasure that remakes "life" far from the austere prescriptions of cinema's neoclassical inheritance. Beatty, too, seeks to *live* experience in her films, polemically insisting that desirable life can be found outside of doctrines of aesthetic and political agency. Jarman likewise brings the pornographic body together with a queer politics of color and the radical potential of art history. Reading the perverse qualities of the pretty allows us to synthesize such texts' intertwined articulations of mise-en-scène, materiality, and desire.

EIGHT

The Sumptuous Charms of Ulrike Ottinger

ULRIKE OTTINGER'S FILMMAKING PRESENTS ANOTHER INSTANCE of how pretty films, even famous ones, tend to become unmoored from the safe harbors of canon formation. Ottinger is an undoubtedly important figure in various fields, including art cinema, feminist film, and New German Cinema, but her films have never fitted smoothly into any of these categories. In the 1970s, critics at the influential German feminist journal *Frauen und Film* found them a poor match for current views on film feminism, and her most famous films predate the queer cinema movements of the 1990s, missing that boat, too. Andrea Weiss considers them not to be art cinema because they reject the realist and psychological impulses that she associates with the category, but Laurence Rickels claims that Ottinger is the epitome of art cinema, precisely because of her formalism.[1] If Ottinger's encounters with sympathetic film movements seem repeatedly doomed to miss, her audience likewise misses out on her films. In the 1970s, Annette Kuhn described the sense, on discovering Ottinger's films, that she had misunderstood New German Cinema because films like Ottinger's had not been distributed in the way that Rainer Werner Fassbinder's or Helma Sanders-Brahms's work had been, and even today Ottinger's films are not commercially available on DVD.[2] Thus even though Ottinger is an important figure for queer and feminist film scholarship, and she has produced significant fiction and documentary films consistently since the 1970s, her films are not nearly as widely viewed as those of her contemporaries. I find this persistent overlooking of Ottinger's films to be symptomatic of their prettiness and the scholarly debates over her value (to feminism, art cinema, and so on) to express similar anxieties about how to read a pretty film. In this chapter, I look *at* rather than over Ottinger's prettiness, mobilizing the pretty to focalize the troublesome questions of spectacle, perversion, and geographical otherness in her cinematic corpus.

Ottinger's films bring into close proximity many of the features of the pretty: an emphasis on visual style, a decorative and composed mise-en-scène, an engagement with the foreign and the perverse, and a mode of relating aesthetics to politics that does not fit with prevailing critical or institutional norms. *Madame X—Eine absolute Herrscherin / Madame X: An Absolute Ruler* (Ottinger, 1978) purports to tell a feminist tale of all-female adventure, but its sisterly piracy bleeds into fetishism, domination, and violence, articulating lesbian desire and orientalist fantasy with a mise-en-scène centered around the various characters' bodies and elaborate costumes. Issuing an invitation to all women to join her for a life of adventure on the China Seas, the charismatic Madame X entices American housewife Betty Brillo, artist Josephine de Collage, and pilot Omega Centauri to join her crew, among a group of women representing various feminine types. Ottinger's deployment of types echoes that of Mikhail Kalatozov and even Baz Luhrmann. Although by no means a prerequisite for the pretty, the recurrence of visually legible characters is provocative as a form of surface-level signification and pleasure in pretty films. Depth of characterization is simply dismissed as a cinematic aim, just as reproductive life is refused in queer decorative aesthetics. In *Madame X*, each woman can be recognized by her exaggerated costuming, and Madame X herself is doubled in the ship's figurehead, which wears a black leather bodysuit and sports a knife instead of a hand. Where the film speaks of gender, sexuality, and power, it does so through a bold visual strategy of embodiment.

Johanna d'Arc of Mongolia (1989), made ten years later, continues Ottinger's interest in nonrealist characters and staging, sending a group—including colonial travel expert Lady Windermere, Broadway singer Fanny Ziegfeld, and adventurous young woman Giovanna—off to Mon-

FIGURE 46 *Johanna d'Arc of Mongolia* (Ottinger, 1989)
Lady Windermere's compartment is an orientalist fantasy of luxury and sexual decadence.

golia on an elaborately constructed Trans-Siberian Railway (figure 46). As in the earlier film, costume, décor, and comedic play on stereotypes construct a prettily composed feminist milieu. Once in Mongolia, however, things change: the train is stopped, and the women are kidnapped by Princess Ulan Iga and taken to the taiga, where they encounter the lives of Mongolian nomads. The film also experiences a break from the theatrical interiority of the train set to location shooting in a wide-open landscape and from completely enclosed fiction to a semidocumentary engagement with its Mongolian nonactors. On both sides of the film, prettiness creates the formal tone, from ornate interior spaces that create meaning from objects to beautifully composed vistas that evoke the picturesque and the exotic. And, as in *Madame X*, lesbian desire, perverse relations, and orientalism run through the film's form and narrative. In just one narrative example of this geosexual play, the beautiful young traveler Giovanna first is seduced by Lady Windermere and then begins a relationship with Ulan Iga and dresses like a Mongolian as the film progresses. Just as many critics found *Madame X* to be unfeminist, so some scholars have rejected *Johanna d'Arc* as imperialist in its Western representation of the East. Ottinger's films are undoubtedly important and yet constantly troublesome, and the pretty names the place where these aesthetic and political ambivalences meet. In this chapter, I argue that the pretty is uniquely able to negotiate the cinema's intertwined regimes of the sexual and the geopolitical and, moreover, that this encounter is integral to the cinematic image itself.

Let us begin with *sumptuousness*, a word that recurs again and again in the critical literature on Ottinger. Almost everyone who writes on her films agrees that they are extremely rich visually: Rickels values the films' formalism, Brenda Longfellow describes *Johanna d'Arc*'s "sumptuous display of oriental objects," and Patricia White notes that "her films feature elaborate costumes, painterly shot composition, anti-realist performances, and eclectic and abundant musical and sound quotations."[3] It is not surprising that critics should notice what is a central stylistic quality of the films, but it is telling that this specific word, *sumptuous*, is repeated. Janet A. Kaplan describes *Johanna d'Arc* in terms of its "sumptuous visual impact," and Roswitha Mueller, writing on *Dorian Gray im Spiegel der Boulevardpresse / The Image of Dorian Gray in the Yellow Press* (1984), says that "like all of Ottinger's films [it] is built around a narrative, a story line so slender and simple that it threatens to be swallowed up by the sumptuous way of its execution."[4] Ottinger's pretty is sumptuous because it is not carefully restrained or tasteful. Its sets are overstuffed; its costumes are outré; and its theatricality blends avant-garde performance with more low-brow cinematic pleasures. Moreover, there is a patriarchal quality to the use of the term *sumptuous* that reiterates a fear that the pretty image might overwhelm masculine narrative. Here, instead of the common anxiety of the seductively feminine image, we have a feminist threat of engulfment, enfolding, or, in Mueller's terms, swallowing. The sumptuous image does not sit around hoping to seduce. Like Madame X herself, it goes too far and ends by eating its lovers. I suggest here a few ways that we might analyze this sumptuousness through the pretty; this is not an exhaustive list (though later, I will be talking about lists) as much as a selection of prisms through which Ottinger's prettiness might be viewed.

First, there is art history. As insistently as early film theorists, Ottinger's films locate their representational practices in relation to other forms of art. In *Johanna d'Arc*, the Yiddish theater star and dandy Mickey Katz describes an excessive meal with reference to nineteenth-century

FIGURE 47 *Johanna d'Arc of Mongolia*
Mickey Katz, the Yiddish theater star and epicurean dandy, prepares for his *zakuska*.

oil painting, sculpture, mosaic, and taxidermy (figure 47). We swoop up
and down the register of aesthetic value, from the decadent sensuality of
food as art up to the peaks of realist oil painting and back down through
the more tactile art of mosaic to the uncanny craft of stuffing dead animals (as opposed to stuffing them in one's mouth, which is what Mickey
does with the caviar and swan of his *zakuska*). The mise-en-scène itself is
stuffed with such resonances: paintings, carvings, tiles, and vases fill the
train's space, and the Mongolian yurt is no less replete with objets d'art.
In an article whose title, "The Mirror and the Vamp," cites the inheritance
of romantic literary theory, Mueller writes, "What comes across immediately is the brilliance of surfaces in the film. Ottinger embraces the notion of surface in much the same sense as the fin-de-siècle artists did, or
Rilke, for example."[5] Surface is a key quality of prettiness, and brilliance
of course resonates with a Platonic dazzle so disliked by Le Corbusier. In
fact, Mueller's positive claim on Ottinger's surfaces constructs a self-reflexive romantic aesthetic that is limited neither to the empty aestheticism of one end of the century nor to the blank parody of the other end.[6]
The fin de siècle is directly thematized in *Dorian Gray*, but *Madame X*,

too, references the aesthetic potential of art nouveau. On the pirate ship *Orlando*, we cut to a close-up of a poster in nouveau style, and a giant tortoiseshell prop reminds us of Joris-Karl Huysman's novel *À rebours / Against Nature* (1884), in which the dandy inadvertently kills his tortoise by sticking jewels to its shell. Even Madame X's opening call to offer women "gold—love—adventure" echoes in another film about sumptuousness in Toulouse-Lautrec's decadent Paris: the motto "truth, beauty, freedom, love" in *Moulin Rouge!* (Luhrmann, 2001). Ottinger's art historical reference does not aim to differentiate film's specificity, but to prize open a queer space for a sumptuous countermodernity.

A second model for the sumptuous pretty is drag, for the putting on of costumes and identities is central to Ottinger's films. The protagonists of several of the early films are played by Tabea Blumenschein, Ottinger's then partner, who is also the films' costume designer. (This is another parallel with Luhrmann, whose romantic and filmmaking partner, Catherine Martin, is his costume designer.) In *Bildnis einer Trinkerin / Ticket of No Return* (1979), Blumenschein dons a series of highly colored and constructed outfits for her unnamed character's attempt to drink herself to death. The film also extends the trope of naming characters allegorically (Social Question, Exact Statistics), making identity a name tag pinned on a body, as much a question of having the right dowdy suit as any interior truth. These ridiculous busybodies are the sort of figure that lead Pamela Robertson to identify Ottinger's work as an example of politically inspired feminist camp, but they also insist on the superiority of the superficial as a mode of reading.[7] *Madame X* also features Blumenschein and takes on that most overdetermined of female drag genres, the pirate adventure. The female pirate promises inversion of gender roles and with it an opening up of queer desires: this is certainly the case with Blumenschein's swashbuckling Madame X, who lures all the women to her cause. But it is clothes that make the woman, and the film constructs Madame X's power and allure out of her sumptuous costumes: the skintight leather worn by the ship's figurehead (a murderous copy of Madame); the ceremonial pink kimono that Madame wears in a striking, frontally composed sequence; and a naked Blumenschein, decorated with pearls and rings, putting on a jeweled bustier and hat. In each case, meaning, desire, and political critique take place on the spectacular surface of the desirable decorated body.

As I argued in the previous chapter, the queer pretty is also perverse, its stylistic moves turning away from proper aesthetic order. As color for

Charles Blanc restrains and dominates masculine line, so the sumptuousness of Ottinger's films joyfully disrupts aesthetic and sexual conven-
tion. *Madame X*, of course, centers a relationship of dominance between
the pirate captain and her crew, with the leather-clad figurehead literally
figuring erotic power and violence. Noa Noa, the South Sea Islander who
survives Madame X's murderous ways, offers herself as a submissive in
a comedic scene in which she presents Madame with vegetable gifts.
Madame accepts the gifts and pulls Noa Noa toward her by her necklace.
Object fetishism is parodied in the vegetable offerings, but the erotically
charged link forged between two bodies by way of a bodily adornment
performs a more serious enunciation of style. A series of similarly overdetermined relationships unfold in *Johanna d'Arc*, first between Lady
Windermere and Giovanna and then between Ulan Iga and Giovanna.
These couplings of a powerful woman with a young, inexperienced one
might imply an exploitative or even clichéd erotics; they certainly do not
stage the radical love of a disprized (homeless) body that Kaja Silverman
finds important in *Ticket of No Return*.[8] But Ottinger, like Silverman, is
not interested in simplistic models of transgression or feminist empow-
erment, and the kinky aesthetic that saturates *Johanna d'Arc*—from
Fanny Ziegfeld's vinyl dress and bright red nails to the women forced to
eat unappetizing kosher meals because Mickey Katz ate all the other
food on board—makes the erotics of fetishism and dominance into a
mode of visual thinking. The apparent inequality in social status between the lovers might not be a significant inequality in sexual exchange,
but it poses questions of dominance that also center the ethnographic
narrative. Giovanna sleeps with the ethnographer and the native princess: as the film's beautiful naif, she might try out an empirical heuristic, but the film's visual erotics build a more complex image of power.

GRAY MICE AND FEMINISTS

Neither Ottinger's sumptuousness nor her intimations of BDSM sexuality were appreciated by her early feminist critics. *Frauen und Film* condemned Ottinger's apparent lack of political engagement, finding, in
Amy Villarejo's words, "worlds of fantasy and visual opulence as poor
substitutes for social realism."[9] In a classic iteration of anti-pretty logic,
visual opulence precludes an articulation of the social that can come
only from ugly realism. Miriam Hansen tells us that *Frauen und Film*
found the emphasis on costume in *Ticket of No Return* to be sexist and

that "Ottinger was accused of indulging in a decadent aestheticism—
instead of dealing with the problem of women's alcoholism in a properly
critical, socially responsible and realistic manner."[10] If the film's fantastic
and aestheticized treatment of "social issues" was a problem for German
feminists, then the perverse sexuality was a further turn of the screw.
Hansen writes, "Ottinger's highly stylized exploration of the erotic
fringe, her foregrounding of sadomasochistic and fetishistic tendencies
as culturally constructed (and constructing) signs, obviously presented a
challenge to essentialist positions which would condemn such tendencies as 'naturally' male."[11] Sadomasochistic sexuality was seen as antifeminist, and, closely aligned to this argument, the stylized image was
understood as ideologically retrograde. Anti-image and anti-kink feminisms aligned to reject Ottinger's mode of queer pretty. Ottinger herself
responded to these accusations with a dismissive rejection of anti-pretty
feminism: "Some women have accused me of sexism and leather fetishism. I do not see it this way. I do not think women should now turn into
grey mice."[12]

"Grey mice": in this neat formulation, Ottinger overthrows the Marxist–feminist association of plainness in the image with radicality in ideology. Gray mice are quiet, hard to see, lacking in individuality or bravery;
they are, in short, "mousy." For Ottinger, this unobtrusive image conjures
the woman without agency, afraid of standing out. Far from embodying
rationality and meaningful line, the colorless woman simply fades even
farther into the background of patriarchy. Ottinger's valuation of the
colorful woman provoked immediate abhorrence in the *Frauen und Film*
critics, but other feminists reacted more ambivalently. In 1981, Claudia
Lenssen reflected that "I was exceedingly bored by all the familiar conventions regarding female beauty; at the same time the aestheticism
fascinated, even seduced me."[13] Here we see an anti-pretty discourse of
seduction—Ottinger represents the evil feminine image that lies through
cosmetics—tied to a feminist critique of looking relations and the spec-
tacularized female body. In the next two decades, however, film scholars sought to reevaluate Ottinger as a feminist and queer artist. Much
of the Anglo-American critical response was positive: White lauds *Madame X*'s "feminist surrealism," and Villarejo explores the "lesbian
impression" figured in the films.[14] Longfellow takes on the problem of
seduction directly, arguing that spectacle in Ottinger does not work in
a Mulveyan fashion, that we are not "seduced into a fantasy of illicit

viewing" but "proffered an invitation to play, an invitation to invest, as a woman looking at other women."[15] Ottinger's spectacular colors and beautiful bodies become, in this reading, a way out of patriarchal image culture, a female adventure for the audience as much as for the films' protagonists.

The feminist and queer reevaluation of Ottinger demonstrates the strong affiliation between these theoretical traditions and potentially pretty qualities of spectacle, surface, and costume that I discussed in the previous chapter. However, what makes Ottinger such a troublesome figure is the difficulty critics have had in maintaining both sides of this affiliation as positive values. Rickels retains a strongly positive assessment of the surface qualities of the image in his study of Ottinger as "the autobiography of art cinema." He contextualizes the early negative reception of her work within histories of aesthetics and politics—indeed, in relation to the most influential of all such texts, Walter Benjamin's essay "The Work of Art in the Age of Its Technological Reproducibility": "The postwar German political imperative of social critique that prayed to the lip service of the equation drawn (out of context) between aestheticization (of politics) and fascism, preyed, under this cover, on what was genuinely new in the arts."[16] Pointing out the misreading of Benjamin that is involved in turning his words into an anti-aesthetic slogan, Rickels finds that the postwar German social critique worked to make aestheticization into a taboo as much as it enabled radical new visual cultures. (This argument intersects with my discussion of art cinema and the Marxist pretty in chapter 5.) He holds on to Ottinger's formalist aesthetic but does so at the expense of her feminism, disdainfully dismissing White's engagement with feminist theory as "dated debates about his and her pleasures."[17] Although Rickels's claim that Ottinger has a broader significance than the ghettoes of feminist film or academic film studies would allow is useful—I agree that she is an undervalued filmmaker—it troubles me that feminism has to be excised (with some rhetorical vigor) for this reevaluation to take place. Rickels aims to deprettify Ottinger's visual style, to strip it of its queer impression, and to install it instead in a masculinist art institution.

What of the second side of the feminist debate? Although a second wave of Ottinger critics rescued her films from accusations of unfeminist visual pleasure, approbation for her colorful bodies was soon displaced by accusations of exoticism and orientalism. Katie Trumpener posits that "probably the most characteristic feature of all of Ottinger's films is their insistence on framing political questions and historical phenomena in aesthetic terms." Whereas Rickels values this formalism, Trumpener accuses *Johanna d'Arc* of being a Western fantasy of the East, in which the Western protagonists can rediscover themselves among the exotic natives. She does see moments of ironic distance from this utopian fantasy structure, but "the overall effects of most of the filming, from its visual rhythm to its vocalizations, is almost a complete capitulation to it."[18] Pausing to note the metaphor of seduction and surrender that Trumpener uses, we see in her turn to orientalism as the aesthetico-political problem with Ottinger the recurrent linkage of sexual to racial or ethnographic spectacle in pretty films. Feminists might find colorful and excessive images of women to be progressive in the right circumstances, but a similar representational mode applied to non-Europeans inevitably invokes neocolonial exploitation. Trumpener argues that "what this version of travelling cultures clearly and deliberately leaves out are conventional histories of persecution and displacement, as well as polemical accounts of uneven development and power relations."[19] It is certainly true that *Johanna d'Arc* is not "about" China's oppression of the Mongolian nomadic population, at least not in any direct way, but the same can be said of a great many unpretty films whose engagement with political histories is allowed to be complex, allusive, and multiform. In rejecting Ottinger's visual style, Trumpener seems to imply that the topic can be addressed legitimately only in an unpleasurable or didactic fashion.

Trumpener's linkage of pretty aesthetics and exoticist politics is clear in a passage where she finds the film to be "exoticisme pur experienced by the aesthete who enters a deeply foreign culture for the first time and, unable to understand its verbal and visual languages, feels free to hear and see the culture as pure music or pure form."[20] There is a strong echo here of the critics of *Soy Cuba / I Am Cuba* (1964) who found Mikhail Kalatozov to be a naive traveler who was unable to understand Cuban culture and was stuck on visualizing its exotic seductions. Is Ottinger such a clueless aesthete? By the end of the process of shooting *Johanna d'Arc*, she was able to speak Mongolian. Like Kalatozov, she spent long years in situ and clearly knew much more about her subject matter than many filmmakers who never face such challenges to their authentic knowledge. Even at the beginning of the filmmaking process, though, does it matter if the filmmaker lacks a particular form of expertise? Cultural authenticity does not seem like a strategy that radical critics should be foregrounding, and presenting Ottinger's engagement with Mongolian culture as aestheticism reveals that the problem is not really with the filmmaker's preproduction research, but with her choice of visual style.

Subsequent readings of *Johanna d'Arc* as orientalist expand Trumpener's connection of exoticism and excessive aesthetic form. Lutz Koepnick, for instance, finds the film to cast a "spell of exotic places" and suggests that "filmmakers such as Ottinger cleanse their Third World of all neocolonial traces only in order to articulate their desire for pastoral ways of life in which there is no separation between art and everyday practice."[21] Again, here are echoes of the Latin American debate on political cinema and of the realism debates discussed in chapter 1. Koepnick, like many anti-pretty critics, considers an outsider view to erase neocolonial power relations rather than, as I would suggest, potentially to prevent an easy ventriloquizing of the supposedly authentic neocolonial subject.[22] The assumption that realism would provide superior access to the conditions of geopolitical alterity can be viewed as a substantially more complicit aesthetic of global power than Ottinger's pastoral charade. In this vein, notice how Koepnick's sign of apolitical pastorality—no separation between art and everyday practice—is for Jorge Sanjinés precisely the measure of Third Cinematic political filmmaking.[23] Ottinger and Sanjinés obviously make films for very different audiences, but insofar as Third Cinema's theoretical claims have already been enormously influential for filmmakers and critics in the West, we should not foreclose on those Third Cinema theories that complicate how European political cinema might look.

Kristen Whissel makes a persuasive case for *Johanna d'Arc*'s implication in historical modes of racist representation, arguing that it "does not subvert traditionally racist cinematic representations of racial difference. Rather, Ottinger's film participates in the cinema's traditional process of producing, reproducing and organizing historical conceptions of racial and ethnic difference from the position of dominant Anglo-American and northern European culture."[24] For Whissel, Ottinger's overvaluation of racial difference partakes in the same system as previous denigrations (for instance, those described by Fatimah Tobing Rony in chapter 3), still representing race through spectacle. It is true that *Johanna d'Arc* deploys and cites histories of ethnographic looking. The scene in which the train stops in stations to reveal a tableau of Central Asian bread sellers, to say nothing of the Mongolian ceremonies of drinking mare's milk and raising the yurt, supports Whissel's claim. And yet Whissel's critique centers on the same double bind of prettiness and race that we have explored previously: the early-twentieth-century aesthetic of the racialized spectacle becomes in postcolonial thought the spectacle as racist. Whissel does allow for the possibility that the film might critically interrogate the problems of cinematic racism through its self-reflexive form, artificiality, and generic pastiche, but what makes this interpretation unlikely, for her, is that even for a more informed spectator the pleasure offered by the film is "the same pleasure offered by the racialized spectacle—namely, the phantasy of an encounter with racial difference that is mediated by the commodity form of the spectacle."[25] In other words, she is saying that if only the visual form of the film were different, it might enable self-critique.

But, as we shall see, *Johanna d'Arc* does offer critiques aplenty of ethnography, realism, and cinema's history as an apparatus of global tourism. However, these critiques do not counterpose bad spectacle to politically radical austerity, allowing the visual to speak only against itself. The film is not, in this way, *self*-critical. Instead, it counters racist and patriarchal knowledge with geographically and culturally grounded images whose meaning is located in their pleasurable composition. Fantastical Yiddish, Mongolian, and Georgian mise-en-scènes insist on wresting spectacle away from the dour and authenticating eye of the colonist. This is where the pretty produces a different intervention, offering a way to think spectacle as a more malleable force that can enable us to envision geopolitical difference otherwise.

CAMELS WITH RIBBONS

Amy Villarejo has incisively articulated the disjuncture between feminist theorists who redeem Ottinger's pretty images as radically queer and those who condemn them as reactionary and orientalist. If Hansen, Judith Mayne, and others are correct, and Ottinger does have a sophisticated visual politics, Villarejo asks, then why are we so quick to believe that she is an unthinking imperialist?[26] For Villarejo, to dismiss Ottinger's fantastical and ironic representations of the non-West as racist is the same rhetorical move as to reject her spectacular and parodic representations of gender as sexist. To demand that Ottinger represent racial and geographical difference only in direct and naturalistic ways would be as limiting as to expect feminist art to hew to the gray mice formula of asexuality and didactic unpleasure. Thus Villarejo aims to connect the redemptive feminist and queer readings with the racial critiques, to make "a bridge, a connection between these two domains—lesbian sexuality and Asia."[27] In proposing this "lesbian impression," she draws from Sabine Hake, who links *Madame X*'s representation of lesbianism with orientalism. Hake finds orientalist images to be "part of the film's distinctly homosexual sensitivity" and argues that "the oriental scenario is alluded to in the film's intimate relations between desire and death, lust and decay, domination and submission, and, in particular, all those subtle hints of perversion . . . that have become the bone of contention in the film's critical reception. Through Ottinger's appropriation of the oriental scenario, these relations are activated in order to link the problem of femininity to colonialism, thereby establishing colonialism as the important other strategy of exclusion within the patriarchal order."[28] This passage yokes orientalism to feminism, lesbianism, and perversion, and it intimates that the pretty is what does the labor of forging those critical links. This imbrication of gendered, sexual, and geopolitical alterities leads to an exploration of how pretty style works in Ottinger's films to create a specifically cinematic mode of thought.

Ottinger's films privilege highly costumed and performative bodies, so the decorated body offers an obvious entry point for thinking aesthetic and erotic spectacle. Noa Noa in *Madame X* evokes a clichéd colonial sex appeal through her layers of necklaces and heavy gold manacles. But as this decorative bondage suggests, ironic reflexivity is complicated by queer erotic investment: when Noa Noa dances, bare breasted like Josephine Baker, the spectator's relationship to histories of primitivism cannot be either outright fetishization or a high-minded pretence of progress. Hake considers that "intimately connected to the film's erotic investment in costume are its references to orientalism. . . . [O]rientalism in *Madame X* functions as an operating principle through which a particular erotic imagery is generated."[29] But orientalism and primitivism are more than erotic principles (if that were all they were, they might rightfully be regarded with suspicion). Instead, the decorated woman forms the principle by which the entire semiotic system of Ottinger's films is elaborated. The princess in *Johanna d'Arc* stands at the center of this system, with

FIGURE 48 *Johanna d'Arc of Mongolia*
Princess Ulan Iga centers a screen oriented to ornamentation.

her complexly braided and beribboned hair; her headdress heavily ornate with red, silver, green, and blue beads; and her deeply colored dresses (figure 48). Even her camel has colorful ribbons about his face. This ornamentation certainly does involve an erotics, but it resists the valuation of plainness by which classical (and much art) cinema would align the male spectator with the aesthetic austerity of the screen. The decorated woman is not the aesthetic exception that signifies male desire, but the central figure in a screen organized along decorative principles. A lesbian (and perverse) visual regime disperses both desire and meaning across the visual field, up and down power relations, and through objects and landscapes as much as through bodies. The princess's yurt opens onto chinoiserie doors, paintings of horses, and a lacquered table, articulating a multiform cultural location as well as an ironic reversal of orientalist desire.

Both White and Hansen have related this style to fin-de-siècle aestheticism, appropriating gay male decadence to stage lesbian style.[30] Benjamin had already connected the lesbian to art nouveau's "stylizing style," and the lesbian who avoids fertility in Benjamin produces an aesthetic in which composed and detailed images refuse heteronormative aims. And like Maria Beatty's kinky Weimar bohemians, Ottinger's adventurers are the descendants of Benjamin's "depraved woman." Far from recapitulating the commodity form, the lesbian decorative style refuses to reproduce. Aestheticism is a crucial vector of historical reflexivity in these films, evoking the contested decorative style of art nouveau as part of a modern discourse on feminine independence, lesbian cultural space, and rapid geopolitical change. Mickey Katz in *Johanna d'Arc* is a comedically Wildean dandy, dressing up in pink and purple with tasseled cap and silk handkerchief. He is also a greedy gourmand, eating all the wild strawberries, and a Jew, leaving nothing but unwanted kosher meals for all the other passengers. This scabrous joke illustrates that the stakes of these decorative references are not at all low for Ottinger: decadent aestheticism is always already intercut with the threat of cultural annihilation, and this holds true for the beautiful Mongolian princess and for *Madame X*'s troupe of adventurous women as much as for the Yiddish theater performers in *Johanna d'Arc*'s eastbound train. Both Villarejo and Rickels have emphasized the European traumas enfolded in these stories, and the persecution of Jews, homosexuals, and nomadic peoples in the Shoah is not irrelevant to the contemporary politics of Mongolia that the film does not overtly narrate. Aestheticism in Ottinger's films— whether Katz's enormous *zakuska*, the princess's elaborate adornments, or the returning cast of characters in *Madame X* who show up after death in a new set of subcultural costumes—is always a joyous refusal of annihilation.

I am concerned here with how a pretty aesthetic can articulate the sexual and geopolitical encounter formally. If aestheticism conjures a specifically European imbrication of aesthetics and politics, queer spaces, and cultural disappearance, then Asian forms provide another modality with which to negotiate the meeting of bodies. Speaking of her documentary *China, the Arts, Everyday Life* (1986), Ottinger says, "I was influenced by Chinese nature-painting: by the use of the scroll, which not only demands a different method of painting, but a different way of viewing— rolling out the scroll, focusing in on details, wandering to and fro, viewing piecemeal."[31] This formal engagement with East Asian aesthetics is similar both to Christopher Doyle's contrast of Asian compositional principles with those of European painting and to Sergei Eisenstein's turn to Japan in his writings on film language and synesthesia. Each of these filmmakers uses Asian art history as a way to access cinematic vision, and although they all have been accused of some form of orientalist appropriation, I argue that they illustrate instead how the pretty inscribes the geopolitical encounter as integral to the cinematic. *Johanna d'Arc's* long takes move around the screen space of the taiga like the viewer's attention to a scroll painting, but this wandering eye also choreographs bodies and spaces, foreground and background, in arabesque form. The arabesque and scroll forms, the cinematic frame and the camera already tell stories of Eastern and Western representational practices mutually encountered and unequally exchanged, with women's bodies at the center of the process. Ottinger's films mobilize this striated formal history at the textual level, rendering it both visible and perversely mutable.

The scrolling camera is one instance of Ottinger's use of Asian form as a pretty mode; another is the list form. I discussed the list form in chapter 4 as a feature of discourse on orientalist art, a way of minimizing the importance of oriental objects by removing their individuality and turning them into a homogenous series. Listing is certainly a hazard in writing on Ottinger because her mise-en-scènes are packed with objects. Longfellow, for example, uses the language of orientalism to evoke its textual elaboration in *Johanna d'Arc*, writing that "the film opens with a track past what appears as a nineteenth-century train compartment, past a sumptuous display of oriental objects, vases, screens, embroidery, heavily scrolled wooden chests, masks, tapestries, paintings and artefacts."[32] But if scholarly writing runs the risk of repeating the imperialism of the list form, the films refuse such a singular orientation, refracting the list form across the bodies of the texts. *Madame X* repeatedly lists its female characters: in several scenes, the women parade through the frame one at a time. Here, the slowing down of narration and the repetition of movement overlays the list of oriental objects (costumed women) with an art cinematic attention to temporality. In *Johanna d'Arc*, the slowed temporality of the list form is reiterated in both narrative and image. The Mongolian messenger and Lady Windermere tell long mythic stories that are made longer by descriptive lists that sometimes make the on-screen audience laugh. Then there are the visual lists of objects. In the opening, the camera pans slowly around Lady Windermere's train compartment, taking in Chinese vases and puppets, European chinoiserie furniture and curtains, a Russian painting of the Virgin and Child, and various European and Asian masks. The camera behaves like Blanc's colorist painter, lovingly attending to a litany of foreign decorative objects. It also materializes the histories of European and Asian style in which these women's experiences are to be embedded. The list form thwarts efficient narration just as the Mongolian women stop the train, diverting patriarchal order and knowledge with a pleasure in superficies and durational spaces. And by closely linking the list form to foreign, queer, and subcultural styles, the film also focuses attention on the stakes of this diversionary tactic for the various bodies it describes.

"Are These the Equestrian Games You Talked About?"

Johanna d'Arc's stopping of narrative splits the film into two parts: the artificial interior fiction of the train and the documentary real space of the taiga. As many critics have noted, this split mirrors that of Ottinger's career between art cinematic fictions and documentary. The doubled narrative also forms a fulcrum for critique: Is the second half an ethnographic fantasy for the European fictional characters and for the real audience, or does it break down such binary models? The film speaks repeatedly of the fantasies at play in this West–East transit. Lady Windermere reads near the start of the film that "Yermak Timofeyevich crosses this border line dividing Europe and Asia and beholds for the first time the unending verdant expanse." At the end, Ulan Iga discusses the "mutual exotic attraction" that led to rococo in Mongolia and chinoiserie in Paris. For Whissel, such self-reflexivity is not enough to dislodge the fundamental racism of the ethnographic gaze, but for Rickels the two sides are "impure in their separation and nonintegrable and nonassimilable in their differentiation inside and out."[33] As Homay King understands the mirroring of the *zakuska* scene with the ritual slaughter of a lamb in Mongolia, "The earlier scene instructs us in how the later one is to be read: not as raw, uncivilised barbarism, but as an equally codified activity. In turn, and as importantly, the slaughter scene retroactively informs its predecessor, reasserting the materiality of flesh and land. The 'white, shining tundra' of Katz's monologue is neither strictly linguistic fiction nor strictly material fact. Like the sign always already placed in the verdant expanse, it is both."[34] In this trope of the colorful sign in the green landscape, we catch sight of the cinematic principle underlying Ottinger's geopolitical spectacle.

As the train passengers enter the Mongolian taiga, there is a scene that might exemplify Ottinger's pretty visual style: a long shot, deep green grass, moving yurts, colored flags. Each of the Mongolian women wears a differently colored dress: pinks, sky blues, deeply dyed colors in the bright daylight. The Western women, too, stand out from the scenery in their glamorous costumes so inappropriate for the setting (figure 49). The locational realism seems the epitome of Siegfried Kracauer's endlessness, the opposite of the artificiality of the train sets, and yet the strong color contrast of reds and blues against the green taiga creates as decorative a spectacle as any seen in the film's first half. Kracauer rejects historical films because of what he regards as a disjuncture between the costumed actors and the real trees,[35] and although *Johanna d'Arc* is not historical, its theatrically costumed bodies look equally out of place in the bright light of the Mongolian exterior. I have argued elsewhere that this diegetic mismatch can be used to political effect, creating a Benjaminian constellation of past and present, political fantasy and disenchanted reality.[36] *Johanna d'Arc* uses the exact same

FIGURE 49 *Johanna d'Arc of Mongolia*
The endlessness of the taiga contrasts with the decorative costumes of both Mongolian and European characters.

effect, but in order to bring about a geopolitical rather than a historical transformation.

The film depends for its most fundamental effect on the extreme disjuncture between the spectacularly costumed women and the endless natural expanse of the Mongolian taiga. Where, for Kracauer, such a visual break prevents films from cohering, *Johanna d'Arc* precisely does not aspire to cohere and asks the audience to experience the causes and implications of this splintering diegesis. What Ottinger's film plays out is the geopolitical and sexual underpinnings of Kracauer's realism: such realism has always depended on locating the woman as decorative other to cinematic life, but it has also depended on the assumed Western value of the endless reality filmed. Placing theatrical women on one side and "real" Asia on the other, *Johanna d'Arc* does not let people, places, and objects settle into their "proper" camps. The film calls attention to the taiga's indexical status, a landscape that can only be a "real" location. But the film's style is also highly formative (scrolling and listing across Asian spaces, the setting no longer looks like the costumed Germany that stands in for China in *Madame X*), as are its inhabitants (in resplendent tribal costume) and their objects (inlaid tables, colored flags, elaborate yurts). Looking at this landscape, we are repeatedly flummoxed regarding where realism lies and complicitly enjoy its knowing critique of ethnographic overdetermination at the same time as we respond with awe to its evidentiary abilities. *Johanna d'Arc* is not interested in rejecting altogether Kracauer's sense of cinema's registrative power, but it does rewrite the opposition of realist and formative tendencies as a dialectic that is resolvable only with a queer orientation.

POSTSCRIPT

Toward a Worldly Image

THE DEVELOPMENT OF THE PRETTY AS A SPACE OF EXCLUSION IN film studies has a long history, complexly imbricated in debates on cinematic specificity, realism, ideology, and film form. This study has attempted to bring the negative space of the pretty into view as an object of study and to define it moreover as a political object worth taking seriously. The polemic qualities of the term *pretty* demand that we look closely at that which we might otherwise regard with disdain. It asks why we assume so easily that certain kinds of aesthetic image are valueless, and it understands that the moment we make such ready judgments, we are assuredly caught in the machinations of ideology. Two central claims of this book are that the decorative image speaks outside and against dominant aesthetic hierarchies and that we must read both the image itself and its critical rejection politically. This is why the book progresses on parallel tracks, intertwining an intellectual history of the pretty's appearances in film theory with analyses of pretty films. We cannot understand Derek Jarman's deployment of queer color without the context of color's exclusion from reason in the history of aesthetics, and, conversely, it is hard to discern what is at stake in teasing out anti-pretty rhetoric without seeing its opposite in a practice of filmmaking that speaks meaningfully through the pretty. My case studies of Jarman, Baz Luhrmann, Mikhail Kalatazov, and Ulrike Ottinger address filmmakers whose prettiness has left them placed awkwardly in their respective genres; their aesthetics and politics do not fit within dominant paradigms, and their films are often seen as misplaced, mistimed, or simply wrong. To reread these troublesome cases is to begin to build a way of reading films for and through the pretty.

This book aims to construct the pretty as a portable concept that other scholars can use, extend, and contest. Much is not addressed here—including, to take only one significant omission, the potential for sound as a pretty quality. Sound, too, can be considered decorative, extraneous, or supplementary, and gendering discourse is certainly at play in music criticism and theory. To take the most obvious example, *Moulin Rouge!* (Luhrmann, 2001) constructs soundscapes as frilly and excessive as its images, keying camera movements to unnecessary sound effects and using scraps of (often) melodramatic and outdated pop songs to create its emotional effects. We might easily consider its soundscape as an important aspect of its prettiness. I have focused on the pictorial as a way of accessing the influence of visual theory and aesthetics on cinema, and this etiology by necessity forecloses on the full spectrum of cinema as a multichannel experience. The issue of iconophobia has been central to my elaboration of the pretty, a discourse that may seem odd to sound scholars used to arguing against the dominance of visual approaches to film. However, there are intriguing parallels. Sergei Eisenstein argues that sound is to image as color is to graphic outline, drawing a comparison between those elements sidelined by the graphic imperative.[1] Both sound and color are considered supplementary, and thus perhaps they can benefit from the renewed perspective of the pretty. This perspective illustrates what I hope is the adaptability of the pretty as a critical term that can prompt new readings of the aesthetic and new debates on the politics of cinematic form.

A major question for the project has been how to define the pretty as a cinematic aesthetic that is uniquely able to negotiate film's commodity form, its investment in a realist ontology, and its ambivalent relationship to pleasurable spectacle. Alois Riegl defines ornament in terms of pattern on a surface,[2] and this simple description can apply equally to the material form of film. The experimental arabesques of Marie Menken and John and James Whitney certainly ask us to look at surface patterning, but a focus on the surface of the screen also characterizes recent film theory. Whether we look at the tableau vivant or the haptic, the sensory or the fantastic, film theory in its current forms is fascinated by the affective potential of cinematic superficies. The pretty articulates a mode of image making that foregrounds the surface of the screen and, with it, cinema's potential for a decorative regime of meaning in contrast to the exigencies of mimesis. The aspects of prettiness that this book has explored suggest the contours of this regime: color that seeps past the limits of line, pattern that supplants representational depth, camera movements that trace arabesque designs, picturesque compositions that demand an aesthetic eye, and an array of bodies, objects, and landscapes that resist supplementarity to articulate an ornamental visual order. The pretty demands that we read film style politically, finding in the decorative patterning of the screen a discourse on power no less rigorous than that of narrative or representation.

If the pretty offers an optic for analyzing film form, it refuses the shibboleths of "formalism," insisting that the decorative is historically and geographically embedded. At stake is the value of the pretty as a critical concept in film studies, able to intersect productively with feminist and queer film theory and with critical models of world cinema. I have argued throughout that the pretty is structurally linked with gender, sexuality, race, and geopolitics. The modern history of anti-pretty aesthetics associates noble beauty and value with the male Western subject, inscribing a devalued feminine, queer, and foreign subject into the language of the decorative image. Discourses of primitivism, effeminacy, and orientalism work, often in combination, to map out a geopolitics of aesthetic disdain. It is crucial, I have argued, for film theory to reassess its reliance on this compromised aesthetic foundation, but more positively to understand how the terrain of the excluded pretty offers rich soil for a radical aesthetics. Filmmakers attuned to the political and aesthetic languages of exclusion turn to pretty styles to speak otherwise about their own place in the world.

Contemporary cinema is distinguished by a bright strand of prettiness that is in productive tension with the more critically acclaimed movements of neo-neorealism and new documentary. Wong Kar-wai and Todd Haynes exemplify the resurgence of self-consciously aestheticized cinematography and production design as defining qualities of the modern. Apichatpong Weerasethakul emphasizes color and tone as well as

compositional balance and elegance in films such as *Sang sattawat /
Syndromes and a Century* (2006) and *Sud pralad / Tropical Malady* (2004).
Indeed, pretty qualities can even be found even in the work of directors
who in general are associated with a much more austere or rigorous
style. Lars von Trier's *Dogville* (2003), for example, plays games with a
minimalist chalk-drawn theatrical set but overthrows its nonexistent diegesis in one stunning moment with a fantastically imagined vision of
richly colored apples in a cart. This emergence of a contemporary pretty
articulates the condition of world cinema, located in the transnational
market of the film festival, but still attempting sporadically to envision
the world outside of colonial or postcolonial looking relations. Prettiness,
in this historical context, offers to create an alternative image of the geopolitical encounter.

I end by pointing toward a possible future for the pretty. French director Claire Denis has consistently explored the French postcolonial condition through elegantly composed and colorful images. *Chocolat* (1988)
has been critically viewed as a kind of French heritage film, nostalgically
bathing the memories of white colonists in rich cinematographic light.
But even in this early film, as scholars such as E. Ann Kaplan have argued,
Denis constructs an ethics of representing the desire of the other.[3] The
film memorably stages oppressive looking relations as the white protagonist, France, and her mother glimpse their black servant Protée show-
ering in the yard; his shame at being seen by these women is exposed by
the scene's framing of his dark skin lathered by white soap. Whereas another film might either fetishize Protée's body in an unthinking repetition
of the white women's violation or absent his body from vision or materiality altogether, *Chocolat* mobilizes an erotics of bodily display to articulate Protée's position. The nostalgic light of the postcolonial heritage
film turns out not to be a reactionary spectacle, but a pretty ethics. Denis's more recent films extend this exploration of prettiness as a worldly
ethics, insisting that decorative images are the only ones capable of rendering the experience of a newly imagined cinematic subject.

Denis's film *L'intrus / The Intruder* (2004) stages globality in a more
abstract way than the postcolonial narratives of *Chocolat* and *Beau Travail* (1999), obliquely tracing the journey of a white Frenchman to Tahiti
to receive a new heart and to find his illegitimate son. But it is not any
direct representation of postcolonial relationships that produces critique,
but what I have called elsewhere an image of incommensurability.[4] *The*

Intruder is in part inspired by Jean-Luc Nancy's memoir of his own heart transplant, and Denis's images are imbued with Nancy's idea of the image as "the obviousness of the invisible. . . . In a single stroke, which is what makes it striking, the image delivers a totality of sense or a truth."[5] In this account of the image, the imagistic is not secondary to representational meaning. Rather, meaning—truth—inheres in the experiential force of the image's visuality (figure 50). *The Intruder* precisely creates this effect in its refusal to center meaning in a linear story. Subordinating narrative coherence, the film is structured around a series of indelible images, such as a woman riding a dog sled through a snowy forest, two men carrying a mattress in the ocean, and a human heart purple and vulnerable on the ground. When we spectators take these strikingly beautiful images individually, we do not always know what they portend, but their compositional clarity demands that we look—at the subject and the body, at France and Tahiti—with close and rapt attention.

Denis's association with Nancy proposes an engagement of the pretty with contemporary philosophy of the image. Nancy certainly thinks of the image rather differently than does the iconophobic tradition so entrenched in French thought. In *The Ground of the Image*, he says that "it is a matter, then, of grasping the passion of the image, the power of its stigma or of its distraction (hence, no doubt, all the ambiguity and ambivalence that we attach to images, which throughout our culture, and

FIGURE 50 *L'intrus / The Intruder* (Denis, 2004)
Streamers in the wind offer an image of incommensurability.

not only in its religions, are said to be both frivolous and holy)." Nancy recognizes the anxiety around the image that has characterized both philosophy and image culture itself. And yet his recuperation of the image seemingly comes at the expense of the decorative. He argues that "the image is desirable or it is not an image (but rather a chromo, an ornament, a vision or representation—although differentiating between the attraction of desire and the solicitation of the spectacle is not as easy as some would like to think)."[6] Nancy presents us with both an example of anti-pretty thinking and a suggestive departure from it. On the one hand, the image is separated from the colorful and the ornament: a good image, a real image, is not a mere ornament. The ornament does not have the draw, the force, or the sacredness of the image in Nancy's terms; moreover, the figure of the bad visual object is once again the prostitute or fake, the feminine cosmetic that hides a lie. On the other hand, he complicates and undermines antispectacular thinking. How do we separate good images from bad spectacles, desire from solicitation? Nancy's implication is that the categories are false and that spectacle is a straw man, for the image contains a force that an insistence on linguistic reason cannot contain. He still views the image in rather Bazinian terms of purity versus decoration, but his insistence on the image's distinctive force offers both a rejection of Platonic suspicion and a way of thinking the image in terms of experience of the world.

Denis takes up this offer to view the image without suspicion, as a mode of experiencing the world, but she also overthrows Nancy's denigration of the ornamental and the chromatic. In *L'intrus* and *35 Rhums / 35 Shots of Rum* (Denis, 2008), pictorial compositions and aestheticized cinematography form the major discourse within which the lives of immigrants and the entwined histories of France and its former colonies can be reimagined without recourse to identitarian narratives. In one striking image in *The Intruder*, a cloud of multicolored streamers waves sinuously across the frame, at once a reference to the christening of a ship in an international port, an abstracted experience of a foreign place and time, and a highly aestheticized surface pattern. This image recalls a description written by Paul Morand in 1900 and collected by Walter Benjamin in *The Arcades Project*: "What M. Arsène Alexandre, then, calls 'the profound charm of streamers blowing in the wind'—this serpentine effect is that of the octopus style, of green, poorly fired ceramics, of lines forced and stretched into tentacular ligaments, of matter tortured for no good reason."[7] We see here many of the rhetorical themes of anti-pretty thought. The sinuous curves of art nouveau are denigrated as animalistic and primitive as well as violent and perverse. The reference to "the octopus style" reminds us of Siegfried Kracauer's critique of Eisenstein, with the tentacular arabesques of the creature abjecting the line of beauty. And the lines that are forced and tortured evoke the patriarchal fears of submissive pretty's revolt and the queer response that Maria Beatty inscribes in cinematic images of desirable violence. Denis's multicolored streamers might contain all of these allusive meanings, transforming the pretty image into a site of geopolitical meaning and affective value. Her films propose a future for the pretty as an aesthetic field uniquely able to voice a cinematic ethics of worldliness through the resonance of the decorative image.

NOTES

INTRODUCTION

1. Quoted in Laia Manresa, *Joaquín Jordá: La mirada lluire / The Free Spirit*, trans. Andrew Stacy (Barcelona: Filmoteca de Catalunya, 2006), 154.

2. See, for example, Wheeler Winston Dixon, *The Transparency of Spectacle: Meditations on the Moving Image* (Albany: State University of New York Press, 1998).

3. There is, of course, a vast philosophical literature on this topic. Here, I point to only two major contemporary critical engagements with Plato's image: Jacques Derrida, "Plato's Pharmacy," in *Dissemination*, trans. Barbara Johnson (Chicago: University of Chicago Press, 1981), 67–185; and Michèle le Doeuff, *The Philosophical Imaginary*, trans. Colin Gordon (London: Continuum, 1989). Le Doeuff's analysis is particularly suggestive for its insistence on gender as intrinsic to the philosophical delegitimization of the image.

4. One of the major works on this topic is Martin Jay, *Downcast Eyes: The Denigration of Vision in Twentieth-Century French Thought* (Berkeley: University of California Press, 1994), to which I return in subsequent chapters.

5. Jean-Luc Nancy, *The Ground of the Image*, trans. Jeff Fort (New York: Fordham University Press, 2005), 31.

6. Dudley Andrew, "A Preface to Disputation," in *The Image in Dispute: Art and Cinema in the Age of Photography*, ed. Dudley Andrew (Austin: University of Texas Press, 1997), viii.

7. Jacqueline Lichtenstein, *The Eloquence of Color: Rhetoric and Painting in the French Classical Age*, trans. Emily McVarish (Berkeley: University of California Press, 1993), 1.

8. Charles Blanc, *The Grammar of Painting and Engraving*, trans. Kate Newell Doggett (Chicago: Griggs, 1891), 169.

9. Anton Kaes, *From Hitler to Heimat: The Return of History as Film* (Cambridge, Mass.: Harvard University Press, 1989), 16.

10. Christian Metz, *Language and Cinema*, trans. Donna Jean Umiker-Sebeok (The Hague: Mouton, 1974); Michel Chion, "Quiet Revolution . . . and Rigid Stagnation," *October* 58 (1991): 69–80.

11. Lichtenstein, *Eloquence of Color*, 42.

12. Umberto Eco, *On Beauty: A History of a Western Idea*, trans. Alastair McEwan (London: Secker and Warburg, 2004), 8.

13. Siegfried Kracauer, *Theory of Film: The Redemption of Physical Reality* (Princeton, N.J.: Princeton University Press, 1997), 30 (my italics).

14. Rebecca Johnson, "*Kawaii* and *Kirei*: Navigating the Identities of Women in Laputa: *Castle in the Sky* by Hayao Miyazaki and *Ghost in the Shell* by Mamoru Oshii," *Rhizomes* 14 (2007), available at http://www.rhizomes.net/issue14/johnson/johnson.html (accessed May 11, 2009).

15. Sianne Ngai, "The Cuteness of the Avant-Garde," *Critical Inquiry* 31 (2005): 811–12.

16. Naomi Schor, *Reading in Detail: Aesthetics and the Feminine* (New York: Methuen, 1987), 3–4.

17. J. Hoberman, "Times of Tumult," *Village Voice*, January 11, 2000, available at http://www.villagevoice.com/2000–01–11/film/times-of-tumult/1 (accessed June 25, 2009); M. G. Radhakrishnan, "Filmmaker with a Focus," *India Today*, December 28, 1998, available at http://www.indiatoday.com/itoday/28121998/profile.html (accessed June 25, 2009).

18. A. O. Scott, "*The Terrorist*: A Guerrilla Grows Up During a Mission," *New York Times*, January 14, 2000, available at http://www.nytimes.com/library/film/011400terrorist-film-review.html (accessed June 25, 2009).

19. Rai Paramjit, "*The Terrorist*," *Sight & Sound* 11, no. 5 (2001): 59.

20. Gayatri Chakravorty Spivak, "Terror: A Speech After 9-11," *boundary* 31, no. 2 (2004): 81–111. *The Terrorist* is not the only recent Indian film to thematize the female bomber; indeed, Sivan worked with director Mani Ratnam on *Dil se / From the Heart* (1998), which tells a similar story, but broadly within the generic format of the Hindi musical romance. *From the Heart* also played to art house audiences outside India and arguably includes a more conventional representation of the mysterious and romantic female extremist, but its twist on a Hindi genre meant that critics did not read its style as too beautiful or its female lead as fetishized.

21. Sivan's film *Tahaan* (2008) is set in the Kashmir Valley and similarly uses picturesque landscapes to figure a traumatic and volatile political environment.

22. I am extremely grateful to Swarnavel Eswaran Pillai, who generously discussed Tamil language and culture with me and shared his encyclopedic knowledge of Tamil film history.

23. Quoted in Dudley Andrew, "Jules, Jim, and Walter Benjamin," in *Image in Dispute*, ed. Andrew, 37; originally published in *Le cinéma selon François Truffaut*, ed. Ann Gillain (Paris: Flammarion, 1988), 132.

24. François Truffaut, "A Certain Tendency of the French Cinema," in *Movies and Methods*, ed. Bill Nichols (Berkeley: University of California Press, 1976), 1:225.

25. See, for instance, Mark Harrison, "Zhang Yimou's *Hero* and the Globalisation of Propaganda," *Millennium Journal of International Studies* 34, no. 2 (2006): 569–72; and, in response, Wendy Larson, "Zhang Yimou's *Hero*: Dismantling the Myth of Cultural Power," *Journal of Chinese Cinemas* 2, no. 3 (2008): 181–96.

26. Theodor W. Adorno, *Aesthetic Theory*, trans. Robert Hullot-Kentor (Minneapolis: University of Minnesota Press, 1997); Theodor W. Adorno, Walter Benjamin, Ernst Bloch, Bertolt Brecht, and Georg Lukács, *Aesthetics and Politics*, trans. Anya Bostock, Stuart Hood, Rodney Livingstone, Francis McDonagh, and Harry Zohn (New York: Verso, 1980).

27. Sean O'Toole, "In Conversation with Zwelethu Mthethwa," *Artthrob: Contemporary Art in South Africa* 83 (2004), available at http://www.artthrob.co.za/04july/news/mthethwa.html (accessed January 9, 2009).

28. João Marcelo Melo, "Aesthetics and Ethics in *City of God*: Content Fails, Form Talks," *Third Text* 18, no. 5 (2004): 475, 478.

29. Karen Backstein, "*City of God*," *Cineaste* 28, no. 3 (2003): 40.

30. Luiz Carlos Merten, "From the Aesthetics to the Cosmetics of Hunger?" *Thinking Eye* 1 (2002), available at http://www.elojoquepiensa.udg.mx/ingles/revis_02/index.html (accessed March 20, 2009). See also Ivana Bentes, "The Aesthetics of Violence in Brazilian Film," in *City of God in Several Voices: Brazilian Social Cinema as Action*, ed. Else R. P. Viera (Nottingham: Critical, Cultural, and Communications Press, 2005), 82–92.

31. Lúcia Nagib, "Panaméricas Utópicas: Entranced and Transient Nations in *I Am Cuba* (1964) and *Land in Trance* (1967)," *Hispanic Research Journal* 8, no. 1 (2007): 79–90.

32. Lúcia Nagib, "Talking Bullets," *Third Text* 18, no. 3 (2004): 239–50.

33. Quoted in Stella Bruzzi, *Undressing Cinema: Clothing and Identity in the Movies* (New York: Routledge, 1997), 35.

34. Charles Tesson, "Lara contre *Amélie*," *Cahiers du Cinéma* 559 (2001): 12.

35. Serge Kaganski, "Rebonds de Serge Kaganski paru dans Libération du 31 mai," *Les Inrockuptibles*, available at http://www.lesinrocks.com (accessed February

4, 2008) (my translation); originally published as "Amélie pas jolie," *Libéra-tion*, May 31, 2001.

36. Dudley Andrew, "*Amelie*, or the fabuleux destin du cinéma Français," *Film Quarterly* 57, no. 3 (2004): 34–46.

37. Quoted in ibid., 38.

38. Serge Kaganski,. "Pourquoi je n'aime pas *Le fabuleux destin d'Amélie Poulin*," *Les Inrockuptibles*, May 31, 2001, available at http://www.lesinrocks.com/cine/cinema article/article/pourquoi-je-naime-pas-le-fabuleux-destin-damelie-poulain/.

39. Kaganski, "Rebonds."

40. Ibid.

41. We might note that *Delicatessen* is similarly white and yet was not put under any pressure on this score. Of course, one can argue that *Delicatessen* was a lesser-known film and that it is only when a film is nominated for Oscars that such issues get raised. Likewise, it is possible to argue that *Amelie* caught so much ire because critics tend to value "dark" texts more than cheerful ones; that, unlike the dystopian setting of *Delicatessen*, Paris is a real place and *might* have been filmed in a more naturalistic manner; or even that Jeunet's career can be mapped, like that of many art house auteurs, as a trajectory from honest and serious films to Hollywood sellout (*Alien: Resurrection* [1997]) or Euro-heritage pap (*Un long dimanche de fiançailles / A Very Long Engagement* [2004]) and that the shift in critical attitude follows his loss of filmmaking integrity. All these arguments are legitimate, but I don't think they can en-tirely or even mostly account for the rabid switch in critical response to two films that have quite similar visual and narrative styles.

42. Rey Chow, *Primitive Passions: Visuality, Sexuality, Ethnography, and Contempo-rary Chinese Cinema* (New York: Columbia University Press, 1995).

43. Tess Do and Carrie Tarr, "Outsider and Insider Views of Saigon / Ho Chi Minh City: *The Lover / L'Amant*, *Cyclo / Xích lô*, *Collective Flat / Chung cu'*, and *Bargirls / Gái nhay*," *Singapore Journal of Tropical Geography* 29, no. 1 (2008): 58.

44. Ibid., 59, 60.

45 Ibid., 65.

46. Hamid Naficy, *An Accented Cinema: Exilic and Diasporic Filmmaking* (Prince-ton, N.J.: Princeton University Press, 2001).

47. Chris Doyle, interviewed on *The Culture Show* (BBC, 2005).

48. Lisa Robertson, *Occasional Work and Seven Walks from the Office for Soft Archi-tecture* (Astoria, Ore.: Clear Cut Press, 2003), 125, 126.

49. Ibid., 130.

1. FROM AESTHETICS TO FILM AESTHETICS

1. See, for instance, Alois Riegl, *Problems of Style: Foundations for a History of Ornament*, trans. Evelyn Kain (Princeton, N.J.: Princeton University Press,

1992); and Heinrich Wölfflin, *Principles of Art History: The Problem of the Development of Style in Later Art*, trans. M. D. Hottinger (New York: Dover, 1950).

2. Walter Benjamin, *The Arcades Project*, trans. Howard Eiland and Kevin McLaughlin (Cambridge, Mass.: Harvard University Press, 1999), 456–88.

3. Walter Crane, *Line and Form* (London: Bell, 1912), 1.

4. Jacqueline Lichtenstein, *The Eloquence of Color: Rhetoric and Painting in the French Classical Age*, trans. Emily McVarish (Berkeley: University of California Press, 1993), 4.

5. Sir Joshua Reynolds, "Seven Discourses on Art," in *The Complete Works* (London: Thomas McLean, 1824), 105–6.

6. Iris Barry, *Let's Go to the Movies* (London: Chatto and Windus, 1926), 44–45.

7. Hugo Münsterberg, *The Film, a Psychological Study* (New York: Dover, 1970), 89.

8. Ibid., 90.

9. Ibid., 49.

10. Ibid., 52.

11. I do not have the space here to cite the full range of Plato's thought on color. Some key passages, however, can be found in *Timaeus*, 67e–68a, 1191, which discusses "dazzle"; in *The Republic*, 557c, 786, where we hear that women and young boys foolishly think that multicolored things are beautiful; and in *Gorgias*, 465b, 247, which also discusses cosmetics (*The Collected Dialogues of Plato*, ed. Edith Hamilton and Huntington Cairns [Princeton, N.J.: Princeton University Press, 1961]). In her description of the influential debate between the Venetian and Roman schools of Italian painting, Naomi Schor describes the argument that the Venetian school was inferior "due to the privilege it accords to sensuality over reason, dazzle over affect, color over line, ornament over severity" (*Reading in Detail: Aesthetics and the Feminine* [New York: Methuen, 1987], 19).

12. Rudolf Arnheim, "Remarks on Film Color," in *Film Essays and Criticism*, trans. Brenda Benthein (Madison: University of Wisconsin Press, 1997), 21. Note here another movement of the line: color in painting is now unproblematic, but in film it is unacceptable.

13. Bela Balázs, *Theory of the Film*, trans. Edith Bone (London: Dobson, 1952), 242.

14. David Batchelor, *Chromophobia* (London: Reaktion Books, 2000), 22–23.

15. Ibid., 52.

16. Dudley Andrew, "The Post-war Struggle for Color," in *Color: The Film Reader*, ed. Angela Dalle Vacche and Brian Price (New York: Routledge, 2006), 44.

17. Siegfried Kracauer, *Theory of Film: The Redemption of Physical Reality* (Princeton, N.J.: Princeton University Press, 1997), 36.

18. Siegfried Kracauer, "The Mass Ornament," in *The Mass Ornament: Weimar Essays*, trans. Thomas Y. Levin (Cambridge, Mass.: Harvard University Press, 1995), 76. I am indebted to filmmaker Katy Hoffer for pointing out the resonance of this phrase.

19. Johann Wolfgang von Goethe, *Theory of Colors*, trans. Charles Eastlake (Cambridge, Mass.: MIT Press, 1970), 55.

20. J. J. Winckelmann, *The History of Ancient Art*, trans. G. Henry Lodge (London: Sampson, Low, Marston, Searle & Rivington, 1881), 308.

21. Charles Blanc, *The Grammar of Painting and Engraving*, trans. Kate Newell Doggett (Chicago: Griggs, 1891), 5; originally published as *Grammaire des arts du dessin* (Paris: Librarie Renouard, 1862).

22. Quoted in Rudolf Arnheim, *Film as Art* (Berkeley: University of California Press, 1957), 159.

23. Batchelor, *Chromophobia*, 13.

24. Richard Dyer, *White: Essays on Race and Culture* (London: Routledge, 1997).

25. See, for instance, Roy Armes, *A Critical History of the British Cinema* (London: Secker and Warburg, 1978); Stephen L. Hanson, "Michael Powell and Emeric Pressburger," in *Film Reference*, available at http://www.filmreference.com/Directors-Pe-Ri/Powell-Michael-and-Emeric-Pressburger.html; and, for an example of the historiographic turn in the 1980s by which this fantastic difference is celebrated, Julian Petley, "The Lost Continent," in *All Our Yesterdays: 90 Years of British Cinema*, ed. Charles Barr (London: British Film Institute, 1986), 98–119. Also striking is Michael Powell's desire for a "composed film" in which, as Ian Christie puts it, "sound and image would be as closely integrated as they are normally in animation" (*Arrows of Desire: The Films of Michael Powell and Emeric Pressburger* [London: Faber and Faber, 1994], 69).

26. Brian Price, "Color, the Formless, and Cinematic Eros," in *Color*, ed. Dalle Vacche and Price, 81.

27. Lichtenstein, *Eloquence of Color*, 62.

28. Vachel Lindsay, *The Art of the Moving Picture* (New York: Liveright, 1970).

29. André Bazin, "The Ontology of the Photographic Image," in *What Is Cinema?* trans. Hugh Gray (Berkeley: University of California Press, 1967), 1:9–16.

30. Balázs, *Theory of the Film*, 47, 84.

31. Ibid., 59.

32. Gotthold E. Lessing, *Laocöon: An Essay on the Limits of Painting and Poetry*, trans. Edward Allen McCormick (Baltimore: Johns Hopkins University Press, 2008).

33. Balázs, *Theory of the Film*, 158.

34. Lichtenstein, *Eloquence of Color*, 62.

35. Münsterberg, *Film*, 62.

36. Jean Epstein, "Magnification," in *French Film Theory and Criticism: A History/Anthology*, vol. 1, *1907–1939*, ed. Richard Abel (Princeton, N.J.: Princeton University Press, 1988), 238.

37. Ibid.

38. Quoted in Ara H. Merjian, "Middlebrow Modernism: Rudolf Arnheim at the Crossroads of Film Theory and the Psychology of Art," in *The Visual Turn:*

Classical Film Theory and Art History, ed. Angela Dalle Vacche (New Brunswick, N.J.: Rutgers University Press, 2003), 158.

39. Immanuel Kant, *The Critique of Judgment*, trans. J. H. Bernard (Amherst, N.Y.: Prometheus Books, 2000).

40. Arthur Danto, in "The Art Seminar," in *Art History Versus Aesthetics*, ed. James Elkins (New York: Routledge, 2006), 52.

41. Kant, *Critique of Judgment*, 197.

42. In addition—following Gayatri Chakravorty Spivak's reading of Kant in *A Critique of Postcolonial Reason: Toward a History of the Vanishing Present* (Cambridge, Mass.: Harvard University Press, 1999), 26–30—we notice that although the woman has a limited access to subjectivity, the colonial subject cannot even be included. Spirit is a closely guarded quality for aesthetics.

43. Balázs, *Theory of the Film*, 114–15.

44. Jacques Aumont, "The Face in Close-Up," in *Visual Turn*, ed. Dalle Vacche, 133.

45. Ricciotto Canudo, "The Birth of a Sixth Art," in *French Film Theory and Criticism*, ed. Abel, 1:62.

46. Victor Freeburg, *The Art of Photoplay Making* (New York: Ayer, 1970), 25.

47. Laura Marcus, *The Tenth Muse: Writing About Cinema in the Modernist Period* (Oxford: Oxford University Press, 2007), 213–20.

48. Hugo Münsterberg, "The Problem of Beauty," *Philosophical Review* 18, no. 2 (1909): 135.

49. Quoted in Marcus, *Tenth Muse*, 209.

50. Kant, *Critique of Judgment*, 72.

51. Ibid.

52. David J. Getsy, "Other Values (or, Is It an African or an Indian Elephant in the Room?)," in *Art History Versus Aesthetics*, ed. Elkins, 196.

53. Spivak, *Critique of Postcolonial Reason*, 26–29.

54. Kant, *Critique of Judgment*, 284.

55. Spivak, *Critique of Postcolonial Reason*, 26–27.

56. Eugène Véron, *Aesthetics*, trans. W. H. Armstrong (London: Chapman, 1879), 119.

57. Assenka Oksiloff, *Picturing the Primitive: Visual Culture, Ethnography, and Early German Cinema* (London: Palgrave, 2001); Catherine Russell, *Experimental Ethnography: The Work of Film in the Age of Video* (Durham, N.C.: Duke University Press, 1999), 55.

58. Ricciotto Canudo, "Les orientales," in *L'usine aux images* (Paris: Séguier, 1995), 247 (my translation).

59. Jean Epstein, "The Senses I (b)," in *French Film Theory and Criticism*, ed. Abel, 1:243.

60. Christian Keathley, *Cinephilia and History, or, The Wind in the Trees* (Bloomington: Indiana University Press, 2006), 99–100. Keathley also points out the Impressionists' enthusiasm for Hayakawa (99n.80).

61. Mary Ann Doane, "The Close-Up: Scale and Detail in the Cinema," *differences* 14, no. 3 (2003): 89–111; Balázs, *Theory of the Film,* 75–76.

62. Sumiko Higashi, "Ethnicity, Class, and Gender in Film: DeMille's *The Cheat,*" in *Unspeakable Images: Ethnicity in Cinema,* ed. Lester Friedman (Urbana: University of Illinois Press, 1991), 112–39; Daisuke Miyao, *Sessue Hayakawa: Silent Cinema and Transnational Stardom* (Durham, N.C.: Duke University Press, 2007). Both Higashi and Miyao connect the threat of Hayakawa's bad guy in *The Cheat* to the ambivalent discourses of the new woman and Japanese style in early-twentieth-century consumer culture.

63. Louis Delluc, "Beauty in the Cinema," in *French Film Theory and Criticism,* ed. Abel, 1:138–39.

64. Lindsay, *Art of the Moving Picture,* 64.

65. See, for example, Catherine Russell, ed., "New Women of the Silent Screen: China, Japan, Hollywood," special issue, *Camera Obscura,* 20, no. 3 (2005); and Matthew Bernstein and Gaylyn Studlar, eds., *Visions of the East: Orientalism in Film* (London: Taurus, 2007).

66. Canudo, "Les orientales," 246.

67. Louis Delluc, *Photogénie* (Paris: De Brunoff, 1920), 8, translated and quoted in Eugene C. McCreary, "Louis Delluc, Film Theorist, Critic, and Prophet," *Cinema Journal* 16, no. 1 (1976): 18.

68. McCreary, "Louis Delluc," 18.

69. Dudley Andrew, "A Preface to Disputation," in *The Image in Dispute: Art and Cinema in the Age of Photography,* ed. Dudley Andrew (Austin: University of Texas Press, 1997), x.

70. Marcel Gromaire, "A Painter's Ideas About the Cinema," in *French Film Theory and Criticism,* ed. Abel, 1:175.

71. Delluc, "Beauty in the Cinema," 137.

72. Ibid., 145.

73. Ibid., 160–61.

74. Anton Kaes and David J. Levin, "The Debate About Cinema: Charting a Controversy (1909–1929)," *New German Critique* 40 (1987): 12.

75. Louis Aragon, "On Décor," in *French Film Theory and Criticism,* ed. Abel, 1:167.

76. Andreas Huyssen, *After the Great Divide: Modernism, Mass Culture, and Postmodernism* (London: Macmillan, 1986), 50–51.

77. Delluc, "Beauty in the Cinema," 137.

78. Ibid., 138.

79. Jacques Aumont, "The Variable Eye, or the Mobilization of the Gaze," in *Image in Dispute,* ed. Andrew, 232–34 (my italics).

80. This shift from a picturesque sensibility to a modern one in which any random bit of nature can be framed raises an interesting issue. The pretty not only encompasses the carefully composed beautiful object but can be found

in the ephemeral—for example, in Derek Jarman's nature shots or in Christopher Doyle's light effects. The work of the camera, however, is such that these ephemeral pieces of nature are rendered visible *as* aesthetic, worked on so that they are never "plucked from nature," as it were, but turned into pretty objects. Doyle's lighting and Jarman's filters are nonnaturalistic, and it is the surplus of color and light on nature that constructs the pretty in these cases.

81. Roland Barthes, *Camera Lucida: Reflections on Photography*, trans. Richard Howard (New York: Hill & Wang, 1982); Ivone Margulies, ed., *Rites of Realism: Essays on Corporeal Cinema* (Durham, N.C.: Duke University Press, 2003).

82. James Lastra, "From the Captured Moment to the Cinematic Image, a Transformation in Pictorial Order," in *Image in Dispute*, ed. Andrew, 263–91; Alpers quoted on 269.

83. Marcus, *Tenth Muse*, 201. Marcus also writes of *photogénie* as a beauty of the moment, "glimpsed rather than held" (182).

84. Le Corbusier, *The Decorative Art of Today*, trans. James I. Dunnett (London: Architectural Press, 1987), 89.

85. Paul Willemen, "Through the Glass Darkly: Cinephilia Reconsidered," in *Looks and Frictions: Essays in Cultural Studies and Film Theory* (London: BFI, 1994), 253.

86. Louis Delluc, "La mauvaise étoile," *Le Film*, September 24, 1917, 7, translated and quoted in McCreary, "Louis Delluc," 20.

87. Balázs, *Theory of the Film*, 269–70, 270, 271.

88. Ibid., 114.

89. Aragon, "On Décor," 168 (italics in original).

90. Balázs, *Theory of the Film*, 77.

91. Ibid., 78.

92. André Bazin, "The Evolution of the Language of Cinema," in *What Is Cinema?* 1:24. By "image," Bazin specifies "everything that the representation on the screen adds to the object there represented" (24). The image is additional, excessive to representation.

93. André Bazin, "*Le journal d'un curé de campagne* and the Stylistics of Robert Bresson," in *What Is Cinema?* 1:138–39.

94. Spivak, *Critique of Postcolonial Reason*, 3–4.

95. André Bazin, "Bresson," in *What Is Cinema?* 1:140–41.

96. It is also significant that Spivak finds in the sublime the heart of Kant's model of humanity. Only those who can experience the sublime can be moral, and the native woman is thus considered less than human because of her lack of access to the sublime. Bazin does not make any such associations, but this is the pernicious structure of the anti-pretty. In importing these aesthetic categories, we import by necessity their moral structures, too.

97. André Bazin, "Painting and Cinema," in *What Is Cinema?* 1:165.

98. André Bazin, "An Aesthetic of Reality: Cinematic Realism and the Italian School of the Liberation," in *What Is Cinema?* trans. Hugh Gray (Berkeley: University of California Press, 1971), 2:26.

99. Bazin, "Ontology of the Photographic Image," 15.

100. André Bazin, "*Farrebique*, or the Paradox of Realism," in *Bazin at Work: Major Essays and Reviews from the Forties and Fifties*, trans. Alain Piette and Bert Cardullo, ed. Bert Cardullo (New York: Routledge, 1997), 106.

101. Bazin, "Ontology of the Photographic Image," 15.

102. André Bazin, "William Wyler, or the Jansenist of Directing," in *Bazin at Work*, 2.

103. Ibid., 3, 5.

104. André Bazin, "*Battle of the Rails* and *Ivan the Terrible*," in *Bazin at Work*, 201.

105. Ibid. It should be noted that many of Bazin's arguments depend on the natural qualities of the filmed object—the true or pure nature of the profilmic as well as the objective nature of the camera. For Bazin, the natural encompasses everything out there to be filmed, but as his concern for the political quality of postwar Italian reality or the spiritual quality of Bresson's *curé* demonstrates, the natural is never without interest either. A feminist or queer reading might have as much cause to suspect the natural as the pure.

106. Ibid., 202.

107. Ibid., 200.

2. COLORS

1. David Batchelor, *Chromophobia* (London: Reaktion Books, 2000).

2. Derek Jarman, *Chroma: A Book of Color* (Woodstock, N.Y.: Overlook Press, 1995), 45.

3. Ibid., 58.

4. See, for example, Roger Wollen, ed., *Derek Jarman: A Portrait* (London: Thames and Hudson, 1996); Andrew Moor, "Spirit and Matter: Romantic Mythologies in the Films of Derek Jarman," in *Territories of Desire in Queer Culture: Refiguring the Contemporary Boundaries*, ed. David Alderton and Linda Anderson (Manchester: Manchester University Press, 2000), 49–67; Chris Lippard, ed., *By Angels Driven: The Films of Derek Jarman* (Trowbridge: Flick Books, 1996); Peter Wollen, "The Last New Wave: Modernism in the British Films of the Thatcher Era," in *The British Avant-Garde Film, 1926–1995: An Anthology of Writings*, ed. Michael O'Pray (London: Arts Council of England and University of Luton Press, 1990), 239–59; Paul Julian Smith, "*Blue* and the Outer Limits," *Sight & Sound* 3, no. 10 (1993): 18–19; and William Pencak, *The Films of Derek Jarman* (Jefferson, N.C.: McFarland, 2002).

5. Tony Rayns, "Unnatural Lighting," *American Film* 11, no. 10 (1986): 46.

6. Simon Field, "Editorial: The Troublesome Cases," in ". . . of Angels & Apocalypse," special issue, *Afterimage* 12 (1985): 3.

7. Serge Paradjanov, *"Shadows of Our Forgotten Ancestors,"* trans. Steven P. Hill, *Film Comment* 5, no. 1 (1968): 47.

8. Steven Dillon, *Derek Jarman and Lyric Film: The Mirror and the Sea* (Austin: University of Texas Press, 2004), 2–13. Dillon's description of Paradjanov's lyricism resonates strongly with the pretty: "the screen is saturated with glorious color, and the sound track is equally full of Oriental instrumentation. . . . Each frame plays out a contrast between formal opposites: linear and arabesque" (18). We will see these elements recurring throughout the case studies of the pretty.

9. Stuart Dollin, "Super 8 Artist," *Movie Maker* 18, no. 7 (1984): 42. Michael O'Pray speaks of Super-8 as "a rather despised medium for serious work" in the context of John Maybury and Cerith Wyn Evans's influential show *A Certain Sensibility* (1981) ("The Elusive Sign: From Asceticism to Aestheticism," in *The Elusive Sign: British Avant-Garde Film and Video, 1977–1987*, ed. David Curtis [London: Arts Council of Great Britain, 1987], 8). These filmmakers were part of Jarman's scene, and, like his, their influences included both avant-garde artists such as Andy Warhol, Kenneth Anger, and Jack Smith and art cinema auteurs such as Pier Paolo Pasolini, Jean Cocteau, and Federico Fellini. These influences were rather looked down on, and we see that even in the avant-garde, prettiness is associated with a love for the more middlebrow or bourgeois that can never accommodate modernist purity and austerity of form.

10. A. L. Rees, *A History of Experimental Film and Video: From the Canonical Avant-Garde to Contemporary British Practice* (London: BFI, 1999), 100.

11. "Derek Jarman: Présenté dans le cadre des sélections étrangères," *Apec Cinema* 13, no. 3 (1975): 73.

12. Peter Gidal, *Structural Film Anthology* (London: BFI, 1976), 2, 47–49.

13. Simon Field and Michael O'Pray, "Imagining October, Dr. Dee and Other Matters: An Interview with Derek Jarman," in ". . . of Angels & Apocalypse," special issue, *Afterimage* 12 (1985): 46.

14. Rees, *History of Experimental Film and Video*, 100.

15. Ibid., 102–3.

16. Richard Porton, "Language Games and Aesthetic Attitudes: Style and Ideology in Jarman's Late Films," in *By Angels Driven*, ed. Lippard, 135, 136.

17. James Tweedie, "The Suspended Spectacle of History: The Tableau Vivant in Derek Jarman's *Caravaggio*," *Screen* 44, no. 4 (2003): 380–81.

18. Jacqueline Lichtenstein, *The Eloquence of Color: Rhetoric and Painting in the French Classical Age*, trans. Emily McVarish (Berkeley: University of California Press, 1993), 3–4.

19. Batchelor, *Chromophobia*, 62.

20. Jarman, *Chroma*, 52.

21. Lisa Robertson, *Occasional Work and Seven Walks from the Office for Soft Architecture* (Astoria, Ore.: Clear Cut Press, 2003), 142.

22. Ibid.

23. Tony Rayns, "Submitting to Sodomy: Propositions and Rhetorical Questions About an English Film-maker," in ". . . of Angels & Apocalypse," special issue, *Afterimage* 12 (1985): 60, 61.

24. Chapter 7 explores the pretty politics of perversion in more detail, but for now we can note the alignment of prettiness (and its attendant anxiety) with the submissive, passive, or secondary, whether we are dealing with male / female or same-sex rhetorics.

25. Brian Price, "Color, the Formless, and Cinematic Eros," in *Color: The Film Reader,* ed. Angela Dalle Vacche and Brian Price (New York: Routledge, 2006), 76–87.

26. Adolf Loos, "The Story of a Poor Rich Man," in *Adolf Loos: Pioneer of Modern Architecture,* by Ludwig Münz and Gustav Künstler (New York: Praeger, 1966), 225. I discuss Loos more fully in chapter 3.

27. Colin MacCabe, "Preface," in *Wittgenstein: The Terry Eagleton Script and the Derek Jarman Film,* ed. Colin McCabe (London: BFI, 1993), 2.

28. Jarman, *Chroma,* 37, 42.

29. The color theories of Arthur Rimbaud, A. W. Schlegel, and Hermann Helmholtz, among others, are discussed in Sergei Eisenstein, *The Film Sense,* trans. Jay Leyda (New York: Harcourt, 1947).

30. Jarman, *Chroma,* 143.

31. Michael O'Pray, *Derek Jarman: Dreams of England* (London: BFI, 1996), 202–3.

32. Henry Adams, *Mont-Saint-Michel and Chartres* (New York: Anchor Books, 1959), 152.

33. Jarman, *Chroma,* 105.

34. Ibid., 105, 14, 36, 37.

35. Robertson, *Occasional Work,* 141.

36. For a discussion of Jarman's interest in alchemy, see Jim Ellis, "Queer Period: Derek Jarman's Renaissance," in *Out Takes: Queer Theory and Film,* ed. Ellis Hanson (Durham, N.C.: Duke University Press, 1999), 288–315.

37. Michael O'Pray, "Derek Jarman: The Art of Films / Films of Art," in *Derek Jarman,* ed. Wollen, 66.

38. I am grateful to Duncan Petrie for this observation.

39. Karen Pinkus, "Nothing from Nothing: Alchemy and the Economic Crisis," *World Picture* 2 (2008), available at http://www.worldpicturejournal .com (accessed June 10, 2009). See also Karen Pinkus, *Alchemical Mercury: A Theory of Ambivalence* (Stanford, Calif.: Stanford University Press, 2009).

40. Peter Schwenger, "Derek Jarman and the Colour of the Mind's Eye," *University of Toronto Quarterly* 65, no. 2 (1996): 420.

41. Porton, "Language Games and Aesthetic Attitudes," 137; Moor, "Spirit and Matter," 49.

42. Peter Wollen, *"Blue,"* in *Color,* ed. Dalle Vacche and Price, 194.

43. Jean-Luc Nancy, *The Ground of the Image*, trans. Jeff Fort (New York: Fordham University Press, 2005), 12.

44. Schwenger, "Derek Jarman and the Colour of the Mind's Eye," 424–25.

45. Jacques Derrida, *The Truth in Painting*, trans. Geoff Bennington and Ian McLeod (Chicago: University of Chicago Press, 1987), 64.

46. Ibid.

3. ORNAMENT AND MODERNITY

1. G. W. F. Hegel, *Aesthetics: Lectures on Fine Art*, trans. T. M. Knox (Oxford: Clarendon Press, 1975), 31.

2. Naomi Schor, *Reading in Detail: Aesthetics and the Feminine* (New York: Methuen, 1987), 49.

3. Rae Beth Gordon, *Ornament, Fantasy, and Desire in Nineteenth-Century French Literature* (Princeton, N.J.: Princeton University Press, 1992), 24.

4. Ibid., 4.

5. Ernest Gellner, "The Gaffe-Avoiding Animal or a Bundle of Hypotheses," in *Individualism: Theories and Methods*, ed. Pierre Birnbaum and Jean Leca (Oxford: Oxford University Press, 1990), 24. See also Alan Sekula, "The Body and the Archive," *October* 39 (1986): 3–64.

6. Charles Blanc, *Grammaire des arts du dessin* (Paris: Librarie Renouard, 1862), and *Grammaire des arts décoratifs* (Paris: Librarie Renouard,1882).

7. Jules Bourgoin, *Théorie de l'ornement* (Paris: Duchet, 1883), 3.

8. Owen Jones, *The Grammar of Ornament* (London: Quaritch, 1856); Augustus Pugin, *Contrasts; or, A Parallel Between the Noble Edifices of the Fourteenth and Fifteenth Centuries and Similar Buildings of the Present Day; Shewing the Present Decay of Taste* (Salisbury, 1836); John Ruskin, *The Works of John Ruskin*, vol. 11, *Seven Lamps of Architecture*, ed. E. T. Cook and Alexander Wedderburn (London: Allen, 1904); Franz Sales Meyer, *A Handbook of Ornament* (London: Duckworth, 1974).

9. Alois Riegl, *Problems of Style: Foundations for a History of Ornament*, trans. Evelyn Kain (Princeton N.J.: Princeton University Press, 1992), 5, 7.

10. Eugène Véron, *L'esthétique* (Paris: Reinwald, 1878), 131 (my translation). Véron argues that beauty and art are not the same because art can include the ugly and all manner of emotions. For him, art that looks for beauty specifically, separate from any ideas or sentiments, is decorative art (130). This view is a reversal of Kant: whereas Kant finds beauty defined by the lack of concepts a good in itself, Véron argues that beauty shorn of ideas is mere decoration. In any case, the decorative is that which lacks ideas / sentiments, and we see how easily we can move from "all beauty without ideas is called decorative" to "all decorative art is without ideas."

11. Sianne Ngai, "The Cuteness of the Avant-Garde," *Critical Inquiry* 31 (2005): 811–12.

12. Ralph N. Wornum, *Analysis of Ornament: The Characteristics of Styles, an Introduction to the Study of the History of Ornamental Art* (London: Chapman and Hall, 1882), 8.

13. Gordon tells us that "French theory shared with British the idea that mimesis was for fine arts, abstraction for applied arts" (*Ornament, Fantasy, and Desire*, 10).

14. Béla Balázs, *Theory of the Film*, trans. Edith Bone (London: Dobson, 1952), 286.

15. Wornum, *Analysis of Ornament*, 9.

16. Sales Meyer describes the Great Exhibition of 1851, which demonstrated excess in ornament by displaying Gothic engines and cathedral bookcases (*A Handbook of Ornament*, 5). The backlash against this kind of excess is characterized by Pugin's call for an honest expression of structure, material, and function. Pugin was a huge influence in the nineteenth century and even into twentieth-century modernisms, according to Brent Brolin, *Architectural Ornament: Banishment and Return* (New York: Norton, 2000), 91–93.

17. Balázs, *Theory of the Film*, 133.

18. Bourgoin, *Théorie de l'ornement*, 7.

19. Balázs, *Theory of the Film*, 133–34.

20. Riegl, *Problems of Style*, 10.

21. Owen Jones, *The Ornament and Design of the Alhambra* (New York: Dover, 2008). E. H. Gombrich cites the tattooed heads in *The Sense of Order: A Study in the Psychology of Decorative Art* (Oxford: Phaidon, 1979), 51.

22. Riegl, *Problems of Style*, 78.

23. Gombrich, *Sense of Order*, 57. See also Gordon, who traces the first European exhibitions of Japanese art in the later nineteenth century in *Ornament, Fantasy, and Desire*, 10.

24. Bourgoin, *Théorie de l'ornement*, 5.

25. Walter Crane, *Line and Form* (London: Bell, 1912), 94.

26. Emile Vuillermoz, "Before the Screen: *La dixième symphonie*," in *French Film Theory and Criticism: A History/Anthology*, vol. 1, *1907–1939*, ed. Richard Abel (Princeton, N.J.: Princeton University Press, 1988), 169.

27. Gombrich, *Sense of Order*, 25; Jean-Jacques Rousseau, *Discours sur les arts et les sciences* (Paris: Gallimard, 1986), 4.

28. Laura Marcus, *The Tenth Muse: Writing About Cinema in the Modernist Period* (Oxford: Oxford University Press, 2007), 324, quoting Kenneth Macpherson, "As Is," *Close Up* 6, no. 2 (1930): 88. The tortoise shell is a repeated trope of bad pretty, deriving from Joris-Karl Huysmans, *Against Nature*, trans. Robert Baldick (London: Penguin, 2003).

29. Germaine Dulac, "L'art du mouvement considéré en lui-même," in *Regards neufs sur le cinéma*, ed. Jacques Chevalier and Max Egly (Paris: Editions du Seuil, 1965), 28 (my translation).

30. Roberto Rossellini, "Je n'aime pas les décors," in *L'art du cinéma*, ed. Pierre Lherminier (Paris: Edition Seghers, 1960), 143.

31. Quoted in Gombrich, *Sense of Order*, 59.

32. Eugène Véron, *Aesthetics*, trans. W. H. Armstrong (London: Chapman and Hall, 1879), 126.

33. Brolin, *Architectural Ornament*, 14.

34. Klaus-Jurgen Sembach, *Art Nouveau* (Berlin: Taschen, 2002), 1.

35. Hal Foster, *Design and Crime (and Other Diatribes)* (London: Verso, 2002), 13.

36. Quoted in Ludwig Münz and Gustav Künstler, *Adolf Loos: Pioneer of Modern Architecture* (New York: Praeger, 1966), 14.

37. Adolf Loos, "Ornament and Crime," in *Ornament and Crime: Selected Essays*, trans. Michael Mitchell (Riverside, Calif.: Ariadne Press, 1998), 167.

38. Adolf Loos, "Potemkin City," in *Spoken into the Void: Collected Essays, 1897–1900*, trans. Jane O. Newman and John H. Smith (Cambridge, Mass.: MIT Press, 1982), 95. The historical reference is to Grigori Potemkin, who in 1797 made fake facades to persuade Catherine the Great that the Crimea was more advanced than it actually was.

39. John V. Maciuika, "Adolf Loos and the Aphoristic Style: Rhetorical Practice in Early Twentieth-Century Design Criticism," *Design Issues* 16, no. 2 (2000): 75.

40. Loos, "Ornament and Crime," 167–68.

41. Quoted in Maciuika, "Adolf Loos and the Aphoristic Style," 75. See also Le Corbusier, *The Decorative Art of Today*, trans. James I. Dunnett (London: Architectural Press, 1987), in which much of the rhetoric owes a debt to Loos.

42. Janet Stewart, *Fashioning Vienna: Adolf Loos's Cultural Criticism* (New York: Routledge, 2000), 6–9.

43. Even within his own Viennese circle, Loos was engaged in a dynamic and interdisciplinary investigation of contemporary culture. His friends included Karl Kraus and Ludwig Wittgenstein, and his critical writings responded to a turbulent moment in Viennese history that was being articulated by Arthur Schnitzler, Robert Musil, and Egon Schiele, not to mention the contemporaneous work of Sigmund Freud. Although Loos was closely identified with Viennese culture, he also traveled extensively in western and central Europe, creating a wide readership for his work. He lectured in Berlin, Prague, Basel, and other cities, and "Ornament and Crime" was published in the German expressionist magazine *Der Sturm* (1912), in the avant-garde *Cahiers d'aujourd'hui* (1913), and in Le Corbusier's *L'esprit nouveau* (1920). He made connections across the European avant-garde, including giving seminars with Walter Gropius and J. J. P. Oud in Prague in 1925 and, in the following year, designing a house for Tristan Tzara in Paris. His central location in European modernist culture might be best demonstrated by the book that was produced in honor of his sixtieth birthday, which included writings by Oscar Kokoschka, Ezra Pound, and Arnold Schoenberg as well as by Kraus and Tzara. See Benedetto Gravagnuolo, *Adolf Loos: Theory and Works*, trans. C. H. Evans (New York: Rizzoli, 1982), 34; and

Jan Otakar Fischer, "White Walls in the Golden City," *Harvard Design Magazine* 15 (2001): 1–8.

44. Theodor W. Adorno, "Functionalism Today," in *Rethinking Architecture: A Reader in Cultural Theory*, ed. Neil Leach (London: Routledge, 1997), 7.

45. Ibid.

46. Max Nordau, *Degeneration* (New York: Fertig, 1968).

47. Sherwin Simmons, "Ornament, Gender, and Interiority in Viennese Expressionism," *Modernism / Modernity* 8, no. 2 (2001): 245–76.

48. Mark Wigley, *White Walls, Designer Dresses: The Fashioning of Modern Architecture* (Cambridge, Mass.: MIT Press, 1995), 78.

49. Umberto Eco, *On Beauty: A History of a Western Idea*, trans. Alastair McEwan (London: Secker and Warburg, 2004), 369.

50. Wendy Steiner, *Venus in Exile: The Rejection of Beauty in Twentieth-Century Art* (New York: Free Press, 2001), 57, 45.

51. Ernst Bloch, "Formative Education, Engineering Form, Ornament," in *Rethinking Architecture*, ed. Leach, 44.

52. Ibid., 45.

53. Ernst Bloch, *The Spirit of Utopia*, trans. Anthony A. Nassar (Stanford, Calif.: Stanford University Press, 2000), 13, 17.

54. Nikolaus Pevsner, "Introduction," in *Adolf Loos*, by Münz and Künstler, 16.

55. Adolf Loos, "The Story of a Poor Rich Man," in *Adolf Loos*, by Münz and Künstler, 225.

56. Jean Epstein, "On Certain Characteristics of *Photogenie*," in *French Film Theory and Criticism*, ed. Abel, 1:317. There is also a geopolitics to this evocation of vitality. In "Magnification," Epstein writes, "There were café terraces. Swings. Races on the grass and through the reeds. Everywhere, men, life swarms, truth" (*French Film Theory and Criticism*, ed. Abel, 1:237). He is speaking of a film called *Souvenir d'été à Stockholm* (which can be translated as *Memory of Summer in Stockholm*, director and year unknown), and, as with Loos, it is healthy northern Europeans who can present cinematic life with ease.

57. Ricciotto Canudo, "The Birth of a Sixth Art," in *French Film Theory and Criticism*, ed. Abel, 1:59.

58. Vachel Lindsay, *The Art of the Moving Picture* (New York: Liveright, 1970), 144.

59. Marcus, *Tenth Muse*, 3.

60. Martin Jay, *Downcast Eyes: The Denigration of Vision in Twentieth-Century French Thought* (Berkeley: University of California Press, 1994), 198.

61. Original French terms from Véron, *L'esthétique*; translated quote from Véron, *Aesthetics*, 136.

62. Siegfried Kracauer, *Theory of Film: The Redemption of Physical Reality* (Princeton, N.J.: Princeton University Press, 1997), 75.

63. Siegfried Kracauer, "The Mass Ornament," in *The Mass Ornament: Weimar Essays*, trans. Thomas Y. Levin (Cambridge, Mass.: Harvard University Press, 1995), 79.

64. Ibid., 76, 78.

65. Adorno, "Functionalism Today," 13.

66. Kracauer, "Photography," in *Mass Ornament*, 48–49.

67. Kracauer, *Theory of Film*, 306.

68. Miriam Hansen, "Introduction," in *Theory of Film*, by Kracauer, xiv. See also Gertrud Koch, "'Not Yet Accepted Anywhere': Exile, Memory, and Image in Kracauer's Conception of History," trans. Jeremy Gaines, *New German Critique* 54 (1991): 95–109.

69. Kracauer, *Theory of Film*, 306.

70. Jeannette Sloniowski, "'It Was an Atrocious Film': Georges Franju's *Blood of the Beasts*," in *Documenting the Documentary: Close Readings of Documentary Film and Video*, ed. Barry Keith Grant and Jeannette Sloniowski (Detroit: Wayne State University Press, 2003), 171–87; Adam Lowenstein, *Shocking Representation: Historical Trauma, National Cinema, and the Modern Horror Film* (New York: Columbia University Press, 2005).

71. Kracauer, *Theory of Film*, 305.

72. Ibid., 37.

73. Ibid., 33–36, 37.

74. Hansen, "Introduction."

75. Adolf Loos, "The Plumbers," in *Spoken into the Void*, 45.

76. Adolf Loos, "Culture," in *The Architecture of Adolf Loos*, by Yehuda Safran and Wilfried Wang, with Mildred Budny (London: Arts Council of Great Britain, 1985), 97.

77. Adolf Loos, "The English Schools in the Austrian Museum," in *Spoken into the Void*, 172.

78. Kracauer, *Theory of Film*, 80.

79. Ibid., 227.

80. Adolf Loos, "Architecture," in *Architecture of Adolf Loos*, by Safran, Wang, and Budny, 104.

81. Maciuika, "Adolf Loos and the Aphoristic Style," 84.

82. Mitchell Schwartzer, "Ethnologies of the Primitive in Adolf Loos's Writings on Ornament," *Nineteenth-Century Contexts* 18 (1994): 225–47.

83. Adolf Loos, "The Luxury Vehicle," in *Spoken into the Void*, 40.

84. Mary Ann Doane, *Femmes Fatales: Feminism, Film Theory, Psychoanalysis* (New York: Routledge, 1991), 209–48.

85. Stewart, *Fashioning Vienna*, 145.

86. Farès el-Dahdah, "The Josephine Baker House: For Loos's Pleasure," *Assemblage* 26 (1995): 75.

87. Ibid., 77.

88. Josephine Baker and Jo Bouillon, *Josephine*, trans. Mariana Fitzpatrick (New York: Harper & Row, 1977), 84.

89. Fatimah Tobing Rony, *The Third Eye: Race, Cinema, and the Ethnographic Spectacle* (Durham, N.C.: Duke University Press, 1996), 10. See also Timothy Mitchell, "Orientalism and the Exhibitionary Order," in *Colonialism and Culture*, ed. Nicholas Dirks (Ann Arbor: University of Michigan Press, 1992), 289–300.

90. Tobing Rony discusses Baker in *Third Eye*, 198–203. See also Ylva Habel, "To Stockholm, with Love: The Critical Reception of Josephine Baker, 1927–35," *Film History* 17 (2005): 125–38.

91. Terry Francis, "Embodied Fictions, Melancholy Migrations: Josephine Baker's Cinematic Celebrity," *MFS: Modern Fiction Studies* 51, no. 4 (2005): 831.

92. Phyllis Rose, *Jazz Cleopatra: Josephine Baker in Her Time* (London: Chatto and Windus, 1990), 16.

93. Tobing Rony, *Third Eye*, 200; Habel, "To Stockholm, with Love," 134.

94. Elizabeth Ezra, *The Colonial Unconscious: Race and Culture in Interwar France* (Ithaca, N.Y.: Cornell University Press, 2000), 98.

95. Jean Gallacher, "H. D.'s Distractions: Cinematic Stasis and Lesbian Desire," *Modernism / Modernity* 9, no. 3 (2002): 407–22.

96. H. D., "The Cinema and the Classics I: Beauty," in *Close Up, 1927–1933: Cinema and Modernism*, ed. James Donald, Anne Friedberg, and Laura Marcus (Princeton, N.J.: Princeton University Press, 1999), 107.

97 Ibid., 109.

98. Le Corbusier, *Decorative Art of Today*, 12.

99 Ibid., 84.

100. Wigley, *White Walls, Designer Dresses*, 78.

101. Walter Benjamin to Franz Glück, December 17, 1930, in Walter Benjamin, *Gesammelte Briefe*, vol. 3, *1925-1930*, ed. Christoph Gödde and Henri Lonitz (Frankfurt: Suhrkamp, 1997), 559. Benjamin's English-language editors highlight the significance of this letter in Walter Benjamin, *Selected Writings*, vol. 2, *1927–1934*, trans. Rodney Livingstone and others, ed. Michael W. Jennings, Howard Eiland, and Gary Smith (Cambridge, Mass.: Harvard University Press, 1999), 839–40.

102. Walter Benjamin, "Little History of Photography," in *Selected Writings*, ed. Jennings, Eiland, and Smith, 2:515.

103. Ibid., 517.

104. Ibid., 510–12.

105. Ibid., 518.

106. Roland Barthes, *Camera Lucida: Reflections on Photography*, trans. Richard Howard (New York: Hill & Wang, 1982); André Bazin, *What Is Cinema?* vol. 1, trans. Hugh Gray (Berkeley: University of California Press, 1967); Philip

Rosen, *Change Mummified: Cinema, Historicity, Theory* (Minneapolis: University of Minnesota Press, 2000); Daniel Morgan, "Rethinking Bazin: Ontology and Realist Aesthetics," *Critical Inquiry* 32, no. 3 (2006): 443–81.

107. Walter Benjamin, "Experience and Poverty," in *Selected Writings*, vol. 4, *1938–1939*, trans. Edmund Jephcott and others, ed. Howard Eiland and Michael W. Jennings (Cambridge, Mass.: Harvard University Press, 2003), 732.

108. Ibid., 733.

109. Miriam Hansen, "Benjamin, Cinema, and Experience: 'The Blue Flower in the Land of Technology,' " *New German Critique* 40 (1987): 179–224.

110. Patrizia C. McBride, " 'In Praise of the Present': Adolf Loos on Style and Fashion," *Modernism/Modernity* 11, no. 4 (2004): 745.

111. Walter Benjamin, "Karl Kraus," in *Selected Writings*, ed. Jennings, Eiland, and Smith, 2:434.

112. We might also note that Benjamin attributes to Loos (via Kraus) an opposition to the impression. This position is quite different from that of anti-ornamental film theory, which valorizes the impression of the real. Benjamin here picks up on a quite different reading of Loos, which might complicate cinema's tendency to conflate the impression with the modern.

113. Benjamin, "Karl Kraus," 456, 438.

114. Ibid., 443.

115. Werner Oechslin, *Otto Wagner, Adolf Loos, and the Road to Modern Architecture*, trans. Lynette Widder (Cambridge: Cambridge University Press, 2002), 114. Gravagnuolo argues that Loos would subscribe to Benjamin's claims on history because both reject historicism (*Adolf Loos*, 36), but this seems to me to stretch Loos's political radicalism beyond plausibility.

116. Walter Benjamin, "The Regression of Poetry, by Carl Gustav Jochmann," in *Selected Writings*, ed. Eiland and Jennings, 4:362.

117. Quoted in ibid., 374.

118. Félix Bracquemond, "Le même mobile qui pousse le sauvage à se tatouer, a etre un anneau dans le nez, nous dirige dans le choix de nos vêtements, de notre toilette" (*Du dessin et de la couleur* [Paris: Charpentier, 1885], 162).

119. Benjamin, "Regression of Poetry," 364.

120. Ibid., 363.

121. Walter Benjamin, "The Work of Art in the Age of Its Technological Reproducibility," in *Selected Writings*, ed. Eiland and Jennings, 4:251–83.

122. Walter Benjamin, *The Arcades Project*, trans. Howard Eiland and Kevin McLaughlin (Cambridge, Mass.: Harvard University Press, 1999), 557.

123. Ibid., 547, 550. Moreover, Sternberger goes on to describe how the owner of a Jugendstil house "loses the power of moving about freely and becomes attached to ground and property," echoing the Poor Rich Man.

124. Ibid., 551.

125. Ibid., 216.

126. Quoted in ibid., 214.

127. Ibid., 218.

128. Ibid., 556.

129. Ibid., 558.

130. Epstein, "On Certain Characteristics of *Photogenie*," 317.

131. Benjamin, *Arcades Project*, 214.

132. Jules Lecomte, *Les lettres de Van Engelgom,* ed. Henri d'Almeras (Paris: Éditions Bossard, 1925), 63–64, quoted in ibid., 223.

133. Hansen, "Benjamin, Cinema, and Experience," 223.

134. Susan Buck-Morss, "Aesthetics and Anaesethetics: Walter Benjamin's Artwork Essay Reconsidered," *October* 62 (1992): 3–41.

135. Ackbar Abbas, "On Fascination: Walter Benjamin's Images," *New German Critique* 48 (1989): 46.

136. Benjamin, *Arcades Project*, 557.

137. Ibid., 556.

138. Eduardo Cadava, "Words of Light: Theses on the Photography of History," *Diacritics* 22, nos. 3–4 (1992): 89.

139. Ibid., 90.

4. Objects

1. Adolf Loos, "Interiors: A Prelude," in *Spoken into the Void: Collected Essays, 1897–1900,* trans. Jane O. Newman and John H. Smith (Cambridge, Mass.: MIT Press, 1982), 20.

2. Walter Benjamin, *The Arcades Project,* trans. Howard Eiland and Kevin McLaughlin (Cambridge, Mass.: Harvard University Press, 1999), 224.

3. José Arroyo, *"Moulin Rouge!" Sight & Sound* 11, no. 9 (2001): 50–51.

4. The only sustained area of research is on *Romeo + Juliet,* where adaptation studies and Shakespeare scholars have written on the film. See, for instance, Angela Keam, "Claire Danes's Star-Body, Teen Female Viewers and the Pluralisation of Authorship in Baz Luhrmann's *William Shakespeare's Romeo + Juliet," English in Australia* 43, no. 2 (2008): 39–46; and Chris Palmer, " 'What Tongue Shall Smooth Thy Name?' Recent Films of *Romeo and Juliet," Cambridge Quarterly* 31, no. 1 (2003): 61–76.

5. This response can also be interestingly historicized: the success of the *High School Musical* films (Ortega, 2006, 2007, and 2008) and the television series *Glee* in 2009 and 2010 changes the debate, with *Glee* in particular finding enormous success by appropriating old pop songs in a way that was perhaps prepared by *Moulin Rouge.*

6. Marsha Kinder, *"Moulin Rouge!" Film Quarterly* 55, no. 3 (2001): 52.

7. Kristin Thompson, "The Concept of Cinematic Excess," in *Film Theory and Criticism: Introductory Readings*, 5th ed., ed. Leo Braudy and Marshall Cohen (New York: Oxford University Press, 1999), 487–98.

8. Charles Blanc, *The Grammar of Painting and Engraving*, trans. Kate Newell Doggett (Chicago: Griggs, 1891), 4–5. Blanc also claims that Europeans have much to learn from the Orient in terms of color and decorative art. Unwilling to give any ground on the question of fine art, he does credit the Orient for its facility with carpets, tiles, ceramics, and other such decorative work, in *Grammaire des arts décoratifs* (Paris: Librarie Renouard, 1882), 223.

9. Blanc, *Grammar of Painting and Engraving*, 169.

10. Sigmund Freud, "Femininity," in *New Introductory Lectures on Psychoanalysis and Other Works*, trans. James Strachey (New York: Norton, 1989), 139. Freud cites Heinrich Heine, *Die Nordsee*, Second Cycle, VII, "Fragen," 146.

11. Thomas W. Kim, "Being Modern: The Circulation of Oriental Objects," *American Quarterly* 58, no. 2 (2006): 383.

12. Sarah Cheang, "What's in a Chinese Room? 20th Century Chinoiserie, Modernity, and Femininity," in *Chinese Whispers: Chinoiserie in Britain, 1650–1930*, ed. David Beevers (Brighton: Royal Pavilion and Museums, 2008), 75.

13. Kim, "Being Modern," 379.

14. Kim's example here is *The Cheat*, returning to the figure of Sessue Hayakawa, who is "surrounded by Oriental objects and obsessively marking them with his brand: here is consumption divorced from production, as well as a hint of avarice and superficiality, a satisfaction in appearances that is also the Oriental's secret" (ibid., 403).

15. Victoria de Grazia, "Introduction," in *The Sex of Things: Gender and Consumption in Historical Perspective*, ed. Victoria de Grazia, with Ellen Furlough (Berkeley: University of California Press, 1996), 14–15.

16. Kim, "Being Modern," 387.

17. Bill Brown, *A Sense of Things: The Object Matter of American Literature* (Chicago: University of Chicago Press, 2003), 4.

18. Iain Chambers, "History, the Baroque, and the Judgement of the Angels," in *The Actuality of Walter Benjamin*, ed. Laura Marcus and Lynda Nead (London: Lawrence & Wishart, 1998), 174.

19. Sumiko Higashi, "Ethnicity, Class, and Gender in Film: DeMille's *The Cheat*," in *Unspeakable Images: Ethnicity in Cinema*, ed. Lester Friedman (Urbana: University of Illinois Press, 1991), 130; Cheang, "What's in a Chinese Room?" 75.

20. Malek Alloula, *The Colonial Harem*, trans. Myrna Godzich and Wlad Godzich (Minneapolis: University of Minnesota Press, 1986), 62.

21. Ibid., 5, 18.

22. Meyda Yegenoglu, *Colonial Fantasies: Towards a Feminist Reading of Orientalism* (Cambridge: Cambridge University Press, 1998), 42.

23. Mike Sell, "Bohemianism, the Cultural Turn of the Avantgarde, and Forgetting the Roma," *TDR: The Drama Review* 51, no. 2 (2007): 49.

24. On the relationship between spontaneous and artificial articulation in the Hollywood musical, see Jane Feuer, *The Hollywood Musical* (London: BFI, 1982).

25. Joseph Boone, "Vacation Cruises; or, the Homoerotics of Orientalism," in *Postcolonial, Queer: Theoretical Intersections*, ed. John C. Hawley (Albany: State University of New York Press, 2001), 44.

26. Quoted in David Beevers, " 'Mand'rin Only Is the Man of Taste': 17th and 18th Century Chinoiserie in Britain," in *Chinese Whispers*, ed. Beevers, 24.

27. Reina Lewis, *Gendering Orientalism: Race, Femininity, and Representation* (New York: Routledge, 1996), 114.

28. John M. MacKenzie, *Orientalism: History, Theory, and the Arts* (Manchester: Manchester University Press, 1995), 63.

29. Ibid., 105.

30. Naomi Schor, *Reading in Detail: Aesthetics and the Feminine* (New York: Methuen, 1987), 42.

31. Linda Nochlin, "The Imaginary Orient," in *The Nineteenth-Century Visual Culture Reader*, ed. Vanessa R. Schwartz and Jeannene M. Przyblyski (New York: Routledge, 2004), 290.

32. Lewis, *Gendering Orientalism*, 113.

33. Sell, "Bohemianism," 48–49.

34. Ibid., 53.

35. *Moulin Rouge*'s Occidental fantasies include Paris but also the erotic Argentina conjured in the tango scene.

36. Beevers, "Mand'rin," 15. Beevers gives as an example Chinese lacquer, which came to be known as "Japanning" or "India work."

37. Oliver Impey, *Chinoiserie: The Impact of Oriental Styles in Western Art and Decoration* (London: Oxford University Press, 1977), 12.

38. Patrick Conner, "Chinese Style in 19th Century Britain," in *Chinese Whispers*, ed. Beevers, 70.

39. Impey, *Chinoiserie*, 14.

40. Kinder, "*Moulin Rouge!*" 55–56.

41. This swooping digital camera movement begins in the 1990s, first in animations such as *Aladdin* (Clements and Musker, 1992) and increasingly in the 2000s in live-action films. Another notable use of the shot is in the opening sequence of *Sweeney Todd*.

42. André Bazin, "An Aesthetic of Reality," in *What Is Cinema?* trans. Hugh Gray (Berkeley: University of California Press, 1967), 1:33.

43. Markus Brüderlin, "Introduction: Ornament and Abstraction," in *Ornament and Abstraction: The Dialogue Between Non-Western, Modern, and Contemporary Art*, ed. Markus Brüderlin (Basel: Fondation Beyeler, 2001), 20.

44. Alois Riegl, *Problems of Style: Foundations for a History of Ornament*, trans. Evelyn Kain (Princeton, N.J.: Princeton University Press, 1992), 229; Eva Baer, *Islamic Ornament* (Edinburgh: Edinburgh University Press, 1998), 15.

45. Riegl, *Problems of Style*, 231.

46. Baer, *Islamic Ornament*, 20.

47. Richard Ettinghausen, Oleg Grabar, and Marilyn Jenkins-Madina, *Islamic Art and Architecture, 650–1250* (New Haven, Conn.: Yale University Press, 2001), 66.

48. Riegl, *Problems of Style*, 237.

49. Winfried Minninghaus gives an overview of these debates in "Hummingbirds, Shells, Picture-Frames: Kant's 'Free Beauties' and the Romantic Arabesque," in *Rereading Romanticism*, ed. Martha B. Helfer (Amsterdam: Rodopi, 2000), 29.

50. Carsten Strathausen, "Eichendorff's *Das Marmorbild* and the Demise of Romanticism," in *Rereading Romanticism*, ed. Helfer, 375n.15.

51. Ibid., 375; Minninghaus, "Hummingbirds, Shells, Picture-Frames," 41–43.

52. Minninghaus, "Hummingbirds, Shells, Picture-Frames," 27.

53. Annemarie Schimmel, "The Arabesque and the Islamic View of the World," in *Ornament and Abstraction*, ed. Brüderlin, 34.

54. Laura U. Marks, "Infinity and Accident: Strategies of Enfoldment in Islamic and Computer Art," *Leonardo* 39, no. 1 (2006): 42.

55. Henry van de Velde, "Die Linie," *Die Zukunft*, September 6, 1902, quoted in Brüderlin, "Introduction," 23.

56. Ernst Beyeler, "Preface," in *Ornament and Abstraction*, ed. Brüderlin, 15.

57. Brüderlin, "Introduction," 21.

58. Viola Weigel, "The War of Signs—Peace in Ornament: The Ornament as a Bridge Between Cultures," in *Ornament and Abstraction*, ed. Brüderlin, 169.

59. Jenny Anger, *Paul Klee and the Decorative in Modern Art* (Cambridge: Cambridge University Press, 2004), 3–4.

60. Ettinghausen, Grabar, and Jenkins-Madina, *Islamic Art and Architecture*, 79.

61. Clare Parfitt, "The Spectator's Dancing Gaze in *Moulin Rouge!*" *Research in Dance Education* 6, no. 1 (2005): 97–110.

62. Ella Shohat, *Taboo Memories, Diasporic Voices* (Durham, N.C.: Duke University Press, 2006), 80–81.

63. P. Adams Sitney, *Visionary Film: The American Avant-Garde, 1943–2000* (Oxford: Oxford University Press, 2002), 161.

64. Quoted in Melissa Ragona, "Swing and Sway: Marie Menken's Filmic Events," in *Women's Experimental Cinema: Critical Frameworks*, ed. Robin Blaetz (Durham, N.C.: Duke University Press, 2007), 20.

65. Ibid., 23. Ragona's reading of Menken opens out a broader engagement with questions of representation and material. She argues that Menken's work is "deeply concerned with ungrounding the easel-based practices of drawing and sculpture through film" (23). Thus she is interested in the relationship of film to art history and in bringing ideas from painting and sculpture into cinema. Shifting the arabesque from the walls of the Alhambra to the movements of the camera turns drawing into movement in a way that meshes productively with the aims of the pretty.

66. William Hogarth, *Analysis of Beauty* (Hildesheim: Olms, 1974), 38–39.

67. Ibid., 49.

68. Jacques Rancière, *Film Fables*, trans. Emiliano Battista (London: Berg, 2006), 127.

69. Francesca Falcone, "The Arabesque: A Compositional Design," trans. Irene Minafra and Brett Shapiro, *Dance Chronicle* 19, no. 3 (1996): 232.

70. Carlo Blasis, *The Code of Terpsichore* (New York: Dance Horizons, 1976), 74, quoted in ibid.

71. Francesca Falcone, "The Evolution of the Arabesque in Dance," *Dance Chronicle* 22, no. 1 (1999): 71.

72. Falcone, "Arabesque," 245.

73. Ibid., 242.

74. Corinn Columpar, "The Dancing Body: Sally Potter as Feminist Auteur," in *Women Filmmakers: Refocusing*, ed. Jacqueline Levitin, Judith Plessis, and Valerie Raoul (New York: Routledge, 2003), 108–16.

75. E. Ann Kaplan, "Night at the Opera: Investigating the Heroine in Sally Potter's *Thriller*," *Millennium Film Journal* 10–11 (1981): 115–22.

76. Susan M. White, *The Cinema of Max Ophuls: Magisterial Vision and the Figure of Woman* (New York: Columbia University Press, 1995), 277.

77. Andrew Sarris, "Films in Focus," *Village Voice*, September 5, 1963.

78. Mary Ann Doane, *Femmes Fatales: Feminism, Film Theory, Psychoanalysis* (New York: Routledge, 1991), 66.

79. Virginia Wright-Wexman, "The Transfiguration of History: Ophuls, Vienna, and *Letter from an Unknown Woman*," in *Letter from an Unknown Woman*, ed. Virginia Wright-Wexman (New Brunswick, N.J.: Rutgers University Press, 1986), 11.

80. Chris Wisniewski, "The Main Attraction," *Reverse Shot* 23 (2008), available at http://www.reverseshot.com/article/lola_montes (accessed January 5, 2009).

81. Riegl, *Problems of Style*, 234.

82. Kaja Silverman, *The Subject of Semiotics* (New York: Oxford University Press, 1983), 226.

83. Ibid., 227.

84. Doane, *Femmes Fatales*, 75; White, *Cinema of Max Ophuls*, 284. We can connect this childless, queer Lola with Benjamin's perverse woman as well as

with a refusal of "life" in Kracauer's or Loos's terms. The decorative always hints at a queer refusal of "life."

85. Wisniewski, "Main Attraction."

86. Schimmel, "Arabesque and the Islamic View of the World," 32.

5. AT THE CROSSROADS

1. Karl Schoonover, *Brutal Humanism: The Neorealist Body and Global Spectators* (Minneapolis: University of Minnesota Press, forthcoming); Laura E. Ruberto and Kristi M. Wilson, eds., *Italian Neorealism and Global Cinema* (Detroit: Wayne State University Press, 2007).

2. Roland Barthes, *Mythologies*, trans. Annette Lavers (New York: Hill & Wang, 1972), 11 (italics in original). For an account of Barthes's relationship to Marxism, see Jean-Jacques Lecercle, "Barthes Without Althusser: A Different Style of Marxism," *Paragraph* 31, no. 1 (2008): 72–83.

3. Raymond Williams, *Marxism and Literature* (Oxford: Oxford University Press, 1978), 154–56.

4. James Roy MacBean, "*Vent d'Est* or Godard and Rocha at the Crossroads," in *Movies and Methods*, ed. Bill Nichols (Berkeley: University of California Press, 1976), 1:93.

5. Quoted in ibid., 94.

6. Ibid., 93.

7. Ibid., 94.

8. Gilles Deleuze argues that Plato's separation of false image from true form produces the foundations of all criticism in *The Logic of Sense*, trans. Mark Lester and Charles Stivale (New York: Columbia University Press, 1990), 253–65.

9. Plato, *Republic*, 509d–510a, 745, 598–599d, 823–24; *Symposium* 212a, 563; *Sophist* 239c–e, 982–83, 264c, 1012, all in *The Collected Dialogues of Plato*, trans. Lane Cooper and others, ed. Edith Hamilton and Huntington Cairns (Princeton, N.J.: Princeton University Press, 1961). In *Images of Excellence: Plato's Critique of the Arts* (Oxford: Clarendon Press, 1995), Christopher Janaway usefully reminds us that Plato is not simply a Philistine with a misguided aversion to the arts and argues that Plato's rejection of art is based on good reason. Nonetheless, although this may be an important correction to previous readings of Plato, it does not alter the influence of Platonic thinking on subsequent image theories. Janaway goes on to compare Plato's censure of poetry with reactionary media critics: "He engages with poetry in the way recent critics have engaged with television, cinema, and video: 'the endless proliferation of senseless images,' 'ubiquitous and intrusive purveyors of bad taste, deformed paradigms, and questionable values,' from which children and others nevertheless learn" (81). Again, although this clarification may helpfully reorient Plato for some

readers, it does not greatly ameliorate the sense of him as fundamentally out of sympathy with image culture.

10. Plato, *Republic*, V, 745c–e, 714–15.

11. Plato, *Symposium*, 212e, 563.

12. Plato, *Greater Hippias*, 297e–299e, 1551–53. These terms are debated throughout Plato's dialogues—for example, in *Gorgias*, 465a, 247, 474c–475b, 256–57—so these categories are by no means fixed.

13. Jacqueline Lichtenstein, *The Eloquence of Color: Rhetoric and Painting in the French Classical Age*, trans. Emily McVarish (Berkeley: University of California Press, 1993), 49.

14. Arthur Danto, *The Philosophical Disenfranchisement of Art* (New York: Columbia University Press, 1986), 13.

15. W. J. T. Mitchell, *Iconology: Image, Text, Ideology* (Chicago: University of Chicago Press, 1987), 8–10, 164. Mitchell does not hold to a vulgar interpretation of ideology as a false image but instead details how the rhetorical history of image metaphors has allowed iconoclastic thinking to find its way into diverse intellectual histories.

16. Ibid., 8.

17. John Peters, "Beauty's Veils: The Ambivalent Iconoclasm of Kierkegaard and Benjamin," in *The Image in Dispute: Art and Cinema in the Age of Photography*, ed. Dudley Andrew (Austin: University of Texas Press, 1997), 10.

18. Guy Debord, *The Society of the Spectacle*, trans. Donald Nicholson-Smith (New York: Zone Books, 1994); Fredric Jameson, *Signatures of the Visible* (New York: Routledge, 1991), 6.

19. Dudley Andrew, "A Preface to Disputation," in *Image in Dispute*, ed. Andrew, viii.

20. Jean-Luc Comolli and Jean Narboni, "Cinema, Ideology, Criticism," in *Movies and Methods*, ed. Nichols, 1:22–30.

21. Ibid., 28.

22. Comolli and Narboni argue that categories "b" and "c" constitute "the essential in the cinema" and "should be the chief subject of the magazine" (ibid., 26). For readings of Douglas Sirk, see Thomas Elsaesser, "Tales of Sound and Fury: Observations on the Family Melodrama," in *Home Is Where the Heart Is: Studies in Melodrama and the Woman's Film*, ed. Christine Gledhill (London: BFI, 1987), 43–69; Laura Mulvey, "Notes on Sirk and Melodrama," in *Home Is Where the Heart Is*, ed. Gledhill, 75–79; Sam Rohdie, ed., special issue on Douglas Sirk, *Screen* 12, no. 2 (1971); and Barbara Klinger, *Melodrama and Meaning: History, Culture, and the Films of Douglas Sirk* (Bloomington: Indiana University Press, 1994).

23. Colin MacCabe, "Theory and Film: Principles of Realism and Pleasure," in *Narrative, Apparatus, Ideology: A Film Theory Reader*, ed. Philip Rosen (New York: Columbia University Press, 1986), 180.

24. Peter Wollen, "Godard and Counter-cinema: *Vent d'Est*," in *Movies and Methods*, ed. Bill Nichols (Berkeley: University of California Press, 1985), 2:508.

25. Gertrud Koch, "Mimesis and *Bilderverbot*," *Screen* 34, no. 3 (1993): 211–22.

26. Theodor W. Adorno, *Negative Dialectics*, trans. E. B. Ashton (New York: Seabury, 1973), 207.

27. Koch, "Mimesis and *Bilderverbot*," 221.

28. Stephen Heath, "On Screen, in Frame: Film and Ideology," in *Questions of Cinema* (Bloomington: Indiana University Press, 1981), 6.

29. Ibid., 8.

30. Stephen Heath, "The Question Oshima," in *Questions of Cinema*, 154, 160 (my italics).

31. Ibid., 151.

32. Jean-Luc Comolli, "Machines of the Visible," in *The Cinematic Apparatus*, ed. Teresa de Lauretis and Stephen Heath (New York: St. Martin's Press, 1980), 124, 123, 141.

33. Martin Jay, *Downcast Eyes: The Denigration of Vision in Twentieth-Century French Thought* (Berkeley: University of California Press, 1994), 14, 150.

34. Marcel Duchamp and Pierre Cabanne, *Entretiens avec Marcel Duchamp* (Paris: Pierre Belfond, 1967), 83–84, quoted in ibid., 162.

35. Mikhail Iampolski, "Russia: The Cinema of Anti-modernity and Backward Progress," in *Theorising National Cinema*, ed. Valentina Vitali and Paul Willemen (London: BFI, 2006), 72–87.

36. Fredric Jameson, *The Geopolitical Aesthetic: Cinema and Space in the World System* (Bloomington: Indiana University Press, 1995), 98.

37. Nigel Andrews, "*Adrift / Hrst plná vody*," *Monthly Film Bulletin* 39, no. 460 (1972): 96.

38. Edith Laurie, "The Film Festival at Karlovy Vary," *Vision* 1, no. 2 (1962): 9.

39. Edith Laurie, "Notes from the Venice Film Festival," *Film Comment* 1, no. 3 (1963): 10.

40. Carlo Lizzani, "Come risolvere il problema del naturalismo nel cinema?" *Cinema Nuovo* 204 (1970): 96–99.

41. John Hughes, "Recent Rossellini," *Film Comment* 10, no. 4 (1974): 16, 17.

42. Jean-Luc Godard, "La nuit, l'éclipse, l'aurore: Entretien avec Michelangelo Antonioni," *Cahiers du Cinéma* 160 (1964): 16.

43. "*Red Psalm*," *Monthly Film Bulletin* 40, no. 471 (1973): 80.

44. Nelly Kaplan, "À propos de Cannes," *Film Comment* 1, no. 5 (1963): 42.

45. Joan Mellen, "*Vent d'Est*," *Film Comment* 7, no. 3 (1971): 67.

46. Philip Strick, "*Zabriskie Point*," *Monthly Film Bulletin* 37, no. 436 (1970): 102; Nigel Andrews, "*Roma*," *Monthly Film Bulletin* 39, no. 467 (1972): 258.

47. Mike Wallington, "*Fellini–Satyricon*," *Monthly Film Bulletin* 37, no. 441 (1970): 200, 201.

48. Marcel Marën, "Another Kind of Cinema," *Film Comment* 1, no. 3 (1963): 15. Immediately before the section where this statement occurs, Marën gives *French Cancan* as an example of what's wrong with such a "totally cinematized universe." Referring again to an intertext of *Moulin Rouge*, he finds bohemian sexual display to exemplify the bad pretty.

49. Thomas Guback, *The International Film Industry* (Bloomington: Indiana University Press, 1969), 199. Mark Betz quotes this passage in "The Name Above the (Sub)Title: Internationalism, Coproduction, and Polyglot European Art Cinema," *Camera Obscura* 46, no. 16/1 (2001): 1–44. However, he is more concerned with how Guback's research has been ignored by scholars than with the reading of art cinema aesthetics that the passage proposes.

50. Strick, "*Zabriskie Point*," 102.

51. Ibid.

52. Bill Nichols, "*Il conformista*," *Cineaste* 4, no. 4 (1971): 19, 20.

53. Jean-Pierre Oudart, "Un discours en défaut," *Cahiers du cinéma* 232 (1971): 11 (my translation). Oudart repeats the terms *semblance* and *false-semblance* (*faux-semblant*).

54. Gianfranco Corbucci, "*La strategia del ragno*," *Cinema Nuovo* 209 (1971): 60–61.

55. Immanuel Kant, *The Critique of Judgment*, trans. J. H. Bernard (Amherst, N.Y.: Prometheus Books, 2000), 73.

56. Corbucci, "*La strategia del ragno*," 61.

57. Rosalind Delmar, "*Amore e Rabbia*," *Monthly Film Bulletin* 38, no. 448 (1971): 91; Amos Vogel, "Bernardo Bertolucci: An Interview," *Film Comment* 7, no. 3 (1971): 28–29.

58. Vogel, "Bernardo Bertolucci," 25.

59. Leonard Quart, "*1900*: Bertolucci's Marxist Opera," *Cineaste* 8, no. 3 (1977–1978): 25, 27.

60. Jan Dawson, "*The Conformist*," *Monthly Film Bulletin* 38, no. 455 (1971): 238.

61. Richard Combs, "*The Bitter Tears of Petra von Kant*," *Monthly Film Bulletin* 42, no. 496 (1975): 100.

62. Richard Combs, "*Fear Eats the Soul*," *Monthly Film Bulletin* 41, no. 490 (1974): 244.

63. Carlos Losilla, "Legislación, industria y escritura," in *Escritos sobre el cine español, 1973–1987* (Valencia: Filmoteca de la Generalitat Valenciana, 1989), 41; translated in Sally Faulkner, *Literary Adaptations in Spanish Cinema* (Woodbridge: Tamesis, 2004), 16–17.

64. Fernando Solanas and Octavio Getino, "Towards a Third Cinema," in *Movies and Methods*, ed. Nichols, 1:49.

65. Glauber Rocha, "The Aesthetics of Hunger," in *Twenty-five Years of the New Latin American Cinema*, ed. Michael Chanan (London: BFI, 1983), 13.

66. Solanas and Getino, "Towards a Third Cinema," 54.

67. Ibid.

68. Julio García Espinosa, "In Search of the Lost Cinema," in *Latin American Filmmakers and the Third Cinema*, ed. Zuzana M. Pick (Ottawa: Carleton University Press, 1978), 194.

69. Julio García Espinosa, "For an Imperfect Cinema," in *Twenty-five Years of the New Latin American Cinema*, ed. Chanan, 28, 33.

70. Rocha, "Aesthetics of Hunger," 13.

71. García Espinosa, "In Search of the Lost Cinema," 195.

72. García Espinosa, "For an Imperfect Cinema," 28.

73. Ibid., 31.

74. Solanas and Getino, "Towards a Third Cinema," 46.

75. Ibid., 50 (italics in original).

76. Jorge Sanjinés, "El cine político no debe abandonar su preocupación por la belleza," in *Teoría y práctica de un cine junto al pueblo* (Mexico City: Editorial Siglo XXI, 1971), 156–57 (my translation).

77. Solanas and Getino, "Towards a Third Cinema," 49.

78. Jorge Sanjinés, "Problems of Form and Content in Revolutionary Cinema," in *Twenty-five Years of the New Latin American Cinema*, ed. Chanan, 34.

79. Comolli and Narboni, "Cinema, Ideology, Criticism," 26–27.

80. Dennis Hanlon, "Traveling Theory, Shots, and Players: Jorge Sanjinés, New Latin American Cinema, and the European Art Film," in *Global Art Cinema: New Histories and Theories*, ed. Rosalind Galt and Karl Schoonover (New York: Oxford University Press, 2010), 351–66.

81. Jorge Sanjinés, "Sobre *Fuera de aquí!*" *Cine Cubano* 93 (1979): 129 (my translation).

82. Sanjinés, *Teoría y práctica*, 156 (my translation).

83. Max Horkheimer and Theodor W. Adorno, *Dialectic of Enlightenment*, trans. John Cumming (New York: Continuum, 1996).

84. García Espinosa, "For an Imperfect Cinema," 30.

6. FORMS

1. Jonathan Rosenbaum, *Essential Cinema: On the Necessity of Film Canons* (Baltimore: Johns Hopkins University Press, 2004), 370.

2. The exhibition information comes from *Hoy* (Havana), June–August 1964.

3. Michael Chanan, *Cuban Cinema* (Minneapolis: University of Minnesota Press, 2004), 166.

4. Rob Stone, "Mother Lands, Sister Nations: The Epic, Poetic, Propaganda Films of Cuba and the Basque Country," in *Remapping World Cinema: Identity, Culture, and Politics in Film*, ed. Stephanie Dennison and Song Hwee Lin (London: Wallflower, 2006), 68.

5. Lúcia Nagib, "Panaméricas Utópicas: Entranced and Transient Nations in *I Am Cuba* (1964) and *Land in Trance* (1967)," *Hispanic Research Journal* 8, no. 1 (2007): 85.

6. In addition to those critics discussed, the film was positively reviewed by José Valdés Rodríguez in *El Mundo*, August 18, 1964, and by Mario Rodríguez Alemán in *Diario de la tarde*, August 3, 1964.

7. Josefina Ruiz, "*Soy Cuba*," *Verde Olivo* 32, no. 9 (1964): 12, 13. All translations are mine unless otherwise noted.

8. Alejo Beltrán, "*Soy Cuba*," *Hoy*, August 8, 1964.

9. Eduardo Mane, "80 minutos con Serguei Urusevski," *Cine Cubano* 20 (1964): 2.

10. Mario Rodríguez Alemán, "Bosquedo histórico del cinema cubano," *Cine Cubano* 26 (1965): 33.

11. Edith Laurie, "To Have or Not to Have a Film Festival," *Film Comment* 3, no. 3 (1965): 18–23.

12. "Liste des films sortis en excusivité à Paris," *Cahiers du cinéma* 233 (1971): 62.

13. Steven P. Hill, "The Soviet Film Today," *Film Quarterly* 20, no. 4 (1967): 51.

14. Josephine Woll, *Real Images: Soviet Cinema and the Thaw* (London: Taurus, 2000), 184.

15. Luis M. López, "No *Soy Cuba*," *Bohemia*, August 21, 1964, 24–25.

16. Ibid., 24, 25.

17. Ibid., 24.

18. The *Iskusstvo Kino* review is cited in Dina Iordanova, "Review of *I Am Cuba*," *Russian Review* 56, no. 1 (1997): 125–26; and Hill, "Soviet Film Today," 52.

19. Steven P. Hill, "Introduction to *Shadows of Our Forgotten Ancestors*," *Film Comment* 5, no. 1 (1968): 39. The issue of Kalatozov as a Georgian director is also significant. Hill, for example, finds Paradjanov's work to be strongly influenced by questions of ethnicity and marginality within Soviet culture. At the very least, Kalatozov's Georgian background should give the lie to his construction by some of the Cuban commentators as a stereotypical dour Russian.

20. López, "No *Soy Cuba*," 24.

21. Ibid., 25.

22. Nagib, "Panaméricas Utópicas," 85. Nagib also quotes camera operator Sasha Calzatti: "As far as Cuba is concerned, we didn't know about their culture or their tongue, we only knew its location on the map." His point is that *before* they went to Cuba, they knew nothing. However, the crew spent a year there before they started filming, and production took almost two years, so in reality there was quite an astonishing amount of research.

23. López, "No *Soy Cuba*," 25.

24. Some recent criticism has been more positive. Iordanova praises the film as a masterpiece of post-1920s Soviet cinema in "Review of *I Am Cuba*." Yannick Lemarié compares Kalatozov to Eisenstein in his ability to use film language to adequate historical change in "*Soy Cuba*: Le mythe de la révolution," *Positif*

512 (2003): 77–78. But these assessments are mostly short reviews of the film's DVD release rather than extended articles, and they focus mostly on the film's technical achievements.

25. Paul Julian Smith, "*I Am Cuba*," *Sight & Sound* 9, no. 8 (1999): 46.

26. Augusto Martínez Torres and Manuel Pérez Estremera, *Nuevo cine latinoamericano* (Barcelona: Anagrama, 1973); Stone, "Mother Lands, Sister Nations," 67.

27. Chanan, *Cuban Cinema*, 167.

28. Mane, "80 minutos con Serguei Urusevski," 5.

29. Richard Gott, "From Russia with Love," *Guardian*, November 12, 2005, available at http://www.guardian.co.uk/film/2005/nov/12/cuba (accessed January 30, 2008).

30. Mane, "80 minutos con Serguei Urusevski," 5.

31. Hill, "Soviet Film Today," 51.

32. Mane, "80 minutos con Serguei Urusevski," 5.

33. Nagib, "Panaméricas Utópicas."

34. Ibid., 84; Ismail Xavier, *Allegories of Underdevelopment: Aesthetics and Politics in Modern Brazilian Cinema* (Minneapolis: University of Minnesota Press, 1997), 89. It may also be productive to think Benjamin's theory of the baroque allegory in relation to the ornamental qualities of *Soy Cuba*'s prettiness.

35. This nationalizing discourse may help explain why Rocha's Brazilian-themed films screen widely, whereas *Cabezas cortadas* (1970), the film he made in Spain in collaboration with members of the Catalan avant-garde, is much less easily available.

7. PERVERSE PRETTINESS

1. Naomi Schor, *Reading in Detail: Aesthetics and the Feminine* (New York: Methuen, 1987), 49.

2. Ibid., 45.

3. As Stella demonstrates, both her belief in this theory of cosmetics and her awareness of its pathetic nature inevitably lead to a reactionary politics. The often cited feminist debate on the film demonstrates that the politics of feminine decoration is a sticky subject for film theory. See E. Ann Kaplan, "The Case of the Missing Mother: Maternal Issues in Vidor's *Stella Dallas*," in *Issues in Feminist Film Criticism*, ed. Patricia Erens (Bloomington: Indiana University Press, 1990), 126–36; and Linda Williams, "Something Else Besides a Mother: *Stella Dallas* and the Maternal Melodrama," in *Home Is Where the Heart Is: Studies in Melodrama and the Woman's Film*, ed. Christine Gledhill (London: BFI, 1987), 299–325. See also Stanley Cavell, "Stella's Taste: Reading *Stella Dallas*," in *Contesting Tears: The Hollywood Melodrama of the Unknown Woman* (Chicago: University of Chicago Press, 1996), 197–222.

4.   I read feminist and queer theories as broadly cognate in regard to the debates of this chapter. This harnessing is by no means intended to collapse the differences between theories of gender and those of sexuality, especially where, as in some streams of queer film theory, feminist theory is criticized specifically as inadequate to or a closing down of lesbian perspectives. See, for example, Chris Straayer, *Deviant Eyes, Deviant Bodies: Sexual Re-orientations in Film and Video* (Edinburgh: Edinburgh University Press, 1996). Because I argue that anti-pretty rhetoric works to exclude both the feminine and the queer, however, I think there is more to be gained by emphasizing structural similarities and pointing out differences where necessary than by treating gender and sexuality as completely separate questions.

5.   E. H. Gombrich, *The Sense of Order: A Study in the Psychology of Decorative Art* (Oxford: Phaidon, 1979), 18.

6.   Barbara Maria Stafford, "The Eighteenth Century at the End of Modernity," in *Good Looking: Essays on the Virtue of Images* (Cambridge, Mass.: MIT Press, 1996), 47.

7.   Martin Jay, *Downcast Eyes: The Denigration of Vision in Twentieth-Century French Thought* (Berkeley: University of California Press, 1994).

8.   Friedrich Von Schiller, *On the Aesthetic Education of Man*, trans. Elizabeth M. Williamson and L. A. Willoughby (Oxford: Clarendon Press, 1967), 201.

9.   Ibid., 201, 191–93.

10.   J. J. Winckelmann, *The History of Ancient Art*, trans. G. Henry Lodge (London: Sampson Low, Marston, Searle & Rivington, 1881), 1:304. Winckelmann does not specify the pretty face as female, although the contrasting beautiful face is a woman's. His own homosexuality offers an interesting complication to the development of a masculinist aesthetics based on the ideal male body of Greek sculpture: he creates a potential point of divergence between feminist critique of women's secondary aesthetic status and queer investment in the centrality of male–male desire to his influential aesthetic criticism. For further reading on the topic, see Whitney Davis, "Winckelmann's 'Homosexual' Teleology," in *Sexuality in Ancient Art*, ed. Natalie Boymel Kampen (Cambridge: Cambridge University Press, 1996), 262–76; and Alex Potts, *Flesh and the Ideal: Winckelmann and the Origins of Art History* (New Haven, Conn.: Yale University Press, 1994). Potts points out that although neoclassicism often lays claim to a manliness in contrast to effeminate baroque forms, "undeniably the most visibly striking aspect of [Winckelmann's] writing on Greek art [is] the unapologetically sensuous homoeroticism of his reading of the Greek male nude" (5).

11.   Winckelmann, *History of Ancient Art*, 311.

12.   J. J. Winckelmann, "Thoughts on the Imitation of the Painting and Sculpture of the Greeks," in *German Aesthetic and Literary Criticism: Winckelmann, Lessing, Hamann, Herder, Schiller, Goethe*, ed. and trans. H. B. Nisbet (Cambridge: Cambridge University Press, 1985), 34.

13. Winckelmann, *History of Ancient Art*, 308.

14. Winckelmann, "Thoughts on the Imitation of the Painting and Sculpture of the Greeks," 43.

15. Umberto Eco, *On Beauty: A History of a Western Idea*, trans. Alastair McEwan (London: Secker and Warburg, 2004), 250.

16. Ralph Wornum, *Analysis of Ornament: The Characteristics of Styles, an Introduction to the Study of the History of Ornamental Art* (London: Chapman and Hall, 1882), 186–87.

17. Quoted in Gombrich, *Sense of Order*, 23.

18. Kaja Silverman, "Fragments of a Fashionable Discourse," in *Studies in Entertainment: Critical Approaches to Mass Culture*, ed. Tania Modleski (Bloomington: Indiana University Press, 1986), 139–52.

19. Barbara Maria Stafford, *Artful Science: Enlightenment Entertainment and the Eclipse of Visual Education* (Cambridge, Mass.: MIT Press, 1994).

20. Stafford, "Eighteenth Century at the End of Modernity," 44.

21. Schiller, *On the Aesthetic Education of Man*, 185.

22. Gottfried Semper, *The Four Elements of Architecture and Other Writings*, trans. Harry Francis Mallgrave and Wolfgang Herrmann (Cambridge: Cambridge University Press, 1989), 54–55.

23. Ibid., 51.

24. Andrew Benjamin, *Style and Time: Essays on the Politics of Appearance* (Evanston, Ill.: Northwestern University Press, 2006), 39.

25. Clyde Taylor, *The Mask of Art: Breaking the Aesthetic Contract—Film and Literature* (Bloomington: Indiana University Press, 1998), 42.

26. Gottfried Semper, "Preliminary Remarks on Polychromatic Architecture," in *Four Elements of Architecture and Other Writings*, 45–73.

27. M. [Antoine-Chrysostome] Quatremère de Quincy, *Lettres écrites de Londres à Rome, et addressées à M. Canova, sur les marbres d'Elgin, ou les sculptures du temple de Minerve à Athènes* (Rome, 1818), and *De l'architecture egyptienne: Considérée dans son origine, ses principes et son goût, et comparée sous les mêmes rapports à l'architecture Grecque* (Paris: Barrois, 1803); David Van Zanten, *The Architectural Polychromy of the 1830s* (New York: Garland, 1977), 7–9, 28–30.

28. Quintilian, *Institutio Oratorio III*, trans. H. E. Butler, ed. T. E. Page, E. Capps, W. H. D. Rouse, L. A. Post, and E. H. Warmington (London: Heinemann, 1922), 8.3.6. Schor also analyzes this debate in *Reading in Detail*, 45.

29. Christine Buci-Glucksmann, *Baroque Reason: The Aesthetics of Modernity* (London: Sage, 1994). See also Christina Degli-Esposti, "Sally Potter's *Orlando* and the Neo-baroque Scopic Regime," *Cinema Journal* 36, no. 1 (1996): 75–93.

30. Peter Galassi, *Before Photography: Painting and the Invention of Photography* (New York: Museum of Modern Art, 1981), 20.

31. Denis Diderot, "Essays on Painting," in *Neoclassicism and Romanticism, 1750–1850*, vol. 1, *Sources and Documents*, ed. Lorenz Eitner (Upper Saddle River, N.J.: Prentice-Hall, 1970), 61.

32. Quoted in Laura Marcus, *The Tenth Muse: Writing About Cinema in the Modernist Period* (Oxford: Oxford University Press, 2007), 188.

33. André Bazin, "Cinema and Theology," in *Bazin at Work: Major Essays and Reviews from the Forties and Fifties*, trans. Alain Piette and Bert Cardullo, ed. Bert Cardullo (New York: Routledge, 1997), 65.

34. Laura Mulvey, "Visual Pleasure and Narrative Cinema," in *Narrative, Apparatus, Ideology: A Film Theory Reader*, ed. Philip Rosen (New York: Columbia University Press, 1986), 198–209.

35. Ibid., 203.

36. Ibid., 205.

37. Quoted in Teresa de Lauretis, "Through the Looking Glass: Woman, Cinema, and Language," in *Narrative, Apparatus, Ideology*, ed. Rosen, 365.

38. Janet Bergstrom, "Enunciation and Sexual Difference," in *Feminism and Film Theory*, ed. Constance Penley (New York: Routledge, 1988), 182; Elspeth Probyn, "This Body Which Is Not One: Speaking as Embodied Self," *Hypatia* 6, no. 3 (1991): 111–24.

39. bell hooks, "The Oppositional Gaze: Black Female Spectators," in *Reel to Real: Race, Sex, and Class at the Movies* (New York: Routledge, 1996), 197–213.

40. Luce Irigaray, *This Sex Which Is Not One*, trans. Catherine Porter (Ithaca, N.Y.: Cornell University Press, 1985), 26.

41. Laura U. Marks, *The Skin of the Film: Intercultural Cinema, Embodiment, and the Senses* (Durham, N.C.: Duke University Press, 2000).

42. Mary Ann Doane, *Femmes Fatales: Feminism, Film Theory, Psychoanalysis* (New York: Routledge, 1991), 45.

43. Elspeth Probyn, *Outside Belongings* (New York: Routledge, 1996). Elizabeth Grosz asks, "Can feminist theory eschew the notion of depth?" in "Refiguring Lesbian Desire," in *Space, Time, and Perversion: Essays on the Politics of Bodies* (New York: Routledge, 1995), 175.

44. Tania Modleski, "Femininity as Mas(s)querade: A Feminist Approach to Mass Culture," in *Feminism Without Women: Culture and Criticism in a "Postfeminist" Age* (New York: Routledge, 1991), 23–34; Andreas Huyssen, *After the Great Divide: Modernism, Mass Culture, and Postmodernism* (London: Macmillan, 1986); Ann Douglas, *The Feminization of American Culture* (New York: Avon, 1977).

45. Modleski, "Femininity as Mas(s)querade," 23–24.

46. Huyssen, *After the Great Divide*, 47.

47. Ibid., 55.

48. Rey Chow, "When Whiteness Feminizes . . . : Some Consequences of a Supplementary Logic," *differences* 11, no. 3 (1999–2000): 1–32. See also Nancy

Armstrong, "Modernism's Iconophobia and What It Did to Gender," *Modernism / Modernity* 5, no. 2 (1988): 47–75.

49. Joan Rivière, "Womanliness as Masquerade," in *Formations of Fantasy*, ed. Victor Burgin (London: Methuen, 1986), 35, 38.

50. Doane, *Femmes Fatales*, 17–32.

51. Ibid., 34.

52. Stephen Heath, "Joan Rivière and the Masquerade," in *Formations of Fantasy*, ed. Burgin, 50.

53. Doane, *Femmes Fatales*, 38.

54. Michèle Montrelay, "Inquiry into Femininity," *m/f* 1 (1978): 83–102. Montrelay writes that "man has always called the feminine defenses and masquerade evil" (93). Linking masquerade to Platonic cosmetics, she suggests pathways among the masquerade, the cinematic screen, and the pretty.

55. Doane, *Femmes Fatales*, 17–32; Heath, "Joan Rivière and the Masquerade," 57–58.

56. Williams, " 'Something Else Besides a Mother,' " 311.

57. Ibid., 317.

58. Ibid.

59. Christine Gledhill, "The Melodramatic Field: An Investigation," in *Home Is Where the Heart Is*, ed. Gledhill, 34.

60. Sue Harper, "Historical Pleasures: Gainsborough Costume Melodramas," in *Home Is Where the Heart Is*, ed. Gledhill, 167, 180.

61. Catherine Constable, *Thinking in Images: Film Theory, Feminist Philosophy, and Marlene Dietrich* (London: BFI, 2006), 2–3.

62. Ibid., 4, 143–47.

63. Barbara Creed, "Lesbian Bodies: Tribades, Tomboys, and Tarts," in *Sexy Bodies: The Strange Carnalities of Feminism*, ed. Elizabeth Grosz and Elspeth Probyn (New York: Routledge, 1995), 86–103.

64. Harry Benshoff, "The Monster and the Homosexual," in *Queer Cinema: The Film Reader*, ed. Harry Benshoff and Sean Griffin (New York: Routledge, 2004), 66.

65. Cindy Patton, "What's a Nice Girl Like You Doing in a Film Like This?" in *Immortal Invisible: Lesbians and the Moving Image*, ed. Tamsin Wilton (New York: Routledge, 1995), 23.

66. An intriguing counterexample here is Michael De Angelis's reading of Keanu Reeves's star persona in *Gay Fandom and Crossover Stardom: James Dean, Mel Gibson, and Keanu Reeves* (Durham, N.C.: Duke University Press, 2001). Reeves is often mocked as the perfect instance of blank surface appeal, prettiness without talent or depth, but in De Angelis's account Reeves's affectless surface actually bespeaks an identificatory complexity. He can be read as white or nonwhite, straight or gay, masculine or feminine: his features and performance style are not so much blank as hard to pin down within dominant

protocols. His prettiness opens out rather than enforcing definitions of race, gender, and sexuality.

67. Thomas Waugh, *The Fruit Machine: Twenty Years of Writings on Queer Cinema* (Durham, N.C.: Duke University Press, 2000).

68. Ibid., 70.

69. Ibid., 69.

70. Ibid., 153.

71. Ibid., 151.

72. Andrea Weiss, "Transgressive Cinema: Lesbian Independent Film," in *Queer Cinema*, ed. Benshoff and Griffin, 51.

73. Mandy Merck, *Perversions: Deviant Readings* (New York: Routledge, 1993), 175.

74. Probyn, *Outside Belongings*, 19.

75. Fabio Cleto, ed., *Camp: Queer Aesthetics and the Performing Subject: A Reader* (Edinburgh: Edinburgh University Press, 1999).

76. Judith Butler, *Bodies That Matter: On the Discursive Limits of "Sex"* (New York: Routledge, 1993), 233–34. See also Judith Butler, *Undoing Gender* (New York: Routledge, 2004).

77. Butler, *Bodies That Matter*, 125.

78. Elisa Glick, "Sex Positive: Feminism, Queer Theory, and the Politics of Transgression," *Feminist Review* 64 (2000): 28, 29.

79. Sara Ahmed, *Queer Phenomenology: Orientations, Objects, Others* (Durham, N.C.: Duke University Press, 2007), 14, 117.

80. Ibid., 16.

81. Barbara Maria Stafford, "Introduction: Visual Pragmatism for a Virtual World," 4; "Eighteenth Century at the End of Modernity," 45; and "The New Imagist," 69, all in *Good Looking*.

82. W. J. T. Mitchell, *What Do Pictures Want? The Lives and Loves of Images* (Chicago: University of Chicago Press, 2005); Christopher Pinney, "Piercing the Skin of the Idol," in *Beyond Aesthetics: Art and the Technologies of Enchantment*, ed. Christopher Pinney and Nicholas Thomas (Oxford: Berg, 2001), 157–80.

83. For example, Gordon Graham, *The Re-enchantment of the World: Art Versus Religion* (Oxford: Oxford University Press, 2007). In a more populist vein, see Thomas Moore, *The Re-enchantment of Everyday Life* (London: HarperCollins, 1996), which sees reenchantment as respritualization, in opposition to a negative secularism.

84. Jane Bennett, *The Enchantment of Modern Life: Attachments, Crossings, and Ethics* (Princeton, N.J.: Princeton University Press, 2001).

85. Wendy Steiner, *Venus in Exile: The Rejection of Beauty in Twentieth-Century Art* (New York: Free Press, 2001), 56.

86. Ibid., xviii.

87. Ibid., 75.

88. Ibid., 86–89, 220.

89. Ibid., xx.

90. Charles Blanc, *The Grammar of Painting and Engraving*, trans. Kate Newell Doggett (Chicago: Griggs, 1891), 168 (my italics).

91. Adolf Loos, "Ladies' Fashion," in *Ornament and Crime: Selected Essays*, trans. Michael Mitchell (Riverside, Calif.: Ariadne Press, 1998), 106–7.

92. See, for example, Teresa de Lauretis, *The Practice of Love: Lesbian Sexuality and Perverse Desire* (Bloomington: Indiana University Press, 1994), which seeks to produce "a formal model of perverse desire" (xiii).

93. B. Ruby Rich, "When Difference Is More Than Skin Deep," in *Queer Looks: Perspectives on Lesbian and Gay Film and Video*, ed. Martha Gever, Pratibha Parmar, and John Greyson (New York: Routledge, 1993), 326.

94. Tanya Krzywinska, *Sex and the Cinema* (London: Wallflower, 2006), 212. The inverse of this approach is demonstrated in the critics who lauded Michael Haneke's *La pianiste / The Piano Teacher* (2001) for its negative representation of BDSM. D. I. Grossvogel finds the protagonist's desire to be desperate and grim ("Haneke: The Coercing of Vision," *Film Quarterly* 60, no. 4 [2007]: 41), whereas Robin Wood praises Haneke for his correlation between masochistic desire and alienated consumer culture under George W. Bush ("'Do I Disgust You?': Or, Tirez pas sur *La pianiste*," *Cineaction* 59 [2002]: 57). For these critics, Haneke's austerity and masculine seriousness stand in direct opposition to the antipolitical work of the perverse image.

95. Andrea Reimann, "Subjection and Power in Monika Treut and Elfi Mikesch's *Seduction—The Cruel Woman*: An Extension of the Configuration of Power in Rainer Werner Fassbinder's Late Oeuvre," in *Queer Cinema in Europe*, ed. Robin Griffiths (Bristol: Intellect, 2008), 182.

96. Barbara Mennel, "Wanda's Whip: Recasting Masochism's Fantasy—Monika Treut's *Seduction: The Cruel Woman*," in *Triangulated Visions: Women in Recent German Cinema*, ed. Ingeborg Majer O'Sickey and Ingeborg von Zadow (Albany: State University of New York Press, 1998), 154, 156.

97. Amber Musser, "Masochism: A Queer Subjectivity," *Rhizomes* 11–12 (2005–2006), available at http://www.rhizomes.net/issue11/musser.html (accessed February 16, 2008).

98. Quoted in Julia Knight, *Women and the New German Cinema* (London: Verso, 1992), 168.

99. Leo Bersani and Ulysse Dutoit, "Merde alors," *October* 13 (1980): 26.

100. Ibid. It is obviously relevant that Pasolini's film represents nonconsensual torture and murder, whereas Treut narrates theatrical but desiring sex acts. However, I do not want to get too caught up in the representational politics of these films because they are not what is at stake in the critical debates on which I focus.

101. Sigmund Freud, "Femininity," in *New Introductory Lectures on Psychoanalysis and Other Works*, trans. James Strachey (New York: Norton, 1989), 139.

102. Judith Halberstam, *Female Masculinities* (Durham, N.C.: Duke University Press, 1998), 35.

103. Katrien Jacobs, "The Lady of Little Death," *Wide Angle* 19, no. 3 (1997): 13.

104. Ibid., 15.

105. See also *Mano destra* (Übelmann, 1986) as an example of an experimental film narrated from the point of view of the submissive and focusing on sound, touch, and temporality rather than on visual mastery. These examples are relatively rare because, as Jacobs points out, "although the institution of S/M has become more available to women in straight and lesbian relationships, the female submissive persona has scarcely been analysed and touched upon by critics and theorists of pornography" (ibid., 20). This lack demonstrates the simplicity of common ideas that dominant women are a reversal of patriarchal relations and should be regarded as "good" by feminists, whereas submissive women merely reiterate patriarchy and are "bad." Where such an account leaves lesbian BDSM partners is only one of the problems inherent in this overly allegorical understanding. Although Jacobs reads Beatty against feminism (and in particular the feminist performance scene that rejected her), I would locate her within a queer and sex-positive feminism.

106. Maria Beatty, Catherine Corringer, Shu Lea Cheang, and Emilie Jouvet, "Femmes, artistes et pornographes" (interview), *Second Sexe*, April 20, 2009, available at http://www.secondsexe.com/magazine/Femmes-artistes-et-pornographes.html (my translation).

107. Tony Rayns, *"Arabian Nights," Monthly Film Bulletin* 42, no. 495 (1975): 79.

8. Bodies

1. Andrea Weiss, *Vampires and Violets: Lesbians in Film* (London: Penguin, 1993), 131; Laurence Rickels, *Ulrike Ottinger: The Autobiography of Art Cinema* (Minneapolis: University of Minnesota Press, 2008), 1–15.

2. This lack is partly Ottinger's own choice: claiming that her films must be seen in a theatrical environment, she has elected not to release them on DVD except in some limited runs for institutional collections. The politics of this kind of created rarity is complex. See, for instance, Brian Price, "Cosmopolitanism and Cinema Today," in *Global Art Cinema: New Histories and Theories*, ed. Rosalind Galt and Karl Schoonover (New York: Oxford University Press, 2010), 109–24.

3. Rickels, *Ulrike Ottinger*, 1–15; Patricia White, "Madame X of the China Seas," *Screen* 28, no. 4 (1987): 81; Brenda Longfellow, "Lesbian Phantasy and the Other Woman in Ottinger's *Johanna d'Arc of Mongolia*," *Screen* 34, no. 2 (1993): 125.

4. Janet A. Kaplan and Ulrike Ottinger, *"Johanna d'Arc of Mongolia*: Interview with Ulrike Ottinger," *Art Journal* 61, no. 3 (2002): 7; Roswitha Mueller, "The Mirror and the Vamp," *New German Critique* 34 (1985): 176.

5. Mueller, "Mirror and the Vamp," 191.

6. Ibid., 192; Fredric Jameson, *Postmodernism, or, The Cultural Logic of Late Capitalism* (Durham, N.C.: Duke University Press, 1991), 17.

7. Pamela Robertson, *Guilty Pleasures: Feminist Camp from Mae West to Madonna* (Durham, N.C.: Duke University Press, 1996), 149–52.

8. Kaja Silverman, *The Threshold of the Visible World* (New York: Routledge, 1996), 39–82.

9. Amy Villarejo, "Archiving the Diaspora: A Lesbian Impression of / in Ulrike Ottinger's *Exile Shanghai*," *New German Critique* 87 (2002): 159.

10. Miriam Hansen, "Visual Pleasure, Fetishism, and the Problem of Feminine / Feminist Discourse: Ulrike Ottinger's *Ticket of No Return*," *New German Critique* 31 (1984): 99.

11. Ibid., 98. See also Sabine Hake, who cites Cillie Rentmeister among German critics who regarded *Madame X* as antifeminist because sadomasochistic in "And with Favourable Winds They Sailed Away," in *Gender and German Cinema*, vol. 1, *Feminist Interventions*, ed. Sandra Frieden, Richard W. McCormick, Vibeke R. Peterson, and Laura Melissa Vogelsang (Providence, R.I.: Berg, 1993), 182n.6; and Cillie Rentmeister, "Frauen, Körper, Kunst: Mikrophysik der patriarchalischen Macht," *Ästhetik und Kommunikation* 37 (1979): 61–68.

12. Quoted in White, "Madame X of the China Seas," 86.

13. Helen Fehervary, Claudia Lenssen, and Judith Mayne, "From Hitler to Hepburn: A Discussion of Women's Film Production and Reception," *New German Critique* 24–25 (1981–1982): 184.

14. White, "Madame X of the China Seas," 81; Villarejo, "Archiving the Diaspora," 159.

15. Longfellow, "Lesbian Phantasy," 134.

16. Rickels, *Ulrike Ottinger*, 2.

17. Ibid., 29.

18. Katie Trumpener, "*Johanna d'Arc of Mongolia* in the Mirror of *Dorian Gray*: Ethnographic Recordings and the Aesthetics of the Market in the Recent Films of Ulrike Ottinger," *New German Critique* 60 (1993): 80, 91.

19. Ibid., 94–95.

20. Ibid., 96.

21. Lutz Koepnick, "Consuming the Other: Identity, Alterity, and Contemporary German Cinema," *Camera Obscura* 44, no. 15/2 (2000): 67.

22. Randall Halle, "Telling Tales They Want to Hear," in *Global Art Cinema*, ed. Galt and Schoonover, 303–19. Halle argues that many supposedly "authentic" national films only appear to come from non-European countries and in fact are funded from within Europe and constructed to present the image of "the East" or North Africa that liberal European audiences imagine to be expressions of political and cultural subjectivities.

23. Jorge Sanjinés, *Teoría y práctica de un cine junto al pueblo* (Mexico City: Editorial Siglo XXI, 1971), 156.

24. Kristen Whissel, "Racialized Spectacle, Exchange Relations, and the Western in *Johanna d'Arc of Mongolia*," *Screen* 37, no. 1 (1996): 42.

25. Ibid., 67.

26. Villarejo, "Archiving the Diaspora," 157–58.

27. Ibid., 160.

28. Hake, "And with Favourable Winds They Sailed Away," 184. Hake's analysis also hints at a tendency to see the Oriental as a mere stand-in for gender, unmasking patriarchy by proxy by means of Oriental images. It is important not to nest these modes of critique, but rather to see them as materially connected.

29. Ibid., 183.

30. White, "Madam X of the China Seas," 283; Hansen, "Visual Pleasure," 107.

31. Quoted in Annette Kuhn, "Encounter Between Two Cultures: A Discussion with Ulrike Ottinger," *Screen*, 28, no. 4 (1987): 75.

32. Longfellow, "Lesbian Phantasy," 125.

33. Whissel, "Racialized Spectacle"; Rickels, *Ulrike Ottinger*, 127.

34. Homay King, "Sign in the Void: Ulrike Ottinger's *Johanna d'Arc of Mongolia*," *Afterall* 16 (2007): 52.

35. Siegfried Kracauer, *Theory of Film: The Redemption of Physical Reality* (Princeton, N.J.: Princeton University Press, 1997), 81.

36. Rosalind Galt, *The New European Cinema: Redrawing the Map* (New York: Columbia University Press, 2006), 62–74.

POSTSCRIPT

1. Sergei Eisenstein, "On Color," in *Eisenstein*, vol. 2, *Towards a Theory of Montage*, trans. Michael Glenny, ed. Michael Glenny and Richard Taylor (London: BFI, 1994), 111.

2. Alois Riegl, *Problems of Style: Foundations for a History of Ornament*, trans. Evelyn Kain (Princeton, N.J.: Princeton University Press, 1992), 2–18.

3. E. Ann Kaplan, *Looking for the Other: Feminism, Film, and the Imperial Gaze* (New York: Routledge, 1997), 154–92.

4. Rosalind Galt, "The Obviousness of Cinema," *World Picture* 2 (2009), available at http://english.okstate.edu/worldpicture/WP_2/Galt.html.

5. Jean-Luc Nancy, *The Ground of the Image*, trans. Jeff Fort (New York: Fordham University Press, 2005), 12.

6. Ibid., 3, 6.

7. Quoted in Walter Benjamin, *The Arcades Project*, trans. Howard Eiland and Kevin McLaughlin (Cambridge, Mass.: Harvard University Press, 1999), 549.

FILMOGRAPHY

Alphabetized by English-language title, followed by original-language title, unless the original-language title was used for release in the United States, there is no English-language title, or the film is best known in its original language.

Adrift / *Hrst plná vody* (Kadár, 1969)
Aladdin (Clements and Musker, 1992)
Alexander Nevsky (Eisenstein, 1938)
Alien: Resurrection (Jeunet, 1997)
All That Heaven Allows (Sirk, 1955)
Amelie / *Le fabuleux destin d'Amélie Poulain* (Jeunet, 2001)
Angel (Ozon, 2007)
Arabesque (Whitney, 1975)
Arabesque for Kenneth Anger (Menken, 1961)
Arabia (Jarman, 1974)
Arabian Nights / *Il fiore delle mille e una notte* (Pasolini, 1974)
L'arroseur arrosé / *The Tables Turned on the Gardener* (Lumière, 1895)
The Art of Mirrors (Jarman, 1973)
Ashden's Walk on Møn (Jarman, 1973)
Australia (Luhrmann, 2008)
Away with Words / *San tiao ren* (Doyle, 1999)

⟵⟶ / *Back and Forth* (Snow, 1969)

Bamako (Sissako, 2006)

Battleship Potemkin / *Bronenosets Potyomkin* (Eisenstein, 1925)

Beau Travail (Denis, 1999)

The Beehive / *La colmena* (Camus, 1982)

The Bitter Tears of Petra von Kant / *Die bitteren Träner der Petra von Kant* (Fassbinder, 1972)

Black God, White Devil / *Deus e o diablo na Terra do Sol* (Rocha, 1964)

Black Narcissus (Powell and Pressburger, 1947)

Blood of the Beasts / *Les sang des bêtes* (Franju, 1949)

Blue (Jarman, 1993)

Borderline (Macpherson, 1930)

Broken Blossoms (Griffith, 1919)

Cabezas cortadas (Rocha, 1970)

Camila (Bemberg, 1984)

The Cheat (DeMille, 1915)

China, the Arts, Everyday Life (Ottinger, 1986)

China Gate (Santoshi, 1998)

Chocolat (Denis, 1988)

Chronically Unfeasible / *Cronicamente inviável* (Bianchi, 2000)

City of God / *Cidade de Deus* (Meirelles and Lund, 2002)

The Class / *Entre les murs* (Cantet, 2008)

Cleopatra (DeMille, 1934)

The Conformist / *Il conformista* (Bertolucci, 1971)

The Cranes Are Flying / *Letyat zhuravli* (Kalatozov, 1957)

Crónica cubana (Ulive, 1963)

Cyclo / *Xích lô* (Tran, 1995)

Damned If You Don't (Friedrich, 1987)

Dante Is Not Only Severe / *Dante no es únicamente severo* (Jordá, 1967)

Death Dance (Jarman, 1973)

Delicatessen (Jeunet, 1991)

Diary of a Country Priest / *Journal d'un curé de campagne* (Bresson, 1951)

Dil se / *From the Heart* (Ratnam, 1998)

La dixième symphonie / *The Tenth Symphony* (Gance, 1918)

Dogville (von Trier, 2003)

La dolce vita (Fellini, 1960)

Ecstasy in Berlin 1926 (Beatty, 2004)

Empire of the Senses / *Ai no corrida* (Oshima, 1976)

Far from Heaven (Haynes, 2002)

Fear Eats the Soul / *Angst Essen Seele auf* (Fassbinder, 1974)

Fellini–Satyricon (Fellini, 1969)

French Cancan (Renoir, 1954)

Les Girls (Cukor, 1957)

Harakiri (Kobayashi, 1962)

Hate / La haine (Kassovitz, 1995)

Hero / Ying xiong (Zhang, 2002)

High School Musical (Ortega, 2006, 2007, and 2008)

I Am Cuba / Soy Cuba (Kalatozov, 1964)

The Image of Dorian Gray in the Yellow Press / Dorian Gray im Spiegel der Boulevard-presse (Ottinger, 1984)

Imagining October (Jarman, 1984)

Inextinguishable Fire / Nicht iöschbares Feuer (Farocki, 1969)

In the Mood for Love / Fa yeung nin wa (Wong, 2000)

The Intruder / L'intrus (Denis, 2004)

It Happened by Chance (Jarman, 1977)

Ivan the Terrible / Ivan Groznyy (Eisenstein, 1944)

Ivan the Terrible, Part II / Ivan Groznyy II (Eisenstein, 1958)

Johanna d'Arc of Mongolia (Ottinger, 1989)

Journey to Avebury (Jarman, 1972)

Joyless Street / Die freudlose Gasse (Pabst, 1925)

Ju Dou (Zhang, 1990)

Jules et Jim / Jules and Jim (Truffaut, 1962)

Knife in the Water / Nóz w wodzie (Polanski, 1962)

Land in Trance / Terra em transe (Rocha, 1967)

The Last of England (Jarman, 1988)

Leave Her to Heaven (Stahl, 1945)

Leche (Uman, 1998)

Lianna (Sayles, 1983)

The Little Foxes (Wyler, 1941)

Lola Montès (Ophüls, 1955)

Madame Satã (Aïnouz, 2002)

Madame X: An Absolute Ruler / Madame X—Eine absolute Herrscherin (Ottinger, 1978)

Mädchen in Uniform (Sagan, 1931)

Mala leche (Uman, 1998)

Mano destra (Übelmann, 1986)

Marie Antoinette (Coppola, 2006)

Moulin Rouge! (Luhrmann, 2001)

1900 / Novecento (Bertolucci, 1976)

Nostalghia (Tarkovsky, 1983)

Now, Voyager (Rapper, 1942)

Paris Is Burning (Livingston, 1990)

The Passion of Joan of Arc / La passion de Jeanne d'Arc (Dreyer, 1928)

Peeping Tom (Powell, 1960)

The Piano Teacher / La pianiste (Haneke, 2001)

Pinocchio (Disney, 1940)

Preludio 11 (Maetzig, 1964)

Princesse Tam Tam (Gréville, 1934)

Psycho (Hitchcock, 1960)

Purple Noon / Plein soleil (Clément, 1960)

Red Desert / Il deserto rosso (Antonioni, 1964)

Red Psalm / Még kér a nép (Jancsó, 1972)

The Red Shoes (Powell and Pressburger, 1948)

The Red Tent / Krasnaya palatka (Kalatozov, 1971)

The Rise of Louis XIV / La prise de pouvoir par Louis XIV (Rossellini, 1966)

Rome, Open City / Roma, città aperta (Rossellini, 1945)

Romeo + Juliet (Luhrmann, 1996)

Salo / Salò o le 120 giornate di Sodoma (Pasolini, 1975)

Salomé (Bryant, 1923)

Salt for Svanetia / Sol Svanetij (Kalatozov, 1930)

The Scent of Green Papaya / Mùi du du xanh (Tran, 1993)

Sebastiane (Jarman, 1976)

Seduction: The Cruel Woman / Verführung: Die grausame Frau (Treut, 1985)

Shadows of Our Forgotten Ancestors / Tini zabutykh predkiv (Paradjanov, 1964)

She Must Be Seeing Things (McLaughlin, 1987)

The Siberian Mammoth (Ferraz, 2005)

Siren of the Tropics / La sirène des tropiques (Étiévant and Nalpas, 1927)

Speed / Lotna (Wajda, 1959)

The Spider's Stratagem / Strategia del ragno (Bertolucci, 1970)

Stella Dallas (Vidor, 1937)

Strictly Ballroom (Luhrmann, 1992)

Strike / Stachka (Eisenstein, 1925)

Sugar Cane Alley / Rue cases nègres (Palcy, 1983)

Sunrise (Murnau, 1927)

Sweeney Todd: The Demon Barber of Fleet Street (Burton, 2007)

Syndromes and a Century / Sang sattawat (Apichatpong, 2006)

Tahaan: A Boy with a Grenade / Tahaan (Sivan, 2008)

Tarot (Jarman, 1972–1973)

The Terrorist / Theeviravaathi (Sivan, 1998)

The Thief of Baghdad (Powell, 1940)

35 Rhums / 35 Shots of Rum (Denis, 2008)

Thriller (Potter, 1979)

Ticket of No Return / Bildnis einer Trinkerin (Ottinger, 1979)

Torrent (Ibáñez, 1926)

Tout va bien (Godard, 1972)

Tropical Malady / Sud pralad (Apichatpong, 2004)

Unknown Pleasures / Ren xiao yao (Jia, 2002)

Valčík pro milión / Vals para un millón (Mach, 1960)

Vent d'Est (Godard / Gorin / Dziga Vertov Group, 1970)

A Very Long Engagement / Un long dimanche de fiançailles (Jeunet, 2004)

La viaccia / The Lovemakers (Bolognini, 1961)

The Virgin Spring / Jungfrukällan (Bergman, 1960)

The Wayward Cloud / Tian bian yi duo dun (Tsai, 2005)

Weekend (Godard, 1967)

The Wicked Lady (Arliss, 1945)

Wittgenstein (Jarman, 1993)

The World / Shijie (Jia, 2004)

Zabriskie Point (Antonioni, 1970)

A Zed and Two Noughts (Greenaway, 1985)

Abbas, Ackbar. "On Fascination: Walter Benjamin's Images." *New German Critique* 48 (1989): 43–62.

Abel, Richard, ed. *French Film Theory and Criticism: A History / Anthology.* Vol. 1, *1907–1939.* Princeton, N.J.: Princeton University Press, 1988.

Adams, Henry. *Mont-Saint-Michel and Chartres.* New York: Anchor Books, 1959.

Adorno, Theodor W. *Aesthetic Theory.* Translated by Robert Hullot-Kentor. Minneapolis: University of Minnesota Press, 1997.

——. "Functionalism Today." In *Rethinking Architecture: A Reader in Cultural Theory,* edited by Neil Leach, 5–19. London: Routledge, 1997.

——. *Negative Dialectics.* Translated by E. B. Ashton. New York: Seabury, 1973.

Adorno, Theodor W., Walter Benjamin, Ernst Bloch, Bertolt Brecht, and Georg Lukács. *Aesthetics and Politics.* Translated by Anya Bostock, Stuart Hood, Rodney Livingstone, Francis McDonagh, and Harry Zohn. New York: Verso, 1980.

Ahmed, Sara. *Queer Phenomenology: Orientations, Objects, Others.* Durham, N.C.: Duke University Press, 2007.

Alderton, David, and Linda Anderson, eds. *Territories of Desire in Queer Culture: Refiguring the Contemporary Boundaries.* Manchester: Manchester University Press, 2000.

Alloula, Malek. *The Colonial Harem.* Translated by Myrna Godzich and Wlad Godzich. Minneapolis: University of Minnesota Press, 1986.

Andrew, Dudley. "*Amelie,* or the fabuleux destin du cinéma français." *Film Quarterly* 57, no. 3 (2004): 34–46.

——, ed. *The Image in Dispute: Art and Cinema in the Age of Photography.* Austin: University of Texas Press, 1997.

——. "Jules, Jim, and Walter Benjamin." In *The Image in Dispute: Art and Cinema in the Age of Photography,* edited by Dudley Andrew, 33–54. Austin: University of Texas Press, 1997.

——. "A Preface to Disputation." In *The Image in Dispute: Art and Cinema in the Age of Photography,* edited by Dudley Andrew, vii–xiv. Austin: University of Texas Press, 1997.

——. "The Post-war Struggle for Color." In *Color: The Film Reader,* edited by Angela Dalle Vacche and Brian Price, 40–49. New York: Routledge, 2006.

Andrews, Nigel. "*Adrift / Hrst plná vody.*" *Monthly Film Bulletin* 39, no. 460 (1972): 96.

——. "*Roma.*" *Monthly Film Bulletin* 39, no. 467 (1972): 258.

Anger, Jenny. *Paul Klee and the Decorative in Modern Art.* Cambridge: Cambridge University Press, 2004.

Aragon, Louis. "On Décor." In *French Film Theory and Criticism: A History / Anthology,* vol. 1, *1907–1939,* edited by Richard Abel, 165–68. Princeton, N.J.: Princeton University Press, 1988.

Armes, Roy. *A Critical History of the British Cinema.* London: Secker and Warburg, 1978.

Armstrong, Nancy. "Modernism's Iconophobia and What It Did to Gender." *Modernism / Modernity* 5, no. 2 (1988): 47–75.

Arnheim, Rudolf. *Film as Art.* Berkeley: University of California Press, 1957.

——. *Film Essays and Criticism.* Translated by Brenda Benthein. Madison: University of Wisconsin Press, 1997.

Arroyo, José. "*Moulin Rouge!*" *Sight & Sound* 11, no. 9 (2001): 50–51.

"The Art Seminar." In *Art History Versus Aesthetics,* edited by James Elkins, 51–90. New York: Routledge, 2006.

Aumont, Jacques. "The Face in Close-Up." In *The Visual Turn: Classical Film Theory and Art History,* edited by Angela Dalle Vacche, 127–48. New Brunswick, N.J.: Rutgers University Press, 2003.

——. "The Variable Eye, or the Mobilization of the Gaze." In *The Image in Dispute: Art and Cinema in the Age of Photography,* edited by Dudley Andrew, 231–58. Austin: University of Texas Press, 1997.

Backstein, Karen. "*City of God.*" *Cineaste* 28, no. 3 (2003): 39–40.

Baer, Eva. *Islamic Ornament.* Edinburgh: Edinburgh University Press, 1998.

Baker, Josephine, and Jo Bouillon. *Josephine.* Translated by Mariana Fitzpatrick. New York: Harper & Row, 1977.

Balázs, Béla. *Theory of the Film.* Translated by Edith Bone. London: Dobson, 1952.

Barr, Charles, ed. *All Our Yesterdays: 90 Years of British Cinema*. London: British Film Institute, 1986.

Barry, Iris. *Let's Go to the Movies*. London: Chatto and Windus, 1926.

Barthes, Roland. *Camera Lucida: Reflections on Photography*. Translated by Richard Howard. New York: Hill & Wang, 1982.

——. *Mythologies*. Translated by Annette Lavers. New York: Hill & Wang, 1972.

Batchelor, David. *Chromophobia*. London: Reaktion Books, 2000.

Bazin, André. *Bazin at Work: Major Essays and Reviews from the Forties and Fifties*. Translated by Alain Piette and Bert Cardullo. Edited by Bert Cardullo. New York: Routledge, 1997.

——. *What Is Cinema?* Vol. 1. Translated by Hugh Gray. Berkeley: University of California Press, 1967.

——. *What Is Cinema?* Vol. 2. Translated by Hugh Gray. Berkeley: University of California Press, 1971.

Beatty, Maria, Catherine Corringer, Shu Lea Cheang, and Emilie Jouvet. "Femmes, artistes et pornographes" (interview). *Second Sexe*, April 20, 2009. Available at http://www.secondsexe.com/magazine/Femmes-artistes-et-pornographes. html.

Beevers, David, ed. *Chinese Whispers: Chinoiserie in Britain, 1650–1930*. Brighton: Royal Pavilion and Museums, 2008.

——. " 'Mand'rin Only Is the Man of Taste': 17th and 18th Century Chinoiserie in Britain." In *Chinese Whispers: Chinoiserie in Britain, 1650–1930*, edited by David Beevers, 13–25. Brighton: Royal Pavilion and Museums, 2008.

Beltrán, Alejo. "*Soy Cuba*." *Hoy*, August 8, 1964.

Benjamin, Andrew. *Style and Time: Essays on the Politics of Appearance*. Evanston, Ill.: Northwestern University Press, 2006.

Benjamin, Walter. *The Arcades Project*. Translated by Howard Eiland and Kevin McLaughlin. Cambridge, Mass.: Harvard University Press, 1999.

——. *Selected Writings*. Vol. 2, *1927–1934*. Translated by Rodney Livingstone and others. Edited by Michael W. Jennings, Howard Eiland, and Gary Smith. Cambridge, Mass.: Harvard University Press, 1999.

——. *Selected Writings*. Vol. 4, *1938–1939*. Translated by Edmund Jephcott and others. Edited by Howard Eiland and Michael W. Jennings. Cambridge, Mass.: Harvard University Press, 2003.

Bennett, Jane. *The Enchantment of Modern Life: Attachments, Crossings, and Ethics*. Princeton, N.J.: Princeton University Press, 2001.

Benshoff, Harry. "The Monster and the Homosexual." In *Queer Cinema: The Film Reader*, edited by Harry Benshoff and Sean Griffin, 63–74. New York: Routledge, 2004.

Benshoff, Harry, and Sean Griffin, eds. *Queer Cinema: The Film Reader*. New York: Routledge, 2004.

Bentes, Ivana. "The Aesthetics of Violence in Brazilian Film." In *City of God in Several Voices: Brazilian Social Cinema as Action*, edited by Else R. P. Viera, 82–92. Nottingham: Critical, Cultural, and Communications Press, 2005.

Bergstrom, Janet. "Enunciation and Sexual Difference." In *Feminism and Film Theory*, edited by Constance Penley, 159–85. New York: Routledge, 1988.

Bernstein, Matthew, and Gaylyn Studlar, eds. *Visions of the East: Orientalism in Film*. London: Taurus, 2007.

Bersani, Leo, and Ulysse Dutoit. "Merde alors." *October* 13 (1980): 22–35.

Betz, Mark. "The Name Above the (Sub)Title: Internationalism, Coproduction, and Polyglot European Art Cinema." *Camera Obscura* 46, no. 16/1 (2001): 1–44.

Beyeler, Ernst. "Preface." In *Ornament and Abstraction: The Dialogue Between Non-Western, Modern, and Contemporary Art*, edited by Markus Brüderlin, 14–15. Basel: Fondation Beyeler, 2001.

Birnbaum, Pierre, and Jean Leca, eds. *Individualism: Theories and Methods*. Oxford: Oxford University Press, 1990.

Blaetz, Robin, ed. *Women's Experimental Cinema: Critical Frameworks*. Durham, N.C.: Duke University Press, 2007.

Blanc, Charles. *Grammaire des arts décoratifs*. Paris: Librarie Renouard, 1882.

——. *Grammaire des arts du dessin*. Paris: Librarie Renouard, 1862.

——. *The Grammar of Painting and Engraving*. Translated by Kate Newell Doggett. Chicago: Griggs, 1891.

Blasis, Carlo. *The Code of Terpsichore*. New York: Dance Horizons, 1976.

Bloch, Ernst. "Formative Education, Engineering Form, Ornament." In *Rethinking Architecture: A Reader in Cultural Theory*, edited by Neil Leach, 43–50. London: Routledge, 1997.

——. *The Spirit of Utopia*. Translated by Anthony A. Nassar. Stanford, Calif.: Stanford University Press, 2000.

Boone, Joseph. "Vacation Cruises; or, the Homoerotics of Orientalism." In *Postcolonial, Queer: Theoretical Intersections*, edited by John C. Hawley, 43–78. Albany: State University of New York Press, 2001.

Bourgoin, Jules. *Théorie de l'ornement*. Paris: Duchet, 1883.

Boymel Kampen, Natalie, ed. *Sexuality in Ancient Art*. Cambridge: Cambridge University Press, 1996.

Bracquemond, Félix. *Du dessin et de la couleur*. Paris: Charpentier, 1885.

Braudy, Leo, and Marshall Cohen, eds. *Film Theory and Criticism: Introductory Readings*. 5th ed. New York: Oxford University Press, 1999.

Brolin, Brent. *Architectural Ornament: Banishment and Return*. New York: Norton, 2000.

Brown, Bill. *A Sense of Things: The Object Matter of American Literature*. Chicago: University of Chicago Press, 2003.

Brüderlin, Markus. "Introduction: Ornament and Abstraction." In *Ornament and Abstraction: The Dialogue Between Non-Western, Modern, and Contemporary Art*, edited by Markus Brüderlin, 17–27. Basel: Fondation Beyeler, 2001.

——, ed. *Ornament and Abstraction: The Dialogue Between Non-Western, Modern, and Contemporary Art*. Basel: Fondation Beyeler, 2001.

Bruzzi, Stella. *Undressing Cinema: Clothing and Identity in the Movies*. New York: Routledge, 1997.

Buci-Glucksmann, Christine. *Baroque Reason: The Aesthetics of Modernity*. London: Sage, 1994.

Buck-Morss, Susan. "Aesthetics and Anaesethetics: Walter Benjamin's Artwork Essay Reconsidered." *October* 62 (1992): 3–41.

Burgin, Victor, ed. *Formations of Fantasy*. London: Methuen, 1986.

Butler, Judith. *Bodies That Matter: On the Discursive Limits of "Sex."* New York: Routledge, 1993.

——. *Undoing Gender*. New York: Routledge, 2004.

Cadava, Eduardo. "Words of Light: Theses on the Photography of History." *Diacritics* 22, nos. 3–4 (1992): 84–114.

Canudo, Ricciotto. "The Birth of a Sixth Art." In *French Film Theory and Criticism: A History/Anthology*, vol. 1, *1907–1939*, edited by Richard Abel, 58–66. Princeton, N.J.: Princeton University Press, 1988.

——. "Les orientales." In *L'usine aux images*, 246–48. Paris: Séguier, 1995.

Cavell, Stanley. *Contesting Tears: The Hollywood Melodrama of the Unknown Woman*. Chicago: University of Chicago Press, 1996.

Chambers, Iain. "History, the Baroque, and the Judgement of the Angels." In *The Actuality of Walter Benjamin*, edited by Laura Marcus and Lynda Nead, 172–93. London: Lawrence & Wishart, 1998.

Chanan, Michael. *Cuban Cinema*. Minneapolis: University of Minnesota Press, 2004.

——, ed. *Twenty-five Years of the New Latin American Cinema*. London: BFI, 1983.

Cheang, Sarah. "What's In a Chinese Room? 20th Century Chinoiserie, Modernity, and Femininity." In *Chinese Whispers: Chinoiserie in Britain, 1650–1930*, edited by David Beevers, 75–81. Brighton: Royal Pavilion and Museums, 2008.

Chevalier, Jacques, and Max Egly, eds. *Regards neufs sur le cinéma*. Paris: Editions du Seuil, 1965.

Chion, Michel. "Quiet Revolution . . . and Rigid Stagnation." *October* 58 (1991): 69–80.

Chow, Rey. *Primitive Passions: Visuality, Sexuality, Ethnography, and Contemporary Chinese Cinema*. New York: Columbia University Press, 1995.

——. "When Whiteness Feminizes . . . : Some Consequences of a Supplementary Logic." *differences* 11, no. 3 (1999–2000): 1–32.

Christie, Ian. *Arrows of Desire: The Films of Michael Powell and Emeric Pressburger*. London: Faber and Faber, 1994.

Cleto, Fabio, ed. *Camp: Queer Aesthetics and the Performing Subject: A Reader.* Edinburgh: Edinburgh University Press, 1999.

Columpar, Corinn. "The Dancing Body: Sally Potter as Feminist Auteur." In *Women Filmmakers: Refocusing,* edited by Jacqueline Levitin, Judith Plessis, and Valerie Raoul, 108–16. New York: Routledge, 2003.

Combs, Richard. "*The Bitter Tears of Petra von Kant.*" *Monthly Film Bulletin* 42, no. 496 (1975): 99–100.

———. "*Fear Eats the Soul.*" *Monthly Film Bulletin* 41, no. 490 (1974): 243–44.

Comolli, Jean-Luc. "Machines of the Visible." In *The Cinematic Apparatus,* edited by Teresa de Lauretis and Stephen Heath, 121–42. New York: St. Martin's Press, 1980.

Comolli, Jean-Luc, and Jean Narboni. "Cinema, Ideology, Criticism." In *Movies and Methods,* edited by Bill Nichols, 1:22–30. Berkeley: University of California Press, 1976.

Conner, Patrick. "Chinese Style in 19th Century Britain." In *Chinese Whispers: Chinoiserie in Britain, 1650–1930,* edited by David Beevers, 65–73. Brighton: Royal Pavilion and Museums, 2008.

Constable, Catherine. *Thinking in Images: Film Theory, Feminist Philosophy, and Marlene Dietrich.* London: BFI, 2006.

Corbucci, Gianfranco. "*La strategia del ragno.*" *Cinema Nuovo* 209 (1971): 60–61.

Crane, Walter. *Line and Form.* London: Bell, 1912.

Creed, Barbara. "Lesbian Bodies: Tribades, Tomboys, and Tarts." In *Sexy Bodies: The Strange Carnalities of Feminism,* edited by Elizabeth Grosz and Elspeth Probyn, 86–103. New York: Routledge, 1995.

Curtis, David, ed. *The Elusive Sign: British Avant-Garde Film and Video, 1977–1987.* London: Arts Council of Great Britain, 1987.

El-Dahdah, Farès. "The Josephine Baker House: For Loos's Pleasure." *Assemblage* 26 (1995): 72–87.

Dalle Vacche, Angela, ed. *The Visual Turn: Classical Film Theory and Art History.* New Brunswick, N.J.: Rutgers University Press, 2003.

Dalle Vacche, Angela, and Brian Price, eds. *Color: The Film Reader.* New York: Routledge, 2006.

Danto, Arthur. *The Philosophical Disenfranchisement of Art.* New York: Columbia University Press, 1986.

Davis, Whitney. "Winckelmann's 'Homosexual' Teleology." In *Sexuality in Ancient Art,* edited by Natalie Boymel Kampen, 262–76. Cambridge: Cambridge University Press, 1996.

Dawson, Jan. "*The Conformist.*" *Monthly Film Bulletin* 38, no. 455 (1971): 237–38.

De Angelis, Michael. *Gay Fandom and Crossover Stardom: James Dean, Mel Gibson, and Keanu Reeves.* Durham, N.C.: Duke University Press, 2001.

Debord, Guy. *The Society of the Spectacle*. Translated by Donald Nicholson-Smith. New York: Zone Books, 1994.

Degli-Esposti, Christina. "Sally Potter's *Orlando* and the Neo-baroque Scopic Regime." *Cinema Journal* 36, no. 1 (1996): 75–93.

De Grazia, Victoria. "Introduction." In *The Sex of Things: Gender and Consumption in Historical Perspective*, edited by Victoria de Grazia, with Ellen Furlough, 11–24. Berkeley: University of California Press, 1996.

De Grazia, Victoria, with Ellen Furlough, eds. *The Sex of Things: Gender and Consumption in Historical Perspective*. Berkeley: University of California Press, 1996.

De Lauretis, Teresa. *The Practice of Love: Lesbian Sexuality and Perverse Desire*. Bloomington: Indiana University Press, 1994.

——. "Through the Looking Glass: Woman, Cinema, and Language." In *Narrative, Apparatus, Ideology: A Film Theory Reader*, edited by Philip Rosen, 360–72. New York: Columbia University Press, 1986.

De Lauretis, Teresa, and Stephen Heath, eds. *The Cinematic Apparatus*. New York: St. Martin's Press, 1980.

Deleuze, Gilles. *The Logic of Sense*. Translated by Mark Lester and Charles Stivale. New York: Columbia University Press, 1990.

Delluc, Louis. "Beauty in the Cinema." In *French Film Theory and Criticism: A History/Anthology*, vol. 1, *1907–1939*, edited by Richard Abel, 137–39. Princeton, N.J.: Princeton University Press, 1988.

——. "La mauvaise étoile." *Le Film*, September 24, 1917, 7–10.

——. *Photogénie*. Paris: De Brunoff, 1920.

Delmar, Rosalind. "*Amore e Rabbia*." *Monthly Film Bulletin* 38, no. 448 (1971): 91.

Dennison, Stephanie, and Song Hwee Lin, eds. *Remapping World Cinema: Identity, Culture, and Politics in Film*. London: Wallflower, 2006.

"Derek Jarman: Présenté dans le cadre des sélections étrangères." *Apec Cinema* 13, no. 3 (1975): 73–74.

Derrida, Jacques. *Dissemination*. Translated by Barbara Johnson. Chicago: University of Chicago Press, 1981.

——. *The Truth in Painting*. Translated by Geoff Bennington and Ian McLeod. Chicago: University of Chicago Press, 1987.

Diderot, Denis. "Essays on Painting." In *Neoclassicism and Romanticism, 1750–1850*, vol. 1, *Sources and Documents*, edited by Lorenz Eitner, 59–64. Upper Saddle River, N.J.: Prentice-Hall, 1970.

Dillon, Steven. *Derek Jarman and Lyric Film: The Mirror and the Sea*. Austin: University of Texas Press, 2004.

Dirks, Nicholas, ed. *Colonialism and Culture*. Ann Arbor: University of Michigan Press, 1992.

Dixon, Wheeler Winston. *The Transparency of Spectacle: Meditations on the Moving Image*. Albany: State University of New York Press, 1998.

Do, Tess, and Carrie Tarr. "Outsider and Insider Views of Saigon / Ho Chi Minh City: *The Lover / L'Amant, Cyclo / Xích lô, Collective Flat / Chung cu',* and *Bargirls / Gái nhay.*" *Singapore Journal of Tropical Geography* 29, no. 1 (2008): 55–67.

Doane, Mary Ann. "The Close-Up: Scale and Detail in the Cinema." *differences* 14, no. 3 (2003): 89–111.

——. *Femmes Fatales: Feminism, Film Theory, Psychoanalysis.* New York: Routledge, 1991.

Dollin, Stuart. "Super 8 Artist." *Movie Maker* 18, no. 7 (1984): 41–43.

Donald, James, Anne Friedberg, and Laura Marcus, eds. *Close Up, 1927–1933: Cinema and Modernism.* Princeton, N.J.: Princeton University Press, 1999.

Douglas, Ann. *The Feminization of American Culture.* New York: Avon, 1977.

Duchamp, Marcel, and Pierre Cabanne. *Entretiens avec Marcel Duchamp.* Paris: Pierre Belfond, 1967.

Dulac, Germaine. "L'art du mouvement considéré en lui-même." In *Regards neufs sur le cinéma,* edited by Jacques Chevalier and Max Egly, 27–28. Paris: Editions du Seuil, 1965.

Dyer, Richard. *White: Essays on Race and Culture.* London: Routledge, 1997.

Eco, Umberto. *On Beauty: A History of a Western Idea.* Translated by Alastair McEwan. London: Secker and Warburg, 2004.

Eisenstein, Sergei. *Eisenstein.* Vol. 2, *Towards a Theory of Montage.* Translated by Michael Glenny. Edited by Michael Glenny and Richard Taylor. London: BFI, 1994.

——. *The Film Sense.* Translated by Jay Leyda. New York: Harcourt, 1947.

Eitner, Lorenz, ed. *Neoclassicism and Romanticism, 1750–1850.* Vol. 1, *Sources and Documents.* Upper Saddle River, N.J.: Prentice-Hall, 1970.

Elkins, James, ed. *Art History Versus Aesthetics.* New York: Routledge, 2006.

Ellis, Jim. "Queer Period: Derek Jarman's Renaissance." In *Out Takes: Queer Theory and Film,* edited by Ellis Hanson, 288–315. Durham, N.C.: Duke University Press, 1999.

Elsaesser, Thomas. "Tales of Sound and Fury: Observations on the Family Melodrama." In *Home Is Where the Heart Is: Studies in Melodrama and the Woman's Film,* edited by Christine Gledhill, 43–69. London: BFI, 1987.

Epstein, Jean. "Magnification." In *French Film Theory and Criticism: A History / Anthology,* vol. 1, *1907–1939,* edited by Richard Abel, 235–41. Princeton, N.J.: Princeton University Press, 1988.

——. "On Certain Characteristics of *Photogenie.*" In *French Film Theory and Criticism: French Film Theory and Criticism: A History / Anthology,* vol. 1, *1907–1939,* edited by Richard Abel, 314–18. Princeton, N.J.: Princeton University Press, 1988.

——. "The Senses I (b)." In *French Film Theory and Criticism: French Film Theory and Criticism: A History / Anthology,* vol. 1, *1907–1939,* edited by Richard Abel, 241–46. Princeton, N.J.: Princeton University Press, 1988.

Erens, Patricia, ed. *Issues in Feminist Film Criticism*. Bloomington: Indiana University Press, 1990.

Ettinghausen, Richard, Oleg Grabar, and Marilyn Jenkins-Madina. *Islamic Art and Architecture, 650–1250*. New Haven, Conn.: Yale University Press, 2001.

Ezra, Elizabeth. *The Colonial Unconscious: Race and Culture in Interwar France*. Ithaca, N.Y.: Cornell University Press, 2000.

Falcone, Francesca. "The Arabesque: A Compositional Design." Translated by Irene Minafra and Brett Shapiro. *Dance Chronicle* 19, no. 3 (1996): 231–53.

——. "The Evolution of the Arabesque in Dance." *Dance Chronicle* 22, no. 1 (1999): 71–117.

Faulkner, Sally. *Literary Adaptations in Spanish Cinema*. Woodbridge: Tamesis, 2004.

Fehervary, Helen, Claudia Lenssen, and Judith Mayne. "From Hitler to Hepburn: A Discussion of Women's Film Production and Reception." *New German Critique* 24–25 (1981–1982): 172–85.

Feuer, Jane. *The Hollywood Musical*. London: BFI, 1982.

Field, Simon. "Editorial: The Troublesome Cases." In ". . . of Angels & Apocalypse." Special issue, *Afterimage* 12 (1985): 2–5.

Field, Simon, and Michael O'Pray. "Imagining October, Dr. Dee and Other Matters: An Interview with Derek Jarman." In ". . . of Angels & Apocalypse." Special issue, *Afterimage* 12 (1985): 40–58.

Fischer, Jan Otakar. "White Walls in the Golden City." *Harvard Design Magazine* 15 (2001): 1–8.

Foster, Hal. *Design and Crime (and Other Diatribes)*. London: Verso, 2002.

Francis, Terry. "Embodied Fictions, Melancholy Migrations: Josephine Baker's Cinematic Celebrity." *MFS: Modern Fiction Studies* 51, no. 4 (2005): 824–45.

Freeburg, Victor. *The Art of Photoplay Making*. New York: Ayer, 1970.

Freud, Sigmund. *New Introductory Lectures on Psychoanalysis and Other Works*. Translated by James Strachey. New York: Norton, 1989.

Frieden, Sandra, Richard W. McCormick, Vibeke R. Peterson, and Laura Melissa Vogelsang, eds. *Gender and German Cinema*. Vol. 1, *Feminist Interventions*. Providence, R.I.: Berg, 1993.

Friedman, Lester, ed. *Unspeakable Images: Ethnicity in Cinema*. Urbana: University of Illinois Press, 1991.

Galassi, Peter. *Before Photography: Painting and the Invention of Photography*. New York: Museum of Modern Art, 1981.

Gallacher, Jean. "H. D.'s Distractions: Cinematic Stasis and Lesbian Desire." *Modernism/Modernity* 9, no. 3 (2002): 407–22.

Galt, Rosalind. *The New European Cinema: Redrawing the Map*. New York: Columbia University Press, 2006.

——. "The Obviousness of Cinema." *World Picture* 2 (2009). Available at http://english.okstate.edu/worldpicture/WP_2/Galt.html.

Galt, Rosalind, and Karl Schoonover, eds. *Global Art Cinema: New Histories and Theories.* New York: Oxford University Press, 2010.

García Espinosa, Julio. "For an Imperfect Cinema." Translated by Julianne Burton. In *Twenty-five Years of the New Latin American Cinema,* edited by Michael Chanan, 28–33. London: BFI, 1983.

———. "In Search of the Lost Cinema." In *Latin American Filmmakers and the Third Cinema,* edited by Zuzana M. Pick, 194–98. Ottawa: Carleton University Press, 1978.

Gellner, Ernest. "The Gaffe-Avoiding Animal or a Bundle of Hypotheses." In *Individualism: Theories and Methods,* edited by Pierre Birnbaum and Jean Leca, 17–32. Oxford.: Oxford University Press, 1990.

Getsy, David J. "Other Values (or, Is It an African or an Indian Elephant in the Room?)." In *Art History Versus Aesthetics,* edited by James Elkins, 194–96. New York: Routledge, 2006.

Gever, Martha, Pratibha Parmar, and John Greyson, eds. *Queer Looks: Perspectives on Lesbian and Gay Film and Video.* New York: Routledge, 1993.

Gidal, Peter. *Structural Film Anthology.* London: BFI, 1976.

Gillain, Ann, ed. *Le cinéma selon François Truffaut.* Paris: Flammarion, 1988.

Gledhill, Christine, ed. *Home Is Where the Heart Is: Studies in Melodrama and the Woman's Film.* London: BFI, 1987.

———. "The Melodramatic Field: An Investigation." In *Home Is Where the Heart Is: Studies in Melodrama and the Woman's Film,* edited by Christine Gledhill, 5–39. London: BFI, 1987.

Glick, Elisa. "Sex Positive: Feminism, Queer Theory, and the Politics of Transgression." *Feminist Review* 64 (2000): 19–45.

Godard, Jean-Luc. "La nuit, l'éclipse, l'aurore: Entretien avec Michelangelo Antonioni." *Cahiers du Cinéma* 160 (1964): 8–16.

Goethe, Johann Wolfgang von. *Theory of Colors.* Translated by Charles Eastlake. Cambridge, Mass.: MIT Press, 1970.

Gombrich, E. H. *The Sense of Order: A Study in the Psychology of Decorative Art.* Oxford: Phaidon, 1979.

Gordon, Rae Beth. *Ornament, Fantasy, and Desire in Nineteenth-Century French Literature.* Princeton, N.J.: Princeton University Press, 1992.

Gott, Richard. "From Russia with Love." *Guardian,* November 12, 2005. Available at http://www.guardian.co.uk/film/2005/nov/12/cuba.

Graham, Gordon. *The Re-enchantment of the World: Art Versus Religion.* Oxford: Oxford University Press, 2007.

Grant, Barry Keith, and Jeanette Slonioski, eds. *Documenting the Documentary: Close Readings of Documentary Film and Video.* Detroit: Wayne State University Press, 2003.

Gravagnuolo, Benedetto. *Adolf Loos: Theory and Works.* Translated by C. H. Evans. New York: Rizzoli, 1982.

Griffiths, Robin, ed. *Queer Cinema in Europe*. Bristol.: Intellect, 2008.

Gromaire, Marcel. "A Painter's Ideas About the Cinema." In *French Film Theory and Criticism: A History/Anthology*, vol. 1, *1907–1939*, edited by Richard Abel, 174–82. Princeton, N.J.: Princeton University Press, 1988.

Grossvogel, D. I. "Haneke: The Coercing of Vision." *Film Quarterly* 60, no. 4 (2007): 36–43.

Grosz, Elizabeth. *Space, Time, and Perversion: Essays on the Politics of Bodies*. New York: Routledge, 1995.

Grosz, Elizabeth, and Elspeth Probyn, eds. *Sexy Bodies: The Strange Carnalities of Feminism*. New York: Routledge, 1995.

Guback, Thomas. *The International Film Industry*. Bloomington: Indiana University Press, 1969.

Habel, Ylva. "To Stockholm, with Love: The Critical Reception of Josephine Baker, 1927–35." *Film History* 17 (2005): 125–38.

Hake, Sabine. "And with Favourable Winds They Sailed Away." In *Gender and German Cinema*, vol. 1, *Feminist Interventions*, edited by Sandra Frieden, Richard W. McCormick, Vibeke R. Peterson, and Laura Melissa Vogelsang, 179–88. Providence, R.I.: Berg, 1993.

Halberstam, Judith. *Female Masculinities*. Durham, N.C.: Duke University Press, 1998.

Halle, Randall. "Telling Tales They Want to Hear." In *Global Art Cinema: New Histories and Theories*, edited by Rosalind Galt and Karl Schoonover, 303–19. New York: Oxford University Press, 2010.

Hanlon, Dennis. "Traveling Theory, Shots, and Players: Jorge Sanjinés, New Latin American Cinema, and the European Art Film." In *Global Art Cinema: New Histories and Theories*, edited by Rosalind Galt and Karl Schoonover, 351–66. New York: Oxford University Press, 2010.

Hansen, Miriam. "Benjamin, Cinema, and Experience: 'The Blue Flower in the Land of Technology.'" *New German Critique* 40 (1987): 179–224.

——. "Introduction." In *Theory of Film: The Redemption of Physical Reality*, by Siegfried Kracauer, vii–xlv. Princeton, N.J.: Princeton University Press, 1997.

——. "Visual Pleasure, Fetishism, and the Problem of Feminine/Feminist Discourse: Ulrike Ottinger's *Ticket of No Return*." *New German Critique* 31 (1984): 95–108.

Hanson, Ellis, ed. *Out Takes: Queer Theory and Film*. Durham, N.C.: Duke University Press, 1999.

Hanson, Stephen L. "Michael Powell and Emeric Pressburger." In *Film Reference*. Available at http://www.filmreference.com/Directors-Pe-Ri/Powell-Michael-and-Emeric-Pressburger.html.

Harper, Sue. "Historical Pleasures: Gainsborough Costume Melodramas." In *Home Is Where the Heart Is: Studies in Melodrama and the Woman's Film*, edited by Christine Gledhill, 167–96. London: BFI, 1987.

Harrison, Mark. "Zhang Yimou's *Hero* and the Globalisation of Propaganda." *Millennium Journal of International Studies* 34, no. 2 (2006): 569–72.

Hawley, John C. *Postcolonial, Queer: Theoretical Intersections.* Albany: State University of New York Press, 2001.

H. D. "The Cinema and the Classics I: Beauty." In *Close Up, 1927–1933: Cinema and Modernism,* edited by James Donald, Anne Friedberg, and Laura Marcus, 105–9. Princeton, N.J.: Princeton University Press, 1999.

Heath, Stephen. "Joan Rivière and the Masquerade." In *Formations of Fantasy,* edited by Victor Burgin, 45–61. London: Methuen, 1986.

——. *Questions of Cinema.* Bloomington: Indiana University Press, 1981.

Hegel, G. W. F. *Aesthetics: Lectures on Fine Art.* Translated by T. M. Knox. Oxford: Clarendon Press, 1975.

Helfer, Martha B., ed. *Rereading Romanticism.* Amsterdam: Rodopi, 2000.

Higashi, Sumiko. "Ethnicity, Class, and Gender in Film: DeMille's *The Cheat.*" In *Unspeakable Images: Ethnicity in Cinema,* edited by Lester Friedman, 112–39. Urbana: University of Illinois Press, 1991.

Hill, Steven P. "Introduction to *Shadows of Our Forgotten Ancestors.*" *Film Comment* 5, no. 1 (1968): 39.

——. "The Soviet Film Today." *Film Quarterly* 20, no. 4 (1967): 33–52.

Hoberman, J. "Times of Tumult." *Village Voice,* January 11, 2000. Available at http://www.villagevoice.com/2000-01-11/film/times-of-tumult/1.

Hogarth, William. *Analysis of Beauty.* Hildesheim: Olms, 1974.

hooks, bell. *Reel to Real: Race, Sex, and Class at the Movies.* New York: Routledge, 1996.

Horkheimer, Max, and Theodor W. Adorno. *Dialectic of Enlightenment.* Translated by John Cumming. New York: Continuum, 1996.

Hughes, John. "Recent Rossellini." *Film Comment* 10, no. 4 (1974): 16–17.

Huysmans, Joris-Karl. *Against Nature.* Translated by Robert Baldick. London: Penguin, 2003.

Huyssen, Andreas. *After the Great Divide: Modernism, Mass Culture, and Postmodernism.* London: Macmillan, 1986.

Iampolski, Mikhail. "Russia: The Cinema of Anti-modernity and Backward Progress." In *Theorising National Cinema,* edited by Valentina Vitali and Paul Willemen, 72–87. London: BFI, 2006.

Impey, Oliver. *Chinoiserie: The Impact of Oriental Styles in Western Art and Decoration.* London: Oxford University Press, 1977.

Iordanova, Dina. "Review of *I Am Cuba.*" *Russian Review* 56, no. 1 (1997): 125–26.

Irigaray, Luce. *This Sex Which Is Not One.* Translated by Catherine Porter. Ithaca, N.Y.: Cornell University Press, 1985.

Jacobs, Katrien. "The Lady of Little Death." *Wide Angle* 19, no. 3 (1997): 13–40.

Jameson, Fredric. *The Geopolitical Aesthetic: Cinema and Space in the World System.* Bloomington: Indiana University Press, 1995.

——. *Postmodernism, or, The Cultural Logic of Late Capitalism*. Durham, N.C.: Duke University Press, 1991.

——. *Signatures of the Visible*. New York: Routledge, 1991.

Janaway, Christopher. *Images of Excellence: Plato's Critique of the Arts*. Oxford: Clarendon Press, 1995.

Jarman, Derek. *Chroma: A Book of Color*. Woodstock, N.Y.: Overlook Press, 1995.

Jay, Martin. *Downcast Eyes: The Denigration of Vision in Twentieth-Century French Thought*. Berkeley: University of California Press, 1994.

Johnson, Rebecca. "*Kawaii* and *Kirei*: Navigating the Identities of Women in La-puta: *Castle in the Sky* by Hayao Miyazaki and *Ghost in the Shell* by Mamoru Oshii." *Rhizomes* 14 (2007). Available at http://www.rhizomes.net/issue14/johnson/johnson.html.

Jones, Owen. *The Grammar of Ornament*. London: Quaritch, 1856.

——. *The Ornament and Design of the Alhambra*. New York: Dover, 2008.

Kaes, Anton. *From Hitler to Heimat: The Return of History as Film*. Cambridge, Mass.: Harvard University Press, 1989.

Kaes, Anton, and David J. Levin. "The Debate About Cinema: Charting a Controversy (1909–1929)." *New German Critique* 40 (1987): 7–33.

Kaganski, Serge. "Pourquoi je n'aime pas *Le fabuleux destin d'Amélie Poulin*." *Les Inrockuptibles*, May 31, 2001. Available at http://lesinrocks.com/cine/cinema-article/article/pourquoi-je-naime-pas-le-fabuleux-destin-damelie-poulin.

——. "Rebonds de Serge Kaganski paru dans Libération du 31 mai." *Les Inrockuptibles*. Available at http://www.lesinrocks.com. [Originally published as "Amélie pas jolie," *Libération*, May 31, 2001]

Kant, Immanuel. *The Critique of Judgment*. Translated by J. H. Bernard. Amherst, N.Y.: Prometheus Books, 2000.

Kaplan, E. Ann. "The Case of the Missing Mother: Maternal Issues in Vidor's *Stella Dallas*." In *Issues in Feminist Film Criticism*, edited by Patricia Erens, 126–36. Bloomington: Indiana University Press, 1990.

——. *Looking for the Other: Feminism, Film, and the Imperial Gaze*. New York: Routledge, 1997.

——. "Night at the Opera: Investigating the Heroine in Sally Potter's *Thriller*." *Millennium Film Journal* 10–11 (1981): 115–22.

Kaplan, Janet A., and Ulrike Ottinger. "*Johanna d'Arc of Mongolia*: Interview with Ulrike Ottinger." *Art Journal* 61, no. 3 (2002): 6–21.

Kaplan, Nelly. "À propos de Cannes." *Film Comment* 1, no. 5 (1963): 40–43.

Keam, Angela. "Claire Danes's Star-Body, Teen Female Viewers, and the Pluralisation of Authorship in Baz Luhrmann's *William Shakespeare's Romeo + Juliet*." *English in Australia* 43, no. 2 (2008): 39–46.

Keathley, Christian. *Cinephilia and History, or, The Wind in the Trees*. Bloomington: Indiana University Press, 2006.

Kim, Thomas W. "Being Modern: The Circulation of Oriental Objects." *American Quarterly* 58, no. 2 (2006): 379–406.

Kinder, Marsha. "*Moulin Rouge!*" *Film Quarterly* 55, no. 3 (2001): 52–59.

King, Homay. "Sign in the Void: Ulrike Ottinger's *Johanna d'Arc of Mongolia.*" *Afterall* 16 (2007): 47–52.

Klinger, Barbara. *Melodrama and Meaning: History, Culture, and the Films of Douglas Sirk.* Bloomington: Indiana University Press, 1994.

Knight, Julia. *Women and the New German Cinema.* London: Verso, 1992.

Koch, Gertrud. "Mimesis and *Bilderverbot.*" *Screen* 34, no. 3 (1993): 211–22.

——. "'Not Yet Accepted Anywhere': Exile, Memory, and Image in Kracauer's Conception of History." Translated by Jeremy Gaines. *New German Critique* 54 (1991): 95–109.

Koepnick, Lutz. "Consuming the Other: Identity, Alterity, and Contemporary German Cinema." *Camera Obscura* 44, no. 15/2 (2000): 40–73.

Kracauer, Siegfried. *The Mass Ornament: Weimar Essays.* Translated by Thomas Y. Levin. Cambridge, Mass.: Harvard University Press, 1995.

——. *Theory of Film: The Redemption of Physical Reality.* Princeton, N.J.: Princeton University Press, 1997.

Krzywinska, Tanya. *Sex and the Cinema.* London: Wallflower, 2006.

Kuhn, Annette. "Encounter Between Two Cultures: A Discussion with Ulrike Ottinger." *Screen* 28, no. 4 (1987): 74–79.

Larson, Wendy. "Zhang Yimou's *Hero*: Dismantling the Myth of Cultural Power." *Journal of Chinese Cinemas* 2, no. 3 (2008): 181–96.

Lastra, James. "From the Captured Moment to the Cinematic Image, a Transformation in Pictorial Order." In *The Image in Dispute: Art and Cinema in the Age of Photography*, edited by Dudley Andrew, 263–91. Austin: University of Texas Press, 1997.

Laurie, Edith. "The Film Festival at Karlovy Vary." *Vision* 1, no. 2 (1962): 6–12.

——. "Notes from the Venice Film Festival." *Film Comment* 1, no. 3 (1963): 8–13.

——. "To Have or Not to Have a Film Festival." *Film Comment* 3, no. 3 (1965): 18–23.

Leach, Neil, ed. *Rethinking Architecture: A Reader in Cultural Theory.* London: Routledge, 1997.

Lecercle, Jean-Jacques. "Barthes Without Althusser: A Different Style of Marxism." *Paragraph* 31, no. 1 (2008): 72–83.

Lecomte, Jules. *Les lettres de Van Engelgom.* Edited by Henri d'Almeras. Paris: Éditions Bossard, 1925.

Le Corbusier. *The Decorative Art of Today.* Translated by James I. Dunnett. London: Architectural Press, 1987.

Le Doeuff, Michèle. *The Philosophical Imaginary.* Translated by Colin Gordon. London: Continuum, 1989.

Lemarié, Yannick. "*Soy Cuba*: Le mythe de la révolution." *Positif* 512 (2003): 77–78.

Lessing, Gotthold Ephraim. *Laocöon: An Essay on the Limits of Painting and Poetry.* Translated by Edward Allen McCormick. Baltimore: Johns Hopkins University Press, 2008.

Levitin, Jacqueline, Judith Plessis, and Valerie Raoul, eds. *Women Filmmakers: Refocusing.* New York: Routledge, 2003.

Lewis, Reina. *Gendering Orientalism: Race, Femininity, and Representation.* New York: Routledge, 1996.

Lherminier, Pierre, ed. *L'art du cinéma.* Paris: Edition Seghers, 1960.

Lichtenstein, Jacqueline. *The Eloquence of Color: Rhetoric and Painting in the French Classical Age.* Translated by Emily McVarish. Berkeley: University of California Press, 1993.

Lindsay, Vachel. *The Art of the Moving Picture.* New York: Liveright, 1970.

Lippard, Chris, ed. *By Angels Driven: The Films of Derek Jarman.* Trowbridge: Flick Books, 1996.

Lizzani, Carlo. "Come risolvere il problema del naturalismo nel cinema?" *Cinema Nuovo* 204 (1970): 96–99.

Longfellow, Brenda. "Lesbian Phantasy and the Other Woman in Ottinger's *Johanna d'Arc of Mongolia*." *Screen* 34, no. 2 (1993): 124–36.

Loos, Adolf. *Ornament and Crime: Selected Essays.* Translated by Michael Mitchell. Riverside, Calif.: Ariadne Press, 1998.

——. *Spoken into the Void: Collected Essays, 1897–1900.* Translated by Jane O. Newman and John H. Smith. Cambridge, Mass.: MIT Press, 1982.

——. "The Story of a Poor Rich Man." In *Adolf Loos: Pioneer of Modern Architecture,* by Ludwig Münz and Gustav Künstler, 223–25. New York: Praeger, 1966.

López, Luis M. "No *Soy Cuba*." *Bohemia,* August 21, 1964, 24–25.

Losilla, Carlos. "Legislación, industria y escritura." In *Escritos sobre el cine español, 1973–1987,* 33–43. Valencia: Filmoteca de la Generalitat Valenciana, 1989.

Lowenstein, Adam. *Shocking Representation: Historical Trauma, National Cinema, and the Modern Horror Film.* New York: Columbia University Press, 2005.

MacBean, James Roy. "*Vent d'Est* or Godard and Rocha at the Crossroads." In *Movies and Methods,* edited by Bill Nichols, 1:91–106. Berkeley: University of California Press, 1976.

MacCabe, Colin. "Theory and Film: Principles of Realism and Pleasure." In *Narrative, Apparatus, Ideology: A Film Theory Reader,* edited by Philip Rosen, 179–97. New York: Columbia University Press, 1986.

——, ed. *Wittgenstein: The Terry Eagleton Script and the Derek Jarman Film.* London: BFI, 1993.

Maciuika, John V. "Adolf Loos and the Aphoristic Style: Rhetorical Practice in Early Twentieth-Century Design Criticism." *Design Issues* 16, no. 2 (2000): 75–86.

MacKenzie, John M. *Orientalism: History, Theory, and the Arts*. Manchester: Manchester University Press, 1995.

Macpherson, Kenneth. "As Is." *Close Up* 6, no. 2 (1930): 88.

Majer O'Sickey, Ingeborg, and Ingeborg von Zadow, eds. *Triangulated Visions: Women in Recent German Cinema*. Albany: State University of New York Press, 1998.

Mane, Eduardo. "80 minutos con Serguei Urusevski." *Cine Cubano* 20 (1964): 1–8.

Manresa, Laia. *Joaquín Jordá: La mirada lluire / The Free Spirit*. Translated by Andrew Stacy. Barcelona: Filmoteca de Catalunya, 2006.

Marcus, Laura. *The Tenth Muse: Writing About Cinema in the Modernist Period*. Oxford: Oxford University Press, 2007.

Marcus, Laura, and Lynda Nead, eds. *The Actuality of Walter Benjamin*. London: Lawrence & Wishart, 1998.

Marën, Marcel. "Another Kind of Cinema." *Film Comment* 1, no. 3 (1963): 14–19.

Margulies, Ivone, ed. *Rites of Realism: Essays on Corporeal Cinema*. Durham, N.C.: Duke University Press, 2003.

Marks, Laura U. "Infinity and Accident: Strategies of Enfoldment in Islamic and Computer Art." *Leonardo* 39, no. 1 (2006): 37–42.

——. *The Skin of the Film: Intercultural Cinema, Embodiment, and the Senses*. Durham, N.C.: Duke University Press, 2000.

Martínez Torres, Augusto, and Manuel Pérez Estremera. *Nuevo cine latinoamericano*. Barcelona: Anagrama, 1973.

McBride, Patrizia C. " 'In Praise of the Present': Adolf Loos on Style and Fashion." *Modernism / Modernity* 11, no. 4 (2004): 745–67.

McCreary, Eugene C. "Louis Delluc: Film Theorist, Critic, and Prophet." *Cinema Journal* 16, no. 1 (1976): 14–35.

Mellen, Joan. "*Vent d'Est*." *Film Comment* 7, no. 3 (1971): 65–67.

Melo, João Marcelo. "Aesthetics and Ethics in *City of God*: Content Fails, Form Talks." *Third Text* 18, no. 5 (2004): 475–81.

Mennel, Barbara. "Wanda's Whip: Recasting Masochism's Fantasy—Monika Treut's *Seduction: The Cruel Woman*." In *Triangulated Visions: Women in Recent German Cinema*, edited by Ingeborg Majer O'Sickey and Ingeborg von Zadow, 153–62. Albany: State University of New York Press, 1998.

Merck, Mandy. *Perversions: Deviant Readings*. New York: Routledge, 1993.

Merjian, Ara H. "Middlebrow Modernism: Rudolf Arnheim at the Crossroads of Film Theory and the Psychology of Art." In *The Visual Turn: Classical Film Theory and Art History*, edited by Angela Dalle Vacche, 154–92. New Brunswick, N.J.: Rutgers University Press, 2003.

Merten, Luiz Carlos. "From the Aesthetics to the Cosmetics of Hunger?" *Thinking Eye* 1 (2002). Available at http://www.elojoquepiensa.udg.mx/ingles/revis_02/index.html.

Metz, Christian. *Language and Cinema*. Translated by Donna Jean Umiker-Sebeok. The Hague: Mouton, 1974.

Minninghaus, Winfried. "Hummingbirds, Shells, Picture-Frames: Kant's 'Free Beauties' and the Romantic Arabesque." In *Rereading Romanticism*, edited by Martha B. Helfer, 27–46. Amsterdam: Rodopi, 2000.

Mitchell, Timothy. "Orientalism and the Exhibitionary Order." In *Colonialism and Culture*, edited by Nicholas Dirks, 289–300. Ann Arbor: University of Michigan Press, 1992.

Mitchell, W. J. T. *Iconology: Image, Text, Ideology*. Chicago: University of Chicago Press, 1987.

———. *What Do Pictures Want? The Lives and Loves of Images*. Chicago: University of Chicago Press, 2005.

Miyao, Daisuke. *Sessue Hayakawa: Silent Cinema and Transnational Stardom*. Durham, N.C.: Duke University Press, 2007.

Modleski, Tania. *Feminism Without Women: Culture and Criticism in a "Postfeminist" Age*. New York: Routledge, 1991.

———, ed. *Studies in Entertainment: Critical Approaches to Mass Culture*. Bloomington: Indiana University Press, 1986.

Montrelay, Michèle. "Inquiry into Femininity." *m/f* 1 (1978): 83–102.

Moor, Andrew. "Spirit and Matter: Romantic Mythologies in the Films of Derek Jarman." In *Territories of Desire in Queer Culture: Refiguring the Contemporary Boundaries*, edited by David Alderton and Linda Anderson, 49–67. Manchester: Manchester University Press, 2000.

Moore, Thomas. *The Re-enchantment of Everyday Life*. London: HarperCollins, 1996.

Morgan, Daniel. "Rethinking Bazin: Ontology and Realist Aesthetics." *Critical Inquiry* 32, no. 3 (2006): 443–81.

Mueller, Roswitha. "The Mirror and the Vamp." *New German Critique* 34 (1985): 176–93.

Mulvey, Laura. "Notes on Sirk and Melodrama." In *Home Is Where the Heart Is: Studies in Melodrama and the Woman's Film*, edited by Christine Gledhill, 75–79. London: BFI, 1987.

———. "Visual Pleasure and Narrative Cinema." In *Narrative, Apparatus, Ideology: A Film Theory Reader*, edited by Philip Rosen, 198–209. New York: Columbia University Press, 1986.

Münsterberg, Hugo. *The Film, a Psychological Study*. New York: Dover, 1970.

———. "The Problem of Beauty." *Philosophical Review* 18, no. 2 (1909): 121–46.

Münz, Ludwig, and Gustav Künstler. *Adolf Loos: Pioneer of Modern Architecture*. New York: Praeger, 1966.

Musser, Amber. "Masochism: A Queer Subjectivity." *Rhizomes* 11–12 (2005–2006). Available at http://www.rhizomes.net/issue11/musser.html.

Naficy, Hamid. *An Accented Cinema: Exilic and Diasporic Filmmaking*. Princeton, N.J.: Princeton University Press, 2001.

Nagib, Lúcia. "Panaméricas Utópicas: Entranced and Transient Nations in *I Am Cuba* (1964) and *Land in Trance* (1967)." *Hispanic Research Journal* 8, no. 1 (2007): 79–90.

——. "Talking Bullets." *Third Text* 18, no. 3 (2004): 239–50.

Nancy, Jean-Luc. *The Ground of the Image*. Translated by Jeff Fort. New York: Fordham University Press, 2005.

Ngai, Sianne. "The Cuteness of the Avant-Garde." *Critical Inquiry* 31 (2005): 811–47.

Nichols, Bill. "*Il conformista*." *Cineaste* 4, no. 4 (1971): 19–23.

——, ed. *Movies and Methods*. Vol. 1. Berkeley: University of California Press, 1976.

——, ed. *Movies and Methods*. Vol. 2. Berkeley: University of California Press, 1985.

Nisbet, H. B., ed. *German Aesthetic and Literary Criticism: Winckelmann, Lessing, Hamann, Herder, Schiller, Goethe*. Cambridge: Cambridge University Press, 1985.

Nochlin, Linda. "The Imaginary Orient." In *The Nineteenth-Century Visual Culture Reader*, edited by Vanessa R. Schwartz and Jeannene M. Przyblyski, 289–98. New York: Routledge, 2004.

Nordau, Max. *Degeneration*. New York: Fertig, 1968.

Oechslin, Werner. *Otto Wagner, Adolf Loos, and the Road to Modern Architecture*. Translated by Lynette Widder. Cambridge: Cambridge University Press, 2002.

Oksiloff, Assenka. *Picturing the Primitive: Visual Culture, Ethnography, and Early German Cinema*. London: Palgrave, 2001.

O'Pray, Michael, ed. *The British Avant-Garde Film, 1926–1995: An Anthology of Writings*. London: Arts Council of England and University of Luton Press, 1990.

——. "Derek Jarman: The Art of Films / Films of Art." In *Derek Jarman: A Portrait*, edited by Roger Wollen, 65–75. London: Thames and Hudson, 1996.

——. *Derek Jarman: Dreams of England*. London: BFI, 1996.

——. "The Elusive Sign: From Asceticism to Aestheticism." In *The Elusive Sign: British Avant-Garde Film and Video, 1977–1987*, edited by David Curtis, 7–10. London: Arts Council of Great Britain, 1987.

O'Toole, Sean. "In Conversation with Zwelethu Mthethwa." *Artthrob: Contemporary Art in South Africa* 83 (2004). Available at http://www.artthrob.co.za/04july/news/mthethwa.html.

Oudart, Jean-Pierre. "Un discours en défaut." *Cahiers du Cinéma* 232 (1971): 4–12.

Palmer, Chris. "'What Tongue Shall Smooth Thy Name?' Recent Films of *Romeo and Juliet*." *Cambridge Quarterly* 31, no. 1 (2003): 61–76.

Paradjanov, Sergei. "*Shadows of Our Forgotten Ancestors*." Translated by Steven P. Hill. *Film Comment* 5, no. 1 (1968): 39–47.

Paramjit, Rai. "*The Terrorist.*" *Sight & Sound* 11, no. 5 (2001): 58–59.

Parfitt, Clare. "The Spectator's Dancing Gaze in *Moulin Rouge!*" *Research in Dance Education* 6, no. 1 (2005): 97–110.

Patton, Cindy. "What's a Nice Girl Like You Doing in a Film Like This?" In *Immortal Invisible: Lesbians and the Moving Image*, edited by Tamsin Wilton, 20–33. New York: Routledge, 1995.

Pencak, William. *The Films of Derek Jarman.* Jefferson, N.C.: McFarland, 2002.

Penley, Constance, ed. *Feminism and Film Theory.* New York: Routledge, 1988.

Peters, John. "Beauty's Veils: The Ambivalent Iconoclasm of Kierkegaard and Benjamin." In *The Image in Dispute: Art and Cinema in the Age of Photography*, edited by Dudley Andrew, 9–32. Austin: University of Texas Press, 1997.

Petley, Julian. "The Lost Continent." In *All Our Yesterdays: 90 Years of British Cinema*, edited by Charles Barr, 98–119. London: British Film Institute, 1986.

Pevsner, Nikolaus. "Introduction." In *Adolf Loos: Pioneer of Modern Architecture*, by Ludwig Münz and Gustav Künstler, 13–24. New York: Praeger, 1966.

Pick, Zuzana M., ed. *Latin American Filmmakers and the Third Cinema.* Ottawa: Carleton University Press, 1978.

Pinkus, Karen. *Alchemical Mercury: A Theory of Ambivalence.* Stanford, Calif.: Stanford University Press, 2009.

——. "Nothing from Nothing: Alchemy and the Economic Crisis." *World Picture* 2 (2008). Available at http://www.worldpicturejournal.com.

Pinney, Christopher. "Piercing the Skin of the Idol." In *Beyond Aesthetics: Art and the Technologies of Enchantment*, edited by Christopher Pinney and Nicholas Thomas, 157–80. Oxford: Berg, 2001.

Pinney, Christopher, and Nicholas Thomas, eds. *Beyond Aesthetics: Art and the Technologies of Enchantment.* Oxford: Berg, 2001.

Plato. *The Collected Dialogues of Plato.* Translated by Lane Cooper and others. Edited by Edith Hamilton and Huntington Cairns. Princeton, N.J.: Princeton University Press, 1961.

Porton, Richard. "Language Games and Aesthetic Attitudes: Style and Ideology in Jarman's Late Films." In *By Angels Driven: The Films of Derek Jarman*, edited by Chris Lippard, 135–60. Trowbridge: Flick Books, 1996.

Potts, Alex. *Flesh and the Ideal: Winckelmann and the Origins of Art History.* New Haven, Conn.: Yale University Press, 1994.

Price, Brian. "Color, the Formless, and Cinematic Eros." In *Color: The Film Reader*, edited by Angela Dalle Vacche and Brian Price, 76–87. New York: Routledge, 2006.

——. "Cosmopolitanism and Cinema Today." In *Global Art Cinema: New Histories and Theories*, edited by Rosalind Galt and Karl Schoonover, 109–24. New York: Oxford University Press, 2010.

Probyn, Elspeth. *Outside Belongings.* New York: Routledge, 1996.

———. "This Body Which Is Not One: Speaking as Embodied Self." *Hypatia* 6, no. 3 (1991): 111–24.

Pugin, Augustus. *Contrasts; or, A Parallel Between the Noble Edifices of the Fourteenth and Fifteenth Centuries and Similar Buildings of the Present Day; Shewing the Present Decay of Taste.* Salisbury, 1836.

Quart, Leonard. "*1900*: Bertolucci's Marxist Opera." *Cineaste* 8, no. 3 (1977–1978): 24–27.

Quatremère de Quincy, M. [Antoine-Chrysostome]. *De l'architecture egyptienne: Considérée dans son origine, ses principes et son goût, et comparée sous les mêmes rapports à l'architecture Grecque.* Paris: Barrois, 1803.

———. *Lettres écrites de Londres à Rome, et addressées à M. Canova, sur les marbres d'Elgin, ou les sculptures du temple de Minerve à Athène.* Rome, 1818.

Quintilian. *Institutio Oratorio III.* Translated by H. E. Butler. Edited by T. E. Page, E. Capps, W. H. D. Rouse, L. A. Post, and E. H. Warmington. London: Heinemann, 1922.

Radhakrishnan, M. G. "Filmmaker with a Focus." *India Today*, December 28, 1998. Available at http://www.indiatoday.com/itoday/28121998/profile.html.

Ragona, Melissa. "Swing and Sway: Marie Menken's Filmic Events." In *Women's Experimental Cinema: Critical Frameworks*, edited by Robin Blaetz, 20–44. Durham, N.C.: Duke University Press, 2007.

Rancière, Jacques. *Film Fables.* Translated by Emiliano Battista. London: Berg, 2006.

Rayns, Tony. "*Arabian Nights.*" *Monthly Film Bulletin* 42, no. 495 (1975): 79.

———. "Submitting to Sodomy: Propositions and Rhetorical Questions About an English Film-maker." In ". . . of Angels & Apocalypse." Special issue, *Afterimage* 12 (1985): 60–64.

———"Unnatural Lighting." *American Film* 11, no. 10 (1986): 44–47, 59–61.

"*Red Psalm.*" *Monthly Film Bulletin* 40, no. 471 (1973): 79–80.

Rees, A. L. *A History of Experimental Film and Video: From the Canonical Avant-Garde to Contemporary British Practice.* London: BFI, 1999.

Reimann, Andrea. "Subjection and Power in Monika Treut and Elfi Mikesch's *Seduction—The Cruel Woman*: An Extension of the Configuration of Power in Rainer Werner Fassbinder's Late Oeuvre." In *Queer Cinema in Europe*, edited by Robin Griffiths, 181–93. Bristol: Intellect, 2008.

Rentmeister, Cillie. "Frauen, Körper, Kunst: Mikrophysik der patriarchalischen Macht." *Ästhetik und Kommunikation* 37 (1979): 61–68.

Reynolds, Sir Joshua. *The Complete Works.* London: Thomas McLean, 1824.

Rich, B. Ruby. "When Difference Is More Than Skin Deep." In *Queer Looks: Perspectives on Lesbian and Gay Film and Video*, edited by Martha Gever, Pratibha Parmar, and John Greyson, 318–39. New York: Routledge, 1993.

Rickels, Laurence. *Ulrike Ottinger: The Autobiography of Art Cinema.* Minneapolis: University of Minnesota Press, 2008.

Riegl, Alois. *Problems of Style: Foundations for a History of Ornament.* Translated by Evelyn Kain. Princeton, N.J.: Princeton University Press, 1992.

Rivière, Joan. "Womanliness as Masquerade." In *Formations of Fantasy,* edited by Victor Burgin, 35–44. London: Methuen, 1986.

Robertson, Lisa. *Occasional Work and Seven Walks from the Office for Soft Architecture.* Astoria, Ore.: Clear Cut Press, 2003.

Robertson, Pamela. *Guilty Pleasures: Feminist Camp from Mae West to Madonna.* Durham, N.C.: Duke University Press, 1996.

Rocha, Glauber. "The Aesthetics of Hunger." Translated by Burnes Hollyman and Randal Johnson. In *Twenty-five Years of the New Latin American Cinema,* edited by Michael Chanan, 13–14. London: BFI, 1983.

Rodríguez Alemán, Mario. "Bosquedo histórico del cinema cubano." *Cine Cubano* 26 (1965): 25–35.

——. *"Soy Cuba." Diario de la tarde,* August 3, 1964.

Rohdie, Sam, ed. Special issue on Douglas Sirk. *Screen* 12, no. 2 (1971).

Rose, Phyllis. *Jazz Cleopatra: Josephine Baker in Her Time.* London: Chatto and Windus, 1990.

Rosen, Philip. *Change Mummified: Cinema, Historicity, Theory.* Minneapolis: Minnesota University Press, 2000.

——, ed. *Narrative, Apparatus, Ideology: A Film Theory Reader.* New York: Columbia University Press, 1986.

Rosenbaum, Jonathan. *Essential Cinema: On the Necessity of Film Canons.* Baltimore: Johns Hopkins University Press, 2004.

Rossellini, Roberto. "Je n'aime pas les décors." In *L'art du cinéma,* edited by Pierre Lherminier, 143. Paris: Edition Seghers, 1960.

Rousseau, Jean-Jacques. *Discours sur les arts et les sciences.* Paris: Gallimard, 1986.

Ruberto, Laura E., and Kristi M. Wilson, eds. *Italian Neorealism and Global Cinema.* Detroit: Wayne State University Press, 2007.

Ruiz, Josefina. *"Soy Cuba." Verde Olivo* 32, no. 9 (1964): 12–13.

Ruskin, John. *The Works of John Ruskin.* Edited by E. T. Cook and Alexander Wedderburn. London: Allen, 1903–1912.

Russell, Catherine. *Experimental Ethnography: The Work of Film in the Age of Video.* Durham, N.C.: Duke University Press, 1999.

——, ed. "New Women of the Silent Screen: China, Japan, Hollywood." Special issue, *Camera Obscura* 20, no. 3 (2005).

Safran, Yehuda, and Wilfried Wang, with Mildred Budny. *The Architecture of Adolf Loos.* London: Arts Council of Great Britain, 1985.

Sales Meyer, Franz. *A Handbook of Ornament.* London: Duckworth, 1974.

Sanjinés, Jorge. "Problems of Form and Content in Revolutionary Cinema." Translated by Malcolm Coad. In *Twenty-five Years of the New Latin American Cinema,* edited by Michael Chanan, 34–38. London: BFI, 1983.

——. "Sobre *Fuera de aqui!*" *Cine Cubano* 93 (1979): 126–32.

——. *Teoría y práctica de un cine junto al pueblo.* Mexico City: Editorial Siglo XXI, 1971.

Sarris, Andrew. "Films in Focus." *Village Voice,* September 5, 1963.

Schiller, Friedrich Von. *On the Aesthetic Education of Man.* Translated by Elizabeth M. Williamson and L. A. Willoughby. Oxford: Clarendon Press, 1967.

Schimmel, Annemarie. "The Arabesque and the Islamic View of the World." In *Ornament and Abstraction: The Dialogue Between Non-Western, Modern, and Contemporary Art,* edited by Markus Brüderlin, 31–35. Basel: Fondation Beyeler, 2001.

Schoonover, Karl. *Brutal Humanism: The Neorealist Body and Global Spectators.* Minneapolis: University of Minnesota Press, forthcoming.

Schor, Naomi. *Reading in Detail: Aesthetics and the Feminine.* New York: Methuen, 1987.

Schwartz, Vanessa R., and Jeannene M. Przyblyski, eds. *The Nineteenth-Century Visual Culture Reader.* New York: Routledge, 2004.

Schwartzer, Mitchell. "Ethnologies of the Primitive in Adolf Loos's Writings on Ornament." *Nineteenth-Century Contexts* 18 (1994): 225–47.

Schwenger, Peter. "Derek Jarman and the Colour of the Mind's Eye." *University of Toronto Quarterly* 65, no. 2 (1996): 419–26.

Scott, A. O. "*The Terrorist*: A Guerrilla Grows Up During a Mission." *New York Times,* January 14, 2000. Available at http://www.nytimes.com/library/film/011400terrorist-film-review.html.

Sekula, Alan. "The Body and the Archive." *October* 39 (1986): 3–64.

Sell, Mike. "Bohemianism, the Cultural Turn of the Avantgarde, and Forgetting the Roma." *TDR: The Drama Review* 51, no. 2 (2007): 41–59.

Sembach, Klaus-Jurgen. *Art Nouveau.* Berlin: Taschen, 2002.

Semper, Gottfried. *The Four Elements of Architecture and Other Writings.* Translated by Harry Francis Mallgrave and Wolfgang Herrmann. Cambridge: Cambridge University Press, 1989.

Shohat, Ella. *Taboo Memories, Diasporic Voices.* Durham, N.C.: Duke University Press, 2006.

Silverman, Kaja. "Fragments of a Fashionable Discourse." In *Studies in Entertainment: Critical Approaches to Mass Culture,* edited by Tania Modleski, 139–52. Bloomington: Indiana University Press, 1986.

——. *The Subject of Semiotics.* New York: Oxford University Press, 1983.

——. *The Threshold of the Visible World.* New York: Routledge, 1996.

Simmons, Sherwin. "Ornament, Gender, and Interiority in Viennese Expressionism." *Modernism/Modernity* 8, no. 2 (2001): 245–76.

Sitney, P. Adams. *Visionary Film: The American Avant-Garde, 1943–2000.* Oxford: Oxford University Press, 2002.

Sloniowski, Jeannette. "'It Was an Atrocious Film': Georges Franju's *Blood of the Beasts*." In *Documenting the Documentary: Close Readings of Documentary Film and Video*, edited by Barry Keith Grant and Jeannette Sloniowski, 171–87. Detroit: Wayne State University Press, 2003.

Smith, Paul Julian. "*Blue* and the Outer Limits." *Sight & Sound* 3, no. 10 (1993): 18–19.

———. "*I Am Cuba*." *Sight & Sound* 9, no. 8 (1999): 46.

Solanas, Fernando, and Octavio Getino. "Towards a Third Cinema." In *Movies and Methods*, edited by Bill Nichols, 1:44–64. Berkeley: University of California Press, 1976.

Spivak, Gayatri Chakravorty. *A Critique of Postcolonial Reason: Toward a History of the Vanishing Present*. Cambridge, Mass.: Harvard University Press, 1999.

———. "Terror: A Speech After 9-11." *boundary* 31, no. 2 (2004): 81–111.

Stafford, Barbara Maria. *Artful Science: Enlightenment Entertainment and the Eclipse of Visual Education*. Cambridge, Mass.: MIT Press, 1994.

———. *Good Looking: Essays on the Virtue of Images*. Cambridge, Mass.: MIT Press, 1996.

Steiner, Wendy. *Venus in Exile: The Rejection of Beauty in Twentieth-Century Art*. New York: Free Press, 2001.

Stewart, Janet. *Fashioning Vienna: Adolf Loos's Cultural Criticism*. New York: Routledge, 2000.

Stone, Rob. "Mother Lands, Sister Nations: The Epic, Poetic, Propaganda Films of Cuba and the Basque Country." In *Remapping World Cinema: Identity, Culture, and Politics in Film*, edited by Stephanie Dennison and Song Hwee Lin, 65–72. London: Wallflower, 2006.

Straayer, Chris. *Deviant Eyes, Deviant Bodies: Sexual Re-orientations in Film and Video*. Edinburgh: Edinburgh University Press, 1996.

Strathausen, Carsten. "Eichendorff's *Das Marmorbild* and the Demise of Romanticism." In *Rereading Romanticism*, edited by Martha B. Helfer, 367–88. Amsterdam: Rodopi, 2000.

Strick, Philip. "*Zabriskie Point*." *Monthly Film Bulletin* 37, no. 436 (1970): 102.

Taylor, Clyde. *The Mask of Art: Breaking the Aesthetic Contract—Film and Literature*. Bloomington: Indiana University Press, 1998.

Tesson, Charles. "Lara contre *Amélie*." *Cahiers du Cinéma* 559 (2001): 5.

Thompson, Kristin. "The Concept of Cinematic Excess." In *Film Theory and Criticism: Introductory Readings*, 5th ed., edited by Leo Braudy and Marshall Cohen, 487–98. New York: Oxford University Press, 1999.

Tobing Rony, Fatimah. *The Third Eye: Race, Cinema, and the Ethnographic Spectacle*. Durham, N.C.: Duke University Press, 1996.

Truffaut, François. "A Certain Tendency of the French Cinema." In *Movies and Methods*, edited by Bill Nichols, 1:224–51. Berkeley: University of California Press, 1976.

Trumpener, Katie. *"Johanna d'Arc of Mongolia* in the Mirror of *Dorian Gray*: Ethnographic Recordings and the Aesthetics of the Market in the Recent Films of Ulrike Ottinger." *New German Critique* 60 (1993): 77–99.

Tweedie, James. "The Suspended Spectacle of History: The Tableau Vivant in Derek Jarman's *Caravaggio*." *Screen* 44, no. 4 (2003): 379–403.

Valdés Rodríguez, José. "*Soy Cuba*." *El Mundo*, August 18, 1964.

Van Zanten, David. *The Architectural Polychromy of the 1830s*. New York: Garland, 1977.

Véron, Eugène. *Aesthetics*. Translated by W. H. Armstrong. London: Chapman and Hall, 1879.

——. *L'esthétique*. Paris: Reinwald, 1878.

Viera, Else R. P., ed. *City of God in Several Voices: Brazilian Social Cinema as Action*. Nottingham: Critical, Cultural, and Communications Press, 2005.

Villarejo, Amy. "Archiving the Diaspora: A Lesbian Impression of / in Ulrike Ottinger's *Exile Shanghai*." *New German Critique* 87 (2002): 157–91.

Vitali, Valentina, and Paul Willemen, eds. *Theorising National Cinema*. London: BFI, 2006.

Vogel, Amos. "Bernardo Bertolucci: An Interview." *Film Comment* 7, no. 3 (1971): 25–29.

Vuillermoz, Emile. "Before the Screen: *La dixième symphonie*." In *French Film Theory and Criticism: A History/Anthology*, vol. 1, *1907–1939*, edited by Richard Abel, 168–71. Princeton, N.J.: Princeton University Press, 1988.

Wallington, Mike. "*Fellini–Satyricon*." *Monthly Film Bulletin* 37, no. 441 (1970): 200–201.

Waugh, Thomas. *The Fruit Machine: Twenty Years of Writings on Queer Cinema*. Durham, N.C.: Duke University Press, 2000.

Weigel, Viola. "The War of Signs—Peace in Ornament: The Ornament as a Bridge Between Cultures." In *Ornament and Abstraction: The Dialogue Between Non-Western, Modern, and Contemporary Art*, edited by Markus Brüderlin, 169–71. Basel: Fondation Beyeler, 2001.

Weiss, Andrea. "Transgressive Cinema: Lesbian Independent Film." In *Queer Cinema: The Film Reader*, edited by Harry Benshoff and Sean Griffin, 43–52. New York: Routledge, 2004.

——. *Vampires and Violets: Lesbians in Film*. London: Penguin, 1993.

Whissel, Kristen. "Racialized Spectacle, Exchange Relations, and the Western in *Johanna d'Arc of Mongolia*." *Screen* 37, no. 1 (1996): 41–67.

White, Patricia. "Madame X of the China Seas." *Screen* 28, no. 4 (1987): 80–95.

White, Susan M. *The Cinema of Max Ophuls: Magisterial Vision and the Figure of Woman*. New York: Columbia University Press, 1995.

Wigley, Mark. *White Walls, Designer Dresses: The Fashioning of Modern Architecture*. Cambridge, Mass.: MIT Press, 1995.

Willemen, Paul. *Looks and Frictions: Essays in Cultural Studies and Film Theory.* London: BFI, 1994.

Williams, Linda. "'Something Else Besides a Mother': *Stella Dallas* and the Maternal Melodrama." In *Home Is Where the Heart Is: Studies in Melodrama and the Woman's Film,* edited by Christine Gledhill, 299–325. London: BFI, 1987.

Williams, Raymond. *Marxism and Literature.* Oxford: Oxford University Press, 1978.

Wilton, Tamsin, ed. *Immortal Invisible: Lesbians and the Moving Image.* New York: Routledge, 1995.

Winckelmann, J. J. *The History of Ancient Art.* Vol. 1. Translated by G. Henry Lodge. London: Sampson Low, Marston, Searle & Rivington, 1881.

——. "Thoughts on the Imitation of the Painting and Sculpture of the Greeks." In *German Aesthetic and Literary Criticism: Winckelmann, Lessing, Hamann, Herder, Schiller, Goethe,* edited and translated by H. B. Nisbet, 32–54. Cambridge: Cambridge University Press, 1985.

Wisniewski, Chris. "The Main Attraction." *Reverse Shot* 23 (2008). Available at http://www.reverseshot.com/article/lola_montes.

Wölfflin, Heinrich. *Principles of Art History: The Problem of the Development of Style in Later Art.* Translated by M. D. Hottinger. New York: Dover, 1950.

Woll, Josephine. *Real Images: Soviet Cinema and the Thaw.* London: Taurus, 2000.

Wollen, Peter. "*Blue.*" In *Color: The Film Reader,* edited by Angela Dalle Vacche and Brian Price, 192–201. New York: Routledge, 2006.

——. "Godard and Counter-cinema: *Vent d'Est.*" In *Movies and Methods,* edited by Bill Nichols, 2:500–509. Berkeley: University of California Press, 1985.

——. "The Last New Wave: Modernism in the British Films of the Thatcher Era." In *The British Avant-Garde Film, 1926–1995: An Anthology of Writings,* edited by Michael O'Pray, 239–59. London: Arts Council of England and University of Luton Press, 1990.

Wollen, Roger, ed. *Derek Jarman: A Portrait.* London: Thames and Hudson, 1996.

Wood, Robin. "'Do I Disgust You?': Or, Tirez pas sur *La pianiste.*" *Cineaction* 59 (2002): 54–60.

Wornum, Ralph N. *Analysis of Ornament: The Characteristics of Styles, an Introduction to the Study of the History of Ornamental Art.* London: Chapman and Hall, 1882.

Wright-Wexman, Virginia, ed. *Letter from an Unknown Woman.* New Brunswick, N.J.: Rutgers University Press, 1986.

——. "The Transfiguration of History: Ophuls, Vienna, and *Letter from an Unknown Woman.*" In *Letter from an Unknown Woman,* edited by Virginia Wright-Wexman, 3–14. New Brunswick, N.J.: Rutgers University Press, 1986.

Xavier, Ismail. *Allegories of Underdevelopment: Aesthetics and Politics in Modern Brazilian Cinema.* Minneapolis: University of Minnesota Press, 1997.

Yegenoglu, Meyda. *Colonial Fantasies: Towards a Feminist Reading of Orientalism.* Cambridge: Cambridge University Press, 1998.

INDEX

Numbers in italics refer to pages on which illustrations appear.

Hitchcock's Romantic Irony
Richard Allen

Intelligence Work: The Politics of American Documentary
Jonathan Kahana

Eye of the Century: Film, Experience, Modernity
Francesco Casetti

Shivers Down Your Spine: Cinema, Museums, and the Immersive View
Alison Griffiths

Weimar Cinema: An Essential Guide to Classic Films of the Era
Noah Isenberg

African Film and Literature: Adapting Violence to the Screen
Lindiwe Dovey

Film, A Sound Art
Michel Chion

Film Studies: An Introduction
Ed Sikov

Hollywood Lighting from the Silent Era to Film Noir
Patrick Keating

Levinas and the Cinema of Redemption: Time, Ethics, and the Feminine
Sam B. Girgus

Counter-Archive: Film, the Everyday, and Albert Kahn's Archives de la Planète
Paula Amad

Indie: An American Film Culture
Michael Z. Newman